T0326890

Journey
through the
Bible

Journey
through the
Bible

LION

Published by
Lion Hudson Limited
Wilkinson House, Jordan Hill Business Park
Banbury Road, Oxford OX2 8DR, England
www.lionhudson.com

ISBN 978 0 74598 131 4
e-ISBN 978 0 74598 132 1

First edition copyright © Monarch Books 1981 published in English under
the title *Journey Through the Bible* by V. Gilbert Beers.
Most of the text and some of the illustrations in this book were first
published as part of *The Victor Handbook of Bible Knowledge* in 1981.

This edition designed for Veritas Press Inc, 2020.

This edition copyright © Lion Books, 2021.

Acknowledgments
Unless otherwise stated, all Scripture quotations are taken from
the Holy Bible, New International Version, copyright © 1973, 1978, 1984
by International Bible Society. Used by permission of Hodder and
Stoughton Ltd. All rights reserved.

Other quotations are from the Good News Bible–New Testament
(GNB): © American Bible Society 1966, 1971, 1976 and the
Authorized (King James) Version (KJV).

A catalogue record for this book is available from the British Library

Printed and bound in China, January 2021, LH54

Contents

Preface   ix

THE OLD TESTAMENT

Creation
Genesis 1–2   2
The Fall
Genesis 3   4
Cain and Abel
Genesis 4   6
Noah Builds the Ark
Genesis 6–8   8
The Tower of Babel
Genesis 11:1–9   10
Abraham's Journeys
Genesis 11:27–12:20   12
Abraham and Lot
Genesis 13:1–13; 14   14
God's Covenant with Abraham
Genesis 17   15
Abraham Entertains Angels
Genesis 18   16
The Destruction of Sodom
Genesis 19   18
Isaac Is Born
Genesis 21:1–7   20
Hagar and Ishmael Are
Sent Away
Genesis 21:8–21   22
Abraham Offers Isaac
Genesis 22   24
A Bride for Isaac
Genesis 24   26
Esau Sells His Birthright
Genesis 25:29–34   28
Jacob Deceives Isaac
Genesis 27:1–40   30
Jacob's Ladder
Genesis 27:41–28:22   32
Jacob Meets Rachel
Genesis 29:1–30   34
Joseph's Cloak
Genesis 37:1–11   36
Joseph Is Sold as a Slave
Genesis 37:12–36   38
Joseph in Potiphar's House
Genesis 39–40   40
Joseph Becomes Governor
Genesis 41   42
Joseph's Brothers Buy Grain
Genesis 42–44; 45:1–15   44

Joseph's Family Moves
to Egypt
Genesis 45:16–47:31   46
Hebrews Become Slaves
Exodus 1   47
Moses Is Born
Exodus 2:1–10   48
Moses Kills an Egyptian
and Flees to Midian
Exodus 2:11–25   50
The Burning Bush
Exodus 3:1–4:17   52
The Plagues
Exodus 4:18–10:29   54
The Passover
Exodus 11:1–12:50   56
The Exodus
Exodus 12:51–13:16   58
Crossing the Red Sea
Exodus 13:17–22; 14   60
Food in the Wilderness
Exodus 15–16; 17:1–7   62
The Ten Commandments
Exodus 20   64
The Golden Calf
Exodus 32   66
The Tabernacle
Exodus 35–36; 39:1–31;
Leviticus 1–9   68
Twelve Spies
Numbers 13–14   70
The Bronze Serpent
Numbers 21:4–9   72
Crossing the Jordan
Joshua 3–4   74
Jericho Captured
Joshua 6   76
Achan's Sin and the
Conquest of Ai
Joshua 7–8   78
The Sun and Moon Stand
Still at Aijalon
Joshua 10:1–28   80
Gideon's Call and Tests
Judges 6   82
Gideon's 300
Judges 7   84

The Birth of Samson
Judges 13   86
Samson the Prisoner
Judges 16:1–31   88
The Story of Ruth
The Book of Ruth   90
The Birth of Samuel
1 Samuel 1:1–20   92
God Speaks to Samuel
1 Samuel 1:21–2:11; 3   94
The Ark Is Captured
1 Samuel 4:1–5:12   96
The Return of the Ark
1 Samuel 6:1–7:2   97
Saul Is Made King
1 Samuel 8–10   98
Saul Sacrifices Wrongly
1 Samuel 13   99
Samuel Anoints David
1 Samuel 16:1–13   100
David Plays for Saul
1 Samuel 16:14–23   102
David and Goliath
1 Samuel 17   104
David and Jonathan
1 Samuel 18:1–4   106
Saul Tries to Kill David
1 Samuel 18–19   107
Jonathan Warns David
1 Samuel 20   108
David Runs From Saul
1 Samuel 21–22   109
Abigail Shares Her Food
1 Samuel 25   110
David Spares Saul
1 Samuel 26   111
The Witch of Endor
1 Samuel 28   112
Saul Dies
1 Samuel 31   113
David Becomes King of Judah
2 Samuel 2:1–11   114
David Captures Jerusalem
2 Samuel 5:1–16;
1 Chronicles 11:1–9   116

The Ark Is Moved
  2 Samuel 6; 1 Chronicles
  13; 15:1–16:3   118
David and Bathsheba
  2 Samuel 11–12   120
Absalom Rebels
  2 Samuel 15–18   122
Araunah's Threshing Floor
  2 Samuel 24   124
Solomon Builds the Temple
  1 Kings 5–8;
  2 Chronicles 2–7   126
Solomon's Glory
  1 Kings 10; 2 Chronicles
  8:17–9:28   128
Solomon Turns from God
  1 Kings 11;
  2 Chronicles 9:29–30   129
The Kingdom Divides
  1 Kings 12:1–24;
  14:21–31; 15:6–8;
  2 Chronicles 10–11   130
Ravens Feed Elijah
  1 Kings 17:1–7   132
The Widow of Zarephath
  1 Kings 17:8–16   134
Elijah and the Prophets of Baal
  1 Kings 18   136
Elijah and the Still, Small Voice
  1 Kings 19:1–18   138

Elijah's Mantle to Elisha
  1 Kings 19:19–21   139
Naboth's Vineyard
  1 Kings 21   140
Elijah Is Taken in a Whirlwind
  2 Kings 2   142
Elisha Raises the
  Shunammite Boy
  2 Kings 4 :8–37   144
Naaman Is Healed
  2 Kings 5:1–19   146
Elisha's Greedy Servant
  2 Kings 5:20–27   148
Elisha and the Syrians
  2 Kings 6:8–23   150
Jehu Overthrows Jezebel
  and Destroys Baal
  2 Kings 9–10   152
The Story of Jonah
  The Book of Jonah   154
The Story of Isaiah
  The Book of Isaiah   156
Israel Taken Into Captivity
  2 Kings 17   158
Sennacherib Goes against
  Hezekiah
  2 Kings 18   160
Josiah Repairs the Temple –
  The Book of the Law Found
  2 Kings 22:1–23:30;
  2 Chronicles 34–35   162

The Story of Jeremiah
  The Book of Jeremiah   164
Judah Falls, Jerusalem Is
  Destroyed and Zedekiah
  Is Blinded
  2 Kings 24–25;
  2 Chronicles 36:5–21   166
Daniel and the King's Food
  Daniel 1   168
The Fiery Furnace
  Daniel 3   169
The Handwriting on the Wall
  Daniel 5–6   170
The Story of Queen Esther
  The Book of Esther   172
Ezra and the People Return
  The Book of Ezra   174
Nehemiah Prays for His
  Homeland
  Nehemiah 1   176
Nehemiah Builds
  Jerusalem's Walls
  Nehemiah 4–7   178
Ezra Reads the Law
  Nehemiah 8–10   180
The Story of Job
  The Book of Job   182
The Prophets and the
  Coming King
  Various prophecy books   184

THE NEW TESTAMENT

John's Birth Announced
  Luke 1:5–25   186
Jesus' Birth Announced
  Luke 1:26–38   188
Mary Visits Elizabeth
  Luke 1:38–56   190
John the Baptist Is Born
  Luke 1:57–80   192
Jesus Is Born
  Luke 2:1–7   194
Shepherds Worship Jesus
  Luke 2:8–20   196
Simeon and Anna Honour Jesus
  Luke 2:21–38   198
Wise Men See a Star
  Matthew 2:1–8   199
Wise Men Visit Jesus
  Matthew 2:9–12   201
The Flight to Egypt
  Matthew 2:13–18   202

The Return to Nazareth
  Matthew 2:19–23;
  Luke 2:39   204
The Carpenter's Shop
  Luke 2:40; Matthew 13:55;
  Mark 6:3   205
Jesus and the Teachers
  Luke 2:41–52   206
John Preaches in the Wilderness
  Matthew 3:1–12; Mark 1:1–8;
  Luke 3:1–18   207
Jesus Is Baptized
  Matthew 3:13–17; Mark
  1:9–11; Luke 3:21–23   208
Jesus Is Tempted
  Matthew 4:1–11   209
The Wedding at Cana
  John 2:1–11   210
Jesus Cleanses the Temple
  John 2:13–22   212
Nicodemus
  John 2:23–3:21   214

The Woman at the Well
  John 4:1–42   215
The Nobleman's Son Is Healed
  John 4:46–54   216
Jesus at the Synagogue
  Luke 4:16–31   218
The Miracle of Fish
  Luke 5:1–11   219
Jesus Calls Four Disciples
  Matthew 4:18–22; Mark
  1:16–20   220
At the Capernaum Synagogue
  Mark 1:21–28;
  Luke 4:31–37   222
Jesus Heals Peter's Mother–
  in–Law
  Matthew 8:14–17; Mark
  1:29–34; Luke 4:38–41   224
A Healing Tour of Galilee
  Matthew 4:23–25; Mark
  1:35–39; Luke 4:42–44   226

Through the Roof to Jesus
Matthew 9:1–8; Mark 2:1–12;
Luke 5:17–26   227
Jesus Calls Matthew
Matthew 9:9; Mark 2:13–14;
Luke 5:27–28   228
A Dinner at Matthew's House
Matthew 9:10–13; Mark
2:15–17; Luke 5:29–32   230
Wineskins and Patched
Garments
Matthew 9:14–17; Mark
2:18–22; Luke 5:33–39   231
At the Pool of Bethesda
John 5:1–47   232
Sabbath in a Wheat Field
Matthew 12:1–8; Mark
2:23–28; Luke 6:1–5   233
The Withered Hand
Matthew 12:9–14; Mark 3:1–6;
Luke 6:6–11   234
Teaching by the Sea
Matthew 12:15–21;
Mark 3:7–12   235
Choosing the Twelve
Mark 3:13–19;
Luke 6:12–16   236
The Sermon on the Mount
Matthew 5:1–8:1;
Luke 6:17–49   238
A Centurion's Servant
Matthew 8:5–13;
Luke 7:1–10   240
The Widow of Nain
Luke 7:11–17   241
The Sower and Other Parables
Matthew 13:1–52; Mark
4:1–34; Luke 8:4–18   242
Jesus Stills a Storm
Matthew 8:18, 23–27; Mark
4:35–41; Luke 8:22–25   243
Jesus Heals a Man with Demons
Matthew 8:28–34; Mark
5:1–20; Luke 8:26–39   244
The Fringe of His Garment
Matthew 9:20–22; Mark
5:25–34, Luke 8:43–48   245
Jairus' Daughter
Matthew 9:18–19, 23–26;
Mark 5:21–24, 35–43;
Luke 8:40–42, 49–56   246
Two by Two
Matthew 9:35–11:1; Mark
6:6–13; Luke 9:1–6   248
John Is Beheaded
Matthew 14:1–12; Mark
6:14–29; Luke 3:19–20,
9:7–9   250

Jesus Feeds 5,000
Matthew 14:13–21; Mark
6:30–44; Luke 9:10–17;
John 6:1–13   252
Jesus Walks on the Sea
Matthew 14:24–33; Mark
6:47–52; John 6:16–21   253
Healing at Gennesaret
Matthew 14:34–36;
Mark 6:53–56   254
The Syro-Phoenician Woman
Matthew 15:21–28;
Mark 7:24–30   255
Jesus Heals a Deaf and
Dumb Man
Matthew 15:29–31;
Mark 7:31–37   256
Jesus Heals at Bethsaida
Matthew 16:5–12; Mark
8:13–26   257
A Visit to Caesarea Philippi
Matthew 16:13–20; Mark
8:27–30; Luke 9:18–21   258
The Transfiguration
Matthew 17:1–8; Mark 9:2–8;
Luke 9:28–36   260
A Fish with Tax Money
Matthew 17:24–27   262
Who Is Greatest?
Matthew 18:1–6; Mark
9:33–37; Luke 9:46–48   264
The Two Debtors
Matthew 18:15–35   265
The Pool of Siloam
John 9:1–41   266
The Good Shepherd
John 10:1–21   268
The Good Samaritan
Luke 10:25–37   270
Mary and Martha
Luke 10:38–42   271
Tears for Jerusalem
Luke 13:31–35   272
The Lost Sheep
Luke 15:1–7   274
The Lost Coin
Luke 15:8–10   275
The Prodigal Son
Luke 15:11–32   276
The Rich Man and Lazarus
Luke 16:19–31   277
Jesus Raises Lazarus
John 11:1–44   278
Ten Lepers
Luke 17:11–19   280
A Pharisee and a Publican
Luke 18:9–14   281
Jesus and the Children
Matthew 19:13–15; Mark
10:13–16; Luke 18:15–17   282

The Rich Young Ruler
Matthew 19:16–30; Mark
10:17–31; Luke 18:18–30   283
The Labourers in the Vineyard
Matthew 20:1–16   284
Blind Bartimaeus
Matthew 20:29–34; Mark
10:46–52; Luke 18:35–43   286
Zaccheus and the Parable
of the Three Servants
Luke 19:1–27   288
Jesus' Triumphal Entry
into Jerusalem
Matthew 21:1–9; Mark
11:1–10; Luke 19:29–44; John
12:12–19   289
Jesus at the Temple
Matthew 21:10–17; Mark
11:11–19; Luke 19:45–48   290
Give to Caesar
Matthew 22:15–22; Mark
12:13–17; Luke 20:20–26   292
The Widow's Mite
Mark 12:41–44;
Luke 21:1–4   293
Figs, Lamps, and Sheep
Matthew 24:32–25:46; Mark
13:28–37; Luke 21:29–36   294
Mary Anoints Jesus' Feet
Matthew 26:6–13; Mark
14:3–9; John 12:2–11   296
Thirty Pieces of Silver
Matthew 26:14–16; Mark
14:10–11; Luke 22:3–6   298
The Last Supper
Matthew 26:17–29; Mark
14:12–25; Luke 22:7–20, 24–30;
John 13:1–20   300
Gethsemane
Matthew 26:36–56; Mark
14:32–52; Luke 22:39–53; John
18:2–12   304
Jesus on Trial
Matthew 26:57–68; Mark
14:53–65; Luke 22:54, 63–65;
John 18:12–14, 19–24   306
Peter Denies Jesus
Matthew 26:58, 69–75;
Mark 14:54, 66–72; Luke 22:54–
62; John 18:15–18, 25–27   308
Judas Hangs Himself
Matthew 27:3–10; Acts
1:18–19   309
Jesus Is Sent to Pilate
Matthew 27:2, 11–14; Mark
15:1–5; Luke 23:1–5; John
18:28–38   310

Jesus is Sentenced to Death
Matthew 27:15–30; Mark
15:6–19; Luke 23:6–25; John
18:39–19:5   312

The Way of the Cross
Matthew 27:31–34; Mark
15:20–23; Luke 23:26–33; John
19:16–17   314

The Day Jesus Died
Matthew 27:27–56; Mark
15:16–41; Luke 23:26–49; John
19:14–30   316

Women Visit Jesus' Tomb
Matthew 27:57–68; Mark
15:42–16:8; Luke 23:50–24:3;
John 19:31–20:8   318

Peter and John Visit
Jesus' Tomb
Luke 24:11–12;
John 20:2–10   320

Mary Magdalene
Mark 16:9–11;
John 20:11–18   321

The Road to Emmaus
Mark 16:12–13;
Luke 24:13–35   322

Doubting Thomas
Mark 16:14; Luke 24:36–43;
John 20:19–31   324

The Miracle of Fish
John 21   326

Jesus Ascends into Heaven
Mark 16:19–20; Luke 24:50–53;
Acts 1:9–12   328

Pentecost
Acts 2   330

Peter and John Heal
a Lame Man
Acts 3   332

Peter and John before
the Council
Acts 4:1–31   333

The Believers
Acts 4:32–5:16   334

The Seven Deacons
Acts 6:1–7   336

Stephen Is Killed
Acts 6:8–7:60   338

Philip and the Ethiopian
Acts 8:26–40   339

Saul Becomes Paul
Acts 9:1–22   340

Saul Escapes
Acts 9:23–31   342

Dorcas
Acts 9:36–42   343

Cornelius
Acts 9:43–10:48   344

Christians at Antioch
Acts 11   346

Peter in Prison
Acts 12:1–23   348

Paul's First Missionary Journey
Acts 13:1–3   350

Paul's Journey Begins
Acts 13:4–52   352

Mistaken for Gods
Acts 14   354

Paul's Second Missionary
Journey
Acts 15:36–41   356

The Macedonian Call
Acts 16:1–10   358

Timothy's Family and Home
Acts 16:1–4; 2 Timothy 1:5 360

Lydia Becomes a Believer
Acts 16:11–15   362

The Philippian Prison
Acts 16:16–40   364

Paul at Thessalonica
Acts 17:1–9   366

The Bereans Accept Paul
Acts 17:10–14   367

Paul at Mars Hill
Acts 17:16–34   368

Paul at Corinth
Acts 18:1–4   370

Gallio Judges Paul at Corinth
Acts 18:5–17   372

Books of Evil Are Burned
Acts 19:17–20   374

Diana of the Ephesians
Acts 19:23–41   376

Eutychus
Acts 20:6–12   378

Paul Is Arrested
Acts 21:17–23:35   380

Paul Before Felix and Festus
Acts 24:1–25:12   382

Paul Before King Agrippa
Acts 25:13–26:32   383

Paul's Journey Toward Rome
Acts 27:1–8   384

Paul's Shipwreck
Acts 27:27–28:10   386

Paul at Rome
Acts 28:11–31   388

Philemon
The Book of Philemon   390

The Seven Churches
The Book of Revelation   392

Index   394

Preface

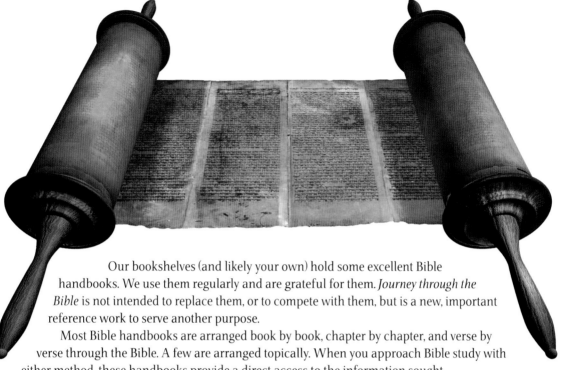

Our bookshelves (and likely your own) hold some excellent Bible handbooks. We use them regularly and are grateful for them. *Journey through the Bible* is not intended to replace them, or to compete with them, but is a new, important reference work to serve another purpose.

Most Bible handbooks are arranged book by book, chapter by chapter, and verse by verse through the Bible. A few are arranged topically. When you approach Bible study with either method, these handbooks provide a direct access to the information sought.

Many people, however, approach the Bible story by story. Millions of teachers, parents, pastors, and Christian education workers focus much of their work on Bible stories. Yet, to our knowledge, there has never been a Bible handbook organized by story through the Bible. Now *Journey through the Bible* does this, moving through the Bible, story by story, with background information in word and picture for almost 250 important Bible stories. It provides a storehouse of authentic material relating to these favourite stories – including hundreds of drawings taken from objects or monuments of Bible times, photos of Bible lands today, archaeological discoveries, reconstructions, and colourful maps which show the Bible in action. Altogether there are more than 500 illustrations, more than any other volume of its kind.

To make this treasury of materials useful to all, including children, the text is written in an easy-to-read style, with much emphasis on interest as well as information.

Many of the stories included in this volume feature common themes, such as shepherds, money, costume, and warfare. We have taken care not to repeat the same information; for this reason, it is important to make good use of the very extensive index to discover additional important facts and illustrations about chosen themes and stories.

Every library – home, church, and school – may find this important reference work widely useful. It will enrich Sunday School lesson preparation, sermon preparation, devotions, and Bible storytelling. It will become an important resource for all Bible study.

The Old Testament

In the wilderness, God delivered the Law to Moses. Joshua told the Israelites to "put away the gods that your fathers served beyond the River and in Egypt, and serve the Lord". The Old Testament is a record of how well (and how poorly) that was done.

Creation

GENESIS 1–2

From nothing, God made the world and all that surrounds it and all that is in it. He spoke the word, and it happened. That was Creation.

Compared with the whole world we know today – as shown in this photo from Apollo 17 – the Bible world was small. Included in the world of Bible events is the ancient Near East, sometimes called "The Cradle of Civilization" because the earliest-known nations have been found there. Countless empires have fallen, but even today this area remains in the world's spotlight.

THE SEVEN DAYS OF CREATION

Day 1

God created light and separated the light from the darkness. The light He called day, and the darkness He called night.

Day 5

God made fish and all other creatures that live in the oceans and lakes. He also made birds to fly above the earth.

Day 2

God made the earth and the heavens (the universe and the skies), and separated the two.

Day 3

God separated the oceans from the dry land. He then created every kind of plant and tree, each bearing its own seed.

Day 4

God created the sun, moon, and stars. He placed them in the heavens to provide light for the earth and seasons for the year.

Day 6

God created man and all the animals, and placed man in charge of the animals. He also told man to multiply and fill the earth.

Day 7

God rested from all the work He had done while creating the world.

The Fall

God created the world and all that is in it and all that surrounds it. He also created a man and a woman, and called them Adam and Eve. God placed them in a beautiful garden in the land of Eden and gave them all they needed. But Satan came and tempted them to want more. That led to sin, and sin led to ruin.

Some have suggested that pomegranate was the tempting fruit. It is common in the Middle East today and was commonly known in Bible times.

Iraq, and Turkey. The other two branches are called the Pishon and Gihon and their locations remain a mystery today. Most scholars believe that the Garden of Eden was located somewhere near the head of the Persian Gulf, at the junction of the Tigris and Euphrates Rivers.

No trace of the beautiful garden has been found and some think that it withered and died when God expelled Adam and Eve. Others believe it was destroyed by the great Flood in the days of Noah. Some think it still exists.

The Garden of Eden
No one knows the exact location of the Garden of Eden, but the Bible offers a clue. It tells of a river that flowed out of the garden and divided into four branches. Two of them, the Tigris and Euphrates, flow through the modern countries of Syria,

Cherubim
The Bible mentions two kinds of spiritual beings created by God – angels, who are in fellowship with God, and demons, who are in rebellion against God. Many believe there are different kinds or ranks of angels and that cherubim fit into one of these ranks.

The appearances of cherubim are mentioned only a few times in the Bible. Ezekiel saw them in a vision but could not express in words their actual appearance. He said that cherubim looked like men (Ezek. 1:5), but had two faces (41:18, a man and a lion), or four faces (1:6, 10; 10:14, a man, a lion, an ox, and an eagle). Some had two wings (1 Kings 6:24) and others

All we know about the serpent before the Fall is that it was "more crafty than any of the wild animals the Lord God had made". Did it walk? Did it fly? We know that after the Fall it would crawl on its belly and eat dust all the days of its life.

four (Ezek. 1:6, 11). Cherubim are usually associated with fire. They and a flaming sword guarded the entrance to the Garden of Eden (Gen. 3:24).

Throughout Bible times carved cherubim were used for idol worship in pagan temples. Heathen cultures such as the Babylonians and Assyrians depicted cherubim as winged humans with an eagle's head or lion's head. Cherubim were also popular as artwork in sculptures and reliefs, but they did not follow the Bible's description of these angels.

The Israelites also made cherubim but did not worship them. Two cherubim of gold were placed on the mercy seat of the ark of the covenant. Cherubim were also embroidered into the tabernacle curtains and two large cherubim of olive wood overlaid with gold were set in Solomon's temple as a symbol of God's greatness.

This Assyrian panel showing a cherub-like being was made in the early 800s BC. Carved reliefs such as this one originally would have been painted.

Cain and Abel

After God created the heavens and the earth, He made a man and a woman and called them Adam and Eve. He placed them in a beautiful garden in Eden and gave them all they needed. But Satan tempted them to want more, and this led to sin. They were expelled, forced to leave their paradise and work for a living. Sin continued, and one day Cain killed his brother Abel in a fit of anger.

The family of Adam and Eve

After expulsion from the Garden of Eden, Adam and Eve started a family. Cain, Abel, and Seth were sons of Adam and Eve, and their only children mentioned by name. But the Bible points out that Adam and Eve had many other sons and daughters. Many of these married and had children of their own.

Cain

Cain was the oldest son of Adam and Eve. Early in his life he was a farmer. Cain "worked the soil" (Gen. 4:2). He was the first man to commit murder (4:8), and God condemned him to a life of wandering away from Eden.

Alienated from his family, Cain was forced to leave and travelled to the land of Nod. There he founded the first city (4:17) and was the ancestor of the earliest musicians and metal-workers (4:21–22). But all of Cain's descendants perished in the great Flood of Noah's time.

Abel

Abel was the second son born to Adam and Eve, Cain's younger brother. Abel was a shepherd, as he "kept flocks" (Gen. 4:2). Abel's offering was accepted by God while Cain's was rejected. As a result, Cain became

A detail from the painting *Cain Slaying Abel* by Peter Paul Rubens

jealous and killed Abel. This was the first murder in history. No descendants of Abel are mentioned
in the Bible, as he probably had none.

Seth

Seth was the third son of Adam and Eve, and only his line of descendants was saved from the great Flood. His family tree was preserved through Noah and continued through Abraham and David. Hundreds of years later, this line reached into the home of Mary and Joseph and culminated in the birth of Jesus Christ.

The land of Nod

After murdering his brother, Cain travelled to the land of Nod. The Bible says that Nod was located east of Eden. There Cain started his family and founded the first city. Nothing else is known about Nod and its location remains a mystery. Some think that Nod is only a play on words used to illustrate a man condemned to wander. Some scholars translate the phrase "land of Nod" into "land of wandering".

Cain was a farmer and probably raised wheat. Abel raised animals, much as shepherds have for many generations.

Noah Builds the Ark

GENESIS 6–8

The years passed after Adam's and Eve's sin in Eden. The world grew worse until God would tolerate it no longer. It grew worse as the years passed, until the time of Noah. God decided to destroy all life on earth, except Noah and his family and a special assortment of animals and birds. After Noah spent 120 years building a big ark, he and his family entered it. Then the Flood began.

Kentucky's "Ark Encounter" features a full-size re-creation of the Ark. This modern engineering marvel amazes visitors young and old.

THE PEOPLE ON BOARD
Eight people are listed as passengers on the ark – Noah, his wife, his three sons, Ham, Shem, and Japheth, and their three wives. No one else is mentioned. As mentioned earlier, Noah apparently had no other children, either at this point, or later. Not only that, but his three sons, though nearly a hundred years old, apparently had no children at this time. They did, however, have children later, after the Flood.

Some say that Methuselah, Noah's ancestor (possibly grandfather), died the year of the Flood, possibly as a result of the Flood, at the amazing age of 969.

Before the Flood

The problems we face today are strikingly similar to those before the Flood. It was a time of population explosion, crime out of control, moral relativism, and decaying marriage and family life.

God was displeased with the marriages between the "sons of God" and the "daughters of men". Some think the "sons of God" were special heavenly beings. Others think they were godly men in Seth's family who married ungodly women from another family.

Noah and his family were the only people who pleased God. Thus God decided to destroy all others and begin life anew through this one family. This decision led to the great Flood.

Most Bible scholars do not give a date for the Flood, though they place it much earlier than the 2350 BC in some chronologies. One respected authority (*Unger's Bible Handbook*) says it was before 5000 BC

The Flood

The Bible says the Flood covered the earth. Some scholars say this means only the populated earth known to Noah. Others say it means the entire earth.

The test of obedience

God's command must have seemed strange to Noah. Build a large ship, fill it with animals, but build it on dry land far from a lake or sea. But the hope for all future humankind rested on Noah's complete obedience, even to a seemingly strange command. The key was the Commander, not the command. We must all remember that!

Noah

A descendant of Seth and ancestor of Abraham, Noah was 480 years old when God told him to build the ark, 600 when the Flood came.

Some believe that Noah was a shipbuilder and thus knew how to make a large boat such as the ark. But there is no way to be sure about this.

Noah had three sons. No others are mentioned in the Bible. Noah lived 350 years after the Flood and died at the age of 950.

Length: 137 m (450 feet)

Height 14 m (45 feet)

SIZE OF THE ARK
If the ark were placed on a football field, it would stretch beyond both goal posts. It was about 1½ times as large as a football field from goal line to goal line. Its width was 23 m (75 feet), and its approximate total deck size was 8,891 square metres (95,700 square feet).

WATERS OF THE FLOOD
There were two sources of water for the Flood. "The springs of the great deep burst forth" suggests a mighty upheaval of the seas or great springs under the earth. "The floodgates of the heavens were opened" suggests the heavy rains which came down (Gen. 7:4, 11).

TIME OF THE FLOOD
Noah was 480 years old when God told him to build the ark. Despite his old age, he apparently had no children yet. Then, strangely, 22 years after God's order to build the ark Shem was born. Japheth came a year later and Ham a year after that. No other children are recorded, even though Noah lived to be 950 years old. It is interesting that the three sons grew up around the ark, from the time they were born until they were almost 100 years old, for it took 120 years for Noah to complete the ark.

WOOD FOR THE ARK
Gopher wood is not mentioned anywhere else in the Bible. Some say it was cypress, pine, or cedar. Others suggest that "gopher" did not refer to the type of wood, but rather to wood covered with pitch, the substance used to seal the cracks in the ark.

PURPOSE OF THE ARK
The ark had one purpose – a floating refuge for Noah, his family, and the animals during the Flood. It had no sails, no oars, and no other way to power it. It had no way for Noah or his family to navigate it toward any certain place. All movement was in the hands of God.

Noah and his family within the ark are excellent examples of people totally committed to God's direction. Once in the ark, they depended completely on God to take them wherever He chose, for as long as He chose, and as fast as He chose.

SPECIAL FEATURES
The ark had three decks. Larger animals or waste materials were probably housed on the lower deck. Living quarters were probably on the top deck, which was covered by a roof. Light and ventilation came from wide windows, 46 cm (18 inches) high, built all around the ark near the roof.

Ham
Ham was probably born about 24 years after God's order to build the ark, and 96 years before the Flood came. He was the youngest of the three sons.

Ham's four sons were Cush, Egypt, Put, and Canaan. Their descendants were the Ethiopians, Egyptians, Libyans, and the Canaanites. Ham's family is listed in Genesis 10:6–20.

Japheth
The Greeks and dwellers of southeastern Europe descended from Japheth, father of seven sons. Japheth helped Shem cover his father when Noah became drunk. Ham was cursed, and his son Canaan because of him, for looking at his father's nakedness. The family of Japheth is listed in Genesis 10:2–5. He was the second son of Noah.

Shem
Abraham's lineage from Noah came through Shem, the father of the Semitic people.

Shem was born 98 years before the Flood, 22 years after God's order to build the ark. He was the oldest of Noah's sons.

Shem's sons were Elam, Asshur, Arpachshad, Lud, and Aram. From them descended the people of Persia, Assyria, Chaldea, Lydia, and Syria. Abraham, and later Jesus, came through the lineage of Arpachshad, also spelled Arphaxad. Shem's family is listed in Genesis 10:21–31.

The Tower of Babel

After God created the universe, Adam and Eve sinned and were driven from their home in the Garden of Eden. From that time on, sin grew worse and worse. By the time of Noah, it was so bad that God destroyed all people except Noah and his family. More time passed until the incident which caused one language to become many.

The Tower of Babel, an oil on copper painting from 1602 by Flanders-born Dutch Golden Age artist Roelant Savery.

The Tower of Babel was built on a plain in the land of Shinar. Throughout the Bible it becomes apparent that Shinar is another name for the land of Babylon. Well-known Babylonian cities are identified as being in the land of Shinar (Gen. 10:10). When Nebuchadnezzar, king of Babylon, sacked Jerusalem, he carried the captives back to his country, the land of Shinar (Dan. 1:2). He placed the spoils in the temple treasuries and asked that certain captives be taught to serve in the king's court. This would have taken place in the capital city, named Babylon, in the land also called Babylon. So it is almost certain that the land of Shinar and the land of Babylon are identical.

The Tower of Babel

After the Flood, the earth once again multiplied with people. A group of these people migrated east, to a plain in the land of Shinar. There they decided to build a large tower that would reach to the heavens. The Bible does not mention the name of the tower, but it is commonly called the "Tower of Babel". In Babylon's native language, Akkadian, "Babel" meant "the gate of God". A similar word in Hebrew means "to mix or confuse".

Ziggurats

The Tower of Babel was probably a ziggurat. A ziggurat was a temple tower common in the land of Babylon about this time. It marked the central place of worship for a city or region.

Here the people gathered to worship their gods and perform religious ceremonies.

The architecture of ziggurats was developed by the Babylonians. Frequently they resembled pyramids, but without the smooth sides. Most ziggurats had seven stories. Each story was slightly smaller than the one below it, creating a step-like appearance. Stairways on the outside of the building connected each level.

Some ziggurats were cone-shaped, and had stairs or ramps that wound around the tower leading to the top. These were the "winding road" variety and very common in the northern Near East. Other ziggurats had four levels instead of seven. Three stairways joined at the top of the first level. From there, one stairway led to the top. Usually, this top section was the size of just one room, and the holiest place in the ziggurat.

Ziggurats were large buildings. At the base, most were 60–90 m (200–300 feet) in each direction. Their height could reach 90 m (300 feet) as well. The Tower of Babel was one of the largest ziggurats, measuring about 90 m (300 feet) on each side. Each level was painted a different colour and the building looked like a large rainbow.

Mud-brick was the common building material for a ziggurat. It was made of either mud and straw, or clay, and then fired at high heat for extra strength. Asphalt was used instead of mortar to glue the bricks together.

The ziggurat was the focal point of a city. It was always the largest building in the area, and could be seen from anywhere in the city. Around the ziggurat were many smaller temples and towers, each devoted to the worship of a particular god.

Ziggurats and the Tower of Babel

Either of two ziggurats uncovered today may have been the ancient Tower of Babel. The temple of Ishtar, built by Nebuchadnezzar II, was constructed over the ruins

The Great Ziggurat of Ur was originally built as a temple for the Sumerian moon god. The partial reconstruction shown here is only the lower portion of what was likely a massive tower.

of an earlier tower. Some say this earlier tower was Babel. At Nimrud, a ruined temple, or ziggurat, has been excavated. According to ancient Jewish tradition this was the Tower of Babel.

The birth of nations

Throughout the years, families continued to multiply. Each new generation had many more people than the previous one. These large families soon formed groups called clans. For organization and protection, different clans joined together and formed tribes. In time, these tribes grew into nations.

Abraham's Journeys

GENESIS 11:27–12:20

A long time had passed since the language of humankind was confused at the Tower of Babel, perhaps more than 2,000 years. One of Noah's descendants, a man named Abraham, who was first called Abram, is found living in Sumer. From there, Abraham migrated northward and westward along the great arc of rich land known as the Fertile Crescent and settled in Haran. Later, he migrated again into Canaan, moving southwestward along the remaining part of the Fertile Crescent. But famine came to Canaan, and Abraham was forced to migrate once more, this time to Egypt.

Abraham was an old man when he left home to follow God.

Ur

On the banks of the Euphrates River stood the ancient city of Ur. Abraham spent his childhood years in this busy centre of trade before migrating to Canaan. Ur was located in the southern section of the region of Mesopotamia. This section was called Sumer and was inhabited by the Sumerians, the dominant people in Mesopotamia at that time.

Ur was an ancient city full of activity. It was surrounded by an intricate system of man-made canals, and for protection an oval wall was built around the city. The average house was a small, one-story mud-brick shelter with no windows. Its unpaved streets were muddy when wet. Ur had no sewers or refuse collection.

The marketplace was the centre of activity. Here the Sumerians gathered to trade their wares and talk about the day's news. Farmers coming in from the fields offered a great variety of food including onions, barley, and apples. Travelling merchants also brought exotic goods from India and other foreign regions.

The Fertile Crescent

As Abraham journeyed from Ur to Canaan, he followed the arc of the Fertile Crescent. This is a large bow-shaped strip of land where fertile soil and plenty of water can be found in the midst of a vast wilderness.

The Fertile Crescent stretches northwest from Ur toward the area of Haran, a city where Abraham lived for a time on his way to Canaan. The crescent then turns southwest and follows the eastern coast of the Mediterranean Sea, spreading across the land of Canaan, later called Israel.

It is no wonder the early civilizations settled in this fruitful land. Cattle and other flocks thrived on the rich pastureland,

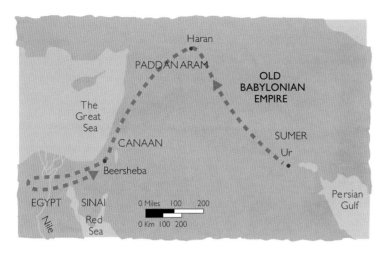
Abraham's journeys – Ur to Haran to Egypt, and back to settle in Canaan.

where wheat, beans, and barley also grew. Numerous rivers fed the area, providing water for vineyards, fields, and gardens. The rivers were also important in travel and communication and helped to form and unify the earliest empires.

Mesopotamia's peoples

In Abraham's time, the Sumerians were the dominant people of Mesopotamia. Later the Babylonians dominated and then the Assyrians. The Persians ruled after the Assyrians fell. Then came the Greeks and Romans.

Abraham's sister

When Abraham told the pharaoh of Egypt that Sarah was his sister, he was not completely lying, but he was not telling the whole truth either. Sarah was Abraham's half-sister on his father Terah's side (Gen. 20:12). In other words, Abraham and Sarah had the same father, Terah, but did not have the same mother. The Bible does not mention their mothers, but it does say they were not the same.

Famine

Imagine entering a grocery store and finding no food on the shelves, and then returning a week later only to see the shelves still empty. By that time there would be many hungry people. But what if those grocery shelves remained empty for months? Where would people get food, and how would they survive?

Abraham faced this kind of problem when famine struck the land of Canaan. A famine is a critical shortage of food

The famous Sphinx of Egypt was built before Abraham's time.

lasting for a long period of time. It may be caused by a number of circumstances. Drought was the main cause of famine. The land of Canaan (later called Israel) depended on two rainy seasons for its crops to grow. If there was no rain in the months when it was supposed to rain, the crops withered and died, and food became scarce. Wealthy people could buy food from foreign countries, but the poor had to live with what little food they could forage from the fields or beg from the wealthy. Life would be difficult at least till the next harvest, which was months away. And some famines lasted for years.

Even with plenty of rain, famine was still feared by the people. Large numbers of insects often devoured the fields before they ripened. Armies invading the land usually attacked during harvest. After taking enough food for themselves, they destroyed the fields, leaving cities and villages without food.

Harems

In the days of Abraham, most people, and especially kings, thought nothing was wrong with having many wives. A king might have as many as 1,000 wives, plus other women who were not married to him. He built a special place for them to live and called on them whenever he pleased. This building, called a harem, was very common among ancient nations.

Abraham and Lot

GENESIS 13:1–13; 14

Abraham and his wife Sarah had migrated from Ur, in Sumer, to Haran, then to Canaan. But a famine came and forced them to move to Egypt. Abraham lied to the king of that land, Pharaoh, telling him that Sarah was his sister, for he was afraid Pharaoh would kill him to marry Sarah. When Pharaoh learned the truth, he forced Abraham and Sarah to leave Egypt. They returned to Canaan. There, a quarrel between Abraham's herdsmen and his nephew Lot's herdsmen forced the two to separate. Not long after that, the city where Lot had moved, Sodom, was involved in a war. Along with others in the city, Lot was carried away captive.

A detail from *Abraham and Melchizedek* by Juan Antonio de Frías y Escalante.

Lot

Lot spent his childhood years in Ur, just as Abraham had. In fact, he was the son of Abraham's brother Haran. But Haran died in Ur, and probably out of a sense of loneliness Lot migrated toward Canaan with his uncle Abraham and his grandfather Terah. He became a wealthy shepherd in Canaan with many flocks and herds. But soon his herdsmen started quarrelling with Abraham's, and the two men decided to split up. Lot chose the fertile Jordan Valley. Though this was a beautiful and well-watered area, it was the home of the wicked people of Sodom and Gomorrah. When God destroyed these cities with fire, only Lot and his daughters escaped.

Canaan – ancestor to Israel

Before the time of the Judges, the land of Israel was called Canaan. This was the land in between the Jordan River and the Mediterranean Sea, the land where Jesus lived and walked. It was also the "Promised Land", the destination of the Hebrews on their Exodus from Egypt.

Abraham's pursuit

When Abraham found out that his nephew Lot had been captured, he set out in pursuit. Leaving his home at Hebron, Abraham and his men travelled northward, finally catching up with the enemy alliance at Dan, a distance of about 210 km (130 miles).

A skilled warrior himself, Abraham made a surprise attack by night and scattered the enemy. He continued the chase as far north as Hobah. The exact location of Hobah is not known for sure, but most think the city was located 80 km (50 miles) north of Damascus, which is about 80 km (50 miles) north of Dan. This means that Abraham travelled a distance of approximately 320–400 km (200–250 miles) north in order to rescue Lot.

Melchizedek

Returning from victory, Abraham was greeted by Melchizedek, the king of Salem who was also a priest of God. Many think that Salem was the city of Jerusalem, about 40 km (25 miles) north of Abraham's home at Hebron.

Melchizedek is mentioned in other places in the Bible. "You are a Priest forever, in the order of Melchizedek" (Ps. 110:4). This psalm apparently refers to Jesus Christ prophetically. Melchizedek is also mentioned in Hebrews 5, in relationship to Jesus as High Priest.

God's Covenant with Abraham

GENESIS 17

Abraham, whose name at this time was Abram, had left Ur to migrate with his family to the north, in Haran, then down to Canaan. But a famine in Canaan forced him to move to Egypt. With a lack of trust in God to take care of him, so unusual for Abraham, he pretended that Sarah (Sarai) was his sister. Pharaoh almost made Sarah a part of his harem, and when he learned the truth, forced Abraham to leave Egypt. Back in Canaan, Abraham and his nephew Lot parted when their herdsmen quarrelled over the land. Lot moved to Sodom and was captured, but Abraham freed him in a swift battle. Now, when Abraham was 99 years old, God appeared to him and renewed His covenant with him.

This clay tablet is an Assyrian record that a loan of silver has been paid. It is a form of an ancient contract, or covenant, and can be seen today in the Metropolitan Museum of Art.

Changing names

In the Old Testament, there were a few people who had their names changed. This almost always marked a very special occasion.

Abram's name was changed to Abraham when God made a covenant with him (Gen. 17:5). Sarai became Sarah when God promised her a son (Gen. 17:15). After wrestling all night with an angel, Jacob's name was changed to Israel (Gen. 32:28). As captives in Babylon, Daniel and his three friends were assigned new names. Daniel was given the name Belteshazzar, Hananiah was called Shadrach, Mishael was named Meshach, and Azariah became Abednego (Dan. 1:7).

Miraculous birth in old age

Sarah was too old to have children. At least that was what Abraham and Sarah thought. But God had promised the couple a child and God does not break His promises. So, at the age of 91, Sarah gave birth to Isaac. At that time, Abraham was 100!

John the Baptist was a "miracle baby" also. His parents, Elizabeth and Zacharias, were both very old when John's birth was promised by God. Zacharias did not believe God's promise and as punishment, God made him speechless until John's birth.

Covenants

In Bible times, there were two types of covenants. The first type was a contract or binding agreement between two people or nations. Both parties were obligated to follow the terms of the agreement which was sometimes sealed by drinking each other's blood or eating a sacrificial meal. God made a covenant with the people of Israel to be their God if they would only follow and obey Him. But Israel rejected God and did not hold up their end of the agreement. So the covenant was broken completely, and the Israelites were carried into captivity.

The second type of covenant was a promise made by one person to another. The one making the promise was bound to keep it, but the one receiving it could accept or reject it. Today, an example of this covenant is a will.

Abraham Entertains Angels

Abraham had moved from his native home in Ur to the land of Haran, and then to Canaan. After a short time in Egypt, during a famine in Canaan, Abraham returned to Canaan to live out the rest of his life. He and his nephew Lot parted ways because of quarrelling herdsmen, but Lot was captured and Abraham rescued him. After that, God renewed His covenant with Abraham. One day God visited Abraham's tent in the form of angels, clothed in men's bodies.

By the oaks of Mamre, Abraham bargained with God for the safety of Sodom and his nephew Lot. *Abraham Receiving the Three Angels of the Lord* by Gerard de Lairesse.

Mamre

When Abraham returned from Egypt after the famine, he "pitched his tent" by the oaks of Mamre, very close to the city of Hebron. It was here that Abraham entertained three angels and bargained with God for the safety of Sodom. Later, near Mamre, Abraham bought the field of Machpelah from Ephron the Hittite. There was a cave at the end of the field where Abraham buried his wife Sarah. Abraham was buried there as well. The Arabic name for Mamre is Ramat el-Khalil, which means "the high place of the friend of God".

How tents were made

The first reference to tents in the Bible is in Genesis 4:20, where a man named Jabal is called "the father of those who live in tents". A tent in Jabal's time was probably made of animal skins crudely patched together. Later, when the Bedouins learned the process of weaving, tents were made by spinning cloth from camels' hair or goats' hair.

The Arabs and Israelites usually made their tents of goats' hair. Because most of the goats were black or dark brown, the tents were this colour as well. When spun together, this goats' hair made a coarse, heavy fabric. In the winter, it protected a family from the cold winds, and in the summer the sides were rolled up to let in the breeze. When dry, the goats'-hair cloth was porous and could "breathe", keeping the tent from getting too stuffy. But after the first rain, the hairs shrunk together making the tent waterproof.

Tents were usually oblong in shape. The size depended on the number of people in a family or

A Bedouin tent in the desert of Qatar.

a person's wealth. Most tents had between one and nine poles. The poles were set in the ground and the tent material was spread over the poles. Leather loops were sewn to the edge of the cloth, and long cords were tied to them. To allow more room inside the tent, these cords were stretched tight and fastened to the ground by iron or wooden pins or pegs.

How people lived in tents

When many Bedouins lived together, they pitched their tents in a circle. Cattle, sheep, and goats were allowed into the circle at night for protection. The sheikh or ruler of the tribe placed his tent in the middle of the circle. Outside the door was his spear, stuck in the ground as a symbol of his authority.

Tents were often large and heavy, and pitching one usually took more than a single person. Some tents had two or three sections. Just inside the entrance were the men's living quarters. Behind a curtain of goats' hair was the women's section, and behind that was an area for the servants or cattle.

Life was simple in a Bedouin tent. Rugs made of skins or goats' hair covered the dirty ground. Sacks of grain supported the tent poles. In the centre of the tent floor a hole was dug for cooking. On hot days the cooking was done outside. Each tent had a hand mill for grinding grain to make bread, and a leather bucket for drawing water from the well.

A hand mill for grinding grain.

The Destruction of Sodom

When the herdsmen of Abraham and Lot quarrelled, Lot moved away to Sodom, a wicked city. Not long after that some kings from the north attacked Sodom and its neighbours and carried Lot away among the captives. Abraham rescued Lot, who then returned to live in Sodom. One day the Lord appeared to Abraham as angels in men's bodies, warning him that Sodom would be destroyed. Lot would be spared for Abraham's sake.

Part of the Dead Sea is coated with minerals.

The city of Sodom

After God totally destroyed Sodom, the city was never again mentioned in the Bible as an active city. It was probably never rebuilt, but this is not known for sure. The exact location of the ruins of the city remains a mystery. Most believe that the ancient ruins of Sodom now lie under the southern part of the Dead Sea. In Lot's time, the sea was probably much smaller, because there is no water outlet and until recently it took in more water than could evaporate.

The Dead Sea area

There is no dry land anywhere in the world lower than the Dead Sea area. Where the Jordan River enters the Dead Sea, the elevation is 390 m (1,285 feet) *below* sea level.

There is no doubt as to how the Dead Sea got its name.

The possible location of the cities of Sodom, Gomorrah, Admah, Zebuuim, and Zoar in the Valley of Siddim.

The Burning of Sodom by Camille Corot shows one angel throwing fire and brimstone on the city of Sodom while another leads Lot and his two daughters away from the destruction – moments after Lot's wife has been turned into a pillar of salt.

Because of the high salt and mineral content of the water, there is no life in the Dead Sea. It is a lifeless body of water, too bitter to drink, often nauseating to smell, and too full of salt, bromide, and sulphur to support any fish or other water life.

The pillar on the left is called "Lot's Wife" and can be found on Mount Sodom – a hill along the Dead Sea.

The Dead Sea is almost 80 km (50 miles) in length, stretching from north to south. Travelling from east to west the widest point is about 18 km (11 miles). There is no water outlet, but most think that if there were, the Dead Sea would be a freshwater sea full of life. The Dead Sea loses water only by evaporation.

The surrounding land is parched and barren. In an entire year, 5–10 cm (2–4 inches) of rain falls. But the sea does have some benefits. With today's modern technology, large amounts of minerals are extracted from the sea and its surrounding area and used for a variety of chemicals, especially fertilizers.

The deception of Lot

After Lot escaped from the burning city of Sodom, he fled to the city of Zoar. But Lot was afraid to live in Zoar, so he left the city and went to live in the mountains, taking his two daughters with him. Soon Lot's daughters grew tired of their lonely life. They wanted children but the only man for miles around was their father. So one night they got him drunk and had children by him. The two children, Moab and Ben-ammi, became the ancestors of the Moabites and the Ammonites, two fierce enemies of Israel who brought much trouble and destruction to the nation.

Isaac Is Born

GENESIS 21:1–7

After Abraham and Lot parted, Lot was captured by some northern kings, but Abraham rescued him. Lot returned to his home in the wicked city of Sodom. One day the Lord told Abraham that Sodom would be destroyed, but Lot would be spared for Abraham's sake. Sodom was destroyed, and Lot was spared. As time passed, God gave Abraham and Sarah a son, as He had promised, and they named him Isaac.

Excavations at Tel Beersheba, to which Abraham moved.

Beersheba

Abraham lived for a time by the oaks of Mamre, near Hebron. But after a while he moved to Beersheba. In all the land of Israel, Beersheba was the farthest city to the south. In fact, there was a saying in Israel "from Dan to Beersheba", which meant from the most northern city to the most southern city.

At Beersheba, Abraham dug a well, and made a covenant of peace with Abimelech (Gen. 21:32). According to the Bible, Abraham gave Beersheba its name, which means "well of the covenant".

Some years later, Isaac had many of his wells stolen by the Philistines. Finally, the Philistines stopped bothering him when he dug a well at Beersheba (Gen. 26:32–33).

Isaac was living at Beersheba when Jacob deceived him to get the family blessing.

The meaning of names

In Bible times, and especially in Old Testament times, a child's name was chosen with great care. Israelites deeply believed that names moulded a child's personality and were responsible for events in their lives. A name was more than just a word to identify a person. Knowing someone's name gave a clue about his behaviour and character.

Abraham's name means "father of a great number". God had promised Abraham that he would be the father of many people, more than the sand on the seashore.

Sarah's name means "princess". Isaac means "laughter", because Sarah was so full of happiness over the birth of her child at such an old age. Jacob's name means "deceiver", which turned out to be prophetic when he tricked Isaac and got the family blessing

Isaac

Isaac was the only son of Abraham and Sarah. It was through him that God chose to fulfil His covenant with Abraham. Through Isaac came the nation of Israel, King David, and most important of all, the birth of Jesus Christ.

When Isaac was born, Abraham was already 100

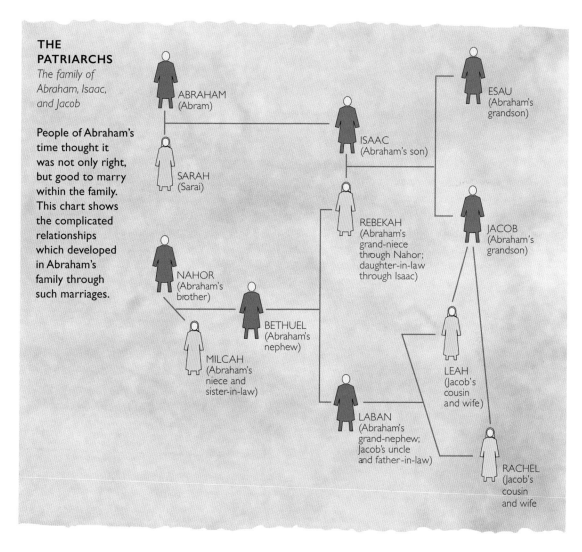

THE PATRIARCHS

The family of Abraham, Isaac, and Jacob

People of Abraham's time thought it was not only right, but good to marry within the family. This chart shows the complicated relationships which developed in Abraham's family through such marriages.

ABRAHAM (Abram)

SARAH (Sarai)

ISAAC (Abraham's son)

ESAU (Abraham's grandson)

REBEKAH (Abraham's grand-niece through Nahor; daughter-in-law through Isaac)

JACOB (Abraham's grandson)

NAHOR (Abraham's brother)

BETHUEL (Abraham's nephew)

MILCAH (Abraham's niece and sister-in-law)

LEAH (Jacob's cousin and wife)

LABAN (Abraham's grand-nephew; Jacob's uncle and father-in-law)

RACHEL (Jacob's cousin and wife

years old. Isaac's birth was a miracle promised by God. But Isaac was not the oldest son of Abraham. His half-brother was Ishmael, the son of Abraham and Hagar. Per Hebrew custom, Ishmael would get the family birthright. But God wanted Isaac to be Abraham's chief heir. So Isaac received his father's blessing and inherited most of his belongings.

Isaac was an excellent example of obedience. When it appeared that he would be sacrificed on Mount Moriah,

he faithfully followed his father's instructions, even when Abraham tied him on the altar.

Through the years, Isaac continued to trust his father and rely on God's guidance. When Abraham's servant Eliezer chose a wife for Isaac, he gladly married her without even seeing her face before the marriage.

But Isaac was not perfect. Like his father, he lied to Abimelech, telling him that Rebekah was his sister instead of his wife. His favouritism

toward Esau over Jacob caused strife in his family and fostered Jacob's deceit. But just before his death, he probably found out that his two sons had again become friends.

Hagar and Ishmael Are Sent Away

GENESIS 21:8–21

After Abraham settled in the land of Canaan, he and Lot separated, for their herdsmen quarrelled over the pasturelands. Lot moved to Sodom, a wicked city which was soon captured by a coalition of kings from the north. But Abraham rescued Lot, who returned to Sodom. The Lord destroyed Sodom and nearby Gomorrah, sparing Lot for Abraham's sake. After that, Abraham and Sarah had a long-awaited son and named him Isaac. But this son, and Abraham's earlier son, Ishmael, caused so much jealousy between the mothers that Abraham had to send his oldest son Ishmael away with his mother Hagar.

Ishmael

Ishmael was the son of Abraham and Hagar, Sarah's Egyptian slave. Ishmael was born because Sarah was unable to have children. It was an embarrassment for a married couple in Bible times not to have children, so Sarah gave her servant Hagar to Abraham to bear children for her.

Hagar gave birth to Ishmael when Abraham was 86 years old. For a long time Abraham thought that Ishmael was the son through whom God would fulfil His covenant. But when Sarah finally had her own son Isaac, the son promised by God, she saw Ishmael as a threat to Isaac, who was now the son to receive the family birthright. Sarah's jealousy forced Hagar and Ishmael to be sent from Abraham's camp and wander in the wilderness of Beersheba. But God did not neglect them. Hagar found Ishmael a wife, and he became the ancestor of the Arab nations of today. Ironically, Isaac's son Esau married Ishmael's daughter.

These Bedouin women remind us of the lifestyle of Sarah and Hagar.

A man carries water in a waterskin near the city of Jerusalem. Hagar probably carried water for herself and Ishmael in one of these kinds of animal skins, illustrated here.

The wilderness of Beersheba

Expelled from the camp of Abraham, Hagar and Ishmael wandered into the wilderness (desert) of Beersheba. The city of Beersheba lies at the most southern part of the land of Israel, just on the outskirts of a vast desert stretching to the south of the city. This was probably the area referred to in Genesis as the "wilderness of Beersheba".

Servant girls as substitute wives

In Bible times, a married woman was shamed and her husband embarrassed if they had no children. Children were a sign of prosperity and good fortune. They were also responsible for helping parents in their work and caring for them in old age. Boys were to master their father's work and carry on the family line. Girls were to help their mother around the home and someday provide their husbands with many children.

If a wife could not provide children for her husband, she was obligated to give to the husband her servant or slave to bear children for her. According to custom, the slave's children were legally the children of the wife, and after birth were taken into the home of the master. Often the children never knew who their real mother was.

Abraham Offers Isaac

GENESIS 22

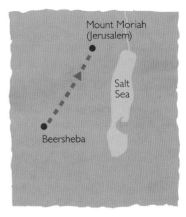

Mount Moriah (Jerusalem)

Salt Sea

Beersheba

Abraham was 100 years old when his long-promised son Isaac was born. Throughout the years he had longed for and waited for this son. Now God asked him to offer Isaac on an altar as a burnt offering.

The route Abraham probably took from Beersheba to Mount Moriah, now in Jerusalem.

A ram took the place of Isaac on the altar.

Isaac and Abraham travelled to the "land of Moriah" around 2050 BC The historian Josephus thinks that Isaac was about 25 years old. In this story, the Hebrew text seems to imply that Isaac might have been just a bit younger, but it is impossible to know his exact age.

Mount Moriah

This mountain was one of the focal points throughout Bible history. It is located just to the north of the city of Jerusalem as it was in David's time. For Abraham and Isaac it was a three-day journey from Beersheba, or a distance of about 80 to 90 km (50 to 60 miles).

On Mount Moriah, God gave Abraham the supreme test of faithfulness, asking him to sacrifice his own son. Because of Abraham's obedience, God started a new nation with Isaac (Gen. 22:1–19).

On this same mountain was Araunah's threshing floor. It was here that God stopped a violent plague from killing the people of Israel because of David's disobedience. David bought the threshing floor and built an altar to God (2 Sam. 24:1–25).

God's holy temple was built on this mountain, first by King Solomon, then by Zerubbabel after it had been destroyed, and finally by Herod the Great. For centuries it was the centre of worship for all Jews (1 Kings 5–8; Hag. 1:12–2:9; John 2:20).

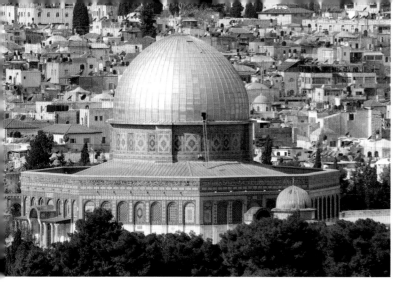

The golden-domed Dome of the Rock stands today over the place where Abraham almost sacrificed Isaac. Solomon's temple once stood there, then later Herod's temple, in the time of Jesus.

The Last Supper took place a short distance down the west side of Mount Moriah. There Jesus and His disciples ate for the last time before His crucifixion (Matt. 26:17–29). Just a few weeks later, the disciples gathered in an upper room, probably this same one, and received the Holy Spirit's power (Acts 2:1–4).

Other important mountains

There were other mountains throughout Bible lands that played an important role in Israel's history. On Mount Ararat, Noah's ark came to rest (Gen. 8:4). Moses received the Ten Commandments on Mount Sinai (Ex. 24:12). Jesus was transfigured on Mount Tabor or Mount Hermon (Luke 9:28–36).

On the Mount of Olives, Jesus was arrested in the Garden of Gethsemane (Matt. 26:30–56). Later, on the same mountain, He ascended into heaven (Luke 24:50–51).

Altars

An altar was much more than a place where an Israelite offered a sacrifice to God. Stepping up to the altar symbolized communion with God and was an act of remembering His covenant. In simple terms, the word "altar" means "to approach". For the Israelites, the altar was a means of approaching God, asking forgiveness for sins, and worshipping Him.

An altar was made of stones, earth, or even metal. Certain Israelite altars could only be made from the stones found in a field. Cutting or shaping the stones for such altars with any type of tool was forbidden, and made the altars unholy and its sacrifices unacceptable to God.

Most altars did not have steps. This was to prevent the priest's body from being accidentally exposed when he walked over to the altar and presented an offering before the people of Israel.

There was a unique design to many Israelite altars. On each corner of the altar at the top, was a horn like a bull's horn. Why these horns were placed on the altar remains a mystery, but most think the idea was to symbolize God's strength and power.

Burnt offerings

The word "offering" today has a much different meaning than it had in Old Testament times. Instead of putting money into a collection plate, the people of the Old Testament placed an animal or food on an altar and burned it before the Lord. Burnt offerings were carried out to ask forgiveness for sins or to give thanks or praise to God.

A Bride for Isaac

For many years the Lord had promised Abraham that he and Sarah would have a son. But they had lost hope, for this son was not born until Abraham was 100 years old. As the child grew, the Lord tested Abraham's faith one day by telling him to offer this only son of his beloved Sarah as a burnt offering. When Abraham obeyed, the Lord stopped him and provided a ram for the offering instead. The years passed and Sarah died at the age of 127 and was buried at Hebron. Abraham then focused his attention on finding the right bride for his son. Isaac was 40 when he married Rebekah. When he was 60, twin sons were born – Jacob and Esau.

Eliezer gave Rebekah rings, which may have been bracelets, nose rings, earrings, or rings for her fingers – like these Egyptian rings from around that time.

Eliezer – Abraham's servant

Eliezer was the most faithful and trusted servant of Abraham. As a result, he was placed in charge of all Abraham's household. This made him responsible for all of Abraham's belongings, as well as all the activities carried on by the other servants.

It is almost certain that Eliezer would have been the servant Abraham chose to travel to Haran and find a wife for Isaac. He was probably chosen for his faith in God, evident when he prayed to God at the well in Haran.

Isaac's wife is chosen for him

In Abraham's day, most young men and women were not allowed to "court" or go on "dates". They could not even go to each other's houses for dinner! Usually, a man did not see his bride until their wedding day.

Sometimes a man could suggest his personal preferences, but usually young men and women were not allowed to choose their mates. The parents, or a trusted servant, had that job. They decided when and where to look for a bride who would be suitable for the son. When she was found, gifts were sent to the woman and her parents. If the father of the woman accepted them and approved of the marriage, the wedding day was then determined.

Eliezer made his way to Haran by camel. The picture above reminds us of his travels. The map shows the possible route Abraham took from Beersheba to Haran.

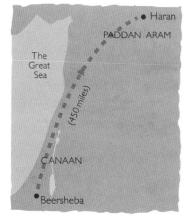

There were probably no wedding ceremonies in Abraham's day, but great wedding feasts that lasted for days.

Wells

Every city and village had a well. The well was obviously a popular place, for in many cities it was the only source of water. They were usually dug just outside a small village in order to keep the dust and crowds of people away from homes and business activities. Larger cities needed wells inside the city as well.

Often a city or village was built next to a well that had already been dug. The well might have been built years before for watering flocks, or along a caravan route.

The well was a busy place early in the morning and just before sunset. Women came to draw cool water for household chores, cooking, and washing. Shepherds also arrived to water their flocks.

Drawing water from a well

In a deep well, a woman dropped a pitcher tied to a rope into the water and pulled it up when it was full. A shallow well often had steps going down to the water, and the pitcher was dipped into the well by hand.

Marriage at an older age

In today's world, the average couple gets married in their twenties, hoping to spend the rest of their lives together. But in early Old Testament times, people lived much longer, and many marriages came at a much older age.

Isaac, for example, did not marry until he was 40 years old, and his two sons, Jacob and Esau, were not born until he was 60. Esau married at 40, but Jacob married years later. It would seem that Jacob was about 80 years old when he first married. But Isaac lived to be 180, and Jacob died at 147. This still gave them plenty of time after their marriages to spend with their families.

Esau Sells His Birthright

GENESIS 25:29–34

Before Abraham died, he arranged for his son Isaac to marry Rebekah. During the last few years of his life, Abraham also arranged for Isaac to inherit all his possessions, except for the gifts which he gave his other children. After Abraham's death, Isaac and Rebekah waited for 20 years to have children, then at last had twin sons, whom they named Jacob and Esau. One day, when these sons had grown, Jacob bought Esau's birthright from him for a bowl of lentil soup.

Lentils grow in pods, much like tiny peas. People in ancient Egypt made lentil soup, just as Jacob did. They recorded this process on the walls of their tombs.

Favourite sons

Many parents have a favourite son or daughter. Often they try hard not to show their favouritism, but it is very difficult. Isaac and Rebekah were this way. As their sons Jacob and Esau grew, Isaac began to prefer Esau over Jacob. The reason for this might be that both Isaac and Esau loved the out-of-doors. Esau was also a hunter and enjoyed bringing venison home to his father. The Bible says that both Isaac and Esau enjoyed the taste of game.

Rebekah preferred Jacob. This was evident when she cunningly helped Jacob steal the family blessing from Esau. According to the Bible, Jacob was a man who "lived in tents". Because of this, he probably spent a lot of time around the family camp and therefore would have spent a lot of time with his mother. Naturally, the two would have developed a strong bond of affection.

The birthright

In a Hebrew family, the firstborn son was very fortunate. He was treated with great respect and honour and given the privilege of the family birthright.

The birthright was the father's special blessing to his oldest son. This gave the son leadership over his brothers, but it also gave him the responsibility of taking care of the family after his father's death. He was to manage the family property and support his widowed mother and unmarried sisters.

When the father died, the oldest son inherited twice as much as his brothers. Israelite custom did not allow the daughters of the dead father to inherit anything, because it was the duty of the son with the birthright to take care of his sisters.

Beersheba today, where Jacob bought Esau's birthright for a bowl of lentil soup.

A birthright could be sold or given away. If the father thought the oldest son did not deserve the birthright, he could give it to a younger son or to someone else. In order to pass the birthright on, the father gave a special blessing to whomever was receiving it. Once this blessing was given, the birthright could not be taken back. This was one reason why the father waited to hand over the family birthright until soon before he was expected to die.

Lentil soup

Jacob was making a very common soup or stew when Esau came in from the fields. This soup was made from lentils, a type of vegetable that was probably so plentiful that it was almost worthless.

In Abraham's day, it is likely that lentils were grown as crops. On the plant grow small, flat pods. Inside these pods are the lentils, which are about the size of a pea. When boiled, they turn the soup into a chocolate-red colour. When Esau was famished, he asked Jacob for a bite of that "red stew" (Gen. 25:30).

Esau

The oldest son of Isaac and Rebekah, Esau was a "hairy man" who enjoyed hunting outdoors and bringing meat, or venison, home to his father. He was Isaac's favourite son.

But Esau did not always please his family. He sold his precious birthright to Jacob, his younger brother, for a bowl of soup. Later, Esau wanted to kill Jacob when he deceived Isaac and received the birthright, but Jacob escaped. Twenty years later however, the two brothers met again as friends.

Esau married two women who were foreigners to the people of Abraham. This showed his lack of concern for God's covenant. Esau became the ancestor of the Edomites, another enemy nation that hated the Israelites.

Jacob Deceives Isaac

GENESIS 27:1–40

Isaac was born when Abraham was 100 and Sarah was 91. He had been promised to them for many years, and God kept His promise in their old age. Isaac did not marry until he was 40, and had no children until he was 60, when he and Rebekah had twin sons, Jacob and Esau. Then, in later years, Isaac moved with his family to Gerar, in Philistine country, where his father Abraham had once lived. Later, he moved to Beersheba. While living there, Jacob deceived his father, Isaac, and took from him a blessing which Isaac had intended to give to Jacob's brother Esau.

The meal before the blessing
Before Isaac would bless Esau and pass on the family birthright, he wanted Esau to prepare for him a "savoury" meal. This meal was sometimes a custom in the ancient Middle East before a covenant or a birthright would be passed on. It turned out to be Esau's undoing, for while he was out hunting for meat, Jacob had time to deceive Isaac and steal the family birthright for himself.

A "savoury" meal probably meant a meal that was cooked with seasonings. Jacob brought Isaac a goat, along with other seasoned food, and Esau brought venison. This meat was cooked by dropping it in a pot of boiling water, or by roasting it over a fire. Meat that was boiled in water left a broth that was eaten with the meal, or saved for another meal.

A widow and the birthright
After the birthright had been passed on, and the man of the house had died, the wife was left with nothing. But this widow was not forgotten. Her welfare was actually a part of the birthright. Whoever inherited the birthright also inherited the responsibility of caring for the widow and her unmarried daughters. This was true regardless of who received the family birthright.

In the guise of his brother Esau, Jacob received the blessing. *Isaac Blessing Jacob*, painted by Nicolas-Guy Brenet.

Rebekah

Rebekah was chosen by Abraham's servant to be the wife of Isaac. Her father, Bethuel, was a nephew of Abraham. For 20 years she had no children, but finally gave birth to two sons, Esau and Jacob. Esau was the ancestor of the Edomites, and Jacob was the ancestor of the Israelites. It was Rebekah's idea to deceive Isaac so that Jacob would receive the family birthright instead of Esau.

Rebekah told Jacob to bring two kids from the herd, and she prepared a savoury meal for Isaac.

Because of Esau's anger, she asked Isaac to send Jacob to Haran, to live with her brother Laban.

Jacob cooked goat meat for Isaac in preparation for the blessing in a vessel like this ceramic Israelite cooking pot (c. 8th–7th century BC) that was found in modern-day Tell ed-Duweir.

Jacob's Ladder

GENESIS 27:41–28:22

When he was younger, Jacob had "bought" his older twin brother's birthright for a bowl of lentil soup. Then when it came time for his father to give the "blessing", which confirmed which son would have the birthright, Jacob pretended to be Esau, whom his father wanted to bless. Jacob received the blessing, but the family was divided. Isaac and Esau were divided from Rebekah and Jacob. To make matters worse, Esau threatened to kill his twin brother. So Rebekah persuaded old Isaac to send Jacob to Haran to find a bride.

These ruins are part of a Christian chapel dating to the time of the Crusades, built next to the site that Jewish tradition says is the place where Jacob dreamed about a ladder.

How far?
When Jacob left for Haran, he had a long trip ahead of him. From his home in Beersheba to Bethel, where he dreamed of the ladder to heaven, was a distance of about 95 km (60 miles). From Bethel, there was still another 645 kilomteres (400 miles) to Haran.

Today that might only take an hour by plane. But then it took many days or weeks. He either walked or rode a camel. Both were slow ways to travel such a great distance.

Bethel
Bethel is about 95 km (60 miles) north of Beersheba, and approximately 16 km (10 miles) north of Jerusalem. It was formerly called Luz, and today it has the name of Beitin, or Beit El.

Long before Jacob had his dream at Bethel, Abraham made a sacrifice there (Gen. 12:8;13:3). In the days of the Judges, the ark of the covenant was kept at Bethel for a time (Jud. 20:26–28). Samuel stopped at Bethel to settle disputes and encourage people to follow God (1 Sam. 7:16).

Bethel became a centre of foreign religion and idol worship. Hosea warned Bethel of its idol worship and called it Beth-aven, which means, "the House of Wickedness". King Josiah destroyed most of the idols in Bethel and led the people to follow God.

Haran
Though the city of Haran was not in the land of Palestine, it played an important role in the history of Israel. The city is located in the arc of rich land, the Fertile Crescent, about

725 km (450 miles) northeast of Beersheba, Jacob's home before travelling to Haran.

Abraham and Sarah lived in Haran before coming to the land of Canaan (Gen. 11:31). Abraham's father, Terah, died there (Gen. 11:32).

When Abraham decided to move to Canaan, he must have

left many relatives behind. In finding a wife for his son Isaac, Abraham sent his servant back to the area of Haran to choose a wife among his relatives (Gen. 24:4). The servant found Rebekah, the daughter of Abraham's nephew, Bethuel.

Years later, Isaac sent his son Jacob to Haran to find a wife. He stayed with Rebekah's brother, Laban (Gen. 28:2). There he fell in love with Laban's daughter, Rachel.

The roads to Haran

In Old Testament times, the best route to a place was not always the straightest. Roads avoided mountains and deserts, and followed rivers or streams whenever possible. This added many miles. Between cities, travel was lonely and dangerous.

The possible route Jacob followed from Beersheba through Bethel to Haran.

33

Jacob Meets Rachel

GENESIS 29:1–30

Isaac had grown old and wanted to give his oldest son Esau the family "blessing", which would confirm that Esau would rule the family. But Jacob and his mother Rebekah deceived Isaac, so that he gave Jacob the blessing instead. Esau was furious and threatened to kill Jacob. Then Rebekah persuaded Isaac to send Jacob away to Haran, where he could find a bride and live away from home until Esau's anger cooled. Along the way, God spoke to Jacob and showed him a ladder that reached from earth to heaven. Confident that God was with him, Jacob continued on to Haran to search for his bride.

When Jacob arrived at Haran, he met a beautiful girl, his cousin, and fell in love with her.

The Bedouin woman reminds us of Rachel, who tended her father Laban's flocks.

Well coverings

A stone was often placed over the opening of a well. This stone sealed the well and helped to keep the water clean.

Most of the wells where shepherds watered their flocks were dug in wide open spaces where the flocks had plenty of room to graze. Strong winds blowing across this almost treeless countryside picked up large amounts of dirt and sand, sometimes enough to clog up an entire well. But when the well opening was covered by a stone, the water remained clean from dirt, sand, and other impurities. These simple stones saved the shepherds countless hours of time cleaning the water and digging their wells again.

Watering flocks at the well

In Bible times, it was usually the custom to wait until all the flocks were gathered at the well before the stone was removed and the flocks were watered. Because the land was often dry and parched, water was precious, and most shepherds wanted the well open for as little time as possible.

Women at the well

Shepherds came to a well to water their flocks, and a weary traveller stopped to draw a cool drink of water. But women also visited the well, probably more often than men.

Men were not the only ones to tend sheep. A woman who tended sheep was called a shepherdess. Rachel was a shepherdess (Gen. 29:9). Every day she came to the well to water her father's flocks. Moses married a shepherdess. After escaping from Egypt, he stopped

by a well in Midian and fought off some evil men who were keeping several sisters from watering their father's flocks (Ex. 2:16–22).

A woman who took care of the home walked to the well twice each day, in the early morning and late afternoon. She drew water for cooking, cleaning, and washing clothes. In a family household, it was almost always the woman's job to make these trips to the well.

Men embracing and kissing
Today it may seem strange for men to greet each other with a hug and a kiss instead of a handshake. But in Bible times, this was the custom, and it still is common today in many Eastern countries.

The nurse
Some families had one or more nurses, or maids, to care for the daughters as they grew up. After the daughter was married, the father gave the nurse to her as a present, and she accompanied the daughter to her new home. There she continued to care for the married daughter. The two often became close friends after the husband brought them to a land of unfamiliar people.

When Rebekah left her family to marry Isaac, she took her nurse along (Gen. 24:59). At Jacob's marriage feast, his wife Leah was given a nurse called Zilpah (Gen. 29:24), and his other wife Rachel received a nurse named Bilhah (Gen. 29:29).

Zilpah and Bilhah
Zilpah was Leah's nurse and Bilhah was Rachel's nurse. These two were a source of competition between Jacob's two wives.

Children were a great blessing and honour to a family. Families with none were ashamed. When Rachel could not have children she became jealous of Leah, and gave her nurse Bilhah to Jacob as a substitute wife in order to have children by her. Bilhah had two sons, Dan and Naphtali. Dan means "justice", implying that God had intervened for Rachel and given her a son. Naphtali means "wrestling", signifying that Rachel was competing with her sister.

Leah had stopped having children for a while. Leah gave Jacob her maid Zilpah as a substitute wife. Zilpah gave birth to Gad and Asher. Gad means "luck" and Asher means "happy".

The marriage feast
When a couple's wedding day arrived, there was often no "official" ceremony like there is today, but rather a great wedding feast that might last as long as two weeks.

The groom dressed in the best clothing he had and was escorted by his friends to the bride's house. There he received his wife, and the entire wedding party made their way back to the groom's house for the feast.

Besides much food, there was dancing, singing, and entertainment. Heathen feasts also included games, contests, and much drinking.

The dowry
Often the bride was not given away unless the groom could offer some compensation for her loss to the family. This might be money, a piece of land, or some animals. Instead of these, Jacob offered his Uncle Laban seven years of work.

The veil
Parents usually decided who their sons or daughters would marry. Often the couple saw each other for the first time on their wedding day. Before the wedding feast, the woman wore a veil which covered her face. If a couple did happen to see each other before they were actually married, the woman could see the man's face from behind her veil, but the man could not see her face. Often he did not see her face until after they were married.

Joseph's Cloak

GENESIS 37:1–11

After Jacob and his family returned to Canaan, they settled at first at Succoth, then moved to a place near Shechem, and finally migrated southward. Near Bethlehem, Jacob's beloved wife Rachel died while giving birth to her second son, Jacob's twelfth son. Jacob returned at last to Mamre, near Hebron, where his father Isaac still lived, and settled there to work as a shepherd. Of all Jacob's 12 sons, Joseph was his favourite. The family noticed this, especially when Jacob gave Joseph a fancy cloak.

Joseph's cloak of many colours
In Joseph's time, most cloaks were very plain, reached to the knees, and had short sleeves or half sleeves. But the cloak that Joseph received from his father was brightly coloured, probably reached all the way down to his ankles, and had long sleeves. Some think that his cloak came from Shinar, also known as the land of Babylon. The Babylonians were highly skilled at this time in making luxurious clothing and embroidery from a variety of materials and colours.

Why did Jacob give a cloak like this to Joseph? It is obvious from the Bible that Jacob favoured his son Joseph over all his other sons, including Benjamin. The beautiful cloak was a sign of Jacob's favouritism. But it was much more than that. A cloak like this was a symbol of distinction and importance. This was the type of cloak that families of royalty wore. Many think that Joseph's cloak was a sign of Jacob's desire to turn the family's birthright over to Joseph. Others believe its purpose was to ward off evil and bring good fortune. But what Joseph's cloak really did was to bring more jealousy and strife to Jacob's already troubled family.

Joseph's unusual cloak provoked jealousy among his brothers, for it clearly showed his father's favouritism. These beautifully woven Bedouin fabrics from Petra, Jordan, remind us of Joseph's cloak.

CLOAKS OF BIBLE TIMES

Cloaks were widely used in Bible times by both men and women. They varied from place to place, and especially from nation to nation. The cloaks pictured here are from monuments of ancient times.

An Egyptian king's cloak

A Persian cloak

A Chaldean cloak

Cloaks with and without girdles (belts)

A Median cloak

An Assyrian cloak

Variety of uses for cloaks

Most people owned only the clothes they wore on their backs. But almost everyone had one other piece of clothing – his cloak. This was certainly the most useful and widely used piece of clothing.

When a person had many things to carry, or when he was moving away, his belongings were wrapped in his cloak and thrown over his shoulder. The Hebrews probably carried many of their personal belongings out of Egypt in this way.

Women carried their babies in their cloaks. Farmers tied their cloaks into a sack which they hung around their necks, and then poured grain into it. From this cloak the farmer would plant his fields by throwing handfuls of grain in front of him as he walked.

When an honoured guest would arrive, the host often spread his cloak on the ground as a place where the guest could sit. At Jesus' triumphal entry, the people of the city laid their cloaks on the ground before Jesus as he rode into Jerusalem on a donkey.

A cloak was also given to someone as a pledge for a debt. When the debt was paid, the cloak was returned. However, the Law of Moses stated that if a cloak was a man's only covering at night, it must be returned to him before sunset.

At night, a person slept under his cloak, or used it as a pillow. Some were made out of goat or camel hair, which kept out most of the dew and rain.

In times of great grief and sorrow, a cloak was often torn to pieces. Others would seize the hem of someone's cloak to beg for mercy.

Dreams

Waking up from a good night of sleep often alarmed people more than it helped them. If they had just had a vivid dream, they would not have laughed about it as most people do today. Dreams in Bible times were highly respected and thought to be predictions or warnings of the future, or uncoverings of the past.

Dream interpreters were always in demand, especially in the presence of kings and rulers. As long as their interpretations were accurate, they were given places of honour and prestige in the kingdom. After Joseph told Pharaoh the meaning of his dream, he was made governor of Egypt (Gen. 41:39–41). Daniel was promoted to a ruler of Babylon under Nebuchadnezzar after he interpreted his king's dream (Dan. 2:46–48).

Joseph Is Sold as a Slave

GENESIS 37:12–36

After returning home to Canaan with his family, Jacob was saddened by the death of his beloved wife Rachel. He had worked 14 years for the right to marry her, and now she had died, while giving birth to her second son, Benjamin. Jacob then settled down near his childhood home, living as a shepherd. As the years passed, it became clear to all that one son was his favourite. That son was Joseph. His jealous brothers brought things to a head by selling Joseph as a slave.

The pit was probably a cistern, which is a deep hole cut down into rock or hard clay that is not porous. Cisterns were used mainly to collect and store rainwater which was used later to water flocks or quench the thirst of travelling caravans.

Cisterns were also used as dungeons when they held no water. The opening was small enough to put a cover on the top, but the bottom was much larger. This pear-shape made it almost impossible for a man to escape once he was dropped into the cistern. Centuries later the Prophet Jeremiah was also put into a cistern that had been dug in a prison courtyard (Jer. 38:6).

Jacob's brothers threw him into a cistern, perhaps much like this one.

Dothan

Joseph left his home around Hebron to search for his brothers. He first travelled northward to Shechem, a distance of about 95 km

The pit or cistern

When Joseph found his brothers in the fields near Dothan, he suddenly became a victim of their jealousy. Jacob's favouritism to Joseph, along with the beautiful cloak and unpopular dreams, had fuelled an intense hatred toward Joseph by his brothers. When they saw Joseph coming across the fields, they immediately wanted to kill him. But Reuben, the oldest, convinced them to throw Joseph into a "pit" until they could decide what to do with him.

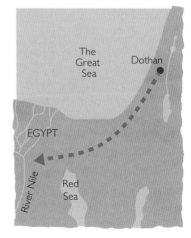

(60 miles). There he learned that his brothers had moved on to Dothan, another 32 km or so (20 miles) to the north.

Dothan is known for its rich pastureland. Even today, many shepherds still take their flocks up to the Dothan area from Jerusalem and elsewhere for good grazing.

In Joseph's time, Dothan was situated on a major trade route which connected Syria in the north with the southern kingdom of Egypt. This was probably the route the Ishmaelite traders were taking when they passed through Dothan and bought Joseph as a slave.

Caravans

Joseph's brothers sold him to Ishmaelite traders for 20 shekels of silver, which was only enough to buy one ram each.

Suddenly Joseph was a member of a caravan, on a long journey to Egypt. Caravans in Bible times were groups of people travelling a common road or toward a common destination. Travelling alone was extremely dangerous, especially when one stopped to rest for the night. Roads had no signs to direct travellers, and robbers and wild animals were frequent. For these reasons, people journeyed in groups whenever possible. The more travellers in a group, the less chance of being attacked by thieves or bands of raiders.

As a caravan made its way along the road, some joined the group, while others left it, having reached the end of their journey. Some caravans had as many as 3,000 people, but most were much smaller. Poor people walked or rode on donkeys, while the rich sat on camels. Because of the dry and dusty roads, those who had to ride at the end of the caravan were breathing clouds of dust for the entire trip.

At nightfall, caravans offered protection from the perils of the dark. Often they stopped at wayside inns, which were usually just empty buildings in which to sleep, or walled courtyards that protected people and animals from robbery or attack.

Caravans caused much excitement when entering a city or village. Often they had come from places far away and brought with them fascinating goods from foreign lands or news that was unknown to many.

A camel caravan today, a reminder of the caravan which took Joseph to Egypt.

A slave's life in Egypt

A slave usually lived a hopeless life, full of despair. Most slaves had no "days off" or holidays. They knew that the rest of their lives would be filled with endless chores and probably difficult, exhausting work.

Joseph was a fortunate slave. Because of his intelligence and good attitude, he was chosen to be a steward. His job was to supervise the activities of a wealthy household.

But most slaves were not so fortunate. Many had to work in copper mines, which meant certain death. Others were oarsmen on Egyptian warships. Some women were forced to be prostitutes. Other slaves were brickmakers or metalworkers.

Joseph in Potiphar's House

GENESIS 39–40

Joseph was clearly his father Jacob's favourite son. This, of course, made his brothers jealous. Joseph aggravated this by telling about two dreams, in which his father, mother, and brothers bowed down before him. Jealousy overcame the brothers, and they sold Joseph as a slave. He was taken to Egypt by caravan and sold to an official named Potiphar. Joseph's faithfulness caught his master's eye, and he promoted him over the entire household. But his faithfulness also angered Potiphar's wife. She lied about Joseph, and he was thrown into prison. There he met Pharaoh's baker and cupbearer, who both dreamed strange dreams and told them to Joseph.

Potiphar's wife might have owned a cosmetic box and mirror like this set (c. 1814–1805 BC).

Potiphar's house may have looked like the country estate shown here, or it may have been a large two- or three-storied city home. The houses in Egypt were built from bricks made of mud from the Nile River. After the walls were built, they would be covered with plaster. The houses had only very small windows and kept cool inside. The rich had big houses with many rooms.

Potiphar

Potiphar was captain of the bodyguard, an official of Pharaoh who bought Joseph from the Ishmaelite traders in Egypt. As captain of the bodyguard, Potiphar was ultimately responsible for the protection of Pharaoh's life. He was also in charge of important prisoners and was often given the job of sentencing them to be executed.

Steward

Joseph was bought as a slave by Potiphar, then taken to Potiphar's house, probably a wealthy home. Joseph's wisdom and attitude soon earned him the job of steward.

A steward in ancient Egypt was in charge of all the activities in his master's house. Joseph ran Potiphar's house so smoothly that the man worried about nothing (Gen. 39:6).

The home of a man like Potiphar would have been very large, with many slaves. Joseph's job was to make sure that each slave was doing his work. As supervisor, Joseph made sure that Potiphar's meal was served on time.

The comfort of the master and his family was a top priority. The house was really to be run like a business, smoothly and efficiently, with excellent service and a minimum of problems.

Prisons

"Guilty until proven innocent." That was the system of justice in ancient times. When a person was suspected of committing a crime, he was thrown into prison until his trial. Often the trial never took place, or it did not come up for years. Until then, the accused person stayed with robbers, murderers, and the insane. A respected man or official who was accused of wrong might be kept in a room of the palace or a house. But most people were thrown into prison cells or dungeons. The rooms were dark and clammy. There were no toilets, and prisoners had to remain in their cells. The stench was unbearable, and sickness and disease were common.

Many prisons offered no food or water. Whatever food the prisoner's family could bring was all that was eaten. Many men thrown into prison far from home starved to death.

A baker's job in ancient Egypt

When Joseph was alive, bread was the most common food in Egypt. It was popular, not because it tasted so good, but because its ingredients were easy to find and bread was inexpensive to make.

Bread was made from wheat or barley, and since the methods for refining the flour were limited, almost all of the grain was left in the bread when it was baked. This probably kept this bread full of calories, fibre, and nutrients, making bread one of Egypt's staple foods .

The first step in breadmaking was to separate the grain from the stalks of wheat or barley. This was done by the farmer. The baker bought this grain from the farmer and then put it into a stone pot called a "mortar". Taking a "pestle", which was a hard stone or wood bar with a large, round end, he crushed the grain into a coarse flour. Running the grain between two millstones produced a much finer flour.

After the flour had been sifted to remove dirt and sand, it was mixed with water and honey to make dough. Yeast was added if the baker wanted the bread to rise. This dough was shaped into loaves and baked in ovens of preheated rocks, or cooked on the outside of heated pottery jars called "*tannurs*". It is obvious that a baker had a hot and tiring job.

A cupbearer's job

Also called a butler, the cupbearer stood before the king every day. His job was to serve the king his drinks, probably wine, though many think that the ancient Egyptians drank no wine.

The cupbearer was also responsible in part for the king's life. Because he was so frequently in the company of the king, the cupbearer had to be a highly trusted man. He was usually an important official with great status and respect in the kingdom.

When offering the king a drink, or refilling the king's drinking cup, the cupbearer first poured the drink into the palm of his hand and tasted it as proof that it was not poisoned. Ancient Egyptian cups usually had no handles, so the cupbearer placed the king's drinking cup directly in the palm of his hand. For this reason, Joseph told the cupbearer that he would "put Pharaoh's cup in his hand", when he had regained his old job (Gen. 40:13).

A limestone relief showing a scribe and a cupbearer approaching Queen Neferu.

Joseph Becomes Governor

GENESIS 41

After Joseph's brothers sold him as a slave, he was taken to Egypt, where he became steward over Potiphar's household. But this official's wife lied about Joseph, and he was thrown into prison. There he met Pharaoh's baker and cupbearer and interpreted strange dreams for them. The cupbearer returned to Pharaoh, and when Pharaoh needed dreams interpreted, told him about Joseph. When Joseph told Pharaoh what his dreams meant, Pharaoh made him governor of all Egypt. Joseph's biggest task lay ahead, though. It was to keep people from starving in the coming famine. Joseph organized the land and set up a system for collecting grain.

Three forms of Egyptian "pillows" or headrests. Two are wood and the one on the right is made of alabaster (c. 16540–2150 BC).

Dreams throughout the Bible

In ancient times, dreams were a serious matter, treated with respect. God often used dreams to tell of some future event or warn people of approaching trouble. Those who were able to interpret dreams quickly rose to positions of importance within the kingdom.

Often God talked directly to people. There is some disagreement as to whether He really conversed with them, or if He spoke in visions or through dreams.

Jacob dreamed of a ladder to heaven when he stopped to rest for the night on his long journey to Haran (Gen. 28:12). Because of this dream, he made a covenant with God. Joseph interpreted the dreams of the butler and the baker (Gen. 40). With God's help, his interpretations were correct, giving him a chance later to interpret Pharaoh's dream. Once again God gave Joseph success in telling Pharaoh the meaning of his dreams. Because of this, Joseph was made governor of Egypt (Gen. 41:1–45).

Many years later, Gideon's courage was renewed when he stole into the Midianite camp and heard a soldier tell his friend of a dream in which their entire army was defeated by Gideon's men (Jud. 7:13–15).

King Nebuchadnezzar was greatly troubled by a dream. He searched his kingdom for a man who could unravel its meaning. When Daniel was able to interpret the king's dream, he was promoted to ruler of Babylon under Nebuchadnezzar (Dan. 2). Later, Daniel had a strange dream about the four winds, the four beasts, and the great sea (Dan. 7).

After Jesus was born, God warned Joseph in a dream to flee to Egypt to escape Herod's anger (Matt. 2:13). Joseph was also told in a dream to return to Israel after Herod's death (Matt. 2:19–20). When Jesus was on trial, Pilate's wife had a traumatic dream which led her to beg Pilate to release Jesus (Matt. 27:19).

An ancient Egyptian signet ring, probably much like the one which Pharaoh gave to Joseph. Note the hieroglyphics carved on it, which become a signature when pressed on clay. This ring depicts Akhenaten and Nefertiti as earth and sky gods standing below the sun and two sacred cobras.

Signet rings

When Pharaoh gave Joseph his royal signet ring, all the people of Egypt knew that Joseph had been given enormous power in the land of Egypt. Handing over the signet ring symbolized the great authority that had been transferred to Joseph by Pharaoh. Next to Pharaoh, Joseph was now the most powerful man in Egypt.

Signet rings were used also to sign documents. Impressing a signet ring into clay or wax was like signing one's signature today. Many men owned signet rings, and each ring had a different mark or symbol engraved on it.

Egyptian storehouses

Before the great famine in Egypt came seven years of abundant harvests. During this time, Joseph, as governor, collected a tax from the people in the form of grain. Joseph knew he had to collect enough grain to carry the people through the seven years of scarcity that lay ahead.

The grain was stored in storehouses or granaries until there was so much of it that it could no longer be measured (Gen. 41:49). Most granaries were buildings with beehive-shaped domes, divided into a series of rooms. Grain was poured into each room from the top, and taken out through a small door near the bottom.

Grain – planting and harvesting

In Israel, farmers depended on two rainy seasons for a good harvest. By contrast, Egyptian farmers relied on the Nile River. During the months of September, October, and November the Nile overflowed its banks, and the river flooded the surrounding land. When the waters receded, a fertile layer of silt was left behind.

While this new soil was still moist, the farmer quickly ploughed his land with a clumsy wooden plough pulled by oxen. Many farmers, however, did not have animals to do their heavy work and were forced to pull their ploughs themselves. After the ploughing and hoeing were done, the farmer began sowing, or planting his seeds. He walked through the fields, throwing the seeds from his hands onto the rich soil. Pigs, sheep, or other animals walked behind him, trampling the seeds into the ground. Then the farmer waited until March or April, the time of harvest.

The job of cutting the stalks of grain and tying them into bundles was given to men and women called reapers. These bundles, or sheaves of wheat, barley, or corn, were then taken to the threshing floor where oxen or donkeys plodded over the stalks, separating the grain from them.

Next the grain was strained, or sifted through a sieve, then thrown into the wind with long wooden forks. The heavier grain fell to the ground, while the chaff was blown away in the wind. This process was called winnowing. The sieve removed the heavier pieces of dirt and sand, while the wind carried away the light and useless chaff.

Now the grain was ready to be stored, until it was needed for making bread or other uses. An official arrived to make sure that some grain went to the temple granaries, for the priests' food, and some grain went to the royal granaries, for the king's food.

What did Joseph look like? Maybe like this wooden statue depicting Merti – a governor like Joseph – who served c. 2381–2323 BC

Joseph's Brothers Buy Grain

GENESIS 42–44; 45:1–15

Joseph's older brothers were jealous because their father Jacob favoured Joseph above them all. The jealousy grew to hatred until they sold Joseph as a slave. In Egypt, Joseph was bought by Potiphar, an official who placed him over all his household when he saw that the Lord was with Joseph. Potiphar's wife lied about Joseph, and he was thrown into prison, where he interpreted some dreams for Pharaoh's baker and cupbearer. When Pharaoh had strange dreams, his cupbearer told him about Joseph, who told Pharaoh a famine was coming. Pharaoh placed Joseph in charge of the land, to prepare for the famine. In time, the brothers who sold Joseph came to buy grain. But they did not recognize Joseph until he revealed himself to them.

Joseph as governor

Joseph was second-in-command over the entire land of Egypt. Only Pharaoh himself had more power and authority. Pharaoh had great trust in Joseph, for he told the people to do whatever Joseph asked (Gen. 41:55). Joseph may have been in charge of Egypt's army, finances, agriculture, and justice system.

Just as Joseph was once a steward in the house of Potiphar, now he had

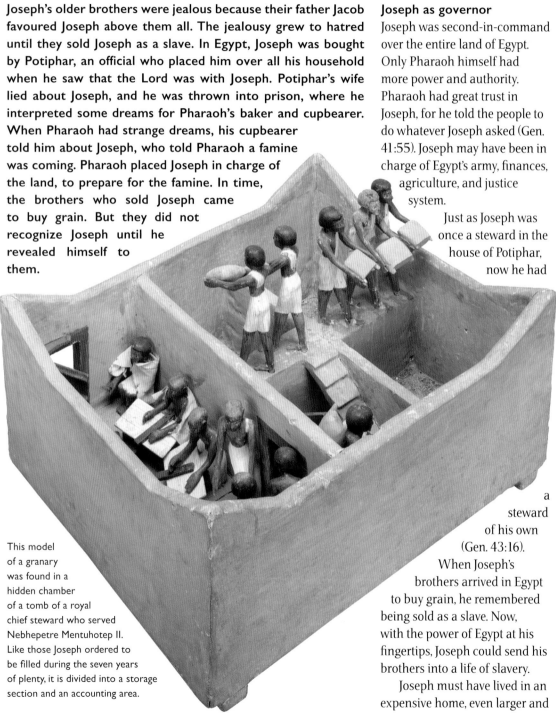

a steward of his own (Gen. 43:16). When Joseph's brothers arrived in Egypt to buy grain, he remembered being sold as a slave. Now, with the power of Egypt at his fingertips, Joseph could send his brothers into a life of slavery.

Joseph must have lived in an expensive home, even larger and

This model of a granary was found in a hidden chamber of a tomb of a royal chief steward who served Nebhepetre Mentuhotep II. Like those Joseph ordered to be filled during the seven years of plenty, it is divided into a storage section and an accounting area.

more beautiful than Potiphar's. It was probably three stories tall and surrounded by a walled courtyard. Slaves kept the house in order, prepared the meals, and looked after Joseph's comfort. Joseph's wife also had many slaves. Some even helped her dress and put on makeup.

Inside, Joseph's home must have been filled with elegant wall hangings and colourful rugs. Decorations of gold, silver, and alabaster were everywhere. The furniture, elaborately carved, was also made of alabaster, or an imported wood like ebony, which was inlaid with ivory.

Joseph's silver drinking cup

Gold was quite common in the land of Egypt, but silver was considered a more precious metal because it was harder to come by. Joseph's personal

drinking cup was made of silver. But this kind of cup was used for more than just drinking.

The cup was called a "divination" cup. Skilled craftsmen engraved symbols, spells, and religious phrases on the cup. Often the owner's name was also inscribed on the cup. When drinking from it, all of the liquid had to be drained from

A silver cup of Egypt, from about the time of Joseph.

the cup in order to repel evil and bring the god's blessings.

In divination (looking into the future), pure water was usually poured into the cup. People thought that the cup answered questions about the future through bubbles, reflections, or calmness. Sometimes hot wax was poured into the water, and predictions were made from the shapes of the hardened wax.

The 11 brothers of Joseph

Though Joseph's brothers were not always kind or honest, God chose to continue the nation of Israel through them. Their descendants became 10 of the tribes of Israel. Reuben was the oldest brother of Joseph. He persuaded his other brothers not to kill Joseph, but to throw him into a pit instead (Gen. 37:12–22).

Simeon was kept in an Egyptian prison by Joseph, while the other brothers returned to Canaan to get Benjamin (Gen. 42:18–24).

Levi was the ancestor of Moses and Aaron. Through Levi came the Levites, Israel's religious leaders and caretakers of the tabernacle (Ex. 32:25–29).

Judah had the idea of selling Joseph into slavery instead of killing him (Gen. 37:26–28). He was an ancestor of King David and Jesus (Matt. 1:1–16).

Issachar was born in Paddan Aram, as were all of Jacob's sons except Benjamin. Descendants of Issachar included Deborah and Barak (Jud. 5:15).

Zebulun was Leah's last son (Gen. 30:19–20). His name meant "dwelling" or "abiding".

Gad was Zilpah's first son (Gen. 30:9–11). His descendants settled east of the Jordan River.

Asher was Zilpah's second son (Gen. 30:12–13). His descendants received the territory that borders the Mediterranean Sea, west of the Sea of Galilee.

Dan was Bilhah's son (Gen. 30:4–6). His descendants eventually settled farther north than any other tribe.

Naphtali was Bilhah's second son (Gen. 30:7–8). The land along the western edge of the Sea of Galilee was given to his descendants.

Benjamin was born to Rachel. His descendants, the tribe of Benjamin, were almost destroyed by the rest of Israel (Jud. 19–21). King Saul and Paul the apostle came from the line of Benjamin (1 Sam. 9:1–2; Phil. 3:5).

Joseph's Family Moves to Egypt

GENESIS 45:16–47:31

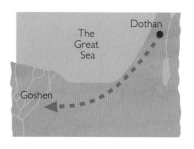

The journey from Canaan to Goshen.

When he was a young man, Joseph was sold into slavery by his brothers. Taken to Egypt, he was bought by an official, Potiphar, who placed Joseph in charge of his household but later threw Joseph into prison because of Potiphar's wife's accusations. There Joseph met Pharaoh's baker and cupbearer and interpreted dreams for them. The cupbearer later told Pharaoh about Joseph, who interpreted two important dreams for Pharaoh, warning of a coming famine. Pharaoh made Joseph governor and placed him over the land to prepare for the famine. In time Joseph's brothers came to buy grain, and he revealed to them who he was. Then Joseph sent them back to Canaan to return with the entire family.

The unsettled life of a herdsman was vulgar to Egyptian men and women, who preferred to live in houses and cities, learning jobs as craftsmen, scribes, or officials. Music and the arts were popular entertainment among Egyptians, but the Hebrews enjoyed gathering in their tents to talk and eat.

The Great Pyramid was standing when Joseph was governor of Egypt.

Egypt – a contrast in living

Arriving in Egypt from the land of Canaan, Jacob and his family faced a new lifestyle. Egyptian customs were very different from those in Canaan, and the landscape was unfamiliar too. Crossing the borders of Egypt, Jacob's family would have noticed the flat and desolate land, quite a contrast to the hills and lush valleys of Canaan. Compared with the small Canaanite villages, the sprawling Egyptian store-cities were certainly awesome and frightening.

Family life was different as well. Egyptian women were allowed to own property and accompanied their husbands to most social functions. This was forbidden in Israelite culture. Hebrew boys learned their father's trade, while Egyptian boys started school at the age of four and trained as scribes or government officials.

An Uncultured Society

Egypt operated a highly skilled and sophisticated society. They considered foreigners from the area of Canaan to be a crude and backward people.

Hebrews grew beards, while Egyptians were clean-shaven.

Goshen

Jacob's nationality and occupation were loathsome in the eyes of the Egyptians, so Pharaoh gave Jacob his own area of land in which to live. This region was in the eastern section of the Nile River delta and was called the land of Goshen. It was a rich land due to the many river branches that watered the area.

The land of Goshen was in the northeastern corner of Egypt. It was one of the first sights in the land of Egypt seen by Jacob's caravan.

Hebrews Become Slaves

EXODUS 1

When Joseph was still in his teen years, his brothers sold him as a slave, and he was bought by an official in Egypt. As the years passed, Joseph died, and a new pharaoh came to the throne. More years passed, and more new pharaohs came until the time when Joseph was almost forgotten. One pharaoh decided to make the Hebrews, descendants of Joseph and his brothers, his slaves.

Taskmasters

The men in charge of supervising the work of the Hebrew slaves were called taskmasters. The word means "chief of the burden" or "oppressor". Their job was to keep the slaves working at a rapid pace and subdue their spirits by oppressing them with beatings and whippings. They were also ordered by Pharaoh to

Brickmaking in Egypt

The name of the pharaoh of Egypt who ruled the land at Moses' birth is not known, but he must have been interested in the wealth and power of Egypt. This pharaoh started many building projects. But before the buildings could be constructed, bricks had to be made. This was probably the main job given the Hebrew slaves. Pharaoh pushed the Hebrew slaves to the brink of death.

Bricks were made by mixing together clay, straw, and water. This mud mixture was poured into wooden moulds in the shape of bricks. The mixture was pressed firmly into the moulds, and placed in the sunlight to dry. The hardened bricks were removed from their moulds and carried to the building site, ready for construction. Because the climate of Egypt is hot and dry, with very little rain, these bricks lasted for centuries.

This wooden frame is an actual Egyptian brick mould (c. 1550–1295 BC) found in the ruins of the Temple of Hatshepsut.

kill as many slaves as necessary to keep their numbers down.

The taskmaster was used not only to ensure that Pharaoh's building projects were carried out, but to see that the Hebrew population did not grow large enough to start a rebellion against Egypt.

Moses Is Born

EXODUS 2:1–10

Almost 400 years before Moses' time Joseph was sold as a slave and taken into Egypt. When he interpreted dreams for Pharaoh, warning of a coming famine, Pharaoh placed him over the land to prepare for this time. But the years and centuries passed, and a pharaoh arose who did not know about Joseph. He enslaved the descendants of Joseph and his brothers. One child born into a Hebrew slave family was Moses.

The bulrushes

Some Bible versions say that Moses was hidden among bulrushes in the Nile River. These bulrushes were large reeds also known as papyrus. They were probably the same reeds that Jochebed, Moses' mother, used to make the basket in which Moses was hidden.

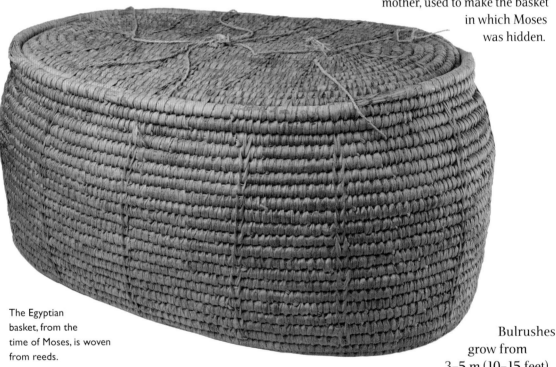

The Egyptian basket, from the time of Moses, is woven from reeds.

The basket

Pharaoh's decree that all Hebrew baby boys were to be killed was put into effect throughout the land. Moses' mother, Jochebed, quickly made a wicker basket, her only hope of hiding Moses from the king's soldiers.

The basket would have been made of papyrus, a hollow reed that grows in abundance along the banks of the Nile River. Most baskets were made by weaving the papyrus reeds together. Egyptian baskets were sturdy as well as beautiful.

Bulrushes grow from 3–5 m (10–15 feet) tall and are as thick as 8 cm (3 inches). They grow along the banks of rivers and lakes, with their roots under the water. They were used in ancient times for paper and boats.

Who was the princess?

Who was the princess who rescued baby Moses from the waters of the Nile? Her identity, as well as that of her father, the reigning pharaoh, remain a mystery. But there are a few clues.

In sorting out the mystery, two main theories have come to light. The first theory is that Moses grew up under the reign of Ramses II, a very cruel pharaoh. Merneptah, the next pharaoh, would have been the king when Moses led the Hebrews out of Egypt.

The second popular theory says that the princess who rescued Moses was Hatshepsut, the daughter of Thutmose I who lived about 200 years before Ramses II.

Hatshepsut was a strong woman who married her half-brother, Thutmose II. When Thutmose I died, his son Thutmose II took over as pharaoh, but it was really the iron hand of Hatshepsut that ruled the land. Hatshepsut had no children, and there must have been bad feelings between the two, because Thutmose II wanted to make one of

This seated limestone statue of Hatshepsut was made around 1479–1458 BC.

his sons, born to a woman from his harem, the next king of Egypt. If this happened, Hatshepsut's power would be stripped from her and her descendants. With no children of her own, Hatshepsut could have raised Moses to be the next pharaoh as an act of revenge against her husband.

Later, Hatshepsut had another motive for raising Moses. After her husband, Thutmose II, died, she seized the throne and became ruler of Egypt for 22 years. With no children, finding Moses would have seemed like a gift from the gods. She would have carefully raised Moses to become the next pharaoh of Egypt.

When was Moses born?

Moses was born in Egypt approximately 300 years after the death of Joseph (1550–1500 BC). He led the Hebrews out of slavery about 400 years after Jacob and his family had first come to Egypt during the famine (Ex. 12:40). Forty years passed from the time Moses escaped from Egypt until the time he led his people from slavery toward the Promised Land.

Moses' parents

The father of Moses was Amram, and his mother was Jochebed. They were also the parents of Aaron and Miriam. Amram was a Levite, an ancestor of the line of priests which began with Aaron.

When Pharaoh started killing Hebrew baby boys, Jochebed made a basket for Moses and hid him in the Nile River. When Pharaoh's daughter found Moses, Jochebed was given the job of caring for her son until he was old enough to live in the palace (Ex. 2:3–9).

Moses Kills an Egyptian and Flees to Midian

EXODUS 2:11–25

Almost 400 years after Joseph's time, a pharaoh arose who did not care about the Hebrews, descendants of Joseph and his brothers. Pharaoh made slaves of them and forced them to work for him. Moses was born into one of these Hebrew slave families. To escape Pharaoh's soldiers, his mother placed him in a basket and laid it in the Nile River. Pharaoh's daughter found him and adopted him as her own. Moses grew up as her son, enjoying all the riches and good education Egypt could offer. Then one day he killed an Egyptian who was beating a Hebrew slave. Moses was forced to run away. At Midian he met and married Zipporah, a shepherdess. He became a shepherd, caring for the flocks of his father-in-law Jethro.

The storage cities of Egypt

Each year the pharaoh of Egypt collected a tax from the people in the form of grain, animals, or other produce. These taxes were collected to provide for the king and his government. During years of a large harvest, taxes were also collected to prepare the country for a "lean" year, or famine.

A place was needed to store all this food, so large cities were built for this purpose. Workmen were necessary, and the Hebrews were forced into slavery to construct great store-cities such as Pithom and Ramses. These two cities were located in the delta of the Nile River, in or near the land of Goshen.

Building these cities was backbreaking work, and none of the Egyptians wanted the job. As slaves, the Hebrews worked hard, provided cheap labour, and were no longer a threat to the Egyptian people. It is easy to see why Pharaoh did not want to let them leave Egypt.

An Egyptian statue of a bound, kneeling slave, c. 2152 BC.

The land of Midian

After Moses knew that his life was in danger, he escaped from Egypt and fled across the desert to the land of Midian. This region was about 320 km (200 miles) southeast of Egypt and probably north and east of the Gulf of Aqaba, an arm of water extending northeast from the Red Sea.

After Abraham's wife Sarah died, he married a woman named Keturah. They had a son called Midian, who became the ancestor of the Midianites.

Moses escaped to the land of Midian and was taken in by Jethro, the priest of Midian. There he married Zipporah, one of Jethro's daughters (Ex. 2:15–22). But despite Jethro's kindness, the Midianites and the Israelites became hostile enemies.

Jethro

Jethro was Moses' father-in-law and the "priest of Midian". His duties as a priest are not certain, but he probably served the different tribes in the area of Midian as a religious leader and a judge. Jethro was also called Reuel (Ex. 2:18). This name might have been given him

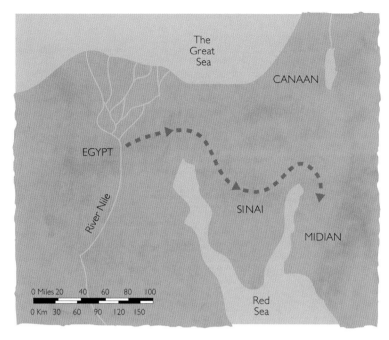

been taught to despise, out of Egypt, his homeland.

Zipporah

Zipporah was one of Jethro's seven daughters. When Moses settled in Midian, he married her (Ex. 2:21). She had two sons, Gershom and Eliezer (Ex. 2:22; 18:3–4). She travelled to Egypt with Moses when he returned to free the Hebrews. Along the way, she circumcised her son, Gershom, because of God's anger at Moses for not doing so (Ex. 4:24–26). Later she returned to her father in Midian and then rejoined Moses in the wilderness.

by a Midianite tribe.

When Jethro learned that Moses had protected his daughters from a band of evil shepherds, he invited Moses to stay and live with him. Moses stayed, and married Jethro's daughter, Zipporah. They lived in the land of Midian for the next 40 years. After Moses had brought the Hebrews out of Egypt, Jethro visited him in the wilderness and helped set up

Israel's first judicial system (Ex. 18:14–27).

Moses settles with shepherds

Born in Egypt, Moses was raised as a prince in the palace of Pharaoh. Here he was fully trained in the skills and customs of the land.

Though Moses was a Hebrew, he was raised as an Egyptian and would have been taught that Hebrews were a crude and backward people and that shepherding was a degrading occupation. What a humbling experience then for Moses, a prince of Egypt, to settle in the land of Midian, where he took a job tending sheep. Later he led the Hebrews, people he had

Moses' 40–year periods

Moses' life is divided into three 40-year periods. The first stretches from his birth in Egypt until his escape to Midian (Acts 7:23–29). During that time Moses was a prince of Egypt, highly trained in language, art, military, and other skills.

Moses' second 40 years begins on his arrival in Midian. During those years he lived in this country, where he tended Jethro's flocks, married Zipporah, had two sons, and met God on Mount Sinai.

After 40 years in Midian, God told Moses to return to Egypt and free His people from slavery. After Pharaoh finally released the Hebrews, they spent 40 years in the desert.

Zipporah was a shepherdess, with a harsh lifestyle very different from that of the sophisticated women of Egypt, like the one depicted in this limestone sculpture (c. 1320–1237 BC). Busts of family ancestors like this were placed in niches in Egyptian homes or in tombs and cemeteries.

The Burning Bush

EXODUS 3:1–4:17

The location of Mount Sinai, as it relates to Egypt and Midian.

Born in a Hebrew slave household, Moses was condemned to die with all other Hebrew baby boys. But his mother hid him in a basket in the Nile River, where Pharaoh's daughter found him and adopted him. Moses grew up as a prince in Egypt until the day when he killed an Egyptian taskmaster for beating a Hebrew slave. Afraid, Moses ran away to Midian, where he married Zipporah, daughter of a shepherd and priest, Jethro. Moses then became a shepherd and cared for Jethro's flocks. One day he noticed a strange sight – a bush that burned but did not burn up.

Though the exact mountain that was called Sinai is not known for certain, tradition says that it is a mountain known today as Jebel Musa (Mountain of Moses). This mountain lies in the southern tip of the Sinai Peninsula, located just north of the Red Sea, between the Gulf of Suez and the Gulf of Aqaba.

The mountain is barren, rugged, and steep, and lies in the midst of other stark and difficult terrain. By the slopes of Jebel Musa a monastery called St Catherine's was built at the traditional site of the burning bush. From there, a good climber can reach the top of the mountain in an hour and a half.

After the Hebrews left Egypt, they camped at Mount Sinai (Ex. 19:1–2, 18). Moses climbed up the mountain to receive the Ten

The barren slopes of Mount Sinai.

As a shepherd, Moses wandered through the wilderness looking for good pasture in and around the land of Midian. While searching for a good grazing area for his flocks, he came to Mount Sinai, or Mount Horeb as it is sometimes called. Here God met him by a burning bush, telling him to return to Egypt to free the Hebrew slaves.

Mount Sinai was probably not in the land of Midian. Many shepherds travelled for weeks into the wilderness looking for good pastureland for their flocks and herds. Moses must have been doing this when he came to Mount Sinai.

These Egyptian sandals are like those in the time of Moses. They are woven from papyrus, palm leaves, and grass.

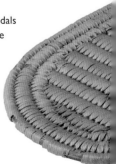

Today the "Sacred Monastery of the God-Trodden Mount Sinai" – or, Saint Catherine's Monastery – is an Eastern Orthodox monastery located at the base of three mountains: Mount Horeb, Jebel Arrenziyeb, and Jebel Musa.

Commandments from God (Ex. 19:20). Centuries later, Elijah visited Mount Sinai, and there God encouraged him (1 Kings 19:8–18).

Sandals

In Old Testament times, sandals were often considered a luxury, for most people went barefoot, especially the poor. But when travelling long distances, or for walking over rocky terrain, sandals were helpful.

Egyptian sandals were made of reeds, papyrus, or leather. Other sandals had wood or leather soles, with leather thongs wrapped around the feet and ankles to keep the sandals in place.

Today, when men enter a house or place of worship, they generally remove their hats. In Bible times, they removed their sandals. In a place of worship, it was a sign of respect. Roads were hot and dusty, so removing a guest's dirty sandals and washing his feet was a way that a host made the guest to feel welcome.

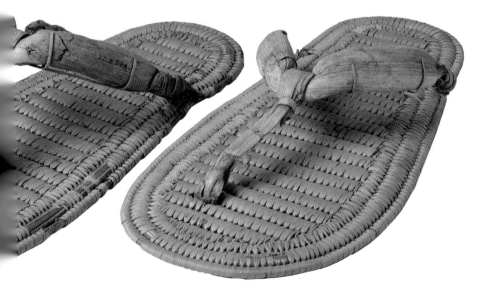

The Plagues

EXODUS 4:18–10:29

Many years before Moses' time Joseph had been sold as a slave and taken to Egypt. There he became governor and saved the land from famine. But many years passed and new pharaohs came to Egypt. One did not know about Joseph and made the Hebrew people slaves. One boy born as a slave was Moses, whom Pharaoh's daughter adopted and raised as a prince. But Moses killed an Egyptian taskmaster and fled to Midian, where he married a shepherdess named Zipporah. For the next 40 years Moses lived in Midian as a shepherd until the Lord spoke to him from a burning bush and ordered him to return to Egypt and lead His people from their slavery. Moses reluctantly returned. Through him the Lord worked ten mighty miracles, ten plagues on the land of Egypt.

Bricks for the Egyptians

One of the primary jobs for the Hebrew slaves was making bricks for the construction of buildings, store-cities, and monuments. These bricks were made of clay mixed with water and sometimes straw.

Egyptian bricks were usually 35–50 cm (14–20 inches) long, 15–23 cm (6–9 inches) wide, and 10–20 cm (4–7 inches) thick. Often they were stamped with a seal which had the name of the reigning pharaoh.

The Nile – lifeline of Egypt

In a great freshwater lake called Victoria, the Nile River begins its long journey northward to the land of Egypt. Until recently, the Egyptians had no idea where the Nile River came from. All they knew was that their lives depended on it, and that every year it kept flowing, emptying itself into the Mediterranean Sea.

In summer, the land of Egypt gets no rain, and throughout the entire winter rain may fall only three or four times. The Nile River provides the main source of water for Egypt. Almost everyone in the country lives near the river, for the lands farther east and west are barren wastelands and deserts where life is impossible.

Statue of Ramses II in the Luxor temple.

Plague 1 (Ex. 7:14–25)
The Nile turned to blood.

Plague 2 (Ex. 8:1–15)
Frogs overran the land.

Plague 3 (Ex. 8:16–19)
Gnats overran the land.

Plague 4 (Ex. 8:20–32)
Flies infested Egypt.

Plague 5 (Ex. 9:1–7)
Egypt's cattle struck by disease.

Plague 6 (Ex. 9:8–12)
Egypt infected with boils.

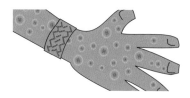

Plague 7 (Ex. 9:13–35)
Hail stones ruined Egypt's crops.

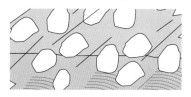

Plague 8 (Ex. 10:1–20)
Locusts devastated the foliage.

Plague 9 (Ex. 10:21–29)
Darkness covered the land.

Plague 10 (Ex. 11:1–12:36)
The firstborn of every Egyptian family was killed.

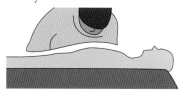

Each year the Nile overflows its banks, leaving a rich layer of silt. When the river recedes, farmers quickly do their planting, and a good harvest is assured. The river is so much a part of everyone's life, that for centuries people worshipped it as a god, always grateful for the prosperity it brought.

The God of Moses against the Egyptian gods

In Egypt, the people worshipped many different gods and goddesses. Each resembled an animal, an object, or a part of nature. God sent most of His plagues to show the Egyptians that He was more powerful than their lifeless gods.

God's plague of frogs proved to the Egyptian people that He was far greater than the frog itself, which was thought to be a god in Egypt. Egyptians also worshipped a cattle-god, and when God's plague struck these animals with disease, He showed His great power once again. God's plague of darkness proved that as the Creator of sunlight He was more powerful than the Egyptian sun-god, Amon-Ra.

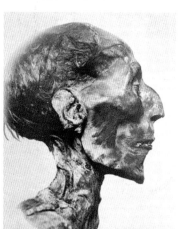

The unwrapped mummy of Ramses II.

The Passover

EXODUS 11:1–12:50

Moses was born into the home of Hebrew slaves in Egypt, but when Pharaoh's daughter found him in a basket in the Nile River, she adopted him and raised him as a prince. One day Moses killed an Egyptian taskmaster who was beating a Hebrew slave and had to flee. At Midian he met and married Zipporah and worked as a shepherd for his father-in-law. Later the Lord called Moses to return to Egypt. Through Moses, the Lord sent ten plagues. The last, the death of all firstborn sons, convinced Pharaoh to free the Hebrews. That night, when the angel of death went through Egypt, it passed over the Hebrews' firstborn sons. That first Passover is still celebrated.

Hyssop, possibly the kind of hyssop plant with which the blood was sprinkled on the doorposts the night of the Passover.

Hebrew culture was loathsome to the Egyptians. So how did Joseph, a Hebrew, come to be governor of Egypt? Who would have permitted this?

From approximately 1800–1600 BC, Hyksos invaders occupied Egypt, and Asian pharaohs sat on the throne. These leaders did not possess the Egyptian blood and culture. Being foreigners themselves, they probably saw nothing wrong with a wise Hebrew ruling as governor. It is almost certain that Joseph ruled sometime during this period.

Moses was born about 300 years after Joseph's death. Eighty years after Moses' birth, he led the Hebrews out of Egypt. The Exodus probably occurred between 1500 and 1400 BC, or according to another popular theory, between 1300 and 1200 BC

Which pharaoh?

Who was the pharaoh who oppressed the Hebrews at the time of Moses' birth, and who was his successor who finally let the slaves go free after watching his country groan under God's plagues? No one knows for sure, but there are two popular theories.

The "early" theory claims that Moses' birth and the Exodus occurred between 1500 and 1400 BC According to this, Thutmose III was the pharaoh at Moses' birth, and his successor, Amenhotep II was pharaoh of the Exodus.

The "late" theory puts the Exodus somewhere around 1300–1200 BC It says that Rameses II, a wicked and brutal pharaoh, oppressed the Hebrews, and that Merneptah, the weak ruler who succeeded him, let the people leave.

The Passover – when it began

The Passover was instituted on the same night that God's angel of death moved across the land of Egypt killing all Egyptian firstborn sons. But death did not enter any Hebrew home that had followed God's instructions.

The Passover – what it is

In the spring of every year, the Passover is still celebrated. This special day is set aside to remember the Israelites' freedom from slavery in Egypt. Over the centuries the Passover has changed but still involves a time of festivity and a ritual meal.

The ritual of the Passover

In the first month of the Jewish year, on the night of the full moon, the Passover begins. In Moses' day it lasted for just 24 hours.

Shortly after sunset, a lamb was killed by the father or head of the household. Its blood was sprinkled on the doorpost of the house. The lamb was then roasted and eaten along with unleavened bread and bitter herbs, symbolizing the bitterness of slavery in Egypt.

The family was to eat quickly, as the Israelites did that night before they left Egypt. Travelling clothes were worn.

On the night of Passover the Israelites were to eat a meal of lamb with unleavened bread and bitter herbs.

To give meaning to the ritual, the youngest son asked his father about the Passover. The story of the Israelites in Egypt was then told.

Phylacteries: little boxes worn on forehead and hand. Among the Lord's Passover instructions were two verses, Exodus 13:9 and 13:16, which were included in the phylacteries in later years.

The Exodus

Though Moses was born as a Hebrew slave, he was adopted by Pharaoh's daughter and raised as an Egyptian prince. But because he killed an Egyptian taskmaster who was beating a Hebrew slave, he had to flee. For 40 years he worked as a shepherd in Midian, until the Lord spoke to him from a burning bush and sent him back to Egypt to lead His people from slavery. Through Moses, the Lord sent ten plagues, including the last, the death of firstborn sons. But the angel of the Lord, who brought death throughout Egypt, passed over the Hebrew firstborn. This was the first Passover. After that, the Egyptians were anxious for their Hebrew slaves to go.

The Jewish calendar

To celebrate the Exodus, the Israelites began their year with the Passover month (Ex. 12:2; 13:4). Canaanites called this month "Abib", and Babylonians named it "Nisan". Tishri marks the beginning of the Jewish civic calendar.

Unleavened bread

During the Passover feast, the Israelites were forbidden to eat any bread that contained leaven, or yeast (Ex. 12:19–20). Without yeast, their bread did not rise. When baked, it was much flatter than the loaves of bread found in grocery stores today.

There were two varieties of unleavened bread. One kind was crispy and very flat, like a cracker. The other type resembled date or nut bread, thick and heavy.

Unleavened bread

THE JEWISH YEAR

The Jewish calendar was ordered both by the movements of the sun, moon, and stars, and also by the national festivals and the agricultural cycle. The year was divided into months marked by the phases of the moon, with an extra month added every few years to adjust as necessary.

JANUARY	Winter	TEBETH
FEBRUARY		SHEBAT
MARCH		ADAR
APRIL	Spring	NISAN
MAY		IYYAR
JUNE	Summer	SIVAN
JULY		TAMMUZ
AUGUST		AB
SEPTEMBER		ELUL
OCTOBER		TISHRI
NOVEMBER		MARCHESVAN
DECEMBER	Winter	KISLEV

Feast of Unleavened Bread

Originally the Feast of Unleavened Bread began the day after the Passover and lasted seven days. The unleavened bread symbolized Israel's haste to leave the land of Egypt. When leaven was added to the dough it sometimes took hours for the dough to rise before it could be baked. The night before the Exodus, the Hebrews did not have time to wait for the rising dough, so God commanded them to leave the next day with unleavened bread.

Like the Passover, the Feast of Unleavened Bread celebrated

Some of the jewellery the Egyptian women gave the Hebrews may have been like these beaded and ribbed penannular earrings, c. 1425 BC

the Israelites' escape from Egypt and their freedom from slavery. Over time, the Passover and the Feast of Unleavened Bread gradually joined together until they became one feast, which lasted seven or eight days. Today the Passover is called a "*seder*" and the unleavened bread is "*matzos*".

Slaves – Egypt's loss, Israel's gain

Overnight, the Egyptians lost the services of about 600,000 men and probably a million women and children (Ex. 12:37). These people were all slaves, responsible for the functioning of Egypt. In Egypt, the Israelites had probably learned construction, brickmaking, weaving, farming, music, metalworking, leathermaking, and glass blowing.

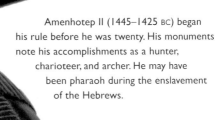

Amenhotep II (1445–1425 BC) began his rule before he was twenty. His monuments note his accomplishments as a hunter, charioteer, and archer. He may have been pharaoh during the enslavement of the Hebrews.

Crossing the Red Sea

EXODUS 13:17-22; 14

When the Lord spoke to Moses in a burning bush, He sent Moses back to Egypt to free His people, the Hebrews. Through Moses, the Lord sent ten plagues to show the Egyptian king, Pharaoh, that He was mightier than all Egyptian gods, and that Pharaoh should obey Him and set His people free. The last plague, death of the firstborn sons, hit all Egyptians, from Pharaoh's palace to the humblest home. After that Pharaoh and his people were anxious to get rid of the Hebrews. The Exodus began, with the Lord leading His people with a pillar of cloud by day and a pillar of fire by night. But trouble came when the Hebrews were caught between Pharaoh's pursuing chariots and the Red Sea. Only a mighty miracle could save these people from certain death. Would the Lord send one?

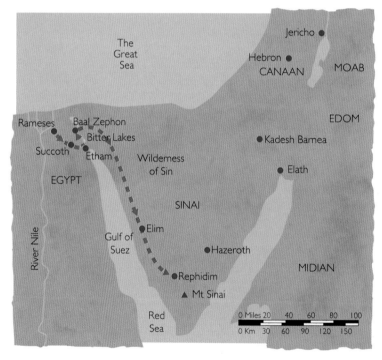

The Israelites were leaving the lush Nile Delta region of Egypt, and heading for Canaan, another beautiful area which God said flowed with milk and honey (Ex. 3:17). But between these fertile areas lay a vast desert with little water and almost no trees.

Nomads lived in the desert, wandering from place to place searching for food and water for their flocks. In years of severe famine, many of these nomads grouped into bands and raided the small villages lying on the edge of the wilderness. Providing for their families' survival led them to a life of thievery.

When the Hebrews crossed this great desert, they had to deal with these nomadic tribes, as well as desert outlaws, lack of water, sparse vegetation, and serpents and wild animals. It was a frustrating experience, and a lesson in trusting God's guidance.

In a few places small springs of water rise to the surface of the desert, and give enough moisture for plants and trees to grow. Such a green island is called an oasis, a most welcome sight to a weary traveller.

The wealth of a pharaoh

The pharaoh of the Exodus lost all of his Hebrew slaves, but he was still one of the richest men in all the world. The life of an ancient pharaoh was filled with the finest of everything the world had to offer.

The reason for a pharaoh's riches lay in the position of Egypt as one of the wealthiest and most powerful nations of civilization in the days of Abraham and Moses. Some pharaohs not only owned their entire country, but all of the people and animals as well.

Gold, silver, and alabaster were common items to an Egyptian ruler. In fact, they were so plentiful that one visiting king once

exclaimed that there was as much gold in the land of Egypt as dust.

But a pharaoh's wealth included much more. Hundreds of slaves attended to him. There were even slaves who dressed and fed him. The finest horses and chariots were his, along with private ships and river barges.

When a pharaoh died, many of his personal belongings, worth millions of dollars, were buried with him in a magnificent tomb or pyramid. But the next pharaoh of Egypt had no worries, for he still had more wealth and riches than he could count.

What the Israelites left behind
As slaves and labourers for Egypt, the Hebrews received no wages for their hard work. But the Egyptian government had the huge task of feeding all of its slaves. When the Hebrews escaped Egypt, they left behind the fertile land, the life-giving water of the Nile River, and a surplus of food and bread (Ex. 16:3).

Where did they cross?
The Red Sea is a great body of water that stretches north-south for nearly 1,930 km (1,200 miles). At its northern tip the sea divides into two arms, the Gulf of Aqaba which extends northeast, and the Gulf of Suez, which reaches to the northwest. Between these two arms of water lies the Sinai Peninsula.

Even farther north, the Gulf of Suez empties into the Bitter Lakes. The Great Bitter Lake is separated from the Little Bitter Lake by shallow straits of water. Continuing north is another lake called Ballah, about 50–65 km (30–40 miles) south of the Mediterranean Sea.

Most believe the Israelites did not cross the Red Sea itself, but one of the bodies of water just to the north. Some of these lakes actually dry up at certain times of the year, making it possible to walk across them. However, the Bible clearly says that the waters parted as a miracle from God.

A painting on wood of the famous "King Tut", riding into battle in a chariot. Similar chariots would likely have been used to pursue the Israelites as they crossed through the Red Sea.

Food in the Wilderness

EXODUS 15–16; 17:1-7

God sent ten mighty miracles to prove to Pharaoh that He is God, and that the king of Egypt should free the Hebrew slaves. At last Pharaoh realized this, and the people left Egypt for the Promised Land. At the Red Sea, God sent another miracle, parting the waters of the sea for the Hebrews to cross, but drowning Pharaoh's cavalry and chariots. God sent a pillar of cloud by day and a pillar of fire by night to guide His people through the wilderness. When the Hebrews got hungry, He sent manna to feed them. When they grew thirsty, He gave them water, even from a rock! Once more God's rod in the hand of Moses proved that God was with His people and would not fail them.

God provided manna for His people to eat. We do not know exactly what it looked like, but it had a shape and size like coriander seeds.

Manna

The Israelites were familiar with the good foods of Egypt – the fish, meat, melons, and a variety of vegetables. But soon they found themselves in a desolate wilderness, hot and thirsty, with no food and little water.

But God did not forget the grumbling Hebrews. He provided yet another miracle for His people. It was a food called manna. The manna looked like a gum or resin and resembled a coriander seed, which was a pearl-shaped seed that grew throughout Palestine.

The manna must have been similar to bread (Ex. 16:12) and tasted like wafers mixed with honey (Ex. 16:31). Each morning, except on the Sabbath, when the dew evaporated, fine flakes of manna covered the ground (Ex. 16:14).

During their 40 year sojourn in the wilderness, the Israelites received manna six days a week. They added variety by boiling it, grinding it, and making cakes of it.

Oasis

For those who have been sailing across an ocean that seems endless, a small tropical island appearing at the horizon is a cause for celebration. Here is a place of rest, to escape the bright sun and hot winds.

The Israelites felt the same way when they spotted an oasis in the hot and barren desert. Springs of water reached to the surface of the sand, and around them grew date palms and other vegetation. Some oases were small, providing only enough water for a brief stop. Others were very large, like Kadesh Barnea, where the Israelites camped for months.

Measures – omer and ephah

When God sent manna, the Israelites were allowed to collect only one omer each per day (Ex. 16:16), which was slightly more than two quarts. An omer was one tenth of an ephah (16:36), about two thirds of a bushel.

The grumblings of Israel

God performed many mighty miracles in the sight of all the Israelites. But despite these wonders, the people largely

remained a group of grumblers and complainers.

Many years of brutal slavery had just ended, thanks to God's miracles of the ten plagues. But no sooner had the Israelites left Egypt, than they started complaining.

Pharaoh and his army were bearing down on the Israelites, who were trapped by mountains and the Red Sea. Since Moses had arrived in Egypt the Israelites had seen God's great miracles and listened to His promises to bring them to their own land. But instead of trusting God, they turned on Moses, bitterly complaining that the Egyptians would soon kill them (Ex. 14:11–12). But God was patient with His people and parted the Red Sea, again proving His guidance.

Soon after, the people grumbled about bitter water at Marah. Once again God provided them with a miracle (Ex. 15: 22–25).

Arriving at Rephidim, the Israelites complained that there was no water, not trusting in God's promises (Ex. 17:1–7).

When Moses spent 40 days on Mount Sinai talking with God, the people thought he was dead and moulded a golden calf to worship. For this they were severely punished (Ex. 32).

Forgetting their hopeless life in Egypt, the Israelites again complained about their surroundings. This time God punished them with a plague of fire (Num. 11:1).

Grumbling continued over lack of meat. God sent flocks of quail, but He also sent a plague (Num. 11:4–33).

Most of the spies sent into the Promised Land brought back a fearful report of giants and walled cities. They forgot that their God had just humbled the mightiest nation in the world. Even the sea obeyed His command.

After seeing miracle upon miracle, and being punished time and again, one would think the Israelites would have learned to trust God. But they grumbled and complained many more times (see Num. 16:1–3; 21:4–9). Despite God's promises, this disobedience and complaining

An oasis provided the necessities of life for weary travellers and local residents in a barren land.

persisted, until centuries later God allowed His people to be utterly defeated and carried off once again into lives of slavery.

Rephidim

Today it is probably called Wadi Feiran, or Wadi Rufaid, but in Moses' day it was called Rephidim. The exact location is unknown, but most think this oasis was in the southern part of the Sinai Peninsula. Here Moses got water from a rock (Ex. 17:6), fought a battle against Amalek (Ex. 17:8–16), and received advice from his father-in-law Jethro (Ex. 18). It must have been a large oasis, for the people of Israel camped here for a while.

The Ten Commandments

EXODUS 20

With a mighty show of miracles, God persuaded Pharaoh to free His people, the Hebrews. With another mighty miracle, He helped them cross the Red Sea on dry land. With a pillar of cloud by day and a pillar of fire by night, He led them in the wilderness, and with more miracles He fed them and gave them water. Now, they had arrived at Mount Sinai. He would perform another mighty work through Moses, sending Laws for His people to obey. With His own finger, God wrote the Ten Commandments and gave them to His people. These, and His other laws, would be guides to His people for generations to come.

This tablet contains the Prologue to the Code of Hammurabi.

Rembrandt's painting of Moses holding aloft the tablets of the Law.

God's Ten Commandments

Moses spent much time on Mount Sinai talking with God. Up on the mountain, God wrote ten basic Laws for the Israelites to follow and apply to their lives:

TEN COMMANDMENTS

1. You shall have no other gods before me.
2. You shall not make for yourself a carved image.
3. You shall not take the name of the Lord your God in vain.
4. Remember the Sabbath day, to keep it holy.
5. Honour your father and your mother.
6. You shall not murder.
7. You shall not commit adultery.
8. You shall not steal.
9. You shall not bear false witness against your neighbour.
10. You shall not covet.

Law codes of other lands

While the Israelite law relied on the power and authority of God, law codes of other countries depended on the power of human beings.

In Egypt, Pharaoh was supreme ruler. His word was the law, and people worshipped him as a god. During this time, there were few written laws, so Pharaoh acted as a judge, using his opinions as the final verdict. The Medes and Persians had a similar justice system. The king was thought to be divine and infallible. When a law was sealed with the king's signet ring, it was irreversible. Not even the king himself could revoke his laws even if he later wanted to. This would contradict himself, which would embarrass a king, who was supposed to be perfect. However, the king could make a new law, which neutralized the old one (Es. 3:13; 8:5, 11).

How did these ancient law codes develop? Thousands of years ago, the earliest nations

One commandment had to do with idols. Never were the Israelites to make an idol. This is a statuette of Amun, considered one of Egypt's most important gods.

Today there are steps going up to Mount Sinai from the monastery below.

had no system to stop the wrongs of society. People who were robbed or abused had nowhere to turn for help. Laws were written in an attempt to stop this widespread evil. The first law codes developed in Samaria and were inscribed on clay tablets.

The Golden Calf

After the people of Israel, the Hebrews, crossed the Red Sea, they went to Mount Sinai, where God gave His Law through Moses. There also God gave the plans for His house, the tabernacle. But while Moses was up on Mount Sinai, receiving the Law from God, the people of Israel were making a golden calf to worship.

When the Israelites turned away from the Lord to worship a golden calf, they were doing what their Egyptian neighbours had done many times before. This ivory statuette (shown at actual size) represents Ptah, an Egyptian god.

something they were familiar with, something which gave them comfort.

Some think the Israelites did not really worship the golden calf itself, but wanted something physical to represent God whom they could not see. But on Mount Sinai, God was forbidding graven images.

Metalworking

The golden calf was fashioned from the golden jewellery and utensils of the Hebrews

The bull: a symbol of worship

The bull has been worshipped throughout history as a symbol of strength, rich crops, and fertile harvests. Even today, in countries such as India, the bull is considered sacred and is never killed.

In Bible times, the bull was set up as an important god in many countries. One of Egypt's most powerful gods was Hapi, the bull god of the Nile River. The Babylonians, Syrians, and Canaanites also worshipped bulls.

The Apis bull was another bull or calf highly revered by the Egyptians. This animal was very rare, and had several strange markings. A square mark on the forehead and a beetle-shaped marking on the tongue were its trademarks. All of Egypt celebrated when one of these bulls was found. It was killed, embalmed, and buried in a coffin of solid granite.

The Israelites lived in the midst of this bull worship for over 400 years. They must have felt afraid and insecure as they camped in the middle of an unknown wilderness, while their leader, Moses, was gone for so many days. Still unfamiliar with God's laws, bull worship was

The Apis bull figure was among several cow and bull deities worshipped by the Egyptians. This bronze bull's head, an ornament for a lyre, is Sumerian and dates from around 2500 BC

(Ex. 32:2-4). But how was this done?

Some Hebrew slaves learned the art of metalworking while in Egypt. They must have helped Aaron make the golden calf. This bull, or calf, was probably made by first carving a wooden image of it. All of the gold was then melted and allowed to partially harden into flat sheets. These sheets were laid over the wooden bull, then moulded and hammered to fit the shape of the wood.

Where did all of the gold come from?

Where did the Hebrews, slaves of Egypt, get all of their gold jewellery? After God's tenth and final plague, the death of the firstborn, the Egyptian people hurried the Hebrew slaves out of Egypt. The Egyptians gave the Hebrews whatever personal belongings they asked for, in an effort to speed them out of the country (Ex. 12:35-36). The Israelites took anything they wanted, plundering the jewellery and vessels of gold and silver from Egypt. The golden calf was made from this gold, as were parts of the tabernacle and its furniture.

To make idols and other items, workers heated metal with bellows and blowpipes. The modern process is more efficient but much the same: heat metal until it melts, then pour it into a mould.

When Moses descended from the mountain, he saw the people worshipping the golden calf and threw the Ten Commandments to the ground.

The Tabernacle

EXODUS 35–36; 39:1-31; LEVITICUS 1–9

While the people of Israel camped at Mount Sinai, the Lord God gave Moses His Law, which His people were to obey. But the people sinned, for at the very time Moses was on the mountain receiving God's Law, they were making a golden calf below, to worship it instead of the Lord. God's instructions to Moses included plans for His tent-home and for a group of people, His priests, and for a system of offerings through which the people would worship Him. The people remained at Mount Sinai until the tabernacle was built.

Arrangement and construction

Gifts of gold, silver, and bronze were used in making God's dwelling place. Fourteen raw materials were used to complete the tent of worship, including animal skins for the roof, insects for the coloured dyes, acacia wood for the beams and carrying poles, and precious metals for its stunning appearance.

The Israelites journeyed from place to place in the wilderness, so the tabernacle was made easy to dismantle. Around the tabernacle was an outer court. Inside the tent itself were two rooms, the Holy Place where the priest entered each morning, and the Holy of Holies, which he entered only once each year.

Furniture

The table of shewbread was on the north side of the Holy Place. Twelve loaves of bread were kept here at all times. The golden candlestick, or menorah, was on the south wall of the Holy Place. It lighted the room. The altar of incense was in the centre of the Holy Place, just in front of the veil which separated the Holy Place from the Holy of Holies. Each morning Aaron burned incense on the altar. Inside the Holy of Holies was the ark of the covenant, which contained the Ten Commandments.

The priests

Only men who were descendants of Aaron, thus born into the tribe of Levi, were eligible to become priests. These men took care of the tabernacle and performed the daily sacrifices along with other services. The priests made a living by taking a share of the temple tax and eating part of the meat of the daily sacrifices. The high priest wore a beautiful embroidered robe with a dark blue tunic and a breastpiece of precious jewels.

Above is a model of the tabernacle, as seen in Israel, Timna Park. On the opposite page is an engraving of the various liturgical vestments and furniture Bezalel made for worship, as well as a diagram showing the arrangement of the tribes camped around the tabernacle.

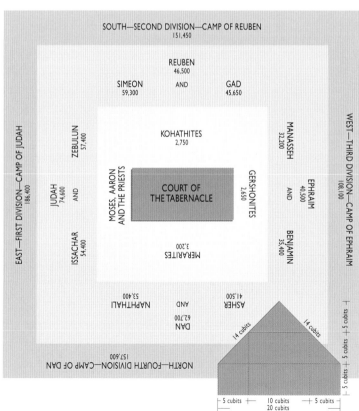

SOUTH—SECOND DIVISION—CAMP OF REUBEN 151,450		
SIMEON 59,300	REUBEN 46,500 AND	GAD 45,650

EAST—FIRST DIVISION—CAMP OF JUDAH 186,400

ZEBULUN 57,400

KOHATHITES 2,750

MANASSEH 32,200

WEST—THIRD DIVISION—CAMP OF EPHRAIM 108,100

JUDAH 74,600 AND

MOSES, AARON AND THE PRIESTS

COURT OF THE TABERNACLE

GERSHONITES 2,650

EPHRAIM 40,500 AND

ISSACHAR 54,400

MERARITES 3,200

BENJAMIN 35,400

NAPHTHALI 53,400 AND

ASHER 41,500

DAN 62,700

NORTH—FOURTH DIVISION—CAMP OF DAN 157,600

14 cubits · 14 cubits

5 cubits · 5 cubits · 5 cubits

5 cubits · 10 cubits · 5 cubits
20 cubits

The offerings

Man's sin destroyed his relationship with God. In Old Testament times, a man could once again come into good standing with God through an offering, or sacrifice. There were many different ways to offer a sacrifice. Often the priest made a sacrifice for the people.

Twelve Spies

From Mount Sinai, the people of Israel moved onward. Behind them lay the wilderness. To the north lay the Promised Land. To the east and south lay still more wilderness. The time had come to test their faith, to see if they were ready to enter the land of promise. But first they would send spies into the land to see what they faced.

When the spies returned from the Promised Land, they confirmed that it truly was a "land flowing with milk and honey". But they were afraid to trust the Lord to help them conquer it. At the time, they were camped at Kadesh Barnea, pictured here.

Kadesh Barnea

Trudging wearily across the desert, the Israelites moved north toward the Promised Land, finally coming to an oasis with four springs, called Kadesh Barnea. Here the people camped for a long time.

Kadesh Barnea was south of the land of Canaan, the Promised Land, about 80 km (50 miles) from Beersheba. A further 80 km (50 miles) to the west lay the Mediterranean Sea.

The Lord told Moses to send 12 spies into Canaan from Kadesh Barnea (Num. 13:2, 26). Ten of the spies returned afraid, and the people lost hope. As punishment for refusing to accept God's guidance, the Israelites of that generation lived the rest of their lives in the wilderness, perhaps much of the time at Kadesh Barnea (Num. 14:26–38).

At Kadesh, the springs dried up. Moses disobeyed God in the way he provided water (Num. 20:1–13). Miriam and Aaron died at this oasis (Num. 20:1, 22–29).

The Promised Land

God called it a land flowing with milk and honey (Ex. 3:8). Moses spent a third of his life trying to get there, but never made it. Joshua spent many years fighting for it. Where was this land, and why was it so special?

The Promised Land was also called the land of Canaan. Later

it became the nation Israel. It was the land that God chose to give to the descendants of Abraham, Isaac, and Jacob (Gen. 12:7).

Travelling from north to south, the country stretches from Dan to Beersheba (1 Sam. 3:20), a distance of about 240 km (150 miles). The nation is bordered on the west by the Mediterranean

Sea and on the east by the Jordan River, a width that is close to 80 km (50 miles).

Canaan – a land of plenty

When the spies returned from their mission in Canaan, they brought back a giant cluster of grapes. But this was only a small evidence of the riches of the Promised Land.

Thirty-eight years after the spies' return, the Hebrews were finally allowed to enter the land God had promised them. This was a land watered by the Jordan River and fed from the gentle rains that formed over the sea and moved inland. There fruits, vegetables, and grain grew in abundance.

After living in the wilderness for over 40 years, the people were filled with delight when they entered a land plentiful in cucumbers, dates, figs, walnuts, lentils, barley, onions, pomegranates, grapes, and olives.

From the Valley of Eshcol the 12 spies brought enormous bunches of grapes. The exact location of this valley is not known, except that it was near Hebron.

Vineyards and olive groves were a familiar sight in this fertile country, along with valleys full of abundant harvests, rippling streams, and lush grass. After barren, windswept hills and a horizon of only sand and rocks, this land looked like a garden paradise.

Grapes

Grapes, also called wine grapes, were a common fruit in Bible times. The Bible mentions grapevines more than any other plant. The grape harvest usually begins in September. They were usually eaten raw, dried into raisins, and pressed into wine.

The Bronze Serpent

NUMBERS 21:4-9

From Mount Sinai the people of Israel journeyed through the wilderness to Kadesh Barnea, where they sent 12 spies into the Promised Land. But ten of the spies gave a negative report, and the people were afraid to go into the land. So the Lord punished them for their lack of faith and sent them back into the wilderness. For the next 38 years, they would wander, unable to claim the land of promise until a new generation arose. Soon both Aaron and Miriam died. Later the people again complained against the Lord, who sent a plague of fiery serpents. Only the people who looked at the bronze serpent would live.

is sometimes 60 cm (2 feet) long, and it often hides in the sand, attacking people without warning. At first the victim feels no pain, but already internal bleeding has started. After a day or two, the person actually feels better, but death soon comes. These carpet vipers might have been the serpents God sent to punish the Israelites for complaining (Num. 21:4–9).

The Egyptians had great respect for snakes. The cobra was their national symbol and worshipped as a goddess named Wadjet or Udjet. Most pharaohs attached cobra figures to their headdresses.

A poisonous sand viper, common to desert areas in the Middle East.

Serpents

The Egyptians and Hebrews had something in common – fear of snakes. From Egypt to Palestine there were a variety of these creatures. Most kinds were harmless, but a few struck quickly, with deadly venom.

As the Israelites trudged through the wilderness, they were most afraid of sand vipers and carpet vipers. The carpet viper

Snake amulet from Egypt, 664–30 BC

The Bible says the spies went through the Negev (some versions call it the way of the south) to investigate the Promised Land. The Negev (Negeb) was the desert region south of Judah. The map below shows the route of the Israelites thus far.

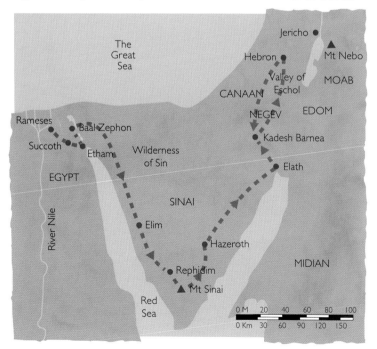

The Negev

This barren desert land stretches south from the land of Canaan. At times during Israel's history, it was included within its borders. Most settlers in this mountainous area took jobs breeding and tending sheep. Later, a major trade route was carved through the region, opening commerce and increasing population.

Crossing the Jordan

JOSHUA 3–4

Under Joshua's wise and courageous leadership, the people of Israel were ready to enter the Promised Land. Before they entered, Joshua sent two spies into the land to see what it was like. There they met a friendly woman named Rahab who helped them. At last the day came to enter the land. This time preparations included the Lord.

The Jordan River

The Jordan River is a landmark of Bible history. It begins near the slopes of Mount Hermon, and flows south into the Sea of Galilee. South of Galilee, the River Jordan runs through the Plain of Zor and the Ghor Valley. Growing wider with each mile, the river meanders close to the Mount of Olives and finally empties into the Dead Sea.

Near Jericho, Joshua parted the waters of the river, and the entire company of Israel crossed into the Promised Land without getting their feet wet! (Josh. 3:14–4:18)

Elijah escaped from King Ahab across the Jordan (1 Kings 17:3, 5). Naaman, a Syrian general, was healed from leprosy when told by Elisha to wash in the Jordan seven times (2 Kings 5:1–15). Elisha also made an axehead float in its waters (2 Kings 6:1–7).

John the Baptist baptized believers in the River Jordan (Matt. 3:6) and later baptized Jesus there (Matt. 3:13-17). In Jesus' day, Jews travelling from Galilee to Jerusalem who wished to avoid the hated Samaritans probably crossed and recrossed the river to keep from walking through Samaria.

The Ark of the Covenant

The most treasured and sacred article in the nation of Israel was the ark of the covenant – a symbol of God's covenant with Israel.

It was made when the tabernacle was first constructed in the wilderness (Ex. 25:10–22; 37:1–9). The framework was made of acacia wood, a strong and durable wood that resisted insects and rot, then overlaid with pure gold. Fastened to each corner was a gold ring which held the carrying poles.

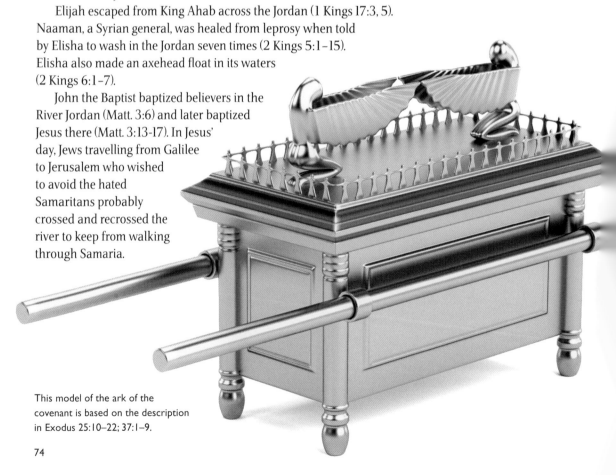

This model of the ark of the covenant is based on the description in Exodus 25:10–22; 37:1–9.

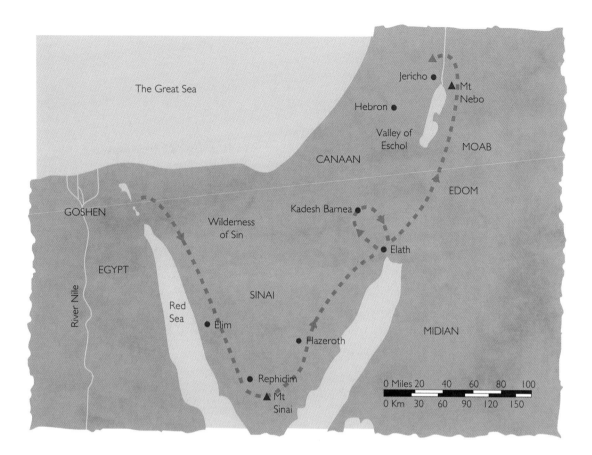

The Great Sea

Jericho ●

▲ Mt Nebo

Hebron ●

Valley of Eschol

CANAAN

MOAB

EDOM

GOSHEN

Wilderness of Sin

Kadesh Barnea ●

Elath ●

EGYPT

River Nile

Red Sea

● Elim

SINAI

● Hazeroth

MIDIAN

● Rephidim

▲ Mt Sinai

0 Miles 20   40   60   80   100
0 Km   30   60   90   120   150

Resembling a large chest, the ark was about 115 cm (3.75 feet) long by 70 cm (2.25 feet) wide. The height was about 70 cm (2.25 feet). Inside the ark the Ten Commandments were kept, along with a jar of manna and Aaron's rod that had budded.

The lid of the ark was called the mercy seat. Once each year, the high priest entered the inner room of the tabernacle called the Holy of Holies, to sprinkle blood on the mercy seat, asking God to offer mercy for the people's sins.

Across the top of the ark, two winged cherubim of gold faced each other. It was believed that God dwelt between these wings, living among His people.

Gilgal
After crossing the Jordan River, the Israelites first camped at Gilgal, about 3 km (2 miles) northeast of Jericho (Josh. 4:19). There all of the males were circumcised. The word Gilgal means to "roll away".

The Israelites set off from Goshen and wandered around the Sinai wilderness for 40 years before they finally entered the Promised Land.

At this place, God rolled away the waters of the Jordan and rolled away the bad memories of Egyptian slavery through the covenant of circumcision (Josh. 5:9).

Jericho Captured

JOSHUA 6

When at last the people of Israel reached the Promised Land, they waited across the Jordan River from Jericho for a report from two spies. The spies returned and encouraged Joshua to lead the Israelites into the land. Thus, while the priests carried the ark of the covenant toward Jericho, the waters of the Jordan River held back and the people crossed on dry land. The people of Jericho shut up the city, afraid of the Israelites and their God. Then Joshua gave the order for the strange silent battle to begin.

Jericho – a fortified city
From the cold winter hills of Jerusalem, one can find a tropical paradise in the warm climate of Jericho, just a six-

When the people shouted at the sound of a trumpet, the walls of Jericho fell outward. Part of these ruined walls have been excavated.

hour hike on foot. The city of Jericho lies about 27 km (17 miles) northeast of Jerusalem, yet is close to 915 metres (3,000 feet) below it. At 245 m (800 feet) below sea level, the summer climate is almost unbearably hot, while the winter months are warm and pleasant.

In Joshua's day, Jericho was by no means the largest city in Canaan, but it was located in a strategic area. It lay a few miles west of the Jordan River, where most nomads and travellers crossed to enter Canaan.

Jericho was a city with walls. Excavations have uncovered ruins that prove it was an ancient city when Joshua arrived. As a fortified city, it was constructed to repel enemy attack. Many fortified cities had walls up to 6 m (20 feet) thick and over 8 m (25 feet) high.

On top of these walls soldiers could see for miles, and were constantly on guard, watching for the enemy. Some cities even had a moat, a large ditch filled with water, that circled their walls. Often another wall was built just outside the moat.

Jericho was a strong city, able to defend itself against a large army. But it could not be built strong enough to stop God's army, and the walls collapsed at His command (Josh. 6:20). Joshua then placed a curse on Jericho (Josh. 6:26), which was fulfilled centuries later (1 Kings 16:34).

Trumpets

Music was strongly woven into Israelite culture. Feasts, festivals, war, worship, and death were just some of the events where music played an important role. Music was also associated with God's supernatural power when the priests blew their trumpets and God destroyed the walls of Jericho (Josh. 6:20).

The trumpet was one of the most popular and important musical instruments in Israel. There were probably two distinct kinds. One was called the *chatsotserah*, which was long and straight, beginning with a very narrow tube at the mouthpiece, and opening at the end into the shape of a bell. It was similar to trumpets today, except that it did not have valves, so it was really a bugle.

The other type of trumpet

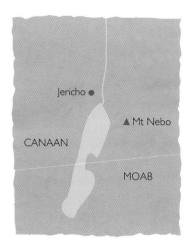

was called the *shophar*. It was probably made from an animal horn and was bent or curved in shape. Many think this horn had a clearer, brighter sound than the *chatsotserah*.

Both of these trumpets were used to announce the beginning of feasts, signal a call to battle, proclaim a victory celebration, and inform people of important events.

Shofar trumpets are made from animal horns.

Achan's Sin and the Conquest of Ai

JOSHUA 7–8

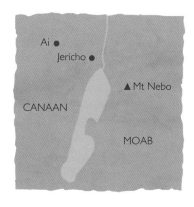

After the people of Israel had crossed into the Promised Land, they followed every instruction carefully, and the Lord gave them a great victory over the city of Jericho. Triumphantly, they expected an equally great victory over Ai, the next target of their conquest. But their defeat caused them to search for a reason.

Gold necklace, pendants, and beads (c. 18th–17th century BC) from Mesopotamia. Soldiers often plundered such valuable spoils from their defeated enemies.

The spoils of battle

Booty, plunder, and spoil are all words that mean the same thing – useful or valuable items taken from a defeated enemy. The victors had the right to take anything they wished from the land and cities of the losers. This included animals, women and children, precious metals, jewellery, weapons, clothing, and a long list of other things.

But at times, God did not want the Israelites to take the spoils of battle. It was sometimes a test of the people's obedience. This was the case at Jericho, where everything was to be utterly destroyed except the precious metals which were to go into the Lord's tabernacle (Josh. 6:18–19, 21, 24).

When a battle had ended, those who had killed someone or even touched a dead body had to follow purification rites which lasted for a week. During this week, the soldiers stayed out of the camp with all the booty. Both the men and booty were sprinkled twice with a special water mixture called the "water of impurity". Soldiers washed their clothes, while the precious metals were "purified" in a hot flame. The booty was then divided among the soldiers, priests, tabernacle, and other people of the camp. One captive of every 500 was often given to the tabernacle service, and the very finest articles were given to the Lord.

Ai

The city's name means a "heap of stones", and today it still lies in ruins. Joshua totally destroyed this city. Years later it was probably rebuilt (1 Chron. 7:28; Neh. 11:31; Isa. 10:28), but once again it must have died off or been destroyed.

No archaeologist can say with certainty they have found the site of the ancient city, but most would agree that it probably stood about 3 km (2 miles) southeast of Bethel, where a large heap of ruins lies today. Recent excavations seem to show that Ai was a beautiful and prosperous city over 1,000 years before Joshua arrived there.

When Joshua first tried to capture the city, his forces were soundly defeated. Achan's sin was the reason for the Israelites' loss. After Achan was punished, Joshua easily destroyed Ai (Josh. 7:1–8:29).

The shekel

After confessing his sin, Achan went into his tent and uncovered the stolen spoil – a beautiful robe, 200 shekels of silver, and a gold bar weighing 50 shekels (Josh. 7:21).

The shekel was the standard weight used in the ancient countries around Palestine. But this "standard" weight seems to have been different from country to country and time period to time period. Kings sometimes used a shekel of a different size and weight from ordinary people. A variety of symbols have also been uncovered, each thought to represent the shekel. Because of this, it is impossible to know the exact weight or amount of Achan's spoil.

These ruins are thought to be of ancient Ai. It lies about two miles southeast of Bethel. and is now called Et-Tell.

Throughout Bible times, the shekel weighed anywhere from 8–16 grams, which is about .3 to .6 ounces. If this were true, then Achan would have stolen from 60–120 ounces of silver, and 15–30 ounces of gold, a value today of between $20,000 and $35,000. In Joshua's day, the silver alone would have bought Achan ten slaves.

A silver half-shekel from Jerusalem. Decorated with a beaded chalice, this coin was minted during the first century AD

The Sun and Moon Stand Still at Aijalon

JOSHUA 10:1-28

Victory had come easily at Jericho, the first conquest in the Promised Land, for the people of Israel had followed the Lord's instructions completely. But Ai was next, and there the Israelites suffered utter defeat. Sin was in the camp. Achan had disobeyed the Lord. With Achan executed, Ai was conquered. Gibeon, a nearby city, was afraid and sent men to trick Joshua into a truce. Before long, Joshua was forced to defend this city, even with a great miracle.

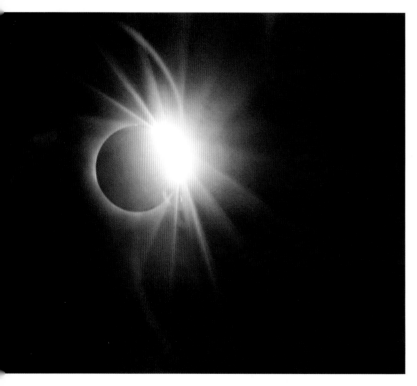

A solar eclipse. What would it be like for the sun and moon to stand still?

invention of chariots, soldiers still fought this way.

When God was with Joshua's army, it made no difference how skilled the enemy was. But years later, the Israelites did not follow God with such enthusiasm and ran into deep trouble when faced with war.

After settling in Canaan, the Israelites were a disorganized people. Farmers and shepherds fought with hammers, axes, sticks, and hunting knives. They were no match for the skilled and organized armies of the Philistines and other Canaanites, who fought in mobilized units with horse-drawn chariots, spears and swords of bronze or iron, and powerful bows with arrows made of metal instead of stone or wood.

A soldier of Israel went into battle with everyday clothes, while Canaanite soldiers wore metal armour, with helmets and shields of iron or bronze instead of wood or leather.

The only way for Israel to win a battle was to keep their army small and disciplined. Without heavy armour, they moved quickly and fought in the hills where chariots were useless. Wise tactics and faith in God were keys to a successful battle in Israel.

Hand-to-hand battle

In Joshua's day, there were no high-powered rifles, grenades, or fighter jets. In battle, each man looked his opponent in the eye, and the more powerful man usually won. This was hand-to-hand combat, and even with the

The Valley of Aijalon today, about 24 km (15 miles) west of Jerusalem.

Military alliances

Joshua marched through Canaan, destroying each city he met along the way. These cities were called city-states, and many were actually small nations in themselves. Alone, they were powerless against Joshua, but united, they formed a strong army with the hope of victory.

The Bible mentions another great alliance where two large groups of kings banded together to fight a great battle in Abraham's time (Gen. 14). But Abraham, like Joshua, was able to defeat four of these kings.

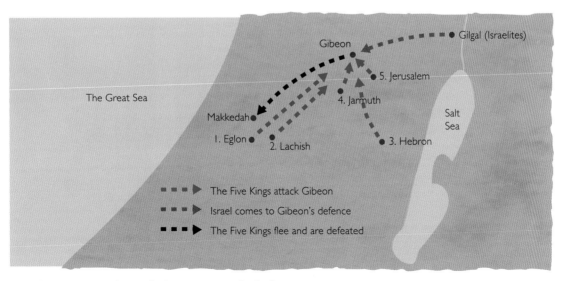

Joshua's battle strategy that resulted in victory over the five kings.

Gideon's Call and Tests

JUDGES 6

The conquest of the Promised Land was never complete. Though Joshua had been a mighty leader, the Israelites did not conquer all of the cities. So they lived among the Canaanites, the people who had inhabited the land before them, absorbing many of their heathen ways. By the time of the Judges, the people of Israel were far from the Lord. Occasionally the Lord raised up a mighty leader to rule as a judge, someone like Gideon.

Baal worship

Coming from Egypt, the Israelites were used to the worship of numerous gods and goddesses. Canaan was no exception, except that in this land, one particular god, Baal, was much more important than the others. He was a symbol of strength and fertility to the Canaanites and the one whom they thought brought life-giving rains to Palestine.

The people of Canaan believed fervently in this god. He was usually represented as a bull, the strongest animal known to them.

They were certain that famine was caused when Baal was worshipped improperly. To win back Baal's favour, the heathen priests of this god might offer hundreds of sacrifices, while dancing around the altar slashing themselves with knives and sharp rocks. Hopefully, Baal would feel sorry for them and once again send his gentle rains over the land.

If this failed, priests urged families to sacrifice their own children, the ultimate expression of devotion and worship to their god.

Over the years, many of the Israelites turned from God to worship Baal. This was strictly forbidden when God had made His covenant with the people. As punishment, God let other nations invade Israel, making life as difficult as it had been in Egypt.

This early second millennium BC bronze represents Baal, "He Who Rides on the Clouds". Scholars believe that this votive sculpture probably was originally dressed in a gold skirt and may have carried a mace. Other depictions of this god show him with a flowering staff in one of his hands.

Beating out wheat

When Gideon was a young man, the Midianites were in control of his people. Periodically, they swept through the land, destroying crops and livestock in order to keep the Israelites weak.

Gideon was fortunate enough to harvest some wheat before it was burned or trampled. He "beat it out" in a winepress, trying to cover up what he was really doing in case the Midianites rode by. In beating out the wheat, Gideon was separating the grain from the stalks of wheat. He did this by trampling on it or by pounding it with a heavy club. Animals usually did the job of beating out the wheat, but Gideon's livestock were probably taken by the Midianites, or possibly the plodding animals would have made Gideon's job obvious.

After the grain was separated from the stalks, it was strained in a sieve to remove the dirt, and then thrown into the wind, where the useless chaff blew away, and the heavier grain fell to the ground. The grain was ground into flour and used in baking bread.

The winepress

A winepress was usually built on the edge of a vineyard. Women picked the grapes from the vines and carried them in large baskets to the winepress, which resembled a large stone tub. The grapes were emptied into the tub, while men trampled on them with their bare feet, keeping their balance by hanging onto ropes tied to a wooden crossbeam. The juice from the squeezed grapes was then stored in wineskins or jars.

Gideon's Cave, on the southern border of the Jezreel Valley.

Gideon's 300

JUDGES 7

The people of Israel had been victorious in conquering much of the Promised Land. But they never conquered it all. Thus they settled among the Canaanites and absorbed many of their heathen ways. Through the years they turned from the Lord, and by the time of the Judges, the nation was far from Him. Occasionally the Lord raised up a great man or woman to lead the nation as a judge. One such man was Gideon. And one of his great battles required 300 dedicated soldiers.

The middle watch

When danger was present, armies, cities, and even family homes kept a watch throughout the night. In Joshua's day, this watch was divided into three four-hour periods. The first watch, also called the beginning of the watches, lasted from 6 P.M. to 10 P.M.. The middle watch continued from 10 at night until 2 in the morning. The morning watch started at 2 A.M. and ended at 6 A.M.

The first watch began at sunset, and the morning watch ended at sunrise. Gideon attacked the Midianite army at the beginning of the middle watch (about 10 P.M.). This was a big surprise, because armies rarely fought after dark.

Gideon's trumpet was probably this type.

Gideon's trumpet

Gideon's men surprised the Midianite army by blowing trumpets and breaking pitchers, uncovering flickering torches.

The horns blown by Gideon and his men were called *shophars*, which means "trumpets", or *kerens*, which means "horns". The *shophar* was usually made from an animal horn that was curved in shape. It sounded only two or three different notes, but these were bright and shrill. The *shophar* was mainly used for announcements of war, rebellion, or some of the great Israelite feasts.

Pottery and pitchers

Gideon and his 300 men threw the Midianite army into confusion when together they broke their pitchers, exposing hundreds of burning torches. In the dead of night, the sound of 300 breaking pitchers must have made quite a noise. But where did these pitchers come from, and how were they made?

Before Abraham's day, all pottery was made by hand. It was rough and awkward. But by Gideon's time, most pottery was fashioned on a potter's wheel. This important invention gave pottery a smooth and symmetrical look. There were even tools designed to hide the seam and impress beautiful patterns.

The pitchers used by Gideon's army were probably made of clay. This was the most common material used in pottery, as well as the cheapest. After the vessel was shaped, it was dried for a

few days, and then heated in an oven called a kiln. This gave the piece of pottery extra strength, preventing the clay from becoming too brittle as time passed.

The Well of Harod in Ma'ayan Harod National Park, where Gideon's men drank the water (Judges 7:1–6).

Torches

Suddenly in the dead of night, 300 brilliant torches sprang up from the darkness. Gideon's men had used the torches as an effective weapon of war, scattering and confusing the Midianite army.

In Bible times, torches were also used as lights when the smaller oil burning lamps did not give off enough light.

This Canaanite jug (c. 1780–1580 BC) from modern-day Tell ed-Duweir is perhaps similar to those used by Gideon to cover the torches.

The Birth of Samson

When the Israelites set out to conquer the Promised Land, they had many victories. But they could not take all of the land, so they were forced to live with the Canaanites. In time, they absorbed many of their heathen ways, especially by the time of the Judges. Israel then was far from the Lord. Judges arose to lead the nation, and a few were strong, such as Deborah and Gideon. Others were weak. Samson was physically strong but morally weak.

Idol worship in Canaan

This small silver sculpture of Baal, the storm god, was made by a Hittite artist around 1400 BC.

Smoke rose in Canaan during certain times of the day called "prayer times". The Canaanites worshipped many different gods and goddesses in the form of idols. This idolatry was gradually absorbed by the Israelites as they lived among the people of Canaan.

Daily the Canaanites burned incense to their gods on incense altars. Many chose to worship on their roofs or on hilltops called "high places", believing that their gods could hear them only if the

Samson was a man of incredible strength.

86

Delilah took advantage of Samson's moral weakness and discovered the source of his great physical strength.

A Nazirite was often punished for any of the vows he deliberately broke. If by accident he touched a dead body, he had to shave his head and face, bury the hair, and start his vow all over again. His vow was increased by 30 days if his hair was cut by mistake.

When the vow had ended, a special sacrifice was made at the tabernacle. The hair was shaved and burned in the fire.

Samson broke some of the conditions of the Nazirite vow. He killed 30 Philistines and touched their dead bodies when he stole their robes (Jud. 14:19). Later, he told the secret of his strength to Delilah, who then cut his hair (Jud. 16:19). His carelessness made him a slave to the Philistines for the rest of his life.

smoke from their altars reached up to the gods.

The two most popular deities in the land were Baal, the god of rain and harvest, and Ashtoreth, the goddess of childbirth and fertility. Metalsmiths were kept busy making idols to represent them. Baal was usually cast as a bull, and Ashtoreth was often made to resemble the figure of a woman.

Incense stands, or altars, came in all shapes and sizes, and were made of pottery or metal, usually bronze. Some were stones, with a small depression carved out to hold the incense. Others were large and elaborate, shaped like houses or temples.

Israel's judges and prophets were always reminding and begging the people to stop their idolatry, but nobody listened. Patiently God waited for His people to turn back to Him,

but when it became obvious they would not, He let them be captured and carried captive from the land He had given them.

The Nazirite vow

Whoever took the Nazirite vow was forbidden to cut his hair or shave his beard. No wine or other strong drink was to touch his lips, and he was not allowed to touch or go near a dead person, even if it was a member of his own family. The vow was taken to set aside one's life in total devotion and service to God.

The Nazirite vow could be taken for as little as 30 days, or for an entire lifetime. Parents could take the vow for their children before they were born, and the children were bound by it. Samson was a lifetime Nazirite because his mother and father had made this promise to God (Jud. 13:5, 7).

Samson the Prisoner

JUDGES 16:1–31

The Lord had promised the land to Israel, so when Israel entered after 40 years in the wilderness, the conquest began. Joshua led his people to many great victories, but even so, the land was never completely captured. Thus Israel settled among the remaining Canaanites and adopted some of their heathen ways. By the time of the Judges, Israel was far from the Lord. Even its leaders, the Judges, were not examples of the Lord's power at work, as can be seen in the life of Samson. Here was a mighty man, more powerful than any other. But he let Delilah take him down the road to ruin. Samson's bitter end is a sign of the times, showing how far Israel had gone from the Lord.

Samson's last days were spent in grinding for the Philistines at Gaza. Grinding grain with a small mill was usually assigned to women. But a large mill was usually powered by an animal. Samson may have been forced to turn a large mill like this.

The lords of the Philistines
Samson was the strongest man on earth. The Philistines were afraid of him, for he had killed countless numbers of their people. When Samson fell in love with Delilah, who was probably a Philistine, the leaders of this nation saw a way of ridding themselves of their hated and feared enemy.

These leaders, or lords, of the Philistines came to visit Delilah one day, each offering 1,100 pieces of silver if she could find the source of Samson's strength. These lords took their offer seriously, for this was a large amount of money.

In the land of Philistia, there were five key cities: Ekron, Ashdod, Ashkelon, Gath, and Gaza. Each of these cities was ruled by a "lord". Together, these five lords made up the Philistine government. These men handled small matters on their own, but large decisions were reached by majority vote. This system of government gave the Philistines an advantage over the Israelites, who were now a group of weak, disorganized tribes.

Gouging out the eyes
Kings and other important people captured by the enemy often had their eyes gouged out. Samson had his eyes put out after he was seized by the Philistines (Jud. 16:21). He had already inflicted great damage on the Philistine nation, and they didn't want any more trouble from him if he escaped.

Weaving on a loom
Delilah wove Samson's hair in a loom, hoping to sap his strength (Jud. 16:14). How was this weaving done?

A vineyard in Israel.

The first step in weaving cloth was called spinning. Fibres taken from cotton, flax, wool, or goat's hair were twisted together with a spindle to form yarn or thread. A spindle looked like a small stick with a hook on the end. A whorl was a small weight tied to the fibre, to help it twist into yarn faster.

When the weaving began, long rows of yarn were tied to the loom, all going in the same direction. This was called the warp. Across the warp were laid other strings of yarn which were passed over and under the strings of the warp. The strings of yarn were then pushed together for extra strength, and the new piece of cloth was ready for sewing.

Grinding grain as punishment

Samson was a strong and mighty man in Israel. When captured, he was humiliated before the Philistines when they gouged out his eyes. Suddenly this great hero was a helpless creature. To degrade him further, he was forced to grind grain, a job usually given to women and slaves.

Gaza

Gaza was an important city along a major caravan route that stretched all the way to Egypt. Located 80 km (50 miles) southwest of Jerusalem and just 5 km (3 miles) inland from the Mediterranean Sea, the city held a vital strategic position for armies marching from Egypt in the south and from Syria and Mesopotamia in the north.

Looking south, the city lay near the edge of a vast and dry wilderness. Gaza had 15 wells, making it an essential stopping point for those who had just come from the desert, and for those who were just entering it.

In the days of the Judges, the Philistines controlled Gaza. It was one of the five key cities of the Philistine government where one of their five ruling "lords" lived.

When Samson visited Gaza, he pulled up the city gates and carried them all the way to Hebron, a distance of over 30 miles (Jud. 16:1–3). Later, when Samson was captured, he spent the rest of his days grinding grain in the Gaza prison (Jud. 16:21).

The temple of Dagon

Dagon was the national god of the Philistines. Many cities built large temples to this god. One of these temples was built in Gaza, the city where Samson was a prisoner.

Most of these temples were constructed after a simple design, where large porch pillars provided the main support for the roof, commonly made of mud or stone.

Inside, heathen priests sacrificed many things to Dagon, even children. Sporting events or the humiliation of prisoners was often carried out in the courtyard, while hundreds of people watched from the roof. It was during one of these times that Samson pulled down the pillars, destroying the temple and killing 3,000 Philistines who were making fun of him.

The Story of Ruth

The time of the Judges was a dark period in Israel's history. Unable to conquer the Promised Land completely, the people of Israel settled among the Canaanites and absorbed many of their heathen ways. By the time the Judges ruled Israel, the nation had gone far from the Lord. But a few bright spots shine out of this period, such as the story of a loyal girl named Ruth.

Fields of grain today found to the north of the area where Boaz and Ruth met.

Descendants of Ruth and Boaz

After Ruth and Boaz were married, they had a son named Obed. Obed grew up and married and had a son called Jesse. Jesse became the father of King David and the grandfather of King Solomon, two of the mightiest and richest kings of Israel.

Centuries later, another descendant of Ruth and Boaz was born in the town of Bethlehem, the same small village where Ruth and Boaz were married hundreds of years before. His name was Jesus, and His birth marked human freedom from sin and death.

Widows

Ruth, Orpah, and Naomi were all widows. Ruth and Orpah became widows at an early age. In ancient times, women depended much on their husbands. If a husband died, all of his property and belongings went to the man who owned the family birthright. The widow was left with absolutely nothing. If no one was willing to help her, the widow spent the rest of her life in extreme poverty. With no one to depend on, she was often taken advantage of.

Israelite law recognized the plight of widows and made some specific laws to help them. If the widow had sons, it was their responsibility to take care of her. But Ruth, Naomi, and Orpah did not have sons.

If a widow had no sons, she could return to her parents as Orpah did. Ruth decided to stay with her mother-in-law, Naomi, but Naomi could not care for her for she also was a widow.

If a widow's husband had brothers, they were required to take her in as their wife, beginning with the oldest. A son born from this kind of marriage was given the name of the widow's husband. But Elimelech, Naomi's husband, apparently did not have any brothers.

In some cases, the closest relative was then obligated to marry the widow. Boaz was the

Ruth in Boaz's Field, a painting by Julius Schnorr von Carolsfeld.

closest relative to Ruth except for one man who could not marry her without jeopardizing his own inheritance. Boaz willingly married Ruth, more out of love than obligation. Naomi was then probably cared for by Ruth and Boaz.

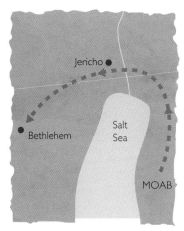

Ruth's journey from her home to the home of her mother-in-law.

Gleaning

When the fields of wheat and barley were ready to be harvested, reapers were hired to cut the stalks of grain and tie them into bundles. According to Israelite laws, any loose stalks that were dropped in the fields were to be left for the gleaners.

Gleaning was done by poor and helpless people such as widows, who without the scraps from the field would have died of starvation. Each day during harvest, the poor walked through the fields and gleaned or picked up any loose stalks that were left behind. Ruth, a widow, was gleaning in a field when she met Boaz, the owner of the field.

Giving away one's sandal

By the city gate, in the sight of many witnesses, Boaz bought the property of Elimelech, which included the right to marry Ruth, as well as the obligation to care for both her and Naomi. The other relative removed his sandal and gave it to Boaz. This was a custom in Israel then, symbolizing that he gave up his right to walk on the land to possess it. Boaz probably returned the man's sandal, though we do not know for sure. The Bible said this legalized the transaction in those early days in Israel (Ruth 4:7).

The Birth of Samuel

I SAMUEL 1:1–20

When the people of Israel were slaves in Egypt, the Lord promised to deliver them, which He did under Moses' leadership. He offered them the Promised Land, but when they arrived at Kadesh Barnea, they were afraid to enter. For 38 more years they remained in the wilderness, entering at last under Joshua's leadership. The land was theirs, but they had to conquer it. Joshua led his people to victory over much of the land, but not all. During the time of the Judges, Israel sank low, going far from the Lord. This dark time in Israel's history lasted about 400 years. At last, a baby was born who became a spiritual leader for Israel. His name was Samuel.

The structure of the tabernacle building had changed since Moses had it made in the wilderness. The front of the tent, covered with curtains in Moses' time, was now a permanent porch with posts.

The yearly sacrifice

Samuel's parents, Elkanah and Hannah, travelled to the tabernacle at Shiloh each year to worship God and attend the "yearly sacrifice" (1 Sam. 1:3, 21). This time of celebration was called the Feast of the Passover, or the Feast of Unleavened Bread, the most important religious event of the year in Israel.

All Israelites were commanded to observe this eight-day feast, and many, especially the men, journeyed to Shiloh each spring to celebrate the feast at the tabernacle.

The journey to Shiloh

Each spring, many of the Israelites went to the Feast of the Passover at the tabernacle in Shiloh, 32 km (20 miles) north of Jerusalem. Samuel's parents made the trip each year from Ramah, a small village 8 km (5 miles) north of Jerusalem. They had a 24-km (15-mile) walk or donkey ride, which would have taken them a day or two at the most. Other Israelites came from the outer borders of the land and beyond, taking a week or more to arrive in Shiloh.

Ramah

The ruins of Ramah lie 8 km (5 miles) north of Jerusalem.

Archaeological excavations around the Tomb of Samuel.

This ancient village is known as the home of Samuel's parents and the birthplace of Samuel, the prophet.

The high priest in full dress must have been a splendid sight. He wore seven articles of clothing, including the ephod and breastpiece, a robe, an embroidered cloak or coat, the belt of the ephod, the mitre, and the diadem or cap. Special underclothing was prescribed also. The high priest's clothing was made of the finest linen. This painting is by Francisco Vieira the Younger (1765–1805).

When Samuel was weaned, his mother brought him to Shiloh, to serve God in the tabernacle. But after the Philistines destroyed Shiloh and the tabernacle, Samuel moved back to Ramah. Here he set up his religious headquarters.

Each year Samuel rode on a circuit through the land, settling disputes, and encouraging the people to follow God, and always returning to Ramah, his home.

Hannah's bargain with God

Hannah and Peninnah were the two wives of Elkanah. Peninnah had children, but Hannah did not. In Old Testament times, a married woman with no children was ashamed before her husband. She was thought to be under a curse from God. So Hannah prayed to God, vowing that if God would give her a son, she would dedicate him to full-time service in the tabernacle. Soon afterward, Samuel was born, and Hannah fulfilled her promise to God, bringing Samuel to Shiloh.

God Speaks to Samuel

I SAMUEL 1:21–2:11; 3

Almost 400 years had passed since the Israelites entered the Promised Land and began its conquest under Joshua's leadership. These years had been dark and discouraging, for Israel had turned far from the Lord, mingling with its Canaanite neighbours and adopting many of their heathen ways. But a godly woman prayed for a son and dedicated that son to the Lord. Samuel, while still very young, went to live at the tabernacle and served the aged priest Eli and the Lord. One night, the Lord spoke to the boy Samuel.

A detail from *Samuel Relating to Eli the Judgements of God upon Eli's House* by John Singleton Copley.

Eli – his duties as high priest

As a young child, Samuel was taken to the tabernacle at Shiloh and dedicated to lifetime service for God. There he grew up under the instruction of Eli, the high priest.

From Aaron, the first high priest, the office was passed down from father to son, and assumed for a lifetime. Eli was, therefore, a direct descendant of Aaron.

As high priest, Eli was ultimately responsible for all of the sacrifices and services offered by the tabernacle. Under him were the priests and Levites, to whom Eli gave the responsibility to carry out most of the work.

The high priest represented the people before God. Each morning and evening, he entered the holy place of the tabernacle and burned incense on the incense altar, which stood in front of the veil. Sometimes the high priest gave this job to other priests.

Once a year, on the Day of Atonement, the high priest alone entered the holy of holies to offer up the sins of the people to God. This was a sacred ceremony, where the high priest begged forgiveness for the people's sins in the presence of God.

Offerings at the tabernacle

The priests at the tabernacle were kept busy caring for the building and preparing the great variety of daily sacrifices, or offerings.

Each day, the priests killed two male lambs. One lamb was burned on the altar of burnt offering in the morning and one in the evening. Anything that was burned with fire on the altar, including animals, plants, or food, was called a burnt offering. But burnt offerings were called by many different names. The daily offering of the two lambs was called the continual burnt offering.

Burned along with the continual burnt offering was the grain offering, a mixture of fine flour and oil, probably olive oil. The drink offering was usually included at this time as well. It consisted of different amounts of wine, varying when a lamb, goat, or bull was sacrificed.

On the Sabbath, and on feast days, many other offerings were included. People approached God with sin offerings, guilt offerings, and offerings of thanksgiving and praise.

This huge menorah outside the Knesset (parliament) in modern Jerusalem is a reminder of the lampstand in the tabernacle.

The menorah

Samuel slept in the sanctuary of the tabernacle, by the golden lampstand known as the menorah. This was a very important piece of furniture to the Israelites and today is still one of the major symbols of the Jewish faith.

Originally, the menorah was carved from a single piece of acacia wood, the same strong and durable wood used to make the other tabernacle furniture. It was then overlaid with 43 kg (96 lb) of pure gold.

The menorah had a long straight stand. Six branches curved out and up from its centre, three on each side. There were seven branches in all, including the centre stand. At the tip of each branch was a small cup. Each morning a priest or Levite filled these seven cups with the finest olive oil, then lighted the wick that floated in the oil. All day the menorah burned and into a part of the evening. These flames were an expression of God's presence.

In the morning, the three right-hand branches were lit first, followed by the three left-hand branches. The centre branch was always the last to be lit. An outside branch could be relit from the centre branch, but the centre branch could only be relit from the altar where the burnt offerings took place.

Many think the menorah was designed to represent the tree of life. Others say the lampstand was patterned after any normal tree, symbolizing fruitfulness and peace in Israel.

Beds

In ancient times, beds were merely mats or blankets, light enough to carry from place to place. In the morning they were easily rolled up and stored in a convenient spot until evening. Samuel probably slept on this kind of bed in the tabernacle sanctuary. Poor people used only their coats, or cloaks, as their beds.

For the wealthy, beds were more comfortable, but still nothing like those enjoyed today. Rich people could afford quilts or even mattresses that were stuffed with soft cotton. Kings slept on elevated beds or couches called divans, with two or three mattresses.

The lamps in Samuel's time (as shown here in this Israelite lamp from the 7th century BC) were shallow and deeper dishes. The wicks lay in the spouts.

The Ark Is Captured

I SAMUEL 4:1–5:12

When the Philistines captured the ark, they took it first to Ashdod, where they put it in the temple of Dagon.

The time of the Judges had been a dark period in Israel's history, a time when the people suffered many defeats because they had turned from the Lord, and thus the Lord had turned from them. But as Samuel grew up, people began to recognize that he was a prophet, a truly godly leader who could help them return to the Lord. During this time, when Eli was still the high priest of Israel, the Philistines were a constant threat. On one occasion the Israelites were so desperate for victory that they took the ark to the battlefield, hoping it would turn the tide of battle. Instead, the Philistines captured the ark and took it home with them. When news of this reached Eli, he died.

Dagon

The chief god of the Philistines was Dagon. He was the god of rain, who brought forth a rich harvest. Later, he was known also as the god of grain.

Against the power of God, Dagon proved ineffective and lifeless. At Gaza, Samson pulled Dagon's temple to the ground, killing 3,000 Philistines inside (Jud. 16:23–30). A few years later, the ark of the covenant was captured by the Philistines and placed in the temple of Dagon at Ashdod. But Dagon's idol could not stand before the ark. Two times it fell before the ark, and the second time it broke into pieces (1 Sam. 5:1–7).

The Philistine's god Dagon was often shown as part fish.

Plagues

Waves of sickness and disease often spread quickly throughout a country in ancient times. This was called a plague and was one of the people's greatest fears.

Plagues moved quickly and seemed to come from nowhere to inflict pain and death on both rich and poor, slave and master. The most common plague in Bible times was the bubonic plague carried by swarms of rats.

Some plagues, sent by God for a specific purpose, may have been this disease (Num. 14:37; 16:47; 25:9). But other plagues of various types also appeared.

The loss of the ark

When the Philistines captured the ark of the covenant, they took Israel's most-prized possession.

In fact, it was so sacred that many believed it alone would provide victory in battle.

The ark was not destroyed when captured because the Philistines understood its importance to the Israelites and wanted to show off this prized treasure to their own people. It was first seized at the battle of Ebenezer, about 40 km (25 miles) west of Shiloh, and brought to the temple of Dagon in Ashdod. When God struck the city with a plague, the ark was moved to Gath, but disease spread to the Philistines there as well. Next it was sent to Ekron, but when the plague broke out again, the Philistines quickly sent the ark back to the Israelites at Beth Shemesh, about 24 km (15 miles) west of Jerusalem. From there it was brought to Kiriath Jearim, where it stayed until David's time.

The Return of the Ark

I SAMUEL 6:1–7:2

While Eli was still high priest of Israel and Samuel had not yet begun a widespread ministry, the Philistines and Israelites fought a battle. But the battle went against the Israelites so much that they brought the ark of the covenant to the battlefield, hoping it would turn the tide for them. Instead, the Philistines captured the ark and took it back to their home territory. However, they had nothing but trouble as long as the ark remained with them, so they made plans to send it back to Israel.

Oxcarts

The Philistines lived along the flat coast of the Mediterranean Sea, and in this region, carts and wagons were very useful. But in Canaan, the land was hilly and rocky. Without roads, travel by cart or wagon was difficult, if not impossible, in many places.

In earliest times, wagon wheels were made from large pieces of wood, carved into a circle. Later, spokes were invented and metal rims added. The ordinary cart of Palestine was made of wood, but some

David brought the ark back to Jerusalem on an oxcart.

were made of reeds, bronze, or iron. The axles turned smoothly in grease made from fish fat or oxen fat.

From Beth Shemesh to Kiriath Jearim

When attacked by plague, the Philistines put the ark of God in an oxcart and sent it back to Israel, to the town of Beth Shemesh, located about 13 km (8 miles) east of Ekron and 24 km (15 miles) west of Jerusalem. But when God killed many of the people of Beth Shemesh for looking inside of the ark, they became afraid. They sent the ark to Kiriath Jearim, about 16 km (10 miles) west of Jerusalem.

The ark stayed here in the house of a man named Abinadab until the days of David, when the king brought the ark to Jerusalem. There it stayed until the days of the Captivity.

Ruins near Beit Shemesh, west of Jerusalem.

Saul Is Made King

I SAMUEL 8–10

Samuel was a godly man, but a poor father, so his sons were unworthy to rule after him. The people of Israel recognized this and demanded a king. Saul was their choice.

The Anointing of Saul, by Jan Victors.

Why the Israelites wanted a king

For years the Israelites had wanted a king, but when Samuel grew old, they were especially demanding. The people gave Samuel three reasons why they thought a king was needed.

First of all, Samuel's sons were evil and corrupt men, unfit to follow in the godly footsteps of their father. Secondly, nearly every nation around Israel had a king as the country's ruler, and the Israelites wanted to be like them. Lastly, they wanted a military commander to make them stronger in the eyes of their enemies (1 Sam. 8:5, 20).

What a king would do

The Israelites wanted a king, but were they willing to accept the responsibilities of one?

A king gave the people better organization and strength, but he also took much of their food, animals, and money in the form of taxes.

A king also gave the nation a military commander, but in return he took the people's sons to fight in his army, and he took their daughters to work in the palace and support him, his servants, and his army. A king also used their horses to pull chariots, and demanded more of their crops to feed his soldiers.

Saul Sacrifices Wrongly

1 SAMUEL 13

During the days of the Judges of Israel, the nation turned away from the Lord. This was still true when Eli led the nation as high priest. But about that time the Lord appointed Samuel to follow Eli, for Eli's sons were unworthy to do this. Samuel served well, leading the nation back to the Lord. But he was also a poor father, and his sons were unworthy to do his work. So the people demanded a king. Saul was made king and served well at first. But when the Lord told Saul to wait for Samuel, he would not do it.

Animal sacrifice was practised in many ancient cultures. This depiction of a sacrifice of a young boar comes from a Greek cup, c. 510–500 BC.

Saul's sacrifices

When Saul would wait no longer for Samuel, he went ahead on his own and sacrificed the burnt and peace offerings. Peace offerings were usually not required, but were a voluntary act of worship and devotion to God.

Burnt offerings often accompanied peace offerings, showing additional devotion to God. They were sometimes given before a battle to uncover the people's sins and ask for God's mercy, as well as to unite the soldiers in preparing for war. Saul disobeyed by offering these sacrifices himself, for God had commanded that Samuel was supposed to offer them.

Archaeological traces of ancient Gilgal where Saul foolishly sacrificed without Samuel.

Gibeah

Saul was born into the tribe of Benjamin and lived in the city of Gibeah. This was Saul's first capital, only 5 km (3 miles) north of Jerusalem. It was the headquarters of Saul's military campaigns.

Philistine garrisons

Garrisons or outposts were military fortresses built by an army near the borders of enemy territory. They were occupied by groups of brave men, usually for defensive purposes.

Philistine oppression

Years before the Israelites arrived in Canaan, the Philistines had moved in. At that time they were called the Sea Peoples, because they came from across the Mediterranean Sea. With their skilled and powerful warriors, they easily swept into the land of Canaan and occupied the territory along the seacoast.

In the days of Samuel and Saul, the Philistines were especially strong. Along with this organized government was a highly organized army of skilled warriors. Only the Philistines knew the secret of making iron, which put the Israelites at a great disadvantage in battle. With their disorganized and bickering tribes, the Israelites were no match for the skilled Philistines, who constantly oppressed Israel until King David united that kingdom and conquered the Philistines.

Samuel Anoints David

I SAMUEL 16:1–13

When it became apparent that Samuel's sons were unworthy to lead the nation after him, the people of Israel demanded a king. Thus Saul was made the first king of Israel. Saul, however, disobeyed the Lord, and Samuel began to realize that he could not endure as a king. One day the Lord told Samuel to go to Bethlehem and anoint David, who would become the next king of Israel.

The Anointing of David by Samuel by François-Léon Benouville.

Why was David anointed?

The king of Israel was called the "Lord's anointed". He was not only a political leader, but one of the nation's spiritual leaders as well, set apart for service to God. It was the religious act of anointing that established the king as God's representative to the people. When anointed, the king was set apart for a special relationship with God. He was supposed to depend on God's wisdom as he served the nation of Israel.

How was David anointed?

A prophet or priest anointed a king of Israel. When the Prophet Samuel anointed David, he filled a horn, probably a curved animal's horn, with a holy anointing oil. This was probably the same special oil used to anoint a high priest. The ingredients for this holy oil were known only to a few priests, who kept the recipe secret. Stealing or copying the recipe was a crime punishable by death. The Bible mentions some of the ingredients as pure olive oil, myrrh, sweet cinnamon, and fragrant cane.

When the anointing horn was filled with the holy oil, the next king would kneel before the prophet or priest, who poured the oil onto the king's head. The king had to be anointed, symbolizing a dedication and

devotion to serve God and His people.

Other occasions for anointing

Anointing a king or high priest was a sacred act, requiring much responsibility. But there were other occasions when anointing was used by just about everyone.

In the hot and dry climate of Palestine, part of a daily routine for most people involved anointing, or rubbing their skin with olive oil to keep it moist. It was also used as a substitute for soap when there was little water.

At special occasions, such as feasts or banquets, an honoured guest was anointed by brushing a dab of oil on his head. People covered themselves with oil during times of celebration as well.

The elders of the city

As Samuel approached Bethlehem to anoint the next king, he was met by the elders of the city. Who were these people?

The elders were a group of men. They were probably heads of families, influential men noted for their wisdom, respect, and

THE KINGS OF ISRAEL AND JUDAH

THE UNITED KINGDOM *about 1025–931*

- ☐ Saul (15) mostly
- ☐ David (40)
- ☐ Solomon (40) mostly

THE KINGDOM DIVIDED *about 931–586*

Judah	Israel
■ Rehoboam (17) 931–913 mostly	■ Jeroboam I (22) 931–910
■ Abijah (3) 913–911 mostly	
☐ Asa (41) 911–870	
	■ Nadab (2) 910–909
	■ Baasha (24) 909–886
	■ Elah (2) 886–885
	■ Zimri (7 days) 885
	■ Tibni (5) 885–880
	■ Omri (7) 880–874
☐ Jehoshaphat (25) 873–848)	■ Ahab (22) 874–853
	■ Ahaziah (2) 853–852
■ Jehoram (8) 848–841	■ Jehoram (12) 852–841 mostly
■ Ahaziah (1) 841	■ Jehu (28) 841–814 mostly
■ Athaliah (6) 841–835	
☐ Joash (40) 835–796 mostly	
	■ Jehoahaz (17) 814–798
	■ Joash (16) 798–782
☐ Amaziah (29) 796–767	■ Jeroboam II (41) 793–753
☐ Uzziah (52) 791–740 mostly	■ Zechariah (6 months) 753–752
	■ Shallum (1 month) 752
	■ Menahem (10) 752–742
☐ Jotham (16) 750–735	■ Pekahiah (2) 742–740
	■ Pekah (9) 740–732
■ Ahaz (20) 736–716	■ Hoshea (11) 732–722
☐ Hezekiah (29) 716–687	*Israel in captivity – no kings*
■ Manasseh (55) 696–642	
■ Amon (2) 642–40	
☐ Josiah (31) 640–608	
■ Jehoahaz (3 months) 608	
■ Jehoiakim (11) 608–597	
■ Jehoiachin (3 months) 597	
■ Zedekiah (11) 597–586	

KEY
☐ Good King
■ Bad King
(40) Years of reign
931–913 Approximate time of reign (years BC). Overlapping dates indicate when two kings were reigning together

fairness. They often sat by the city gate, acting as judges for the people, giving advice, and running the city's government.

Bethlehem was David's home at the time of his anointing. These Herodion ruins are near Bethlehem.

David Plays for Saul

I SAMUEL 16:14–23

When the leaders of Israel saw that Samuel's sons were not worthy to rule after him, they demanded a king. Samuel anointed Saul, who became Israel's first king. But Saul was not obedient to the Lord, so the Lord told Samuel to anoint David, who was still quite young at that time. Not long after this, David went to Saul's palace to play music for the troubled king.

Harps and lyres

David was a skilled musician. He probably knew how to play the harp and the lyre, two similar musical instruments.

A lyre had a sound box as its base, where the rich musical tones came from. Over the base was a crossbar, and the strings were stretched taut between the sound box and the crossbar. Many lyres had four strings, but one of the most common lyres of Israel had three. Still others used six or nine strings.

The harp had no crossbar. Instead, its strings of animal gut were stretched across a curved piece of wood, or between a sound box and a piece of wood attached at a right angle to the box.

Harps were very important instruments in ancient orchestras. They provided gentle music for quieting the heart and soothing the mind and soul. There were as many different kinds of harps and lyres as

David and Saul by Ernst Josephson.

there were countries. Many had elaborate carvings of bulls, cows, and stags, which may have represented the different musical sections of a choir.

Music and musicians

Music was a language understood by everyone in ancient times. Monuments and writings dating from Bible times show that music was greatly loved and appreciated. Musicians were respected and in constant demand.

Rarely did a day slip by without the rhythm of music in some homes. Feasts, parties, rituals, wars, celebrations, and even funerals were filled with music and song. Kings and wealthy families had their own musicians. Orchestras often performed while walking through the streets, similar to the marching bands of today.

Many men and women became musicians to fight loneliness. David, as a shepherd, must have spent many weeks alone in the quiet hills of Canaan. The pleasant sound of his harp pushed back the fears of the night and was also effective in keeping wild animals back in the shadows.

Tell el-Ful, the site of biblical Gibeah. Many of the events surrounding David and Jonathan, as well as King Saul, happened at Gibeah. David lived here with the king and Jonathan for a while. Gibeah just north of Jerusalem.

Messengers

David was well-known as an excellent musician, and when Saul was troubled, the king sent messengers to quickly bring David to the palace. A king's messengers were reliable men and fast runners, who could be trusted to relay the king's messages correctly. Some messengers to foreign lands served as spies, while others brought back news of battles to the king.

Limestone carving of a musician playing a lyre.

David and Goliath

1 SAMUEL 17

When Saul, first king of Israel, became disobedient to the Lord, it became obvious that he would not be a lasting king. The Lord told Samuel to anoint David, a young man of Bethlehem, to become the next king. Meanwhile David went to Saul's palace to live and to play music for the troubled king. About that time the Israelites and the Philistines went to war. David took food to his older brothers, who served in the army of Israel. David found the soldiers of Israel terrified by a giant, Goliath. Though David was probably a teenager, he challenged Goliath and killed him. This immediately made David a hero.

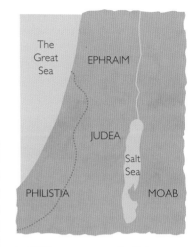

In Old Testament times, the Philistines occupied a strip of coastal land on the Mediterranean, west of Jerusalem, known as Philistia. The Philistines were among the "People of the Sea" who invaded Syria and Egypt in the twelfth century BC Philistia was a league of five important Philistine cities: Gaza, Ashdod, Ashkelon, Ekron and Gath. The Philistines were skilful potters and iron workers. During the time of the Judges, the Philistines were the most feared of Israel's enemies, but King David finally defeated them (2 Sam. 8:1). The Philistines gave their name to Palestine.

The sling
What kind of weapon did David use to defeat the giant Goliath?

David's victory weapon against Goliath was the common sling of the time. Slingers were respected warriors in some nations. Goliath foolishly ignored the fact that a young man could have such skill.

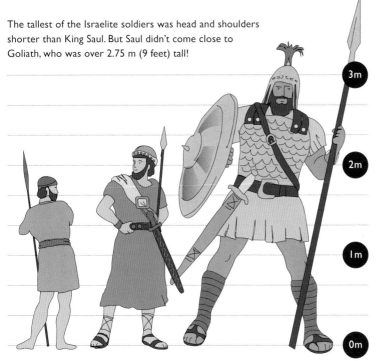

The tallest of the Israelite soldiers was head and shoulders shorter than King Saul. But Saul didn't come close to Goliath, who was over 2.75 m (9 feet) tall!

The valley where David fought Goliath.

It was a common sling, but it was not a boy's toy, for armies had been fighting battles with slings for centuries.

In the days of the Judges, some Israelite soldiers were excellent slingers in battle. The tribe of Benjamin had 700 left-handed warriors who could sling at a hair and never miss (Jud. 20:16).

The centre of a sling, sometimes called the pan, was a wide piece of leather which held the stone. A long strip of leather, or a cord made of goat's hair, was tied to each side of the pan. Sometimes one cord had a loop at the end, for the slinger's wrist. The slinger held the end of the other cord in his hand.

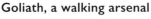

With a stone in place, the slinger whirled his weapon around his head several times, then released the end of the cord from his hand, sending the stone to its mark. Goliath's people learned too late that David's sling was a deadly weapon of war and not a boy's toy.

Goliath, a walking arsenal
For years, the Israelites had looked up to their King Saul as a giant. He was head and shoulders taller than anyone else in Israel, perhaps 2 m plus (6.5–7 feet) in height (1 Sam. 10:23).

But Saul didn't come close to Goliath, who was over 2.75 m (9 feet) tall. He was half as tall again as nearly every Israelite soldier!

Goliath was as powerful as he was tall. On his shoulders and chest he wore a coat of mail that weighed about 55 kg (125 lb). The iron point of his

javelin alone weighed 7 kg (15 lb). With bronze leggings, bronze helmet, and his great shield and sword, Goliath must have carried 90 kg (200 lb) of armour. He was a walking arsenal.

But Goliath was a deadly soldier too. He was a champion of all the Philistines, a giant who used every piece of armour with the precision of a modern pro football player. No wonder the Israelites feared him!

David and Jonathan

I SAMUEL 18:1–4

King Saul had failed as king, not because he ruled poorly, but because he would not obey the Lord. Thus the Lord told Samuel to anoint David, who was still quite young, as the next king of Israel. David went to Saul's palace to live and played music to soothe the troubled king. In time, David challenged giant Goliath in a battle and killed the Philistine. Jonathan, Saul's son, was so impressed with David that the two became lifelong friends.

Since the Israelites' weapons were made only of wood and stone, Jonathan's iron sword was probably the most highly prized weapon in Israel. But without a second thought, he gave it to his friend David.

A rare friendship

Jonathan was not only a mighty warrior, but the prince of Israel. As the son of King Saul, he was next in line to inherit the throne of Israel. According to the custom of the day, Jonathan had every right to become Israel's next king.

But because of Saul's sin, God had taken the kingship away from Saul's family, and given it to David. Jonathan did not know this at first, and after David killed Goliath, the two young men became inseparable. Together, Jonathan and David made a lifelong covenant of friendship (1 Sam. 18:3).

Later, Jonathan learned that David, and not he, would be the next king of Israel. But an unusual thing happened. Jonathan loved David even more, and their friendship grew stronger. Recognizing God's will, Jonathan preferred to lose the throne of Israel, than to lose his companion David. What a rare friendship!

Jonathan's gifts for David

When David and Jonathan met, they became lifelong friends. Jonathan was so serious about their friendship that he made a covenant with David and sealed it by giving him his robe, tunic, sword, bow, and belt (1 Sam. 18:4).

The word robe as used in the Bible meant an expensive and elegant cloak worn by royalty. It was made from the finest cloth. Some were imported from faraway countries like Babylon. This in itself would have been a valuable gift to a trusted friend.

But Jonathan gave his friend more. In all Israel, only Saul and Jonathan had swords and spears of iron (1 Sam. 13:22). The Philistines alone knew the secret of forging the strong metal.

A bronze-age sword like Jonathan's.

106

Saul Tries to Kill David

1 SAMUEL 18–19

Saul was a strong king in many ways, but he did not like to obey the Lord. So the Lord chose David to be the next king instead of a member of Saul's family. After David killed Goliath, the people praised David much more than Saul. This made Saul so jealous that he wanted to kill David.

David fled from Gibeah, in fear of his life because of King Saul's jealousy. He went first to Ramah to visit Samuel, then spent months on the run from Saul, living in the Judean hills, where a large number joined him.

A city celebrates after victory

Victorious in battle, David and Saul must have ridden back to the palace together. When entering a city on their homeward trip, throngs of happy people greeted them in the streets, shouting and dancing.

Women sang a special song as they circled around their heroes. Musicians shook their tambourines, symbolic of victory.

Often the song leader shouted a verse and the other singers repeated it in an exaggerated form. As David and Saul moved through the city, the song leader praised Saul for killing thousands of men, and the singers repeated by praising David for killing tens of thousands. Though this was a common custom in Israelite songs, Saul grew angry and jealous of David's greater praise. After this, Saul kept a suspicious eye on his popular commander.

The spear that missed its mark

What did Saul's spear look like? Though some spears looked more like short knives, Saul's spear probably had a long wooden shaft, almost as tall as he was. The spearhead was made of stone or metal, and the tip often had two hooks or barbs which left a mortal wound when the spear was pulled from a wounded soldier. These long spears were sometimes called javelins. Just the spearhead of Goliath's javelin weighed over 7 kg (15 lb)! Some of these long spears were designed to spin through the air, inflicting even greater injury.

Bronze javelin,
c. 1479–1458 BC.

Jonathan Warns David

I SAMUEL 20

Ancient bronze and bone arrowheads.

After David killed Goliath, Jonathan became his best friend. Jonathan admired David's courage and grew to love him more than a brother. So when Saul, Jonathan's father, grew insanely jealous of David and tried to kill him, Jonathan remained loyal and friendly to David. He would not betray his friend, even for his father.

The deadly bow and arrow

Jonathan used his bow and arrow to warn David of Saul's anger. But bows and arrows were mainly used in battle during war times and for hunting in times of peace.

On the battlefield, an archer's bow and arrows was one of his most deadly and effective weapons. Instead of fighting in hand-to-hand combat, an archer with a sharp aim could pierce the heart of an enemy soldier from a distance of 40 yards or more.

The ancient Egyptians used the simple reflex bow, a curved piece of wood or bone, with a taut string of animal gut tied between the ends. These bows were often as tall as a man, and powerful enough to send a flying arrow completely through a man's body.

Canaanite hunters and soldiers used more complicated bows of wood, bone, metal, or a combination of these materials. They made a bronze battle bow so powerful that even a mighty warrior had trouble pulling the bowstring.

The arrows had a shaft, usually about 90 cm (3 feet) long, made of reed or wood. One end was notched to fit into the bowstring. The arrowhead, attached to the other end, was sometimes tied to the shaft with a cord of leather. Most arrowheads were made from flint, bone, iron, or bronze. Some were dipped in poison before battle to make sure the enemy died, even if he wasn't mortally wounded. Arrows were kept in a quiver, a leather bag strapped over one's shoulder.

Sitting at the king's table

Few people earned the privilege of eating with the king. Persian kings often ate alone, while Israelite kings usually ate only with their closest friends and advisers. During large feasts and festivals, kings sometimes ate with a crowd of people.

The king's table was the place of highest honour. Guests were seated according to their rank or importance. If an unimportant guest took a seat too close to the king, he would be asked to move to a lower position. The Greeks and Romans thought the middle of the table was the greatest place of honour. Other nations made the head of the table the most prominent place. King Saul's seat was at the back of the room against the wall, where he could easily see everyone who was eating with him. To his left was Abner, his army general, and to his right was his son Jonathan.

Festival of the New Moon

The Israelites were festive people. Almost every moment of the day was filled with hard work, so the people eagerly looked forward to the days set aside for feasting and festivity.

One of these festivals was always celebrated at the time of each new moon. It was called the Festival of the New Moon. Though it included religious ceremonies, it was primarily a time for the community to get together and rejoice over the fruits of the land wand its bountiful harvests.

David Runs from Saul

I SAMUEL 21–22

From the day David killed Goliath, the people of Israel praised him more than King Saul. This made Saul jealous, to the point of insanity, so that he often tried to kill David. At last David had to leave the palace and run from Saul, who pursued him with soldiers.

Where was Nob?

David soon realized that Saul wanted to kill him. To save his life, David escaped from Saul's capital at Gibeah and fled to Nob, where many of the priests lived, just to the southeast.

After Shiloh was destroyed, Israel's religious headquarters were probably set up at Nob. It is likely that the tabernacle was destroyed along with Shiloh, and a temporary building might have been set up at Nob to replace it. As the new religious centre of Israel, Nob was the home of many priests and Levites.

David knew he would not be safe so close to Saul's capital. He asked Ahimelech, the high priest who lived at Nob, for Goliath's sword and some of the holy showbread. Then he ran farther into the wilderness.

The shewbread

Inside the tabernacle was a table on which 12 round loaves of special bread were placed. This holy bread was called shewbread and symbolized that God was the Bread of Life for the nation of Israel.

Each Friday afternoon before the Sabbath, certain priests carefully baked the loaves of bread. Only the priests from the Garmu family knew the secret recipe, which contained only the finest flour and the purest oil.

On Saturday morning, the day of the Sabbath, eight priests took part in a special ceremony and replaced the week-old loaves with the freshly baked ones. The bread was arranged in two stacks of six loaves, with a golden bowl of sweet frankincense placed on the top of each stack.

The old bread was divided between the high priest and the other priests and was to be eaten and not thrown away. The old frankincense was poured out over the altar and burned before God. The fresh bread remained on the table until the next Sabbath, when the ritual ceremony was performed again. There was never a day when the shewbread was not present in the tabernacle.

The Bell Cave at Adullam Park might be where David and his men hid from Saul.

Abigail Shares Her Food

I SAMUEL 25

While Saul pursued David with his army, David and his loyal followers moved from place to place. Naturally, David and his men had to find food, so they often asked local farmers and shepherds to share theirs. When they asked Nabal, an incident took place that led to David's marrying Abigail.

Carmel and Maon

In this incident, Nabal was shearing sheep at Carmel, about 11 km (7 miles) south of Hebron. His home in Maon was about a mile farther south of Carmel.

These two places lie in an area of gently rolling hills and rich pastureland, ideal for Nabal's work of tending sheep. Years later, King Uzziah of Judah might have planted his many vineyards on this good soil (2 Chron. 26:10).

Sheep

Life in Palestine and the presence of sheep always seemed to be woven together. In some way, these animals played a very important part in the life of almost every Israelite.

Many men and women made their living tending sheep. Shepherding is one of the best known occupations of Israel. This was because of the many uses of the sheep and their products.

From the sheep came wool, which was spun into yarn, woven into fabric, and then made into clothing. Sheepskin was used to make tents, providing an excellent cloth that kept out the biting winds and resisted the cold and dreary rains.

Even more important was the food provided by sheep. Since they were considered by the Hebrews as "clean" animals, their meat and milk became staple foods in the diet of Israel. Meat for the evening meal and milk to drink kept many of the Israelites well fed. A lamb was also a major part of the Passover meal (Ex. 12:3–11). In addition, the Israelites' worship often called for offering a sheep or a lamb. They were sacrificed in burnt offerings, and in sin, guilt, and peace offerings.

Sheep are often quite particular about what they eat and usually need richer pastureland than goats or cattle. Because of the spotty winter rains in Palestine, the shepherds wander through the countryside, searching for the better grazing areas.

As quiet and non-aggressive animals, sheep willingly follow their shepherd wherever he leads. Sheep are also defenceless, unable to cope with the dangers of attacking animals or thieves. For this reason, the shepherd must always be on the lookout, watching his flock at all times. He alone can save his sheep from approaching disaster.

Shearing the sheep

Once each year, in the middle or end of spring, all the sheep were gathered into pens. One by one they were caught and their thick, warm wool coats were shorn off. One sheep might have up to 4.5 kg (10 lb) of wool removed. After the shearing, a large festival was held, celebrating the prosperity of another good year.

David Spares Saul

I SAMUEL 26

Because the people showed more favour to David than to him, Saul was insanely jealous of David. After Saul tried to kill David at the palace, David fled, and Saul pursued him from place to place. Once David could have killed Saul in a cave, but did not. Now, a second time, David found Saul unguarded and could have killed him, but spared him instead.

The army encampment

After a hard day of marching, an army stopped to set up camp. Often the soldiers stayed in their camp for more than one night, and sometimes for as long as a month or even a year, when besieging a city.

In late afternoon, as the sun was slipping in the western sky, the army commander started to look for a good place to stop. He halted when he found two important things – plenty of water and a natural barrier of defence such as a long ridge or hillside.

When the right place was chosen, the soldiers pitched their tents in a large circle. Any animals they had brought with them or had captured were driven inside the circle after sunset for protection. Sometimes the commander's tent was pitched in the centre of the circle. It was larger than the others, and just outside the tent door his spear was stuck in the ground as a symbol of his authority.

Watchposts were set up on all sides of the army encampment, and throughout the night, men peered into the darkness, looking for any sign of the enemy.

Some armies, like the Assyrians, went to great lengths to protect their camps. Large walls of stone and mud were built around the tents, and tall earthen watchtowers looked out over the surrounding countryside.

The hill of Hakilah

Saul and his army set up camp by this hill when pursuing David. As Saul slept, David and Abishai crept into the camp and stole the king's spear and water jug, but did no harm to Saul himself.

The exact site of the hill is not known today, but it was somewhere in the wilderness of Ziph, a barren wasteland stretching south and east of Hebron.

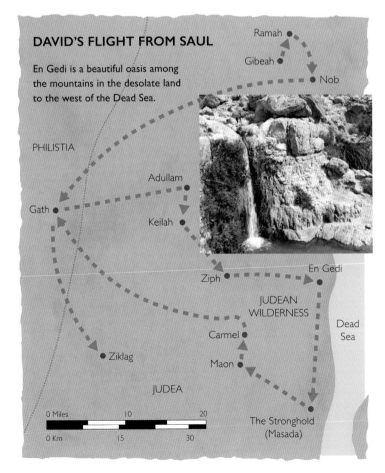

DAVID'S FLIGHT FROM SAUL

En Gedi is a beautiful oasis among the mountains in the desolate land to the west of the Dead Sea.

Ramah
Gibeah
Nob
PHILISTIA
Adullam
Gath
Keilah
Ziph
En Gedi
JUDEAN
WILDERNESS
Dead
Sea
Carmel
Ziklag
Maon
JUDEA
The Stronghold
(Masada)

0 Miles   10   20
0 Km   15   30

The Witch of Endor

I SAMUEL 28

Saul had pursued David with his army, hoping to kill him. David went from place to place, but finally decided to move into the land of the Philistines to hide, for Saul would not pursue him there. When the Philistines went to war against Saul, they refused to let David go with them, for they feared that he would side with Saul in battle. Saul, in the meantime, grew frightened and went to a witch at Endor to see how this battle would go and what would happen to him.

Magic and the occult

Though forbidden by God, magicians, witches, sorcerers, and wizards continued to be popular among the Israelites. Many people sincerely believed that evil spirits and supernatural powers dictated their lives. By looking into the future, they hoped to change the course of their lives to avoid approaching disaster. Clever people were sensitive to these people's pagan beliefs and became wizards or sorcerers to supply their demand.

These wizards, sorcerers, and magicians were called mediums and were supposedly able to communicate with demons, evil spirits, and the spirits of the dead. By speaking with them, they could learn of future events. There was a big business for this, but more often than not the customers were fooled by the trick of ventriloquism. In ventriloquism, the wizard uttered sounds without moving his mouth, making noises that sounded like spirits coming up from the ground.

Reading the future, also known as divination, was practised in other ways as well. "Magic potions" were poured into a cup, and the bubbles and reflections were read as a prediction of what lay ahead. Casting lots was done frequently as well.

God warned the Israelites through His prophets and judges that magic and sorcery were evil and dangerous. Anyone caught using these occult practices was supposed to be stoned to death. But despite God's warnings, the mystery of this evil magic continued.

Nebi Samwil

On a high hill overlooking Jerusalem from the north is a mosque, covering a traditional site of Samuel's tomb. In Arabic it is called Nebi Samwil. But this place is filled with controversy.

Samuel's birthplace and home was at Ramah, thought by many to be modern Er Ram, just east of Nebi Samwil. The Bible says that Samuel was buried at Ramah (1 Sam. 25:1). If Er Ram was Ramah, then Samuel was buried there.

Like many places in Bible lands, the exact location is unknown. But Nebi Samwil remains one traditional site of Samuel's tomb.

Endor

The village where the witch of Endor lived was a small town 13 km (7 miles) northeast of Mount Gilboa, where Saul fought his last battle the next day.

The Urim and Thummim

In times of great trouble, the ephod was often consulted to determine God's will. It was a beautiful sleeveless vest worn by the high priest. Attached to it was a breastpiece containing 12 precious stones, one for each tribe of Israel. Inside the breastpiece were the Urim and Thummim, which might have been two more precious stones that were probably used like lots to receive a yes or no answer to a question asked of God.

Saul Dies

I SAMUEL 31

While David was hiding among the Philistines, the enemies of Israel, the Philistines went to war against Saul. Terrified by the thought of defeat, Saul consulted a witch to see what would happen. Through her, he learned that he would die in battle the next day.

Endor was not far north of Mount Gilboa.

Gilboa – Saul's last battle

Saul fought his last battle on the slopes of Mount Gilboa. The Philistines killed him, along with three of his sons, including Jonathan.

Mount Gilboa rises from the Jezreel Plain. Saul wanted to avoid fighting on the plain itself, because his troops were no match for the sophisticated Philistine weapons and chariots. The battle occurred about 95 km (60 miles) north of Jerusalem or close to 32 km (20 miles) southwest of the Sea of Galilee. It probably started because the Israelites were threatening to close off a major trade route of the Philistines called The Way to the Sea, which ran from Egypt to Damascus.

Prisoners of war

It is little wonder that Saul fell on his sword and killed himself when faced with the prospect of being captured by the Philistines, enemies who hated the Israelites. As a prisoner of war, and especially as a captured king and commander in chief, Saul would have been humiliated before all of the Philistines and brutally tortured.

The Philistines enjoyed humiliating their captives by making them dance or sing before crowds of people. But the Babylonians and Assyrians were known for their brutal tactics of torture. When a city was captured, most of the men were killed, and the rest of the people were carried back to Babylon or Assyria with rings hooked through their lips or noses. Over the long trip, many died from exposure and starvation.

Some captives were bound alive to a table and had their skin stripped off. Others, especially great warriors, had their eyes gouged out and lived the rest of their lives as helpless creatures. Still others were thrown into small prison cells, each chained to the body of a dead man.

Not all captives were tortured. Some were killed instantly with axes or spears, while others were thrown into furnaces. Those not killed or tortured were forced into lives of slavery.

In Babylon, however, a slave's life was not all misery. He could own property and run his own business. If he earned enough money, he could even buy back his freedom!

Beth Shan

Sifting through the plunder on the day after battle, the Philistines found the dead bodies of Saul and his sons. With great rejoicing they carried their bodies about 16 km (10 miles) southwest along the Jezreel Valley to the town of Beth Shan, later called Beth Shean, where they hung the corpses on the city walls. They remained there until brave men from Jabesh Gilead, a small village 24 km (15 miles) farther southwest, recovered the bodies of their king and princes and buried them.

David Becomes King of Judah

While David lived at Ziklag, a city which the Philistines had set aside for his home, the Israelites and Philistines went to war. Saul, king of Israel, was killed in battle with his son Jonathan. After this, David became king of Judah, and Saul's son Ish-Bosheth became king of Israel.

Dating Bible events in Israel's history becomes much more accurate at the start of David's reign than previously. Most authorities agree that David was crowned king of Judah between 1011 and 1000 BC.

But how was such an accurate date determined? Archaeologists have uncovered ancient Assyrian texts which mention every year in Assyrian history from 891–648 BC and the important events which occurred in these years.

For example, ancient Assyrian texts inscribed on stone or clay tell of the battle at Qarqar, where Ahab, king of Israel, clashed with Shalmaneser III, king of Assyria, in 853 BC. They also mention that Jehu, the third Israelite king after Ahab, paid tribute to Shalmaneser III in 841 BC. The Bible mentions all of the kings of Israel and the lengths of their reigns, as well as the kings of Judah who were ruling during their reigns.

The Assyrian texts provide a fixed date, and the Bible tells how long each king ruled. By combining the two, Bible events in the time of the kings can be estimated closely.

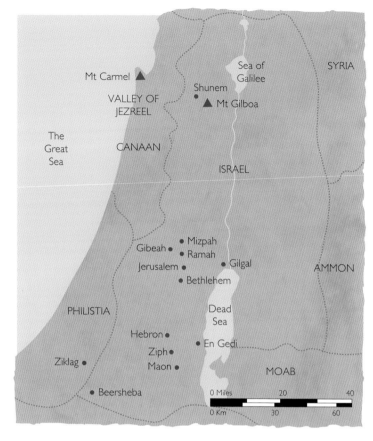

and fertile olive groves, Hebron had an abundant food supply. There was also plenty of water from the many springs which bubbled up around the city.

But the most important reason David chose Hebron was for its central location in the tribe of Judah. His hometown of Bethlehem was too far north.

Hebron today.

David chooses his capital

Why did David choose to make Hebron his capital when crowned king of Judah? As one of the first cities built in the land of Palestine, Hebron was already old and well established when David arrived there as king.

Lying on gentle slopes and surrounded by rich vineyards

Hebron was also the largest city in Judah when David became king and the most secure against enemy attack. Located at the intersection of many vital trade routes, the city was bustling with business activity.

This cuneiform tablet is a letter from the last Assyrian king, Sin-sharra-ishkun, to the Babylonian king Nabopolassar. By combining the biblical accounts and information from ancient texts like this, the dates of Bible events can often be estimated closely.

David Captures Jerusalem

After Saul died in combat, the people of Judah made David their king. But the other Israelites, prompted by Saul's army commander, Abner, made Saul's son Ish-Bosheth their king. Before long, fighting broke out between the two factions, and as time passed, David's forces grew stronger while the forces of Ish-Bosheth became weaker. One day Ish-Bosheth insulted his army commander, Abner, and this caused Abner to change his loyalties to David. But Abner was quickly murdered by David's army commander, Joab. Soon after that, Ish-Bosheth was murdered. The people of Israel then turned to David and made him king over all Israel. As king of all the people, David wanted to move his capital to a more central place than Hebron, so he led an expedition against Jerusalem, held at that time by the Jebusites.

Jerusalem in David's day

During the period of the Judges, and until David's time, the city of Jerusalem was called Jebus and occupied by the Jebusites, who were a mixed Canaanite people. The city had stood for hundreds of years and was well fortified when David marched toward it.

It was a very imposing sight, commanding the summit on the hill of Ophel with its fortified walls of stone and sturdy battlements that looked down over miles of surrounding countryside. David quickly realized that his small army was no match for the strong defences of the city. He probably looked back to his days as a desert raider in Philistine country, remembering that surprise was often the most effective weapon. With that in mind, he attacked Jerusalem through the underground water tunnel built to bring water into the city in times of a siege.

When David was anointed king over all Israel, he chose Jerusalem as his new capital. It was centrally located among all of Israel's tribes and almost impervious to enemy attack. No tribe of Israel owned the city, because David had captured it from the Jebusites. And no tribe could really lay claim to it, because it was on the border between the tribes of Judah and Benjamin.

In David's day, Jerusalem was much smaller than it is today. The king began extensive building projects, beginning with his palace and a strong fortress. He hired skilled craftsmen from Phoenicia to help with the work.

The tunnel through which water was brought from the Gihon spring to Jerusalem. An illustration of Gihon Spring by David Roberts (1796–1864).

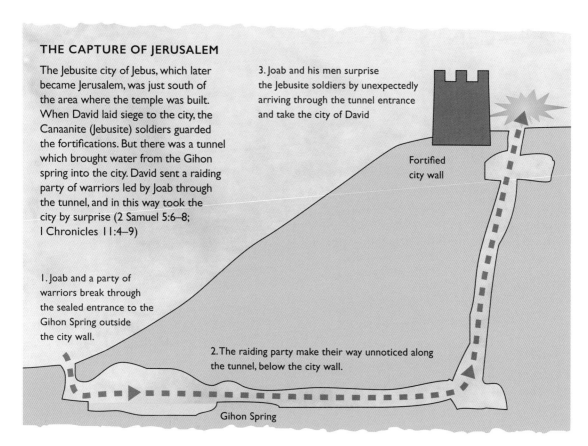

THE CAPTURE OF JERUSALEM

The Jebusite city of Jebus, which later became Jerusalem, was just south of the area where the temple was built. When David laid siege to the city, the Canaanite (Jebusite) soldiers guarded the fortifications. But there was a tunnel which brought water from the Gihon spring into the city. David sent a raiding party of warriors led by Joab through the tunnel, and in this way took the city by surprise (2 Samuel 5:6–8; 1 Chronicles 11:4–9)

3. Joab and his men surprise the Jebusite soldiers by unexpectedly arriving through the tunnel entrance and take the city of David

Fortified city wall

1. Joab and a party of warriors break through the sealed entrance to the Gihon Spring outside the city wall.

2. The raiding party make their way unnoticed along the tunnel, below the city wall.

Gihon Spring

Carpenters at work for David

When David started the work on his palace, there were probably few if any Israelite carpenters. So David made friends with Hiram, the king of Tyre, a nation to the northwest on the coast of the Mediterranean Sea.

Hiram sent David skilled carpenters to construct the palace and perform the detailed woodworking. Their tools, some of the best in the world, were quite primitive in light of today's power equipment. Everything was done by hand. Wooden mallets were used as hammers, flax and reeds passed for rulers, and crushed sandstone was the ancient world's sandpaper.

When David captured Jebus and made it his capital, he began an extensive building programme. This mallet, made from wood, quartzite, and leather, is like one that might have been used for building. It dates from c. 1981–1975 BC

The Ark Is Moved

2 SAMUEL 6; 1 CHRONICLES 13; 15:1–16:3

After King Saul died, David was made king over Judah, and Saul's son Ish-Bosheth was made king over the rest of Israel. But two years later Ish-Bosheth was murdered, and the people of Israel joined in making David king of all the nation. After that, David captured Jerusalem and made it his capital. Then he made plans to move the ark of the covenant to Jerusalem.

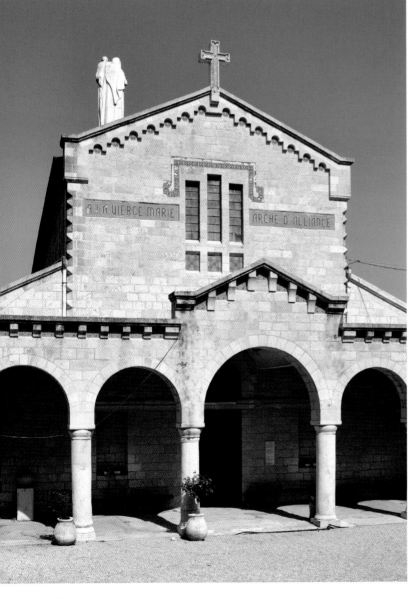

Kiriath Jearim

Kiriath Jearim was built over a large hill. Looking east from the city one can see the golden walls of Jerusalem about 13 km (8 miles) away, gleaming in the late afternoon sun.

The Philistines, plagued by disease after capturing the ark of the covenant, sent the ark back to Israel, to Beth Shemesh, a town on the northern border of Judah about 24 km (15 miles) west of Kiriath Jearim. When a group of men looked inside of the ark, God struck them dead, and the rest of the town begged the men of Kiriath Jearim to take the ark from them.

In Kiriath Jearim, the ark was kept in the house of a man named Abinadab. Today, a church called the Church of the Ark of the Covenant stands over the traditional site of Abinadab's house. Years later King David retrieved the ark from Kiriath Jearim and brought it to Jerusalem.

Celebrating in song and dance

The Israelites loved to come together and celebrate during times of feasts, festivals, and other important occasions.

The ark of the covenant was brought to Jerusalem from Kiriath Jearim. Today, the Church of the Ark of the Covenant stands over the traditional site of Abinadab's house.

DANCING

The Israelites danced at many of their festivals and as part of worship. Dancing occurred during the wine harvest and grain harvest festivals, and at weddings and feasts. The Israelites did not dance in couples, but in groups, and clapped and sang as they danced. There are many examples of dancing in both the Old and New Testament:

- The dance around the Golden Calf (Ex. 32:19).
- Dancing to God in thanks after the Hebrews crossed the Red Sea (Ex. 15:20).
- Dancing in the Temple (Psa. 149:2–3; 150:4).
- David's dance in front of the Ark of the Covenant (2 Sam. 6:12–14).

- There was dancing when the prodigal son returned (Luke 15:25).
- Children danced at play (Matt. 11:17).
- Salome danced a solo at a Greek-style feast (Mark 6:22).

A joyful and natural part of these grand occasions was singing and dancing.

Song and dance were used as an expression of worship, praise, and thanksgiving to God. Much of Israel's history was also passed down through the years in songs. The Book of Psalms is a collection of songs, with many telling of the nation's history.

As the ark was brought from Kiriath Jearim to Jerusalem, David danced ahead of it, making a joyful noise to the Lord. David was also a musician. As a young man he played the harp, or lyre, to soothe King Saul, and probably sang many songs to please the king. When David was king, he started and organized the tabernacle music programme, making sure that each day there were priests and Levites singing to God in praise and worship.

The Bible contains many beautiful songs. Moses and Miriam sang songs of praise to God after crossing the Red Sea to safety (Ex. 15:1–18, 21). After Deborah and Barak had routed the forces of Sisera of Hazor, they sang together a song of victory (Jud. 5). Hannah praised God in a beautiful song of thanksgiving when God gave her a son after years of prayer (1 Sam. 2:1–10). Mary, Jesus' mother, sang of the fulfilment of God's promises to Abraham (Luke 1:46–55).

The music of the tambourine

The timbrel, or tambourine, was a popular musical instrument in ancient times. It was not allowed in the temple, but was used in festivals and other celebrations. It was played mostly by women.

The tambourine was shaped like a circle, often hollow in the centre. Pieces of bronze were set in the rim and rattled when the instrument was shaken.

A replica of the ark of the covenant.

David and Bathsheba

2 SAMUEL 11–12

After David became king over all Israel, he strengthened his power by conquering the nations around him and making Jerusalem, a central city, his capital. But during one of these conquests, David foolishly had a loyal officer killed so that he could marry Bathsheba, the officer's wife.

The Assyrians of Old Testament times left many drawings of warfare. While we cannot assume that the Israelites did things exactly the same way, we may find in these drawings some glimpses of warfare at that time. A king besieges a city while inhabitants defend it from city towers.

How a city was captured

Invading armies and war were common events in ancient times, so before a city was built, careful attention was given to its location, which often meant the difference between defeat and victory.

Most large and important cities were built on natural barriers of defence, like hills or ridges. Huge walls of stone reaching as high as 7.5 m (25 feet) and as wide as 6 m (20 feet) also defended the city. Warriors commanded the tops of the walls, spraying a deadly shower of arrows onto the enemy below. Gates were overlaid with iron and bronze, and great wooden beams locked them shut.

With all this defence, how did an enemy army ever hope to conquer a city? David's army used their wits when besieging the city of Jerusalem by crawling through the city's underground water system and surprising the enemy.

Other armies far outnumbered the soldiers defending the city and used brute force. Thousands of warriors streamed up to the city walls with ladders and battering rams. The casualties were many, but the city was helpless against such great numbers.

At other times the invading army surrounded the fortified city and kept its people inside until they were weakened by starvation. Sometimes the city held out for a year, but finally they had no strength left to resist the attacking enemy.

Bathing

Water was hard to find in ancient times, even for a great king like David. There was no indoor plumbing, and any water had to be drawn from deep wells or saved from the rain in rock cisterns.

Baths were not taken often, for it was a long process that was considered a luxury. Soap was made mostly from the ashes of certain burnt plants. In between baths, people rubbed themselves with olive oil to cover up their bad odours and stay "clean".

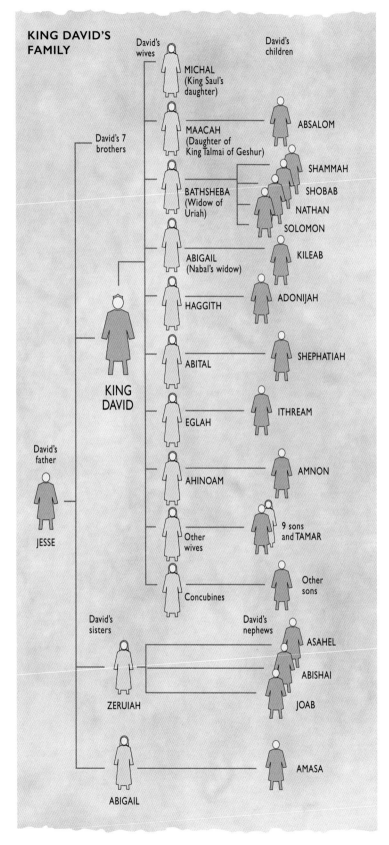

KING DAVID'S FAMILY

David's wives

David's children

MICHAL
(King Saul's daughter)

David's 7 brothers

MAACAH
(Daughter of King Talmai of Geshur)

ABSALOM

BATHSHEBA
(Widow of Uriah)

SHAMMAH

SHOBAB

NATHAN

SOLOMON

ABIGAIL
(Nabal's widow)

KILEAB

HAGGITH

ADONIJAH

KING DAVID

ABITAL

SHEPHATIAH

EGLAH

ITHREAM

AHINOAM

AMNON

David's father

Other wives

9 sons and TAMAR

JESSE

Concubines

Other sons

David's sisters

David's nephews

ZERUIAH

ASAHEL

ABISHAI

JOAB

ABIGAIL

AMASA

David's palace

David had built a palace for himself (1 Chron. 15:1). He saw Bathsheba while he was walking on his roof. Though it may seem strange to us, walking on one's roof was not unusual in Bible times, for most buildings were made with flat roofs, and many of the day's activities were carried out there.

Another wife for David

When King David made Jerusalem his capital, he already had seven wives. Bathsheba became his eighth. She was formerly the wife of Uriah the Hittite, one of David's mighty warriors who was killed in combat through David's sin.

David's other wives

Before David became king at Hebron, he had married Michal (1 Sam. 18:27), Abigail (1 Sam. 25:42), and Ahinoam (1 Sam. 25:43). At Hebron he married Maacah (who became the mother of Absalom) (2 Sam. 3:3), Haggith (1 Chron. 3:2), Abital (1 Chron. 3:3), and Eglah (1 Chron. 3:3). David married Bathsheba, who became the mother of Solomon, at Jerusalem (2 Sam. 11:27).

Absalom Rebels

2 SAMUEL 15–18

Peace had come to the land at last, for David was king. He had risen in power, conquering his enemies and establishing his capital in Jerusalem. But trouble was brewing in David's own family, as his son Absalom made plans to rebel and steal the kingdom from his father.

City bustle inside the Damascus Gate, Jerusalem.

Absalom at the city gate

Unknown to David, Absalom was plotting to seize his father's throne and become the new king of Israel. Absalom carried out his plan with patience, knowing that the best place to begin winning people over to his side was at the city gate, the busiest and most popular place in the city.

The city gate was always bustling with activity. Early each morning, merchants set up their wares just inside the gate. That is where the city elders gathered, to settle small disputes and witness business transactions.

Absalom spent much of his day around the city gate (2 Sam. 15:2). Here he boasted about his wisdom and ability to carry out the people's concerns. Gradually King David's support began to fade.

The mountain of tears

David left Jerusalem by way of the Mount of Olives when he learned of Absalom's plot to take over the kingdom. As he climbed over the summit of the mountain, he looked back over his shoulder across the Kidron Valley and cried as he gazed down on his city (2 Sam. 15:30).

One thousand years passed, and Jesus, probably standing near that same spot, wept for the sins of Jerusalem and predicted its coming destruction (Luke 13:34).

En Rogel – hideout for spies

Not everyone defected to Absalom's side during his revolt. Many brave and loyal men stayed with David and followed him into the wilderness. Two of David's loyal followers remained behind by a spring of water named En Rogel, to learn Absalom's plans and report them to David.

En Rogel is a deep spring lying just south of Jerusalem in the Kidron Valley. It was opened when men cut down into the solid rock and found an underground stream of water. Over the centuries, the valley has filled in considerably from the erosion of the surrounding hills. Today, builders have had to add their own water shaft to reach down to the stream, now many feet below the soil.

The Tomb of Absalom, or Yad Avshalom, though named for David's rebellious son, was probably built during the 1st century. The Bible records that the body of Absalom was thrown into a large pit in the woods and covered with stones.

Absalom's defeat

David fled from his son Absalom across the Jordan River to a town named Mahanaim, about 70 km (45 miles) northeast of Jerusalem. Absalom gathered the entire army of Israel and marched in pursuit of his father. The battle took place in the forest of Ephraim, just north of the Jabbok River and about 5 km (3 miles) northwest of Mahanaim. But some of David's loyal followers were the greatest warriors in all Israel, and Absalom's forces were soundly defeated.

Watchman

David waited nervously in Mahanaim while the battle against his son Absalom raged on. Standing on top of the city wall was a watchman, whose duty it was to warn the king of anyone approaching the city (2 Sam. 18:24).

En Rogel –
a deep spring in
the Kidron Valley
where David's
spies hid.

Araunah's Threshing Floor

2 SAMUEL 24

Toward the end of King David's reign, he decided to count his fighting men. We are not sure why, but this displeased the Lord. Even Joab, David's hardened army commander, knew that this was wrong and told David so. But David insisted, the count was taken, and the Lord punished David by sending a plague. When the plague ended, David bought Araunah's threshing floor and built an altar. Later Solomon's temple, and still later, Herod's temple, stood at this place.

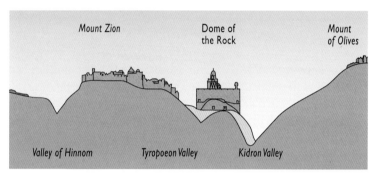

A cross section of the hills on which Jerusalem is built, showing Mount Zion, three famous valleys, and the Dome of the Rock where the temple, and Araunah's threshing floor, once stood. Threshing floors were usually built on high hills so the wind could blow away the chaff.

From Dan to Beersheba

"From Land's End to John o' Groats" is a phrase meant to signify all of the Great Britain. In Israel it was the same way. When talking about the entire country, the popular phrase "from Dan to Beersheba" was often used (Jud. 20:1; 2 Sam. 3:10; 24:2). Dan was a city located at the extreme northern border of Israel, and the city of Beersheba lay on the southern border. When messengers were instructed to deliver news "from Dan to Beersheba", it meant that the message was intended for all 12 tribes of Israel.

Araunah's threshing floor

Long before the judges led Israel and the kings ruled the land, God asked Abraham, the ancestor of the Israelites, to sacrifice his only son on Mount Moriah. The man was puzzled, but faithfully made the trip to the mountain, ready to sacrifice the only heir to the nation that God had promised through him.

But God was merely testing Abraham's faithfulness to Him, and at the last moment stopped Abraham from killing his son. In gratitude, Abraham made an offering to God. This was the first worship service on Mount Moriah, but over the centuries it would see more services than could be counted. For on this same site David bought

Araunah's threshing floor, and Solomon built God's holy temple.

Throughout the years to follow, hundreds of thousands came from all over the world to worship God here. In Old Testament times, priests offered daily sacrifices to God, and musicians sang His praises. Planned by David and built by his son Solomon, the temple was the focal point of Jerusalem. It remained the worship centre for the Jews of the world until after the time of Jesus. Today a Muslim mosque called the Dome of the Rock rests on the same spot.

The threshing sledge

On his threshing floor, the farmer separated the kernels of grain from the stalks of wheat, corn, or barley. To do this he often used a threshing sledge. It was made of wood planks, and looked like a sled or toboggan, only heavier. On the bottom were attached sharp stones or metal. After the stalks were thrown

Threshing floors in the 1940s near Nazareth.

onto the floor, the sledge was hitched to oxen and dragged over the crops while men or children sat on top of it for extra weight.

Threshing sledges from Bible times.

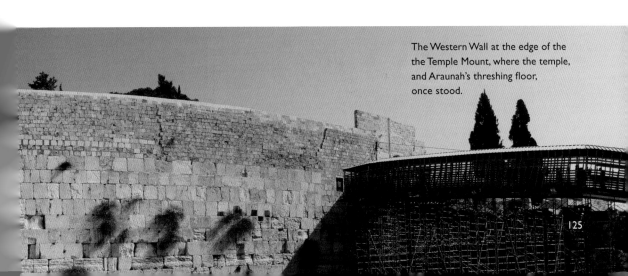

The Western Wall at the edge of the the Temple Mount, where the temple, and Araunah's threshing floor, once stood.

125

Solomon Builds
the Temple

I KINGS 5–8; 2 CHRONICLES 2–7

King David wanted to build a temple for the Lord. But the Lord told him not to do it, for he was a warrior. Instead, David's son Solomon would build the temple. Before David died, he made plans for the temple and helped gather many materials for it. After he died, Solomon built it. After Solomon removed his enemies, he made an alliance with Pharaoh, king of Egypt, and married his daughter. While Solomon made plans to build his palace and the temple, he moved his Egyptian princess to the city of David. Then Solomon went to Gibeon to offer sacrifices to the Lord. While there, he had a dream in which the Lord offered him whatever he wanted. Solomon chose wisdom above all other gifts. His wisdom was soon revealed, when two women came to him with a seemingly impossible problem.

Solomon's palace

After the temple was finished, Solomon built his own palace. It was a magnificent structure, made of stone and cedar and called the Palace of the Forest of Lebanon. Extensive details are given in 1 Kings 7. It took 13 years to construct and was about 150 feet (46 m) long, 75 feet (23 m) wide, and 45 feet (about 13.5 m) high. The roof was cedar, and the walls were stone. The high-quality stone was cut into blocks.

This palace was located just south of the temple and was connected to it by a gate of some sort. It is thought that the palace was destroyed by Shishak, Egyptian ruler, when he came against Jerusalem. Today the El Aksa mosque stands on the site where it is thought Solomon's palace once stood.

This model of the temple of King Solomon was built in 1883 as the centrepiece of an Anglo-Jewish Historical Exhibition in the Royal Albert Hall. The model is faithful to the description found in Scripture, while also applying some extra-biblical imagination, as in the domed-roof.

Solomon's temple

David wanted to build the temple himself. But the Lord refused to let him, for David was a bloody warrior. The task of building God's house went to David's son, King Solomon.

David drew up extensive plans, gathered materials, and arranged for the people who would conduct the temple services. But he could not begin its construction. In fact, he did not live to see any construction begin, for Solomon did that after his father's death. This is an example of how God uses the talents of one person for one job and the talents of another person for a different job.

The altar of burnt offering

The focal point of the temple services would be the altar of burnt offering, for on it sacrifices were made to the Lord. This altar was made of bronze, 9 m (30 feet) wide and 4.5 m (15 feet) high.

Sacrifices were placed on a bronze grating that stretched across the inside of the altar and burned before the Lord. Sacrifices were usually animals, such as sheep, goats, or bulls. But grain and wine were also put on the altar for certain offerings.

The temple area

Since the time of Solomon, the temple area has remained a place of worship. Three times the Israelites built, or rebuilt, a temple on this site and each time it was destroyed. In AD 691, the Muslims built a mosque over the temple ruins. During the days of the Crusaders, it was converted into a Christian church. Today, it is under Muslim control again and is called the Dome of the Rock.

The cedars of Lebanon

The precious wood from cedar trees was the finest in the Middle East. It had an elegant dark-red colour, a sweet fragrance, and a durability that made it an ideal building material.

Solomon bought these beautiful trees from King Hiram of Tyre, in the north. The logs were tied into rafts, and floated down the seacoast to a port city in Israel. From there, the cedar logs were dragged overland to Jerusalem, then cut into attractive wood panels.

Quarrying stones

Cedar wood, magnificent and expensive, was used for the inside of Solomon's temple, but the structure itself was built of stone. Solomon got his stone from large quarries just north of Jerusalem. Here, stonecutters and stonemasons toiled for years in the stone pits, cutting and shaping the white limestone for the temple.

The rock was usually cut along natural cracks or grooves and then smoothed and squared with chisels, mallets of wood, and plumb lines. The cut stones were then moved to the building site and lowered into place with pulleys, rollers, and sledges. Skilled craftsmen squared the stones so perfectly that mortar was seldom used.

Solomon's Glory

I KINGS 10; 2 CHRONICLES 8:17–9:28

David had been a great warrior and had brought peace to the land by military might. Solomon's way to keep peace was to marry the princesses of surrounding nations. With no wars to wage, Solomon concentrated on trade and wealth, making himself and his nation famous.

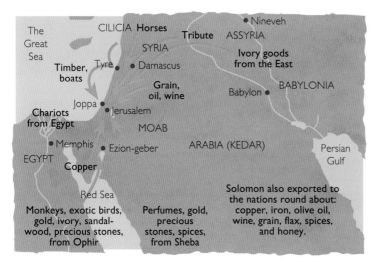

The extent of Solomon's trading interests.

Solomon's wealth

With David on the throne, Israel had established itself as one of the strongest military nations in the Middle East. When Solomon became king, his desire was to make Israel one of the richest nations.

Solomon built a beautiful temple to God, an elaborate palace for himself, and a mighty fortress called the Millo. He built his own fleet of ships and established trade with other countries, which brought in millions of dollars of gold, silver, rare ivory, fine linen, precious woods, spices, and even monkeys and peacocks.

Solomon became wealthier than any other king in the world. But how did he acquire such riches?

The king opened trade to new and unfamiliar lands. Fleets of ships were sent to faraway countries loaded with copper from Solomon's mines, and they returned to Israel's ports laden with millions of dollars in gold.

Due to Israel's central location, numerous trade routes passed through the country, connecting lands to the north and south. Solomon charged huge excise taxes for goods passing through his kingdom.

Solomon's enemies brought him even greater wealth. Nations defeated by his father David paid tribute into Solomon's treasuries to avoid further conflict.

But the high cost of supporting an empire that stretched from Egypt in the south to Mesopotamia in the north was staggering. Solomon levied heavy taxes on his people to help offset these costs.

Where was Sheba?

When the queen of Sheba arrived at Solomon's palace, her caravan had travelled more than 1,600 km (1,000 miles)! Her country, in southwest Arabia, southeast of Palestine, gained great wealth from trade of perfumes and incense, important items in the daily life and religious worship of the ancient world.

Solomon Turns from God

I KINGS 11; 2 CHRONICLES 9:29–30

The lampstand, sometimes called the candlestick or menorah, on which a light was kept burning before the Lord. This and other objects of worship in the temple were associated with holiness and forgiveness of sin.

To keep peace with neighbouring kings, Solomon married their daughters. Who would wage war against his son-in-law? But when these foreign women came to live in Jerusalem, they brought their foreign gods with them. In time, his wives persuaded Solomon to build shrines for their gods. Then he permitted his people to worship them, too. Eventually, Solomon turned far from God himself.

The beginning of Solomon's troubles – a multitude of wives

Polygamy, marrying more than one woman, was tolerated in the Law of Moses, but not advised.

Kings were given special warnings in God's law against marrying a great number of wives (Deut. 17:17). But, like other kings of his day, Solomon followed the custom of marrying numerous wives for pleasure, political alliances, and prestige. In fact, King Solomon had 700 wives and 300 concubines, who lived as wives without full privileges.

Most of Solomon's wives did not follow the Lord, but worshipped idols of stone, wood, or metal. Trying to make them feel comfortable away from home, the king

Heathen objects of worship, shrines or idols, like this Astarte statuette, pointed to gods of wood or stone, made by human hands, and not the Lord who created life.

did not stop this idolatry. Soon it spread across Israel, and before long, Solomon himself accepted these foreign gods.

The age of peace and prosperity, often called Israel's "golden age", was about to end. The nation and its ruler had turned far from God, and that meant trouble.

More polygamy in the Bible

Solomon was not the only man to run into trouble with more than one wife. Jacob had two wives, Rachel and Leah, who were constantly at odds with each other (Gen. 30:1–24). This intense rivalry was continued by their sons and resulted in Joseph being sold as a slave into Egypt (Gen. 37).

Elkanah, Samuel's father, had a wife named Peninnah who had many children. She taunted his other wife Hannah for having none. Elkanah loved Hannah more.

But her inability to bear children caused her much grief (1 Sam. 1:1–18).

The idol-gods of Solomon's wives

ASHTORETH This was the goddess of love and fertility, known as the giver of life. Ashtoreth was worshipped throughout Palestine and other countries. She is thought by some to be Athtar, or Ishtar, a universal goddess named after the planet Venus.

CHEMOSH Solomon built a shrine for Chemosh, the Moabites' national god. Some think Chemosh and Molech were the same god. King Josiah later destroyed Solomon's shrines to Chemosh, Ashtoreth, and Molech (2 Kings 23:13).

MOLECH Molech was the national god of the Ammonites. He was called "king", and children were sacrificed in his worship. According to Moses' law, any Israelite who worshipped Molech should be put to death (Lev. 18:21; 20:5).

The Kingdom Divides

I KINGS 12:1–24; 14:21–31; 15:6–8; 2 CHRONICLES 10–11

King Solomon had supported his luxurious living with high taxes. When he died, his son Rehoboam was advised to lighten the tax load. He refused, and the nation rebelled, dividing into a Southern Kingdom, Judah, under his rule, and a Northern Kingdom, Israel, under the rule of Jeroboam, one of Solomon's officers. The split weakened the people militarily and spiritually. Idolatry was widely accepted in the land, and under most of the kings, evil was common.

This copper plaque (c. 1479–1458 BC) depicts a cow goddess with a lotus flower hanging from its neck and a sun disc between its horns. The golden calves Jeroboam set up to worship may have looked similar to this.

After Pharaoh Shishak of Egypt invaded Judah during Rehoboam's reign, he carved an image of a captive Jew on a wall at Thebes with the inscription "The kingdom of Judah". Some think this is a picture of Rehoboam himself who, while not captured, was humiliated, especially since he was the son of Solomon.

When

In 931 BC the kingdom of Israel split, dividing the tribes of Judah and Benjamin to the south from the ten northern tribes. The two sides were never again united into one nation.

Shishak invades Palestine

Inscribed on the walls of the Amon temple in Karnak, Egypt, is a description of Pharaoh Shishak's invasion of Palestine. He marched his armies into Judah and Israel just five years after the kingdom was divided.

King Rehoboam of Judah could not repel Egypt's forces, and Shishak broke into Jerusalem, stripping the temple and palace of all the wealth that David and Solomon had acquired.

Shishak was not strong enough to defeat Israel and Judah, but his invasion crippled the already weakened and divided kingdoms.

The golden calves

The revolt of the ten northern tribes which suddenly separated them from Judah also separated them from Jerusalem, their centre of religious worship. Jeroboam quickly set up two golden calves in Bethel and Dan to prevent his people from worshipping in Jerusalem, where they might change their allegiance back to Judah. The calves were made to represent God, but being confused with the Canaanite bull god Baal, they were worshipped as idols.

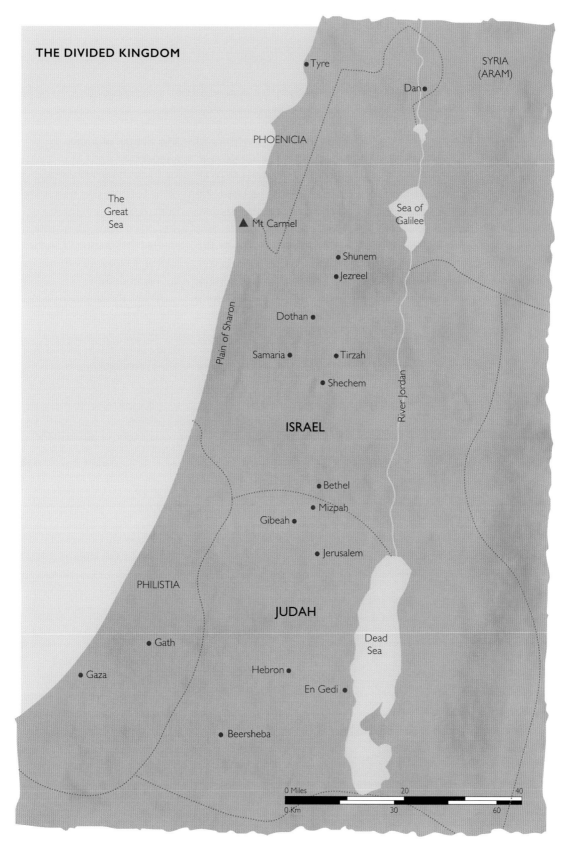

THE DIVIDED KINGDOM

SYRIA (ARAM)

- Tyre
- Dan

PHOENICIA

The Great Sea

▲ Mt Carmel

Sea of Galilee

- Shunem
- Jezreel

Plain of Sharon

- Dothan

- Samaria
- Tirzah
- Shechem

River Jordan

ISRAEL

- Bethel
- Mizpah
- Gibeah
- Jerusalem

PHILISTIA

JUDAH

Dead Sea

- Gath
- Hebron
- Gaza
- En Gedi
- Beersheba

0 Miles | 20 | 40
0 Km | 30 | 60

Ravens Feed Elijah

I KINGS 17:1–7

To keep peace in the land, Solomon married the daughters of foreign kings. These women brought their foreign gods and, before long, corrupted the land, enticing many Israelites to worship their gods. Solomon himself turned from the Lord. He lived a life of luxury, supported by heavy taxes on the people. When Solomon died, the land was ripe for rebellion. It split into two kingdoms, the Southern Kingdom, Judah, ruled by the heirs of David and Solomon, and the Northern Kingdom, Israel, ruled by others. Both kingdoms had a succession of many kings, mostly evil. The kingdom divided in 931 BC. An evil king named Ahab began to rule the Northern Kingdom 57 years later. During his rule a godly prophet named Elijah spoke to the conscience of Israel. On one occasion, Elijah said there would be no rain until the Lord spoke through him. Elijah then went away to hide from Ahab and his evil wife Jezebel. While hiding during the famine, Elijah was fed for a while by ravens.

The names of Judah and Israel

Solomon's kingdom, consisting of the 12 tribes who descended from the 12 sons of Jacob, was called Israel. These tribes entered the Promised Land with Joshua, who gave them specific land boundaries.

When the kingdom divided after Solomon's death, the 10 northern tribes wanted their land to be ruled by Jeroboam. They kept the name Israel for their new nation. Samaria became their capital in the days of Ahab.

The tribe of Judah to the south gave its own name to their new kingdom. They and Benjamin were the only tribes to remain loyal to Rehoboam, who was a descendant of Judah. Jerusalem, once the capital of Israel, was now Judah's capital.

The tribe of Levi owned no land, but lived in designated cities, so they were not included in the revolt.

The reason for famine

The Israelites do not divide their year into the four common seasons. Instead, the weather cycle of Palestine is separated into the rainy season and the dry season.

Early October marks the beginning of Israel's rainy

Elijah Fed by the Raven, an oil painting by Giovanni Girolamo Savoldo.

One traditional site of the Brook Kerith, in the gorge known as Wadi el Qelt, near the Saint George Monastery south of Jericho. Some say it was located farther east, beyond the Jordan River.

Kerith Brook, a small stream of water near the Jordan River, possibly in the land of Gilead.

season. The summer months from June to September produce little or no rain. By the end of September the ground is too dry and hard to plough or plant. The first rains of October, called the "early rains", are welcomed with joy and celebration. If October and November bring no moisture, the planting is delayed, and the harvest will be slim.

Rain often falls during the winter months, watering the growing crops and returning the land to life. The heaviest rainfalls occur in December and January. Often the deluge is so strong that dry riverbeds swiftly change into wild torrents of moving water, washing away everything in their path. Without these winter rains, the country would remain withered and parched from the intense summer heat. Planting could not begin, and with no harvest famine would strike the land.

By the end of April, the rains have usually stopped. May is harvest time, a month of beautiful flowers and rich crops. But the arrival of June completes the cycle, and once again the land simmers under the summer heat.

The Brook Kerith
Elijah hid from Ahab's anger by the

During the early part of the famine which swept the land, ravens fed Elijah at the Brook Kerith. The raven is like a large crow. Noah sent a raven from the ark, but it did not return (Gen. 8:6–7) for it was strong enough to fly back and forth until the waters went down. Ravens fed Elijah at God's command. Ravens are mentioned by Job (38:41 – God feeds them) and Isaiah (34:11 – they dwell in places previously inhabited).

The Widow of Zarephath

I KINGS 17:8–16

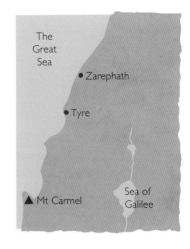

During the days of King Ahab, the prophet Elijah warned that there would be no rain until he said so. Without rain, the land soon dried up, and crops failed. Famine came, and water was scarce. Elijah hid for a while by a brook, where ravens fed him. Then the Lord sent him to Zarephath, where a miracle provided oil and flour for a widow and Elijah until the famine ended.

Zarephath – glassmaking and dyes

Many towns are well known for the unique products or services they produce. The small town of Zarephath became famous for its beautiful glass industry. The brightly coloured glass vessels looked like ice or shiny still water, an exciting change from the objects of wood, metal, and stone that most people were used to.

Elijah the prophet moved to Zarephath after the brook where he was hiding from Ahab dried up. The village lay huddled by the Mediterranean Sea, north of Israel, between the cities of Tyre and Sidon. Zarephath lay within the borders of Phoenicia, and, like other towns of this region, it probably produced deep purple dyes which were harvested from sea snails or murex seashells. Dyes were also extracted from certain plants in the area.

Widows – the first to suffer

When a country was struck with hard times, widows were often the first to suffer the effects. When the severe famine struck Palestine in Elijah's day, the poor widow who lived in Zarephath was certainly one of the first to feel the pinching fingers of starvation. She was gathering

Breadmaking at this time involved grinding grain into flour using a mortar and pestle.

firewood for her last meal when she met Elijah (1 Kings 17:12).

In ancient times, most women were left with nothing when their husbands died. The average man worked long hours every day just to put enough food on the dinner table. Israelite law called for the dead husband's sons or brothers to take the widow in and care for her. But life was difficult and short in Bible times, and often the husband's sons or brothers had also died. The widow at Zarephath had a son, but he was probably too young to care for her.

When Elijah visited the widow, she said, "I don't have any bread – only a handful of flour in a jar and a little oil in a jug". Jugs similar to those of Elijah's time.

In those days, few women had the strength or skill to make a living on their own. Ploughing fields required the strength of a man, and only a few women were fortunate enough to learn the art of dyes and dyemaking, or the skill of sewing fine clothing. But in hard times, even these jobs paid little. Left alone in life, greedy men took advantage of widows, offering help, but providing none.

Baking bread in an oven

The widow might have baked her bread on an oven called a "tannur". It was shaped like a pottery jar. Sticks were placed inside the jar and lit. The dough was plastered on the outside and baked.

A modern-day Bedouin woman baking bread over an open fire.

135

Elijah and the Prophets of Baal

1 KINGS 18

During the days of King Ahab of Israel, the Prophet Elijah warned that there would be no rain until the Lord said so, through him. For a while, Elijah was fed by ravens, but then the Lord sent him to Zarephath, where He provided for both Elijah and a widow who lived there. Elijah challenged the priests of Baal to a contest on Mount Carmel one day, to determine whether their god or his God could send fire to an altar. The priests of Baal cried out and cut themselves, but nothing happened. Elijah prayed to the Lord, and He sent fire in a miraculous way.

The rich life of a heathen priest

The Israelites were not the only nation to have priests as leaders of religious worship. Nearly every country around Israel had their own priests who made sacrifices and performed religious ceremonies to their gods.

Egyptian priests had immense wealth and power. These heathen priests demanded large sums of money for maintaining and protecting temples built by pharaohs and other wealthy people. For this service, they also inherited large amounts of people's property, money, and livestock when the people died.

The Canaanite priests of Baal did not have this kind of wealth, but those Elijah challenged were supported by Queen Jezebel and influenced the affairs of the nation through her. These priests often performed strange dances while slashing themselves with knives or stones. Sometimes they sacrificed children.

A stone carving of Baal.

Rainclouds gather over Mount Carmel.

Elijah and Elisha – God's prophets

We are familiar with most of the prophets in the Bible because of the books they wrote. But two of God's greatest prophets, Elijah and Elisha, did not write a book of the Bible. However, many chapters in other books of the Bible are devoted to their lives and ministries (see 1 Kings 17–19; 21; 2 Kings 1–9).

The importance of rain

Life in Egypt depends on the ceaseless flow of the Nile River, for almost no rain falls in the land. But the region of Palestine would wither into a desert without the arrival of the winter rains. The people rejoice when the first rains begin to fall, for farmers can begin their planting, and wells and cisterns fill again after becoming dangerously low over the hot and dry summer months.

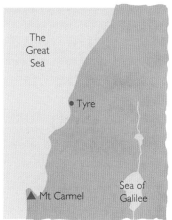

A fresco of the miracle on the walls of the Dura-Europos synagogue.

Elijah and the Still, Small Voice

I KINGS 19:1–18

When Elijah challenged the priests of Baal to a contest on Mount Carmel, the Lord sent fire on the altar there, proving that He, not Baal, is truly God. After that, rain fell, and the drought was broken. But Ahab's queen, Jezebel, was furious. Elijah had not only humiliated her prophets but had executed them. She vowed to murder him. Afraid, Elijah ran away to Mount Horeb to hide. There, the Lord spoke to him, not in wind, earthquake, or fire, but in a still, small voice.

Elijah's long journey
Israel's wicked Queen Jezebel, Ahab's wife, became furious when she learned that Elijah had killed all of her heathen priests of Baal. She vowed to kill Elijah, who escaped to Mount Horeb, also called Mount Sinai. But his journey was not an easy walk, for Mount Horeb stood over 320 km (200 miles) south of Mount Carmel, where Elijah destroyed the priests of Baal. To get to Mount Horeb, the prophet had to cross a wild, barren wilderness.

Rain and harvest
Some things never change with time. Today, as in ancient times, people frequently talk about the weather. In Elijah's day, famine became the main topic of conversation as each new morning dawned clear and dry.

People's lives depended on the rain. Storms that rolled across the land from the sea watered the crops growing in the fields, assuring a bountiful harvest.

In summer, rain rarely fell. Gentle showers marked the beginning of the winter months. If these "winter rains" did not come as expected, the ground turned hard as stone. Ploughing and planting were impossible, and in a few months famine arrived. Without a harvest, food became very scarce, and many people died of starvation.

Baal
Wicked Queen Jezebel worshipped a god named Baal, the most popular and supposedly the most powerful Canaanite god. Baal was the god of rain and abundant harvests. Idols of Baal sometimes looked like bulls, animals which symbolized strength and fertility.

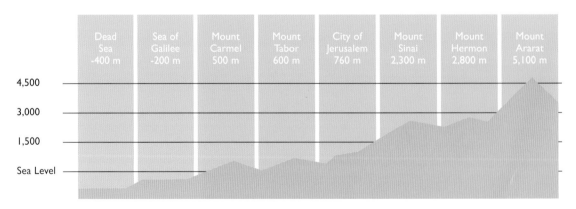

| Dead Sea -400 m | Sea of Galilee -200 m | Mount Carmel 500 m | Mount Tabor 600 m | City of Jerusalem 760 m | Mount Sinai 2,300 m | Mount Hermon 2,800 m | Mount Ararat 5,100 m |

4,500

3,000

1,500

Sea Level

Many Bible events happened in mountains and valleys. The diagram shows how high and how deep some of them were – from the deepest point on earth, the Dead Sea, to the highest point mentioned in Bible events, Mount Ararat (where Noah's ark came to rest after the flood).

Elijah's Mantle to Elisha

I KINGS 19:19–21

During the ninth century BC, a series of evil kings, and a few good ones, ruled in the divided kingdom, while the prophets Elijah and Elisha ministered, especially in Israel. Elijah was first, but when it was time for him to choose a successor, he placed his mantle on Elisha.

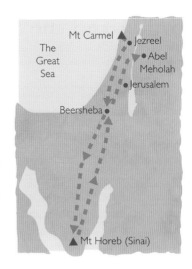

The map shows Elijah's travels in this and surrounding Bible events. It begins at Mount Carmel, where he defeated the prophets of Baal. From there he ran away to Mount Horeb (Sinai), stopping at Beersheba. Then he returned again to Beersheba (the way he came, 1 Kings 19:15). From there, he went north, to Abel Meholah, where he called Elisha to leave farming and become God's prophet.

When Elijah called Elisha to become a prophet, Elisha was ploughing with 12 yoke of oxen. Two oxen were yoked together so they would pull equally.

The important uses of a cloak

Almost everyone owned a cloak, but most people had just one. Cloaks were similar to the outer coats of today, but much more versatile and taken almost everywhere.

Most cloaks were made from animal hides, goat or camel hair, or from wool. Because it took so much time to make them, cloaks were valuable and were not thrown away until completely worn out. It was a common sight to see a cloak that had been patched many times.

A cloak was worn as protection against the burning sun and for warmth in the cold night. But these were just two of its uses.

On a warm night, a cloak made a soft pillow. At a meal, it was laid on the ground and represented a special seat for an honoured guest.

A bundle of goods was carried home from the village in a cloak. A farmer tied his cloak into a bag, emptied his seeds into it, and planted his fields by hand.

A cloak was also used symbolically. By spreading his cloak over a woman, a man was announcing that he would care for her. Throwing a cloak over another's shoulders represented a transfer of power or position. Sometimes it meant a call to discipleship.

A cloak was sometimes given to a lender as a pledge for a debt. And when torn into pieces, a cloak symbolized great sorrow or grief.

Elijah and Elisha

Elijah and Elisha were two of the greatest prophets Israel had ever known. But the two men's personalities were quite different. Elijah liked to live outdoors in the wilderness. Elisha lived in homes and liked the city. Elijah was rugged and forceful in speech, while Elisha was more diplomatic. Elijah wore a cloak of camel's hair, but Elisha usually dressed like other people.

Ploughing and ploughs

Ancient ploughs were crude. The earliest were simply a light tree trunk with two strong branches forking at the end. Later, the ploughshare was developed. This was a piece of wood carved into the shape of a large chisel and attached to the plough. It was the part which moved through the ground and broke up the soil. In the time of the Kings, ploughshares were made of iron.

Naboth's Vineyard

1 KINGS 21

King Ahab of Israel was a wicked king, but his wife was even more wicked. Jezebel did not want her people to worship the Lord, so she tried to force Baal on them. When Ahab wanted a nearby vineyard, his wife Jezebel was not afraid to murder its owner. Naboth was the victim.

Ahab – a wicked king

After the nation Israel divided into the Northern and Southern Kingdoms, God was often forgotten. Until its captivity, the Northern Kingdom of Israel was ruled by a succession of evil kings. Ahab was probably one of the worst.

During the 22 years of Ahab's reign, sin and idolatry went unchecked in Israel. Ahab's greatest mistake was his marriage to Jezebel, a wicked woman who worshipped Baal and tried to force this god on the rest of the Israelites. King Ahab soon found himself following her sinful practices.

Ahab was a strong military leader and a great builder, but he rarely listened to God. He finally died in battle against the Syrians.

Vineyards – peacetime plants

When Elijah lived in the land of Israel, life was closely woven to the land and its products. Most people worked outdoors, and their work depended on favourable weather. Famine affected everyone, from farmers to shepherds.

Vineyards were one important industry in Israel. When the rain was plentiful, clusters of grapes grew plump and delicious on the vines which covered the valleys and mountain slopes.

Ahab's palace and Naboth's vineyard were located at Jezreel. Naboth's ancestors had owned the vineyard there, and he was entitled to keep it. But Naboth was executed so that King Ahab could claim his vineyard. For this sin, Ahab's 70 sons were later beheaded and their heads heaped beside the gate at Jezreel (2 Kings 10:1–11). Jezebel was thrown from her palace window when Jehu came. While Ahab was alive, many of the meetings between him and Elijah took place here.

Vineyards yield their best crops during times of peace, because the vines require constant care and pruning if they are to be fruitful. When men went to war, the vines grew shabby and were picked over by birds and thieves.

When the grapes began to ripen in July, there was never a minute when the vineyard watchtower was not occupied. Day and night, a man stood in the tower that was built on the edge of every vineyard, and searched for any sign of approaching thieves.

September was the month of the grape harvest. If the crop was good, the month was filled with joy and feasts of celebration. As the grapes ripened, women picked them from the vines, and men trampled them with their bare feet to squeeze out the juice, which was fermented into wine. Grapes were also eaten from the vine as food and dried under the sun to make raisins.

The king's seal

Seals took the place of signatures. A seal might be a piece of metal shaped like a ring, or a cylinder-shaped lump of hard clay. A special marking was engraved on each seal. When pressed into wet clay or warm wax, the seal left a "signature". The king's seal was a royal order demanding swift action (1 Kings 21:8–14).

Elijah Is Taken in a Whirlwind

2 KINGS 2

Elijah served for quite some time as the Lord's prophet. At the right time, he chose Elisha to be his successor, and Elisha served as Elijah's helper after that. At last God's appointed time came for Elijah to leave the earth and leave his work in the hands of Elisha. While Elisha watched, Elijah went to heaven in a whirlwind.

Kings and God's prophets

The kingdom of Israel divided because King Solomon had turned away from the Lord and led the nation deep into idol-worship. The kingdom remained divided because most of the succeeding kings from both north and south continued these evil ways, disobeying God.

As a result, God chose special men and women to be prophets. Some were called into a lifetime of service to God, like Elijah and Elisha, while God asked others to perform one simple, yet important job. But every prophet of God was filled with a desire to tell kings and ordinary people God's messages of warning.

Kings often turned to prophets in times of trouble or danger, after all of their idols seemed to fail them. Sometimes kings grew very angry when God's prophets predicted terrible events, for people in Israel believed that when someone prophesied a bad event in public, there was a greater chance of it happening.

But God's prophets were not out to make friends or earn positions of importance in the kingdom. Good or bad, they told God's messages to the people, sometimes at the risk of losing their lives.

The kings of Elijah's time

Jehoshaphat (873–848 BC) was the king of the Southern Kingdom of Judah when God called Elijah to be a prophet. Jehoshaphat was a good king for the most part, obeying the laws of the Lord.

But the Northern Kingdom of Israel was a wicked nation at this time, so Elijah's ministry was concentrated there almost completely. The Bible first mentions Elijah prophesying to King Ahab (874–853 BC), predicting that no rain would fall until Elijah said so (1 Kings 17:1). This was a result of Ahab's continued idol worship.

Elijah also dealt with Ahab's son Ahaziah (853–852). Sometimes God's prophet had to escape from the anger of these wicked kings and especially from Ahab's evil wife Jezebel.

After Jehoshaphat died, his son Jehoram took the throne (848–841). He was a very evil king and not like his father. Elijah sent him a letter, predicting that calamity would strike because of his failure to obey God.

The kings of Elisha's time

Many kings came and went during Elisha's ministry. Both Judah and Israel had many wicked kings at this time, but

A late Bronze-age statue (c. 1550–120 BC) of Baal found at Megiddo.

142

Elisha spent almost all of his time as a prophet to Israel.

In the Northern Kingdom of Israel, Elisha worked under the reigns of Ahaziah (853–852 BC), Joram, or Jehoram (852–841), Jehu (841–814), Jehoahaz (814–798), and Joash, or Jehoash (798–782). Only Jehu and Jehoash showed a desire to serve the Lord, but later even they turned from God to worship idols.

In the Southern Kingdom of Judah, Elisha lived during the reigns of Jehoram (848–841), Ahaziah (841), Queen Athaliah (841–835), Joash (835–796), and Amaziah (796–791). At times, Joash and Amaziah brought the nation back to God, but later they worshipped idols.

Chariots were an important means of transportation for dignitaries in Elisha's and Elijah's time. They also symbolized power and might. *Elijah Taken Up in a Chariot of Fire* by Giuseppe Angeli.

In this medieval illustration depicting Elijah being taken to heaven, we see that Elisha is receiving the prophet's mantle.

Elisha Raises the Shunammite Boy

2 KINGS 4:8–37

For almost a hundred years Elijah, and then Elisha, ministered for the Lord in Israel. The exact dates of their ministries are not known, but correspond with the reigns of King Ahab through King Joash, approximately 874–782 BC. Elisha moved about through the land, ministering from place to place. While in Shunem, he and his servant stayed in a guest room prepared for him by a kind couple. One day this woman's son became violently sick and died. Elisha was called and raised the boy to life.

Elisha Raising the Shunammite's Son by Benjamin West.

Many farmers lived in the Jezreel Valley. The fertile soil grew rich crops and gave abundant harvests. The town of Shunem stood at the edge of this fruitful valley, about 32 km (20 miles) north of Samaria, Israel's capital city.

A married couple from Shunem treated Elisha the prophet with great kindness each time he passed through their village.

A room on the roof – a sign of prosperity

The man and woman who took care of Elisha might have been a prominent couple in their town of Shunem.

The couple made friends with Elisha, who frequently passed through their village. One day they decided to build Elisha a room on the rooftop of their house. This would be a cool and delightful place, secluded from the busy street activity.

Privacy was rare in Israelite houses, which were not built for comfort, but for shelter and protection during the night. Most houses had one main room where the entire family slept on reed mats. It took much time and money to build a house, and only a wealthy man could afford to add another addition to his home.

The perfect gift

The Shunammite couple showed Elisha great kindness each time he passed through their village. They invited him in for a meal and asked him to stay in their home. Because they built a room for him on the roof of their house, Elisha wanted to repay them for their kindness. But they refused.

But Elisha knew what the man and woman wanted, for they had no children. In Israel, children were considered the greatest joy and blessing a husband and wife could have. A woman who bore no children was deeply ashamed, and her husband was embarrassed. In fact, Israelite law gave husbands the legal right to divorce wives who could bear no children. The Shunammite woman knew this law well and might have been afraid. So Elisha gave her the perfect gift in payment for her kindness. He promised her a son, and within a year the baby was born.

When the son he had promised them died, Elisha raised the boy from the dead (2 Kings 4:18–37).

Ancient household furniture

The average house was simple and had only one or two rooms. Curtains woven by hand separated the main room into a side for men and one for women. The family often sat on reed mats to eat and slept on them at night. If a table was used for eating, it was plain, wooden, and very low, for the family always ate while sitting on the floor. On the table was a lamp, a small clay bowl filled with olive oil. Along the wall stood a few clay jars for cooking and storage, and a primitive hand mill for grinding grain into flour.

A woman's daily life in Palestine

An Israelite woman spent almost all of her time working around the home. She had no time or money to spend on beauty care. Baths were rarely taken, and olive oil was rubbed liberally into the skin as a perfume and deodorant. The fragrant oil was also used as a skin moisturizer. Only a few women were wealthy enough to own makeup. Hair was seldom cut, for long hair was a symbol of womanhood in Israel. Ointment was combed through the hair to repel the swarms of insects.

A woman spent most of her day preparing food and spinning cloth for clothing. It took hours

A ceramic jug – with a built-in strainer! This vessel was crafted in Israel during the late 8th–7th century BC.

to grind grain into flour by hand or on a primitive hand mill of stone. After the flour was made, it was baked into bread. Everything had to be done by hand.

Each morning and evening, it was the woman's job to walk to the well and draw water for the family's needs. On the way home, she gracefully balanced the large water jar on her head. At night, she awoke several times to refill the lamp that kept burning till morning.

The courtyard of a Bible-time home, with stairs leading to the roof, where a room was sometimes added.

Naaman Is Healed

2 KINGS 5:1–19

The Prophet Elisha, who ministered during the reigns of Jehoram, Jehu, Jehoahaz, and Joash, worked numerous miracles. By these, people knew that he was truly God's prophet. One of his great miracles involved a Syrian general named Naaman, a man with leprosy who came to Israel for healing.

Patients in a remote leper colony in rural India gather together as a community.

The life of a person with leprosy

A person with leprosy was often driven from town and forced to live in caves or "leper" villages. This seems cruel, but it was the only way a community thought it could protect itself against the disease. Until healed, a person with leprosy lived as an outcast from society, not hated, but greatly feared.

Although the Syrian general Naaman had leprosy (2 Kings 5:1), he was not treated as an outcast. This suggests that he had the milder form of leprosy. With this type, the skin forms pale patches which often do not spread over the whole body. Within one to three years, the victim is usually healed completely. This type was apparently not contagious.

In the mildly infectious type of leprosy, the skin forms paler patches, but they spread quickly over the entire body. A person with this type of leprosy cannot feel burns or cuts in these areas. Large boils appear, and the hands and feet become deformed. During this stage the disease is the most contagious.

It takes from 10 to 20 years for leprosy to heal. The body may become so weak from sickness that when other diseases strike, there is not enough strength to fight back.

In the Law of Moses, a person with leprosy had to be declared "clean" by a priest before returning to the community. Special offerings went along with this ritual of purification. It must have been a wonderful feeling to return to normal after so many years!

After Solomon's great kingdom declined and split into the Northern and Southern Kingdoms, Israel and Aram (the Syrians) warred for about 150 years. But at one time, when Ahab was king, Israel and Aram joined in an alliance to protect themselves from Assyria. The people of Aram were known as Aramaeans, or Syrians. Naaman, a Syrian army general, had captured the little slave girl from a raid on Israel. No wonder the king of Israel was upset when Naaman returned to Israel for healing. The map traces the path Naaman followed from Damascus to Dothan, where he found Elisha. From there he went to the Jordan River to bathe, then back to Dothan before returning to Damascus.

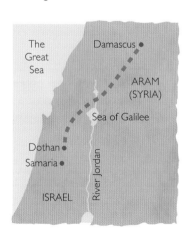

What did a servant girl do?

When a battle had ended, it was common for winners to take anything they wanted from the cities and villages of the losers. This included people, who were taken from their homes to be slaves in a new land.

Naaman captured a girl from an Israelite village. As a slave, she performed household chores, cooked the meals, and even helped Naaman's wife dress and bathe.

Letters

The king of Syria sent a "letter" to the king of Israel, seeking a cure for Naaman's leprosy. What did these ancient letters look like?

The king's letter may have been written on any of several different materials. A scribe, who was a professional writer, might have inscribed the king's message into a tablet of wet clay. Instead of a pen, he would use a "stylus", a short stick with a sharp triangular point.

The muddy Jordan River.

In neighbouring lands, the words were written in cuneiform, a system of writing developed by the Canaanites. Writing was also scratched on clay pottery fragments, used mainly by the poor.

Papyrus was used in letter writing, too. The material looked like paper and was made from reeds which were beaten flat and then rubbed smooth with a shell or with a piece of ivory.

Ink was used on papyrus. It was made from black soot, resin, and olive oil. Reeds with frayed tips were used as pens.

Elisha's Greedy Servant

2 KINGS 5:20–27

Naaman, general of the Syrian army, had captured a little girl on one of his raids in Israel. When Naaman's wife told her he was a leper, the little girl suggested that he go to Elisha for healing. Naaman went and was healed, but Elisha refused the rich gifts he offered. However, Elisha's servant became greedy and tried to get these rich gifts for himself. For this, he was punished with Naaman's leprosy.

Ancient pottery tells a story

Over the years, styles change. Clothing becomes shorter or longer, brighter or duller. And everyone can recognize a very "old" car when it passes by.

Ancient pottery was a timepiece of history. Over the centuries, styles changed and new pottery-making techniques were invented. Archaeologists have learned to identify when these styles were popular and which countries developed them. Of course, they are sometimes deceived. A colourful vase found in Babylon might have been made by the Babylonians, or it might have been carried to the land as part of the spoils from a distant battle.

Before the days of David and Solomon, Israelite pottery was often painted with bright colours. Animals and geometric shapes were the common design. But during the time of Solomon, a new technique called "burnishing" was developed, which gave the pottery a more subtle, softer appearance. Before the clay was dry, it was rubbed with a stone or piece of bone, and baked in an oven called a "kiln". When the vessel cooled, it looked glossy, which enhanced the original colour of the clay.

Pottery also had a distinct style during the period of the kings after Solomon. Vases and jars had long necks, and the sides were often angled instead of curved. Handles were attached in a variety of places. Before this time, handles were moulded on opposite sides of the vessel and called "ears".

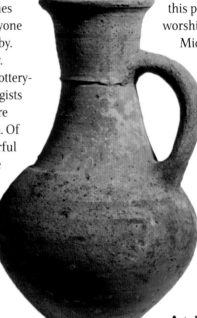

A long-neck ceramic jug from Israel, c. 7 BC.

Rimmon – god of Syria

The country of Syria, just north of Israel, worshipped a god named Rimmon. In other parts of Syria and Canaan, probably this same god was called Baal or Hadad and is known as the god of storms and rain. Rimmon was simply a local name for this popular god that was worshipped throughout the Middle East.

There was a temple to Rimmon in Damascus, the capital of Syria. Naaman, the Syrian army commander, worshipped there with his king (2 Kings 5:17–19). The god is usually pictured as a thunderbolt or a bull.

A talent of silver

When kings ruled the land of Israel, money was weighed instead of counted. The basic unit of money was called the shekel, which weighed between 8 and 16 grams, (0.3 to 0.6 of an ounce). A talent was worth 3,000 shekels. In Bible times, one talent was usually the price of a good ox.

Over the years, the shekel's weight varied, so its exact value remains uncertain.

"Is this the time to take money, or to accept clothes, olive groves, vineyards, flocks, herds, or menservants or maidservants?" Elisha asked his servant. Gehazi had seen Naaman's riches offered to Elisha and had coveted them. *Elisha Declining Naaman's Presents* by Abraham van Dijck.

Damascus

Damascus was the capital of Syria, located about 160 km (100 miles) northeast of Samaria. The two capital cities were always fighting in order to keep important trade routes open.

A large sculpture of the weather god Rimmon, that is, Baal Haddad.

149

Elisha and the Syrians

2 KINGS 6:8–23

During the time of Elisha's ministry in Israel, the Syrians went to war against the Israelites. Elisha often warned the king of Israel about the whereabouts of the Syrian army. This angered the king of Syria, who determined to capture Elisha. When Elisha's servant woke one morning to find their city, Dothan, surrounded by Syrian forces, he was frightened. But Elisha prayed, and the Lord revealed an angel army, waiting to come to aid them, if necessary. The servant knew then that the Lord's army was greater than the Syrian army. Elisha then prayed for the Syrian soldiers to be struck blind and led them to Israel's king. After the Israelites fed the enemy soldiers, they sent them home in peace.

Angels as warriors

Artists often depict the angels of heaven as gentle and docile creatures, wearing long white robes and playing sweet music on their golden harps. But many times the Lord calls His angels to be fearless warriors.

In the Book of Revelation, John sees a mighty angel with feet that look like pillars of fire and a voice that sounds like thunder (Rev. 10:1–3).

When Jesus was arrested, He told Peter that He could call 12 legions of angels at an instant if He wanted (Matt. 26:53). A single Roman legion was made up of 3,000–6,000 trained and valiant soldiers.

God revealed to Elisha and his servant the vast multitudes of His army, with its fearless angel

The ruinous remains at Tel Dothan, where Elisha and his servant saw the angel army.

Who were the Syrians?

The Syrians lived just to the north of Israel, and should not be confused with the Assyrians, another powerful nation.

Most of the Syrian provinces paid tribute to King David, but after his death, they regained their independence under Rezon. For years Syria and Israel remained enemies. Only a few times did they unite in battle.

When Ahab was king of Israel, he fought against the Syrians three times. Ben-Hadad, the Syrian king, started the conflicts by laying siege to Ahab's capital of Samaria. After two victories, Ahab died in battle.

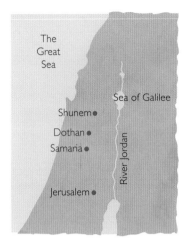

The map shows: The Great Sea, Sea of Galilee, Shunem, Dothan, Samaria, Jerusalem, River Jordan

When Elisha prayed, the Lord revealed an angel army to his servant. Elisha was then in Dothan. He prayed for the Lord to send blindness to the Syrians, and then led them to Samaria. See the map for these cities, as well as Shunem, where Elisha had a room in the home of a wealthy couple.

warriors and their chariots of fire (2 Kings 6:17).

Jacob wrestled with an angel (Gen. 32:24–30), and cherubim guarded the entrance to the Garden of Eden with a flaming sword (Gen. 3:24). These cherubim were probably not angels, but other heavenly creatures.

The archangel Michael and Gabriel from a seventeenth-century Ethiopian illuminated manuscript.

Seeing the unseen

This story suggests that all around us, supernatural events are happening which are invisible to the human eye. At times, God "opens" the eyes of certain people and lets them witness these remarkable incidents.

God showed Elisha and his servant the army of heaven to calm their fears over earthly enemies. Years later, shepherds near Bethlehem witnessed a great choir of angels praising God at Jesus' birth (Luke 2:8–15).

Syria/Israel struggles

There was a good reason why Syria and Israel were always locked in a power struggle. Damascus, Syria's capital, wanted to increase its trade, but Israel controlled all of the important caravan routes to the southern countries of Egypt and Arabia.

On the other hand, Israel's trade to the north was limited due to the strategic location of Syria's capital. Through Damascus ran all of the vital trade routes from the wealthy countries of Mesopotamia. When Ahab defeated Ben-Hadad for the second time, he forced the Syrian king to allow Israelite traders into Damascus.

The politics of peace

Elisha was a diplomat. He understood that peace is not always achieved through war.

After God struck the Syrians blind, Elisha led the enemy army into the city of Samaria. When the soldiers received their sight once again, they found themselves prisoners of war.

It is likely that most of the Israelites wanted to kill the Syrian soldiers and claim a great battle victory. They must have been astounded when Elisha and the king prepared a great feast for the enemy instead! But the plan worked. When the Syrians were freed, they returned to their homes and didn't bother the Israelites for several years.

Samaria – the city and region

After the division of the kingdom, King Omri and his son Ahab built the city of Samaria, capital of the Northern Kingdom of Israel. After the Captivity, the entire region of the Northern Kingdom was called Samaria. The Assyrians populated the Israelite cities with captured foreigners from other lands and called them Samaritans. Over the years, the Samaritans and Israelites became bitter enemies.

Why banquets were given

Feasts, or banquets, were used for celebrating religious festivals (Ex. 12:14), anointing kings (1 Sam. 9:22–24), and showing kindness (2 Kings 6:23).

Jehu Overthrows Jezebel and Destroys Baal

2 KINGS 9–10

King Ahab ruled Israel from about 874 to 853 BC. He was an evil king who married Jezebel, a woman even more evil than he. During Ahab's rule, the prophet Elijah ministered in Israel and was often in conflict with Ahab and Jezebel. Jezebel especially hated him and tried to kill him. Ahab was killed in battle against Ramoth Gilead, going to war against the counsel of a prophet named Micaiah, and Ahab's son Ahaziah became king. But Ahaziah fell from a second-story window and injured himself. He died of his injuries, and another of Ahab's sons, Jehoram, ruled instead. During his rule, Elisha anointed Jehu to be the next king of Israel, and Jehu drove his chariot to Jezreel, where he executed Jezebel, and the kings of Israel and Judah. Jehu then ruled as king and tried to rid the country of Baal worship.

The zealous reign of Jehu

Jehu was a very intense, high-strung man. He even drove his chariot "like a madman" (2 Kings 9:20). While he was still an army commander, Elisha anointed him as Israel's next king.

At the beginning of his reign (about 841 BC), Jehu listened to the advice of Elisha. Only Jehu had the zeal to carry out the bloody job of killing Ahab's entire family, including wicked Queen Jezebel. After this, the new king executed all of Baal's ministers, trying to regain the Lord's favour. But as a ruler, Jehu was a weak king. He was forced to pay tribute to the Assyrian king, Shalmaneser III. Later, Jehu turned from the Lord and Israel declined even further.

The black obelisk of Shalmaneser III, with a drawing from it opposite, showing Jehu bowing before Shalmaneser.

Face painting

In Jezebel's day, women painted their faces with bright colours (2 Kings 9:30) and drew heavy black lines around their eyes. The coloured paints, as well as lipstick and rouge, came from iron or copper ore mixed with water. Ancient nail polish was a dye taken from the flower of the henna plant which actually stained or tinted the fingernails. Olive oil was a perfume and moisturizer. Reddish-brown stains on the skin were also thought to make a woman look beautiful.

Obelisk of Shalmaneser III

This is a basalt monument telling the history of Shalmaneser III's battle campaigns. Chiselled into its side is a picture of Jehu bowing before the Assyrian king, the only ancient "photo" ever found of an Israelite king.

COSMETICS

The women of Egypt and Assyria coloured their eyelashes and the edges of their eyelids with *kohl,* a fine black powder moistened with vinegar or oil, to give an effect similar to mascara. Some Jewish women also painted their eyelashes and eyes, but this was not generally accepted. Jezebel was criticized for her makeup, and eye paint is condemned in the prophets (2 Kings 9:30, Jer. 4:30, Ezek. 23:40).

Perfume was used very commonly by women of Bible times, much as it is today. Perfumes included frankincense and myrrh from Arabia and Africa, stacte and saffron from Palestine, and aloes and nard from India.

Egyptian cosmetics: a monkey-shaped perfume bottle and two kohl jars – one with its lid and applicator.

The Story of Jonah

THE BOOK OF JONAH

Jonah became a prophet of God not long after the time of Elisha, perhaps even overlapping Elisha's ministry during the reign of King Joash. Jonah tried to run away when the Lord told him to preach to the people of Nineveh. Jonah was afraid, so he took a ship headed toward Tarshish, possibly in southern Spain. But the Lord sent a storm at sea, and the sailors realized at last that Jonah must be thrown into the sea, where a great fish awaited him. The fish took him to land, and Jonah then went obediently to Nineveh to preach.

Nineveh

Just east of the Tigris River in modern-day Iraq lie the ruins of Nineveh. In Jonah's day, it was one of the world's largest and most impressive cities. Since it was the capital of the Assyrian empire, it is little wonder why Jonah was afraid to go there.

In 700 BC, King Sargon moved the capital to Khorsabad, 21 km (13 miles) to the north, and Nineveh's importance declined. But his son, Sennacherib, restored the city to its greatness with a grand palace and mighty walls. Zoos and exotic gardens surrounded the city.

This fragment of a bas-relief sculpture of an Assyrian warship – a bireme – comes from king Sennacherib's Southwest Palace in Ninevah.

God told the prophet Jonah to travel to an Assyrian city called Nineveh and preach against their idolatry. Nineveh was destroyed by the Babylonians in 612 BC, so Jonah's ministry must have been before this, probably during the reigns of Jehoash, or Joash (798–782) and Jeroboam II (793–753) of the Northern Kingdom. At this time, Assyria was a serious threat to Israel, and Jonah's message might also have been an appeal for peace.

Numerous ships sailed the waters of the Mediterranean Sea in Jonah's time. From Joppa, Jonah may have sailed on a Phoenician merchant ship such as the one shown here.

Ships and sailing

Ancient ships were fragile vessels. Their styles varied little from country to country. A ship sailed only during the fair-weather months between April and October. Merchant ships were wide and made of pine. Large sails caught the wind, while stars guided their paths.

This illustration of Jonah comes from the Hortus Deliciarum ("Garden of Delights"), a medieval manuscript compiled at the Hohenburg Abbey to teach novices at the convent. It is the first encyclopaedia written by a woman and was completed in 1185.

155

The Story of Isaiah

THE BOOK OF ISAIAH

One of the great prophets of the Southern Kingdom, Judah, was a man named Isaiah. It has been said that he was of royal blood, that his uncle was King Amaziah of Judah and his cousin was King Uzziah. In the year King Uzziah died, Isaiah was called to minister as a prophet. His ministry is thought to have lasted 50 years.

The world in which Isaiah ministered.

Isaiah was a prophet of Judah during the reigns of Jotham (750–736), Ahaz (736–716), and Hezekiah (716–687).

Isaiah the prophet

Isaiah was a prophet who was obedient to God. During his lifetime, the Assyrian Empire was a world threat, but it is interesting to note that as long as Isaiah advised Judah, it was the only nation throughout the Middle East that was not conquered by the powerful Assyrians. However, Judah did have to pay tribute to the Assyrians.

Isaiah by Jean Louis Ernest Meissonier.

Judah in the days of Isaiah

Uzziah restored some of the military and economic strength to Judah. But King Ahaz was evil and ignored Isaiah's warnings. With Israel and Syria ready to attack, Ahaz allied with Assyria and was forced to accept their religion along with their military help. Judah turned to idol-worship until Hezekiah's reign.

Assyrians leading captives, perhaps Israelites.

Bas-relief sculpture of an Assyrian prince (c. 704–681 BC) from the Southwest Palace in Ninevah.

THE PROPHETS
AND THE KINGS WHO REIGNED DURING THEIR LIFETIMES

		KINGS & QUEENS OF ISRAEL	KINGS & QUEENS OF JUDAH
NINTH century BC 900–800	Joel Obadiah	Jehu, Jehoahaz, Joash, Jehoram, Jehu	Queen Athaliah, Joash, Jehoram, Ahaziah, Queen Athaliah
EIGHTH century BC 800–700	Amos	Jeroboam II, Zachariah, Shallum, Menahem	Uzziah
	Hosea	Jeroboam II, Zachariah, Shallum, Menahem, Pekahiah, Pekah, Hoshea	Uzziah, Jotham, Ahaz, Hezekiah
	Isaiah	Shallum, Menahem, Pekahiah, Pekah, Hoshea	Uzziah, Jotham, Ahaz, Hezekiah, Manasseh
	Micah	Pekahiah, Pekah, Hoshea	Jotham, Ahaz, Hezekiah, Manasseh
SEVENTH century BC 700–600	Nahum	None – Israel in exile	Josiah
	Zephaniah	None – Israel in exile	Josiah
	Jeremiah	None – Israel in exile	Josiah, Jehoahaz, Johoiakim, Jehoiachin, Zedekiah
	Habakkuk	None – Israel in exile	Josiah
SIXTH century BC 600–500	Daniel	None – Israel in exile	Jehoiakim, Jehoiachin, Zedekiah
	Ezekiel	None – Israel in exile	Jehoiachin, Zedekiah
	Zephaniah	None – Israel in exile	Josiah
	Haggai	After time of kings – during exile	
FIFTH century BC 500–400	Malachi	After time of kings – during exile	

Israel Taken into Captivity

2 KINGS 17

Israel's golden age was during the reign of King David, from about 1010–970 BC. David was a mighty warrior who subdued his enemies but ruled fairly and with a deep respect for the Lord. David's son Solomon began his reign devoted to the Lord, but tried to keep peace with neighbouring kingdoms by marrying the kings' daughters. These foreign women brought their heathen gods into the land, built shrines to them, and encouraged Solomon's people to worship them. By the end of his reign, Solomon had turned from the Lord and had given himself to luxurious living supported by heavy taxes. Solomon's son Rehoboam planned even heavier taxes, but the people rebelled, and the kingdom divided, forming a Southern Kingdom called Judah and a Northern Kingdom called Israel. Occasionally, a godly king arose, but generally these kingdoms declined spiritually until they were weak and open to enemy attack. Assyria rose as a mighty power in the north and by the reign of King Hoshea (732–722 BC) destroyed Samaria and carried the people of Israel into captivity.

The North falls before the South

After the kingdom divided, Israel had only evil kings. Only a few were even partially good. Judah had many evil kings as well, but it also had some very good kings. Unlike Israel, it depended on the Lord from time to time. As a result, the weaker and more evil nation of Israel was destroyed first (722 BC).

Judah's later captivity pays off

The Assyrians earned a reputation for their brutal treatment of captives. They enjoyed flaying people alive, leading them with hooks fastened through their lips and noses, or just watching them starve to

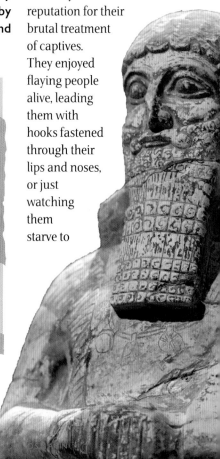

Assyrians invade the eastern Mediterranean. Israel was conquered in 722 BC, and most of the population was exiled, never to return.

The siege of Samaria was begun by the Assyrian king Shalmaneser V (726–722 BC). Sargon II, his successor, actually took the city in 722 BC. This alabaster bas-relief carved on the walls of his palace in Khorsabad (modern Iraq) picture Sargon in his royal chariot, under a parasol, trampling a dying enemy as he inspects his army's attack on a city.

death. The captured Israelites were subjected to this torture..

Judah was not conquered for another 136 years because of the godliness of such kings as Jehoshaphat, Uzziah, and Hezekiah. By this time, Assyria had crumbled, and the Babylonians were in power. They were much more merciful to their captives and even elevated captives such as Daniel to positions of authority.

Kings of Assyria

Shalmaneser III (859–824 BC) was a strong

A statue of Shalmaneser III.

Assyrian king, the first to battle against Israel at Qarqar. The kings who followed him were Shamsi-Adad V (824–815), and Adadnirari III (808–783). These men were weak rulers, setting the stage for the long and prosperous reigns of Jeroboam II of Israel, and Uzziah in Judah.

Tiglath-Pileser III (745–727) attacked Israel in 734 BC and carried many people into exile. His successor, Shalmaneser V (726–722), began the siege of Samaria.

Many think his son Sargon II (722–705) destroyed Samaria, ending the existence of Israel.

Bronze sculpture of Sargon.

Sennacherib Goes against Hezekiah

2 KINGS 18

For more than 150 years, Assyria had been growing as a world power in the north. Israel and Judah, weakened spiritually and militarily, became increasingly attractive to Assyria. By 722 BC the Assyrians had swept down into Israel, the Northern kingdom, and had conquered it. They destroyed Samaria, Israel's capital city, and took its important people back to Assyria as captives. A few years later, the Assyrian King Sennacherib came against Judah. But he found a king there, Hezekiah, who depended on the Lord.

Between the captivities
The Northern Kingdom of Israel ended as a nation in 722 BC when the Assyrians carried the people into captivity. But Judah survived for another 136 years, until the Babylonians captured them in 586 BC.

As you can see, God gave Judah plenty of time to turn from its evil practices of idolatry. Godly kings such as Hezekiah and Josiah had long and prosperous reigns while uniting the nation behind God. But their efforts were soon forgotten, and God's anger fell on Judah, as it had on Israel.

The reign of Hezekiah
No king of Judah had been able to match the religious reforms of David and Solomon until King Hezekiah took the throne in 716 BC. His father Ahaz was a wicked ruler, but Hezekiah must have noticed that Israel's destruction was a result of its disobedience to God.

Within 16 days, the temple was reopened, repaired, and

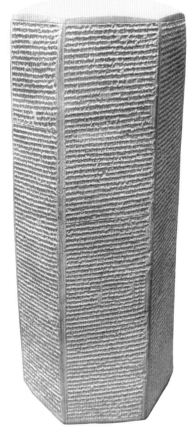

Sennacherib's prism records events of his reign. There are three prisms (in the British Museum, the Oriental Institute of Chicago, and in the Israel Museum in Jerusalem) and among the things they speak of is the siege of Jerusalem during the reign of king Hezekiah.

swept clean of heathen idols. The daily sacrifices were started once again, and the temple was filled with singing and music. The king also brought back the Passover Feast and invited all of Judah and the remaining Israelites to attend.

Some years later, Sennacherib surrounded Jerusalem. Faithful Hezekiah did all he could to prepare his city for the attack (2 Kings 18:19–20; 2 Chron. 32:1–5). But he also trusted God for the amazing victory which He gave (Isa. 36–37).

Sennacherib – a mighty king
At their height of power, the Assyrians defeated everyone in their path, including Egypt. In about 701 BC, Sennacherib marched into Palestine, conquering many cities of Judah, and demanding heavy tribute from Hezekiah, who stripped the temple of its silver and gold.

To prepare for an attack on Jerusalem, Hezekiah dug an underground tunnel through 540 m (1,777 feet) of solid rock, bringing plenty of fresh water into the city. But just as Sennacherib was about to advance on Jerusalem, he received news that Merodach-baladan had revolted in Babylon. One view claims that Sennacherib was forced to leave, but returned around 689–686 BC to continue the siege. Afraid of

defeat, Hezekiah prayed to God, reminding Him of his faithful reign. God answered by sending a plague which destroyed 185,000 of the Assyrian soldiers. Though Judah was a relatively weak nation at this time, the mighty Assyrian king was no match for the power of God.

The Assyrian war machine

As the Assyrians grew in strength, they developed clever battle tactics and weapons which seemed unstoppable. So they extended their borders in all directions.

When the Assyrians first marched against a city, they surrounded it and set up camp.

Sennacherib's cavalry on the march.

In a few days, they built great walls of earth around their tents, along with towers, ramps, and roads. With their camp well fortified, the Assyrian soldiers started to tease the enemy with small raids and fires near the city walls.

When the attack began, the Assyrians struck quickly. Iron-capped battering rams ceaselessly pounded the city walls and gates. Soldiers scaled the walls with numerous ladders. When the gates were broken, the rest of the army poured into the city and destroyed it.

An Assyrian battering ram with archers attacking a fortified city.

Josiah Repairs the Temple: The Book of the Law Found

2 KINGS 22:1–23:30; 2 CHRONICLES 34–35

After the death of King Solomon, his son Rehoboam tried to squeeze unreasonable taxes from the people, hoping to support a life of luxury like Solomon's. But the people had had their fill of such things and rebelled, forming a Northern Kingdom, Israel, with 10 tribes, leaving only the tribes of Judah and Benjamin for a Southern Kingdom, which Rehoboam ruled. This happened in 931 BC. For the next 209 years, both kingdoms declined spiritually, and with that decline weakened militarily. The Northern Kingdom was conquered in 722 BC. Judah, the Southern Kingdom, held on for another 136 years, mostly because godly kings such as Hezekiah and Josiah depended on the Lord instead of military might. Josiah ruled from 640 to 608 BC. During his reign he led a major campaign to rebuild the temple. While doing this, the workmen found a copy of the Book of the Law, which King Josiah read to the people.

Judah's last good king

Josiah was the last of Judah's godly kings. Like Hezekiah, he instituted sweeping reforms throughout the land, abolishing idolatry and demanding that worship be directed only toward the Lord.

The Assyrian Empire was declining at this time. Josiah took advantage of its weakness to expand his borders. His military victories included recapturing territories around Samaria and Megiddo.

Josiah was killed in battle by Pharaoh Necho of Egypt. After his death, the kingdom of Judah declined rapidly until soon it was destroyed by the mighty nation of Babylon.

The Book of the Law

When Moses and the Israelites camped at Mount Sinai, God gave them many important laws to live by. These laws were guidelines for the lifestyle of people who were obedient to God.

Moses wrote these laws in a book and frequently read them to the people to remind them how to live. The Ten Commandments formed the core of this Book of the Law.

The Book of the Law was probably not found on a dusty shelf or in a forgotten corner of the temple. In ancient times, it was common for important documents to be placed in the cornerstone of a new building. In Josiah's day, his workmen were making extensive repairs to the

The fragment of Leviticus shown below is one of the last of the Dead Sea scrolls to be found in what is now known as "Qumran Cave 11". It is written in a script used before the Exile.

This ivory carving may represent Astarte, who was also known as Ashtaroth or Ashtoreth.

temple. The old cornerstone that Solomon had laid over three and a half centuries before was probably cracked or broken, and when the workmen arrived to fix or replace it, they found the important book.

The Book of the Law was God's blueprint for successful living. It was the Word of God written by Moses, who first read this book to the Israelites (Ex. 24:7). On entering the Promised Land, Joshua again read this book before all the people as a reminder of God's blessings to those who obey Him (Josh. 8:32–35).

Scrolls

Most ancient books were called scrolls. They looked nothing like the books of today. In fact, books were not bound into pages until after the time of Christ, and paper was not invented until the 10th century AD.

In Josiah's day, most writing was done on sheets of papyrus, which came from papyrus reeds, that grew along the Nile River. The Egyptians had used papyrus for over 2,000 years, but the Israelites had just started using it to replace the clay tablet.

Sheets of papyrus were made by weaving papyrus stems across each other, much like cloth was woven on a loom. The strips were then beaten until flat, and dried in the sun. One side was rubbed smooth with a piece of ivory or a shell. The finished sheet of papyrus looked similar to paper.

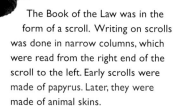

The Book of the Law was in the form of a scroll. Writing on scrolls was done in narrow columns, which were read from the right end of the scroll to the left. Early scrolls were made of papyrus. Later, they were made of animal skins.

These sheets were then sewed or glued into long rolls called scrolls. Some scrolls found in Egypt have been unrolled to a length of over 30 m (100 feet)! Handles were fastened to each end of a scroll, to make rolling it easier.

Scribes and writing

Reading and writing were skills learned by only a select few in Bible times. Scribes were the writers of the ancient world, and an Israelite man was usually trained for 15–20 years to become one.

Scribes were in great demand. They kept records for the kingdom and wrote letters for the king, who often could not read or write. Scribes also sat by the city gate and recorded business transactions for the people.

When the Book of the Law was found, it was the only "Bible" in the entire land of Judah. It would take months for a scribe to write a few extra copies, and even so, most people could not read or write. For this reason, the Book of the Law was read aloud by a scribe at the temple or in a public square.

The Story of Jeremiah

THE BOOK OF JEREMIAH

The world of Jeremiah.

After the Northern Kingdom, Israel, and its capital, Samaria, were conquered in 722 BC, the Southern Kingdom, Judah, held on for another 136 years, until 586 BC, when it fell. During this time, Judah was ruled by eight kings. Hezekiah (716–687) was a godly man who did much to keep Judah alive. The next two kings, Manasseh (696–642) and Amon (642–640), were evil. Josiah followed (640–608) and was a godly king, returning his nation to the Book of the Law and worship in the temple. After he died, Jehoahaz ruled for three months, followed by three evil kings, Jehoiakim (608–597), Jehoiachin (597), and Zedekiah (59–586). During the reigns of Josiah through Zedekiah, a prophet ministered in Judah, counselling kings and religious leaders, often under persecution. His name was Jeremiah. His name remains today on the book of the Bible he left for us.

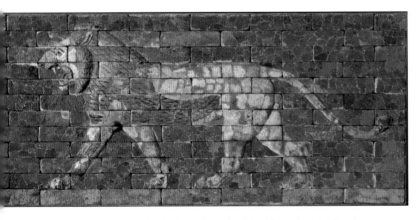

A series of these lions lined the road north of the Ishtar Gate, leading the Babylonians to their city's temple, and worship of Ishtar, goddess of love and war.

The rise of the Babylonian Empire

The great kingdom of Babylon enjoyed its position as a world power for less than a century (605–539 BC). Nabopolassar, the governor of Babylon (625–605), overthrew the Assyrians and gained independence for the Babylonians. But his son, Nebuchadnezzar II, is really given the credit for founding the empire.

Nebuchadnezzar was the only strong king his nation ever had. Under him, trade and culture blossomed and the economy grew prosperous. The city of Babylon was strengthened and became known as a world leader.

The fall of Assyria

In 689 BC, Sennacherib, king of Assyria, destroyed the city of Babylon. The king immediately wrote a law demanding that Babylon remain in ruins for 70 years. But Sennacherib's son Esarhaddon revoked the law and rebuilt the city. This was a fatal mistake, for the city soon grew into an empire which was to destroy the Assyrians.

During the 18-year reign of Esarhaddon, Assyrian might was declining rapidly. Heavy taxes were forced on the people to pay for the nation's building projects and military expeditions. The leaders neglected their country, spending most of their time trying to conquer the world. Soon rebellion broke out, weakening the country further. In 612 BC, the Babylonians took advantage of this weakness and sacked the Assyrian capital of Nineveh, marking the end of the Assyrian Empire.

Jeremiah, by Michelangelo, from the ceiling of the Sistine Chapel.

Jeremiah the prophet

The Northern Kingdom of Israel had been destroyed for over a century because of its failure to obey God. Jeremiah was called as a prophet to try to prevent this from happening to the Southern Kingdom of Judah.

Jeremiah saw the decline of Assyria and the rise of Babylon. At this time Judah was weak. The prophet knew that obedience to God was their only hope of withstanding the Babylonians.

Jeremiah was understanding and sympathetic, but his book is bold in predicting Judah's destruction at the hands of Babylon because of its continued sin, especially idolatry.

THE GREAT EMPIRES OF THE BIBLE

EGYPT
Egypt's greatest achievements in agriculture, crafts, literature, and architecture came in the Middle Kingdom. In the New Kingdom, c. 13th century BC, Egypt conquered countries as distant as the Euphrates.

ASSYRIA
The Assyrian Empire reached its peak of power between 880 BC and 12 BC Assyria destroyed Israel in 722 BC.

BABYLON
The Babylonians captured Nineveh, the Assyrian capital, in 12 BC. The Babylonian Empire reached its peak under Nebuchadnezzar, who destroyed Jerusalem in 586 BC during the time of Daniel.

PERSIA
The Medes and Persians took control of the Babylonian Empire the night Daniel interpreted the handwriting on the wall. Esther lived in the time of the Persian Empire, c. 481 BC.

GREECE
The Greek, or Macedonian, Empire, formed by Alexander the Great, lasted from about 359 to 63 BC. When Alexander died in 323 BC, the Greek Empire broke up into several parts.

ROME
Roman rule of Palestine commenced in 63 BC and continued until well after New Testament times.

Judah Falls, Jerusalem Is Destroyed, and Zedekiah Is Blinded

2 KINGS 24–25; 2 CHRONICLES 36:5–21

After the death of King Josiah of Judah, the Southern Kingdom declined quickly. Within 25 years, four kings had ruled, and the nation was ripe for conquest. Babylon, now the world power in the north, swept down and conquered Jerusalem and with it, Judah. King Zedekiah was forced to watch the murder of his sons and was then blinded. It was the sad end of a once-great nation under Kings David and Solomon.

Destruction of a great city

Over the centuries, Jerusalem was the heartbeat of Israel's life and history. Abraham first journeyed there when the city was called Salem, to honour its King Melchizedek (Gen. 14:18–22). Later, Abraham almost sacrificed his son Isaac on Mount Moriah, the future site of the temple (Gen. 22:1–19).

In the days of the Judges, Jerusalem, then Jebus, was conquered by Joshua (Josh. 10:1–27). But over the years, the city returned to the control of the Canaanites.

King David finally brought Jerusalem back under Israelite control. He defeated the city, and proclaimed it his capital (2 Sam. 5:6–12). David made Jerusalem strong and prosperous and drew plans for God's house.

When Solomon built God's temple, Jerusalem became the focal point in the nation of Israel. Many times each year Israelites travelled to Jerusalem from all parts of the nation to observe various feasts and festivals and to worship at the temple. The city had beauty and wealth and soon came to be known as one of the finest cities in the ancient world.

But when Israel split in two, Jerusalem lost much of its importance. Evil kings outnumbered good, and the city became wicked. After numerous warnings from God's prophets, the once-beautiful city was totally destroyed by the Babylonians.

Treatment of enemy kings

A captured king was a prized prisoner. A victorious king placed his foot on his enemy's neck to symbolize dominance.

Zedekiah, king of Judah, was blinded as is shown in this Assyrian picture.

The Babylonian empire

The kingdom of Babylon rose as quickly as it fell. Within a century, it had overthrown the Assyrians, risen to a world power, and crumbled into extinction by the might of the Persians.

Nebuchadnezzar was Babylon's mightiest ruler. Three times he carried captives from Judah to suppress their revolts. The last time, in 586 BC, Jerusalem was completely destroyed, and Judah lost its existence as a nation.

But Nebuchadnezzar's successors were weak, and soon

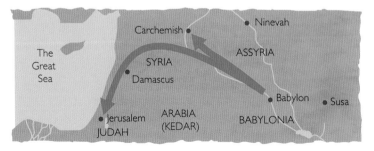

Judah is conquered and exiled to Babylon. Nebuchadnezzar leads Babylonian invasions. Egyptians defeated at Carchemish 605 BC. Jerusalem besieged 597 and 587 BC. Falls in 586 BC. Judean captives taken to Babylon.

THE STORY OF JERUSALEM

Jerusalem, sometimes known as the city of Zion, after one of the hills on which it is built, is situated on a high plateau in the Judean Hills, about 2,670 feet (800 m) above sea level. It had ideal characteristics for a city; it was easily defensible, with steep slopes on its east, west and south sides; and it also had a number of nearby springs, the Gihon spring being of particular importance, for the supply of water.

SALEM
We know that Jerusalem was already in existence in the time of Abraham, when it was known as Salem (Gen. 14:1). It is also believed that Mount Moriah, where Abraham travelled to sacrifice his son, Isaac, is the site where the Jerusalem temple was built centuries later (2 Chron. 3:10).

JEBUS
At the time when the Israelites crossed the Jordan and began to take possession of the Promised Land, Jerusalem was known as Jebus and was populated by the Jebusite tribe (Josh. 15:63; Jud. 1:21; 19:10; 1 Chron. 11:4). The city was already strongly defended with surrounding walls and gates.

CAPITAL OF ISRAEL
When David became king, he conquered the city of Jerusalem, defeating the Jebusites by having some warriors enter the city through an underground water tunnel. David now made Jerusalem the capital of his unified kingdom (2 Sam. 5:7; 1 Chron. 11:7). David also brought the ark of the covenant, which had been captured by the Philistines, into Jerusalem and made the city the centre of worship of the God of Israel. David bought from a man named

Araunah the site of his threshing-floor, and it was probably on this site that the temple was built by David's son Solomon, years later (2 Sam. 24:18–25; 1 Chron. 21:18–27).

SOLOMON'S TEMPLE
David's son, Solomon, built a new defensive wall around the city and constructed the temple that his father had not been permitted to build (1 Kings 6:7; 9:15). The temple was richly decorated and built with the help of materials and craftsmen from Lebanon.

HEZEKIAH'S TUNNEL
King Hezekiah further strengthened the fortifications of the city and also built a tunnel, some 537 m (1,750 feet) long, to carry water from the Gihon spring into the city (2 Kings 20:20). This was particularly important in time of siege. It was during Hezekiah's reign that Jerusalem was besieged – by Sennacherib, king of Assyria; but the siege was lifted, and the city survived (2 Kings 18:13–19:36).

NEBUCHADNEZZAR INVADES
In 597 BC the city was taken by Nebuchadnezzar of Babylon, who took away the leaders of the people into captivity in Babylon and plundered the treasures of the temple (2 Kings 24:10–16). Later, the puppet king Zedekiah revolted against Babylon; as a result Nebuchadnezzar besieged and

took Jerusalem in 586 BC, this time tearing down the walls and burning the temple (2 Kings 25).

REBUILDING
Around 539 BC, some Jews returned to Jerusalem, with the permission of Cyrus, and started to rebuild the temple and some private houses. In 445 BC Nehemiah became governor and oversaw the reconstruction of Jerusalem's defensive walls and gates. Although, about a century later, Alexander the Great captured Jerusalem, he did not destroy the city.

HEROD THE GREAT
In 37 BC Herod the Great was installed as king of Israel, under Roman rule. He put in hand a major programme of public buildings, expanding the city, strengthening the walls and enlarging and ornamenting the temple. He also built a palace for himself and the Antonia Fortress for the Roman garrison.

DESTRUCTION
In AD 66 the Jews revolted against Rome and, after a long struggle, were defeated. The Roman commander Titus destroyed the city and the temple; almost the only parts to survive were some layers of stonework known today as the Western Wall, or Wailing Wall.

Babylon began to decay. Its vast army and great capital city cost too much to support, and rebellion broke out. Within a few short years, King Cyrus and the Persians overthrew Babylon, in 539 BC.

But Cyrus was a merciful man, and one of his decrees allowed the Israelites to return to their homeland. In captivity, the people had learned much about obedience to God.

Daniel and the King's Food

DANIEL I

Nebuchadnezzar's army swept down from Babylon against Jerusalem. In one final conquest, they took the city and the land of Judah surrounding it. They burned the city and took the people of Jerusalem and Judah as prisoners. Many were taken into exile in Babylon, among them Daniel and his friends, who were placed in special training. But these four friends had a problem. Some of their food consisted of meat offered to heathen idols and strong wine, which Daniel and his friends knew would not please the Lord. But what should they do?

King Nebuchadnezzar of Babylon

"Nebuchadnezzar" is perhaps the Aramaic form of the Akkadian word *Nabu-kudurri-usur*, which means "Nabu has protected by inheritance" (Nabu was one of Babylon's deities). Nebuchadnezzar was the eldest son of the founder of the Neo-Babylonian Empire, which succeeded the Assyrian Empire. As crown prince in 605 BC he led the Babylonian armies in their victory over Egypt at the Battle of Carchemish. This may have been the time when Daniel and his companions were captured and taken to Babylon. Just before Nebuchadnezzar had returned to Babylon, he learned of his father's death. He immediately

made a 23-day journey across the desert to establish his kingship. He remained king for the next 43 years. In 601 BC, and again beginning in 599 BC, the Babylonians clashed with Egypt. Judah was inevitably involved in this international warfare. In 597 BC and more completely in 587 BC Judah became a vassal of Babylon.

Babylon

Once the great and lavishly wealthy capital of the foremost empire of its day, Babylon today is only a series of excavated mounds extending over several square kilometres near the village of Jumjummah, southwest of Baghdad in Iraq. The proximity of the Euphrates River has made excavation extremely difficult, but over the last two centuries the upper levels have been uncovered. Earlier travellers mistakenly identified the city with the remains of ziggurat towers west of Baghdad.

Ancient Babylon was a rectangular-shaped city bisected from north to south by the Euphrates River. About 80 km (50 miles) of double walls, the inner one 6.5 m (21 feet) thick, surrounded the city. The waters of the Euphrates River were diverted to form a moat around the walls.

Reconstruction of the famous Ishtar Gate of Babylon.

The Fiery Furnace

DANIEL 3

After Jerusalem was destroyed and the people of Judah were taken captive, Daniel and his friends were forced to go to Babylon to live. There they were trained to be leaders in the new kingdom. But when Daniel's three friends refused to bow to the king's golden statue, he sentenced them to be burned alive in a fiery furnace.

The Plain of Dura

The word "dura" is a common word used in naming ancient Babylonian places. It means "the wall" and probably refers to the walls built around cities to protect them.

We do not know for sure where the Plain or Valley of Dura was. In 1863, a French archaeologist, Jules Oppert, discovered the pedestal of an enormous statue just southeast of Babylon. Ever since then that area has been called Tulul Dura (the Tells of Dura).

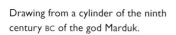
Drawing from a cylinder of the ninth century BC of the god Marduk.

The image of gold

What did the image of gold set up by King Nebuchadnezzar of Babylon look like?

The Bible doesn't say. But from the way the inscriptions of Nebuchadnezzar glorify the Babylonian god Marduk, it may have been an idol of that god.

Marduk was one of the chief gods in the kingdom of Babylon. Each spring the Babylonians celebrated a New Year's Festival. At that time Marduk was officially honoured. The statues of all other Babylonian gods were transported to the city of Babylon by ship or wagon and brought before the statue of Marduk in the great hall of Marduk's temple. Together, these gods were supposed to help determine and shape each man's life for the coming year.

The Furnace

King Nebuchadnezzar's fiery furnace was more like a giant oven called a kiln. Mud bricks were baked inside the kiln. These bricks were used for the numerous building projects undertaken across the city of Babylon.

Most furnaces, or kilns, had both a top opening and a side opening. King Nebuchadnezzar probably talked with the three men in the furnace through the side opening.

King Nebuchadnezzar in his rage ordered the great furnace to be heated to a temperature seven times hotter than normal. Next the king commanded several of his strongest and bravest soldiers to tie up Shadrach, Meshach, and Abednego and throw them into the flames.

Without a second thought, his soldiers obeyed the king's order, knowing that the heat of the flames would almost certainly kill them, too. Why then did they do it?

In Babylon, the king was the supreme ruler. To disobey a king's command meant death, not always a quick death from the flames of a furnace, but sometimes a slow and painful death at the hands of torturers.

The Handwriting on the Wall

Born into a Judean nobleman's family, Daniel was probably only 16 when captured by Nebuchadnezzar's forces and taken from his conquered land to Babylon. There he and a select group of friends were trained to be leaders in this new land. Daniel became one of the Hebrew leaders in Babylon and rose to the highest levels of power. When Daniel was about 70 years old, Belshazzar became king of Babylon. About 10–15 years later, Daniel was called into one of Belshazzar's drunken feasts to explain some mysterious handwriting on a wall, which told Belshazzar that his kingdom would be taken from him and given to another. That night the army of Cyrus entered the city and took over without a struggle. Darius the Mede took over the rule of Babylon for Cyrus and ruled about two years until Cyrus could do it. During this time he appointed presidents, including Daniel, to help him rule. But the other presidents grew jealous of Daniel and tricked Darius into signing a law prohibiting prayer to anyone other than him. Daniel was found guilty and sentenced to die in a den of lions.

King Belshazzar of Babylon

In the six years after King Nebuchadnezzar's death in 562 BC, Babylon had many rulers: his son Evil-Merodach, his son-in-law Nergal-Shar-Usur, and his grandson, the young Labashi-Marduk. Then Nabonidus became king in 556 BC. His son Belshazzar ruled by his side from about 550 until Nabonidus' death in 539. The Bible says that Nebuchadnezzar was the father of Belshazzar, but this simply means that he was an earlier Babylonian king.

Nabonidus was peace-loving and much preferred to build temples and learn to read and write. This gave Belshazzar the opportunity to be a co-ruler with his father. These two rulers explain why Daniel was proclaimed the third highest ruler in the kingdom.

The Medes

The Medes were a people who lived in Media, a region some distance northeast of Babylon and the Tigris River. Little is known of this ancient people. Only a few words of their language have survived, and their origins are almost totally unknown. One of their rulers, named Cyaxares, rose to power and extended the borders of his kingdom, including Persia. His granddaughter, Amytis, married

EMPIRES OF THE ANCIENT WORLD

THE BABYLONIAN EMPIRE
(about the 6th century BC)

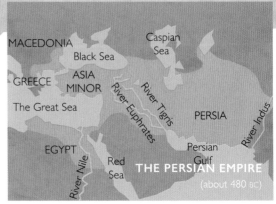

THE PERSIAN EMPIRE
(about 480 BC)

When using scales and balances, a person in ancient times put a fixed weight on one side, like this lion-shaped weight from the Palace of Darius.

walls was a space built for spectators. A small entrance near the bottom of the wall was probably the opening which Darius sealed with a stone (Dan. 6:17).

Darius the Mede

Darius the Mede should not be confused with Darius I, a Persian king who ruled some years later. When King Cyrus took Babylon in 539 BC, he appointed Darius the Mede to rule there as the "governor". The Book of Daniel calls Darius the Mede a "king". This was a natural title to call any ruler of a city or province.

King Nebuchadnezzar. But in 550 BC, Cyaxares' successor, Astyages, was betrayed by his own army to King Cyrus, and the Median empire fell to Persia.

The Persians

Persia lay to the east of both Babylon and Media. In 559 BC, King Cyrus of Persia joined forces with Nabonidus (Belshazzar's father) to conquer much of southwest Asia. In 550 Media's ruler was betrayed and turned over to Cyrus. Then in 539 Cyrus overthrew the weak King Belshazzar of Babylon.

Purple clothing

Purple was a sign of wealth and importance in Bible times. Most purple dye was patiently extracted from the murex shellfish found in the Mediterranean Sea. This slow process made the purple dyes rare and expensive, but in great demand. A purple robe was a symbol of status and considered to be very valuable.

The lions' den

As a means of execution, hungry lions were kept within a small enclosed area. On top of the

THE GREEK EMPIRE
(359–323 BC)

MACEDONIA
Black Sea
Caspian Sea
GREECE
ASIA MINOR
The Great Sea
River Tigris
River Euphrates
PARTHIA
River Indus
EGYPT
Persian Gulf
River Nile
Red Sea

THE ROMAN EMPIRE
(around the time of Jesus)

BRITAIN
GAUL
MACEDONIA
Black Sea
GREECE
CRETE
ASIA MINOR
SPAIN
CYPRUS
The Great Sea
River Tigris
River Euphrates
JUDEA
EGYPT
Red Sea

The Story of Queen Esther

THE BOOK OF ESTHER

After the time of King Solomon, the nation of Israel began to weaken. As the people turned away from God, He permitted the gradual destruction of the nation. First, Israel divided into Northern and Southern Kingdoms. Then wicked kings began to rule over the divided land. At last, from 745 BC until 587 BC the Assyrians and Babylonians captured large numbers of the Israelites and forced them to leave their homes and live in new lands. Assyria was the great world power until 612 BC. Then Babylon ruled as the world power until 539 BC when Cyrus the Great, king of the Persian Empire, conquered it. The story of the handwriting on the wall (Dan. 5) tells of the night when Cyrus' army took the city without a fight. Cyrus ruled the Persian Empire for nine more years until he died in 530 BC, with Darius the Mede ruling the first two years for him. During those nine years he permitted about 50,000 Jews to return to their homeland and lay the foundation of the temple.

During the reign of Cyrus' son, Cambyses II (530–522 BC), work on the temple was stopped. But when Darius I (not Darius the Mede) became king in 522 BC, he permitted the work on the temple to continue. During his reign Haggai and Zechariah ministered to the Jews. By 515 BC the temple was completed by Zerubbabel.

When Darius I died in 486 BC his son Xerxes (Ahasuerus) became king of the Persian Empire and ruled until 465 BC. It was this king who became dissatisfied with his queen Vashti and banished her, marrying Esther.

Xerxes was a warrior king. After he put down a rebellion in Egypt, he invaded Greece. For a while the Persians seemed to be winning. But in a battle at Salamis, the Persians lost their fleet. Sensing defeat, Xerxes turned over his army to a general and went home. Later Xerxes was killed by one of his guards.

Esther's name
Esther had two names. Her Hebrew name, Hadassah, meant "myrtle". Her Persian name, Esther, meant "star". It may have come from the goddess "Ishtar", or may have simply referred to Esther's sparkling beauty.

A Persian chariot. Esther probably rode in a chariot similar to this.

Esther before King Xerxes.

Xerxes' name

The king also had two names. Ahasuerus is the Hebrew name for Xerxes, which was the king's historical name. Actually Xerxes is the Greek form of his name. The meaning of the name is unknown.

Shushan Palace

The kings of Persia had more than one royal city. Shushan Palace was at Susa, in what is now southwestern Iran. Persepolis was another royal city. Esther probably lived from time to time in each of these cities.

The name of God

The name of God is never mentioned in the Book of Esther. Nor is the Book of Esther referred to in the New Testament. But the book speaks clearly of God's care for His people.

Mordecai

Esther's cousin who raised her as a daughter was probably a lower official at the king's royal palace. Both Esther and Mordecai were Jewish exiles who lived in Persia.

Time

Esther lived during the time of Xerxes, who reigned from 486–465 BC.

Persepolis, a palace of Xerxes that was destroyed by Alexander the Great.

Ezra and the People Return

THE BOOK OF EZRA

Daniel was a young Judean nobleman when he was captured by Nebuchadnezzar's army and taken to Babylon. There he was trained and became a leader in Babylon for many years. When he was an old man, he interpreted handwriting on a wall for another king, Belshazzar, which told how the army of Cyrus, king of the Persian Empire, would take over the land. After he did take over, Cyrus immediately gave an edict that the captured Hebrews could return to their native land and rebuild their temple.

Bas-relief reproduction of Cyrus the Great, based on the original in Pasargad, Iran.

Cyrus

Cyrus II of Persia (559–530 BC) began his reign over Babylon in 539 BC. In the first year of his reign Cyrus gave the Jews the temple valuables Nebuchadnezzar had brought to Babylon in 586 BC. He allowed them to return to their homeland. With the support of their neighbours, the Jews gathered offerings for the journey to Jerusalem. Cyrus founded a dynasty that was to last until Alexander the Great conquered Persia, in 336 BC.

Zerubbabel

It is easy to miss the name of Zerubbabel as you read Ezra 2 and 3. He was the heir to the throne of Judah, but when he arrived in Jerusalem with about 50,000 of his people around 539 BC he only became governor. With Jeshua's help he began the second temple, but those who had seen the splendour of Solomon's temple wept when they saw how inferior the new temple was going to be (Ezra 3:12).

Zerubbabel's enemies

Zerubbabel's enemies were Jews who had not been carried into exile in 586 BC. They had remained in the land and intermarried with the people the Babylonians had brought there to settle. Sanballat is mentioned in the Elephantine Papyri of 407 BC as governor of Samaria. Josephus says he built the Samaritan temple on Mount Gerizim (see John 4:20). To Zerubbabel and his companions Sanballat and his associates were no longer God's people because they had married non-Jews and worshipped their gods.

King Darius I (522–486 BC)

When Zerubbabel's enemies, the Samaritans, tried to stop the activities of the returned exiles, King Darius searched for the decree of his predecessor, King Cyrus. He found

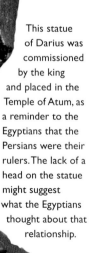

This statue of Darius was commissioned by the king and placed in the Temple of Atum, as a reminder to the Egyptians that the Persians were their rulers. The lack of a head on the statue might suggest what the Egyptians thought about that relationship.

it at Ecbatana, the old capital of Media. Zerubbabel finished the second temple in 516 BC, the seventh year of Darius' rule.

Tattenai

Tattenai was the military governor of Judea. He reported to the king of Persia. Zerubbabel reported to him.

Xerxes and Artaxerxes I

After the death of King Darius (the Great), Xerxes became king of Persia. Also called Ahasuerus, he is known to Bible readers as the husband of Queen Esther. Though he was a weak king, he ruled from 486–464 BC.

Artaxerxes I was Xerxes' son and heir. He helped Ezra and Nehemiah. He ruled the Persian Empire from 464–424 BC.

The Judean countryside. Ezra and the people returned to their own land with Cyrus' permission.

Ezra

Ezra took silver and gold from the province of Babylon and with the blessing of Artaxerxes went to Jerusalem in 458 BC, the seventh year of Artaxerxes' rule. The temple had been rebuilt. Now Ezra taught the Law of God and ended the people's pagan marriages.

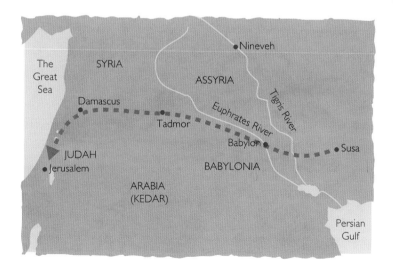

The general route that Ezra and his people followed on their journey. The exact location of the Ahava Canal (River) is not known.

Nehemiah Prays for His Homeland

NEHEMIAH 1

Belshazzar was ruling Babylon when it was captured by the armies of Cyrus, who absorbed Babylon into the Persian Empire which he ruled. Cyrus appointed Darius the Mede to rule in his behalf for a few years. Cyrus immediately gave orders for the Jewish people, the Hebrews, to be permitted to return to their native land and rebuild the temple. Work on the temple began but was halted under the reign of Cyrus' successor, Cambyses I. When Darius I became ruler, Haggai and Zechariah resumed the work and the temple was at last finished about 515 BC. About 34 years later, Esther became queen, with Darius' son Xerxes as her husband. After Xerxes died, his son Artaxerxes I became ruler. Nehemiah was his cupbearer, and when he made his request known to Artaxerxes, the king let him go to Jerusalem to rebuild its walls. Nehemiah worked on the walls about 445 BC.

Homes of Persian kings

The kings of Persia had great power and wealth. Many of them were not content to live in just one home, or palace. Others, on taking the throne, named a different city as the Persian capital, or built an entirely new city to be the chief centre for the kingdom. Some did this simply because they did not like to rule from the same city where the former king had ruled. In any case, kings moved around quite a lot and built palaces in many important cities.

One home of Darius the Great

When Darius the Great became king in 522 BC, he made the city of Susa one of his royal homes. There a beautiful palace was built which became the centre of royal activity for Xerxes (Ahasuerus), Darius' son. Esther was the wife of Xerxes and lived in Susa as queen. The events in the Book of Esther take place in Susa.

Another home of King Darius

Darius the Great was not content with just one royal city or royal home. The king built Persepolis, which was about 320 km (200 miles) southeast of Susa. The city was built near a hill, and to keep most of it flat, Darius placed huge stone blocks together and joined them with iron staples covered with lead. On this flat terrace he set 72 great columns, some as high as 20 m (65 feet), topped by carvings of bulls and horned lions.

The magnificent palace and the city surrounding it were enclosed by three separate walls along with

many watchtowers. Many walls with their stairways may still be seen, with the elaborately carved figures of leaves and people bringing tribute to the king.

A stone relief sculpture from Persepolis of two servants climbing a stairway, bringing food and drink for a royal feast. Scholars believe that this fragment is from the time of Artaxerxes III and may have decorated the palace of Darius.

Homes of Xerxes and Artaxerxes

Susa was probably the principal capital for King Xerxes and his son Artaxerxes. But both kings carried out many of their activities from Persepolis. Queen Esther probably made many trips to Persepolis with Xerxes.

Nehemiah had an important job in the palace at Susa. As the cupbearer, he would have held ornate vessesls like this silver rhyton.

177

Nehemiah Builds Jerusalem's Walls

NEHEMIAH 4–7

The Northern Kingdom, Israel, was conquered in 722 BC and many of its people taken to Assyria. In 586 BC Judah, the Southern Kingdom, and its capital city, Jerusalem, fell and many of its people were taken to Babylon. By this time Assyria had faded as a world power, and Babylon had taken over. Daniel and some friends were among the noble young men deported to Babylon. They were trained as leaders. During Daniel's time Babylon was conquered by the Persians and was swallowed into the Persian Empire. Esther was queen about 481 BC, married to the Persian Emperor Xerxes I (Ahasuerus). Xerxes' successor was Artaxerxes I (464–424 BC). Under his rule Ezra went to Jerusalem. The king's cupbearer Nehemiah also went and rebuilt the walls of Jerusalem (about 445 BC).

Ancient cities had walls to keep out the enemy. The only way to enter was through gates in those walls. At the time of Nehemiah, Jerusalem was a city having three sides, golf tee-shaped, with the shortest side facing northward. On the west wall were the Dung Gate and the Valley Gate. On the north wall were the Old or Jeshanah Gate, the Fish Gate, and the Sheep Gate. On the east wall were the Inspection, Muster, or Miphkad Gate, the East gate, the Horse Gate, the Water Gate, and the Fountain Gate.

King Artaxerxes

King Artaxerxes was the son of Xerxes I, also known as Ahasuerus. This means that Queen Esther could have been Artaxerxes' mother, though it is doubtful that she was his natural mother. Artaxerxes was kind to the Jews and issued the decrees that allowed Ezra and Nehemiah to return to Jerusalem. The king hoped that his helpful attitude to these Jews would keep peace in that corner of his empire.

Workers on the walls

Rebuilding the Jerusalem wall was such a success because all types of people willingly helped. Priests and Levites, perfumers, goldsmiths, merchants, and many women worked in repairing the walls.

Nehemiah is remembered most as the king's cupbearer who rebuilt the walls of Jerusalem. Shown above is the Zion Gate.

THE PEOPLE IN THE STORY

NEHEMIAH
The hero of the book, Nehemiah, was the cupbearer of King Artaxerxes I of Persia (464–424 BC). This was a position of great trust and importance. Everything we learn about Nehemiah from the Book of Nehemiah shows he was a wise, prudent person who studied matters carefully before he acted. Notice how astutely he dealt with his opponents, both those from the surrounding area and those under his leadership, such as the wealthy Jews who charged too-high interest and even enslaved fellow Jews who could not pay back their debts.

SANBALLAT THE HORONITE
Sanballat was the leader of Nehemiah's opponents. He probably came from Beth Horon, northwest of Jerusalem. That is why he was called a Horonite. His name was Sin-uballit in Babylonian, meaning "May Sin give him life". Sin was a Babylonian moon god. Sanballat probably wanted to add Judah to his governorship, and Nehemiah's arrival threatened that possibility. The fact that both his sons, Delaiah and Shelemiah, had Jewish names and his daughter later married the high priest's son may mean that he later became reconciled to Nehemiah's people.

TOBIAH THE AMMONITE
Tobiah was probably an official employed by the Persian government. Both he and his son married Jewish women. The high priest, Eliashib, welcomed him into his rooms in the temple, but Nehemiah later expelled him.

GESHEM THE ARAB
With Sanballat and Tobiah, Geshem was an opponent of Nehemiah. His description as "the Arab" may mean that he was the governor of Edom for the Persians. Or it may mean that he was the governor of Dedan, across the Gulf of Elath east of Mt. Sinai, in the ancient land of Midian.

The story of Jerusalem's walls
The story begins around 1800 BC, when Jerusalem's walls were first erected. Walls were a symbol of strength and prosperity in Bible times. They were a sign that a city was thriving and important.

Over the centuries, Jerusalem's walls were built and destroyed many times. Sometimes the walls were not rebuilt in exactly the same place, and the new walls never looked just like the old.

When King David captured Jerusalem around 1000 BC, he rebuilt the old walls and added some of his own to make the city larger. Three hundred years later, enemy invasions forced King Hezekiah to make extensive repairs to the walls. These didn't last long, for in 586 BC, the Babylonian army destroyed Jerusalem and tore down its great walls. They remained in ruins for over a century, until Nehemiah began his amazing rebuilding programme. Since that time, Jerusalem has seen countless battles and skirmishes, with the walls being in on the activity. Now Nehemiah's walls lie far below those that stand today.

Jerusalem at the time of Nehemiah

- Original Zion
- Extended by the kings
- Extended after the exile

Tower of Hananel
Temple
Lower city
Kidron Valley
Cheesemaker's Valley
Gihon Spring
City of David (Ophel)
Hinnom Valley
Hezekiah's Tunnel
Pool

Ezra Reads the Law

NEHEMIAH 8–10

About 30–40 years after Queen Esther, Nehemiah served as cupbearer to the successor of Esther's husband, whose name was Artaxerxes I. This king permitted Ezra and Nehemiah to return to Jerusalem, where Nehemiah governed and rebuilt the city walls. Ezra established certain religious reforms which had been seriously neglected and read the Law of Moses to the people.

As the workers rebuild the walls, Ezra leads the people in worship.

The Water Gate

Along the east wall that Nehemiah rebuilt and about two thirds of the way down that wall, south of the Hill of Ophel, is the Water Gate, one of the many gates listed in the Book of Nehemiah. On each side of it was a projecting tower. Here in an open square Ezra assembled the people and read the five Books of Moses in 444 BC. For this occasion, people built booths on the roofs of their houses and lived in them to remind them of life during the Exodus.

Ezra the scribe

Ezra was the priest who led about 5,000 people back from Babylon to Jerusalem in 458 BC, several years after Zerubbabel had led the first group back and started to rebuild the temple. By 444 BC. Nehemiah had finished the walls, and Ezra was able to rekindle the people's devotion to God. He put an end to the practice of Jews marrying non-Jews and made a list of all those who had married pagans. Ezra's name means "the Lord helps".

Though Ezra is called "the second Moses" because he reintroduced the Law after the Jews returned from their exile in Babylon, little is known about him. He was not called governor of Judah, but he played a prominent leadership role.

Sackcloth

As a symbol of repentance for sins, the Jews wore sackcloth and put dust on their heads; these were traditional signs of mourning.

Sackcloth was a rough cloth made from camel or goat hair. When made into a sack, it was used to hold grain, much as hessian sacks are used today. But in the ancient world sackcloth was most frequently used for clothing, especially on such solemn occasions as funerals. It was especially common in undergarments. Because it was rough and scratchy, it came to be

seen as an appropriate cloth for self-punishment and repentance.

Scrolls

When Ezra read from the "Book" of the Law of Moses, he was not reading from a book like those today. Instead he was reading from a scroll. A scroll was a sheet of leather, papyrus, or parchment. It was usually about 30 cm (1 foot) high and as much as 10.5 m (35 feet) long. Both ends were wound on wooden rollers. Since writing went from right to left in columns, the right roller was wound and the left one unwound to read a book. The wooden rollers were most interesting. The bottoms were round to make them easier to hold in the hands. The middle parts were wrapped in the scroll. The tops were ornately decorated knobs and balls. A scroll was usually kept in a container. The

Book of the Law of Moses from which Ezra read (what we know as Genesis, Exodus, Leviticus, Numbers, and Deuteronomy) was probably five scrolls.

The tithe

The people promised to bring a tithe of their crops to the Levites, the assistants to the priests. The Levites, under the supervision of priests, travelled from city to city to collect the tithe. They in turn paid one tenth of what they received to the temple treasury to support the priests and help care for the poor. A tithe means one tenth.

The tithe was known in other countries, too. Sometimes it was religious, but often it was a tax. Egyptians, for example, paid a fifth of their crops to the pharaoh.

Various sects of Jews read from the Torah, the Law of Moses, at the Western Wall in Jerusalem.

The Story of Job

Somewhere back in Old Testament times, perhaps as early as the time of Abraham, lived a wealthy man named Job. This man was severely tested, and his story is recorded in a book of poetry bearing his name.

Job heard God speak from a whirlwind and bowed in humble submission.

The good man and the evil man

Most people in Bible times believed that God blessed good people and punished bad ones. Our everyday experience confirms the fact that usually a person who lives the way God wants him to live is happier and better off than one whose life is spent breaking God's laws.

But what about the exceptions? Sometimes people who are corrupt get rich. And sometimes good people experience much suffering. Jesus is the best example of a good person who suffered persecution, and ultimately crucifixion, from wicked men.

The author of the Book of Job seeks to give us God's answer to this problem.

The Book of Job – plot

The Book of Job begins and ends with a story in prose (chapters 1–2 and 42:7-17). But almost everything between is in poetry.

The first two chapters tell us that Job was a good man who lost his seven sons and three daughters, his servants, and all his livestock when Satan was given the right to test Job's faith. The Lord then allowed Satan to further test Job by afflicting this good man with painful sores, from the top of his head to the bottom of his feet. Job's three friends then came for a week's visit to comfort him in his loss and suffering .

The long poem (chapters 3–31) contains the discussions between Job and his friends concerning his losses and why he is suffering. Eliphaz the Temanite, Bildad the Shuhite, and Zophar the Naamathite argue that since God blesses

The story of Job shows the measure of a man's wealth at that time. Flocks of sheep – like these shown on an hillside in Israel – and goats, and camels and donkeys were as important, perhaps more so, than silver and gold.

The Bedouin reminds us of Job, who led a similar lifestyle.

good people and punishes those who are wicked, Job must have sinned. Job insists that he has not sinned, and the three friends stop talking when they find that Job is righteous in his own eyes.

When a younger man named Elihu sees Job's self-righteousness and the inability of Job's three friends to answer him, he jumps angrily into the discussion (chapters 32–37), but he is no more successful than they were in proving his point.

In the climax of the book, the Lord speaks from a storm (chapters 38–41). When Job hears God speak, he bows in humble submission to God's omnipotence and wisdom.

The book concludes with an epilogue in which the Lord criticizes Eliphaz and his friends and tells them to make a sacrificial offering. God also restores Job's family and wealth.

The land of Uz

Job and his family lived in the land of Uz. This area, somewhere in "the East" (Job 1:3), was named after one of the three people named Uz in Genesis (10:23; 22:21; 36:28). Bible scholars believe it was located in the Wadi Sirhan, a valley some 320 km (200 miles) long and 32 km (20 miles) wide, about 80 km (50 miles) east of Edom, the country south of the Dead Sea.

The Prophets and the Coming King

VARIOUS PROPHECY BOOKS

During this time of the divided kingdom, God raised up prophets. These were men of God who spoke out against the sin of the people and warned of God's judgement. They also told of a new King who would come some day to rule. This King would be the Messiah, the Saviour.

With the exception of Elijah and Elisha, the great prophets we remember wrote books contained in our Bible. Four prophets – Isaiah, Jeremiah, Ezekiel, and Daniel wrote long books and were therefore called major prophets. Twelve others wrote shorter books and were called minor prophets.

Sunset in the Negev desert of southern Israel.

Between the time of Malachi and Matthew the Greeks gave the world a unified language, helping the gospel spread quickly after Pentecost. This Corinthian helmet is from the 5th century BC

The New Testament

The New Testament tells us about Jesus, the Good Shepherd, who laid down His life for His sheep, as represented in this Early Christian marble sculpture.

John's Birth Announced

LUKE 1:5–25

The ageing priest Zacharias burned incense in the holy place of the temple in Jerusalem. While there, he saw the angel Gabriel, who appeared to him and told him that he and his wife Elizabeth, both too old to have children, would have a son and would name him John. Zacharias doubted the angel's message, and for this he became speechless until John was born.

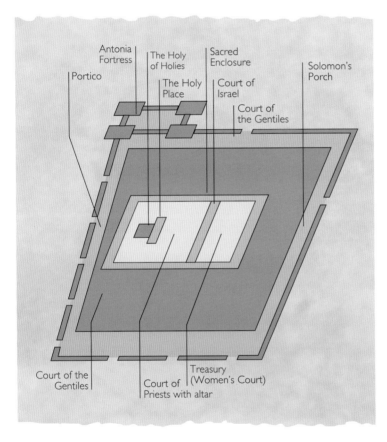

Antonia Fortress | **The Holy of Holies** | **Sacred Enclosure** | **Solomon's Porch**

Portico | **The Holy Place** | **Court of Israel**

Court of the Gentiles

Court of the Gentiles | **Court of Priests with altar** | **Treasury (Women's Court)**

Herod the Great was a prolific builder, and the temple in Jerusalem was one of his most ambitious projects. This model clearly shows the Women's Court and the temple proper, which held the Holy Place and the Holy of Holies.

When

Jesus' birth was announced to Mary six months later, approximately 6–5 BC. John's birth was nine months after the announcement to Zacharias, and Jesus' birth was 15 months after it.

The temple

The temple was built by King Solomon in 949 BC on land which King David bought from Ornan or Araunah (1 Chron. 21:18-30). When the Kingdom divided, King Jeroboam, of the Northern Kingdom, Israel, set up golden calves in Bethel and Dan, so the temple at that time ceased to be the central place of worship for the northern 10 tribes. As the kingdom of Judah weakened, part of the temple treasures were captured by Shishak, king of Egypt; then later part were given to Ben-hadad, king of Syria, to purchase his help. When Judah fell, Jerusalem was burned, and its people were taken to Babylon. In 520 BC the temple was rebuilt by Zerubbabel and other Jews who returned from

Babylon. But it was far less than the one Solomon had built. Five hundred years later, when the Romans ruled the land, Herod the Great began to rebuild the temple (about 21–20 BC), a task that continued for more than 80 years, until about AD 64.

The order of Abijah (Abia)
During the time of David, when plans were made for the temple, the priests who had descended from Aaron were divided into 24 divisions. The eighth of the 24 was named for Abijah (1 Chron. 24:10). Zacharias served in this order, still in service almost a thousand years later. He was probably not a direct descendant of Abijah, for many records were lost during the captivity. But his order was on duty at the temple that day, taking turns with the other 23 orders. Lots were cast among the 50 or so priests on duty to see who would be highly honoured to burn incense in the holy place. A priest was fortunate if he had this honour once in a lifetime, for he was only one of some 20,000 priests in the 24 orders.

The Holy Place
The Holy Place, was the second most holy place in the temple, with only the Holy of Holies above it. Separating the two was the veil. In the Holy Place was the seven-branch candlestick, or lampstand; the golden incense altar, on which red coals glowed; and the table of shewbread.

The angel Gabriel strikes Zacharias dumb in this painting by Alexandr Ivanov.

Zacharias and Elizabeth
Both were descendants of Aaron, a double honour for a priestly family. But the honour was marred by the shame of Elizabeth's childlessness, a shame so great that some rabbis said that separation was a religious duty.

Jesus' Birth Announced

LUKE 1:26–38

In the sixth month after Elizabeth conceived, the angel Gabriel appeared to Mary at Nazareth, announcing to her that she would become the mother of the Messiah, God's Son, and this child's Father would be God Himself. Mary was already betrothed to Joseph, but not married. Though this would be viewed by some as having a child out of wedlock, Mary willingly agreed to do it.

Mary's prayers interrupted by the angel Gabriel.

It was probably October, in 6–5 BC, when Gabriel appeared to Zacharias, so it would have been April when he appeared to Mary.

Augustus Caesar was emperor when Jesus was born.

Nazareth
The hometown of Joseph and Mary was a small, unimportant village, one stop on a caravan route from the seacoast to Damascus. Nazareth is not mentioned by name in the Old Testament, though some think it may have been Sarid. The town must have had a weak reputation, for Nathanael asked, "Can any good thing come out of Nazareth?" (John 1:46) The village is known primarily as the place where Jesus lived throughout His childhood and early life. During His early ministry, Jesus was rejected by the people of Nazareth, so He moved to Capernaum.

Gabriel
Gabriel's name is mentioned in the Bible four times: Daniel 8:16 and 9:21, and in Luke 1:19 (announcement of John's birth to Zacharias) and Luke 1:26 (announcement of Jesus' birth to Mary). In Daniel, Gabriel is called "the man Gabriel", and his voice is called "a man's voice". He flew swiftly (Dan. 9:21) and promised the coming of the Messiah (Dan. 9:24–27). Gabriel was a supernatural messenger, an angel who, as he said, stood in the presence of God (Luke 1:19). Gabriel was sent from God to both Zacharias and Mary to bring God's special news to them.

Betrothal
When Gabriel appeared to Mary, she was betrothed to Joseph. At this time, betrothal was a serious matter, a legally binding promise to marry. It was essentially marriage without living together.

NAMES OF JESUS

Alpha and Omega (Rev. 1:8)
Anointed One (Ps. 2:2)
Author of Life (Acts 3:15)
Branch (Zech. 6:12)
Bright and Morning Star
    (Rev. 22:16)
Christ (Matt. 1:16)
Daystar (2 Peter 1:19)
Everlasting Father (Isa. 9:6)
Gate (John 10:9)
Good Shepherd (John 10:14)
Holy and Righteous One
    (Acts 3:14)
I Am (John 8:58)
Immanuel (Isa. 7:14)
King of Kings (Rev. 19:16)
Lamb (Rev. 5:–13)
Lamb of God (John 1:29)
Lion of Judah (Rev. 5:5)
Lord of Lords (Rev. 19:16)
Mighty God (Isa. 9:6)
Nazarene (Matt. 2:23)
Prince of Peace (Isa. 9:6)
Rabbi (John 1:38)
Root of David (Rev. 5:5)
Root of Jesse (Isa. 11:10)
Son of David (Matt. 15:22)
Son of God (Mark 1:1)
Son of Man (Matt. 8:20)
True Vine (John 15:1)
Wonderful Counsellor
    (Isa. 9:6)
Word (John 1:1)
Word of God (Rev. 19:13)

The actual wedding ceremony marked the time when the husband took his wife home with him. There were three ways to become betrothed at this time: with a *piece of money* in the presence of witnesses; with a *written contract*; or by *living together*. The third way was not approved of in Jesus' time. A breach of vows during betrothal was considered adultery and was dissolved only by divorce. Thus, when Mary expected a child, Joseph considered divorcing her privately, though he could have shamed her publicly.

Two miracles

The two pregnancies were miracles. Elizabeth was too old to have children, and so was her husband Zacharias. Physically, there was no hope that two older people could have a child. Mary was quite young, perhaps still in her teen years, so her miracle was not age, but that she had not yet lived as a wife with her husband-to-be. She was a virgin. Thus her Child had no earthly father, because His true Father was God. Upon this truth is based one important point, that Jesus is the Messiah, God's Son.

The name of Jesus

Jesus was named, not by Mary or Joseph, but by the angel Gabriel, probably under orders from God. The name "Jesus" is the Greek form of the Hebrew name "Joshua", which means "God saves", or "Saviour". Many men at this time were named Jesus, for it was a common name. Thus Jesus is often called Jesus Christ in the Bible, probably to distinguish Him from others who were named Jesus. The word "Christ" means "anointed one", and referred to the One anointed by God to be the Saviour. Jesus had many other names throughout the Bible, such as Wonderful, Counsellor, the Mighty God, the Everlasting Father, the Prince of Peace (Isa. 9:6), Son of Man (Matt. 8:20), Son of God (2 Cor. 1:19), King of Kings, Lord of Lords (1 Tim. 6:15), the Lamb (Rev. 17:14). He is also called the Bread of Life (John 6:48), the Light of the World (John 9:5), the Good Shepherd (John 10:11), the Resurrection and the Life (John 11:25), the true Vine (John 15:1), and the Way, the Truth, and the Life (John 14:6).

Jesus' name is more than just a name. Demons were cast out and sick people healed in the name of Jesus (Acts 3:6; 4:10), and sins were forgiven and salvation given in His name (Acts 4:12; 10:43; 22:16).

Nazareth today. The Church of the Annunciation is built where it is thought Gabriel appeared to Mary.

Mary Visits Elizabeth

LUKE 1:38–56

When Mary heard the news that she would become the mother of the Messiah, she travelled from her home in Nazareth to visit Elizabeth, who lived in a small village west of Jerusalem, traditionally Ein Karem. When Elizabeth saw Mary, she was filled with the Holy Spirit and greeted her with a beautiful "song" which recognized Mary's child as the Messiah, God's Son. Mary responded with another beautiful "song" which has come to be known as the Magnificat. For three months, Mary remained with Elizabeth.

Denarius featuring Pompey, c. 49–48 BC.

A detail from the *Visitation of the Virgin Mary* altarpiece in the Basilica of Saint Frediano, Lucca, Tuscany, Italy.

Mary and Elizabeth

Mary and Elizabeth were closely related. Some Bible versions say cousins (Luke 1:36). Other sources say that Elizabeth was actually Mary's aunt, for she was probably about 40 years older than Mary. It is likely Elizabeth was around 60 at this time, while Mary was probably in her late teens or early 20s. However, the ages of these two women are uncertain.

The times to which Jesus came

Approximately 400 years had passed since the last great Old Testament figure, Malachi, had lived. During that time the land which Israel called home was ruled by the Persians (430–332 BC); then the Greeks (331–167 BC), including a group of Greek kings of Egypt called the Ptolemies. Then a group of Greek kings of Syria called the Seleucids ruled, followed by a little more than a century of independence, called the Maccabean, Asmonean, or Hasmonean period.

In 63 BC the Roman general Pompey took over the old Seleucid Empire of Syria and then laid siege against Jerusalem. Thousands of Jews died before Pompey broke through the city walls and rode to the temple, where he walked into the Holy of Holies, flinging aside the veil to see what was inside. Finding nothing, he went out and ordered the Jewish worship continued.

Antipater, governor of nearby Idumea, was appointed ruler of Palestine under the Jewish high priest. He was an Edomite, a descendant of Esau.

Almost 20 years passed before Antipater was poisoned and his sons struggled for his power. Then Antigonus, son of the last Maccabean king, tried to revolt. In 40 BC Herod the Great, one of Antipater's sons, was appointed king of Judea,

A PALESTINIAN HOUSE

which at that time was most of Palestine. By 37 BC Herod executed Antigonus and ruled all the land.

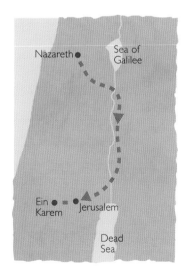

The location of Ein Karem.

These were difficult times for the Jewish people, for they were now ruled by an Idumean under Roman domination. Gentiles were everywhere throughout the land, ruling and taxing the people.

A movement began to search the Scriptures to see what the future held. Many believed that the time had come for the Messiah. The fullness of time was ripe for God to bring forth His Son.

Ein Karem

Many Christians believe that Ein Karem, now at the western edge of Jerusalem, was the birthplace of John the Baptist, the home of Elizabeth and Zacharias, where Mary visited for three months. The road from Jerusalem winds down into a terraced valley with olive trees and vineyards. Ein Karem means "Spring of the Vineyard". Four churches have been built here to commemorate John's birth. Some consider the surrounding countryside as the "desert" in Luke 1:80.

John The Baptist Is Born

LUKE 1:57–80

Eight days after John the Baptist was born, the relatives and neighbours gathered with Elizabeth and Zacharias to circumcise and name him. They wanted to name the baby Zacharias, for his father. But Elizabeth said no, that he would be named John. The relatives and neighbours were surprised, for no family member had that name, so they motioned to Zacharias if this should be his son's name, for Zacharias hadn't been able to speak since the angel Gabriel had announced John's birth to him. Zacharias called for a writing tablet and wrote, "His name is John". Then Zacharias could speak again, and he began to praise God, prophesying John's work as the forerunner of the Messiah. The people who had gathered were afraid, for they wondered what kind of child this would be.

Circumcision

The ceremony of circumcision was a time of great joy and sacredness, for it symbolized the son joining the covenant relationship of his people, to live under the Law of God. In a sense, the father acted as a high priest, offering his child to God with love and gratitude. For the parents of a miracle child, this was an especially meaningful time, for their childlessness had ended.

Zacharias Writes Down the Name of his Son, a fresco by Domenico Ghirlandaio.

Zacharias' loss of speech

Zacharias had been struck dumb when he doubted the message of the angel Gabriel nine months earlier (Luke 1:20). But he also could not hear, for they had to make signs or motions to him concerning the child's name. Doubt had caused Zacharias' speech to leave. It returned with a hymn of praise.

Nazirite

John the Baptist was a Nazirite (Luke 1:15), not by choice, not by his parents' choice, but by God's appointment. A Nazirite was to refrain from three things: grapes and their products, including wine, raisins, grape juice, vinegar, and even grape seeds; cutting one's hair; and touching a dead body. Usually a person was a Nazirite because he had made a vow to be one, but sometimes, as with John the Baptist, he had no choice. The main purpose was not merely to abstain from certain things, but to consecrate himself to holy service to God.

The Nazirite vows appear first in Numbers 6:1–21, revealed to Moses by God. Samuel and Samson were also Nazirites, given to God from birth.

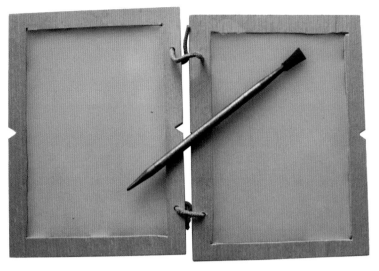

Even early civilizations used writing to preserve records of events. Wax or damp clay was rolled into the wooden frame. Marks could be made with a wood or bone stylus. After use the tablets could be re-coated. Above is a wax tablet and metal stylus as would have been used at the time of Christ.

Writing tablet

Paper was not in use at this time, so writing was done on papyrus (reeds hammered together to make a form of paper), wax-covered wood tablets, broken pieces of pottery with scratch marks or ink on them, or animal skins. Papyrus and animal skins were too expensive for general use, so broken pottery (called potsherds) was often used. Wax-covered tablets made of wood could be erased by smoothing the wax again.

Ink was dry ink, moistened when it was time to write. Black ink was a mixture of lampblack and gum. Red ink was made of sikra, a red powder also used in women's cosmetics.

Pens were made of reeds, not goose quills, which became common much later. These reeds were cut at a curve and split at the end to let the ink flow. A brush or stylus was also used to apply ink to the writing surface.

Forerunner of the Messiah

John's chief purpose in life was to pave the way for the coming Messiah. For that he was born. Mark (1:2–4) tells of John's role as the forerunner, which was also prophesied in Malachi (3:1). Isaiah (40:4–8), who also spoke of John the Baptist, is quoted in Luke 3:1–6. John clearly proclaimed Jesus as the Messiah, the Lamb of God, the Son of God, and placed Jesus far above himself (John 1:29-34). John told also that he himself was not the Messiah, but only the forerunner of the Messiah (John 1:19–27). On another occasion, John said that he must decrease while Jesus must increase, for Jesus had come from above (John 3:25–36). "Forerunner" meant simply that John's work was to tell the world that this Man was truly the Messiah and in other ways prepare people to receive Jesus.

John and Jesus as relatives

Elizabeth was either Mary's cousin or her aunt. Thus Jesus was either John's first or second cousin. Some believe that James and John were also cousins, pointing to John 19:25 (compared to Matt. 27:56 and Mark 15:40), where it appears that Salome, the mother of James and John, was Mary's sister.

Jesus Is Born

LUKE 2:1–7

Caesar Augustus, emperor of the entire Roman world, ordered a census to be taken. In Palestine, the Jews were to return to their ancestral homes, which for both Mary and Joseph was in Bethlehem in Judea. Leaving Nazareth near the time when Mary was to have her baby, they travelled south to Bethlehem, where their ancestor King David had lived as a lad. But they arrived too late in the day to find lodging, so they were forced to stay in the stable with the animals. That night, Mary gave birth to her baby, who was already named Jesus by the angel Gabriel.

A stone manger, perhaps much like the one where Jesus was laid.

Our traditional Christmas fixes the birth of Jesus on 25 December. When our calendar was invented, in the 5th century AD, people thought Jesus was born around the beginning of AD 1 (AD = *Anno Domini*, in the year of our Lord). However, through the years, research into the census has shown that the birth of Christ was actually somewhere around 4–5 BC. No one is sure of the day of the year. During the 4th century AD, the Western Church settled on 25 December, and the Eastern Church settled on 6 January. However, some point out the sheep were still on the hillsides and usually would not be in midwinter. This was true of most sheep, but the temple sheep near Bethlehem usually did stay out all year. Since no one knows for sure, 25 December or 6 January is as good a date as any.

A winter night

Winter in Palestine is the cold, rainy season while summer is the hot, dry season. The heaviest rainfall is between December and February, sometimes with

The front and back of a coin of Caesar Augustus. The coin is called a *denarius*, though in some versions of the Bible it is translated "penny". The *denarius* was the usual payment for a day's labour in New Testament times.

Bell tower of the Church of the Nativity in Bethlehem, Palestine.

caravan routes there were some public buildings in New Testament times, where travellers could stop for the night with their animals and find safety with others. In some cases, these inns had a lower courtyard for the animals, with upper space for the travellers to sleep – certainly not with private room, bath, and restaurant! In some places "inns" were little more than guest rooms adjoining a private home. Such may have been the inn of Bethlehem. The manger may have been a stone feeding trough such as the one opposite.

Bethlehem of Judea

There were two Bethlehems, one in Judea and one in Galilee, only 11 km (7 miles) northwest of Nazareth. Luke writes that Joseph and Mary went "into Judea, to the city of David, which is called Bethlehem". This leaves no doubt concerning which city became Jesus' birthplace. Boaz and Ruth met in the fields near Bethlehem and lived there after they married. David cared for his father's sheep, perhaps in the same fields. Micah (5:2) prophesied that Bethlehem would become the birthplace of the Messiah. The name Bethlehem means "house of bread" or "house of food", perhaps because of the rich fields east of the town where sheep grazed and wheat and barley grew.

hail, thunder, and lightning. The coldest temperature recorded in Palestine is -7°C (19°F), much colder than a normal winter night, which on the Bethlehem hills was probably not down to freezing temperatures. However, a 4°C (40°F) night on a lonely hillside in a rainy season can be quite cold. The rain was almost more unpleasant than the cold. Rainfall in Palestine averages from less than an inch in the south at Eilat to about 1 m (40 inches) per year in the north at Metulla. Jerusalem averages about 64 cm (25 inches) per year with only slightly less in Bethlehem.

The inn and the manger

Bible-time inns were not at all like our modern motels. Along

Shepherds Worship Jesus

LUKE 2:8–20

On the night when Jesus was born in Bethlehem, shepherds watched over their flocks on the nearby hills. Suddenly an angel of the Lord appeared to them, and the glory of the Lord shone about them. The angel told the frightened shepherds the good news that the Messiah, Christ the Lord, had been born in nearby Bethlehem. Then a great heavenly choir praised God. After the angels left, the shepherds went to Bethlehem to see this baby for whom their people had waited so long. No one knows what happened there when they visited with Joseph and Mary, but they returned to their flocks, "glorifying and praising God for all the things that they had heard and seen". They also told others what the angels had said, perhaps even at the temple when they took their next sheep for sacrifice, stirring the hearts of people like Anna and Simeon.

Swaddling clothes

The shepherds found Jesus in the swaddling clothes which Mary had wrapped around Him at birth (Luke 2:7). This was an ancient form of clothing for newborn infants. Sometimes this was called a "swaddling band". It was a square piece of cloth on which the infant was laid with its head at one of the four corners and its feet at the opposite corner. The corner at the head was tucked under the head, and the one at the feet was folded over the feet. The other two corners were folded together over the midsection, then the whole thing was wrapped with bands of cloth.

A shepherd guides fat-tail sheep through fields in Israel.

The Mishnah, the traditional Jewish doctrine collected before the third century AD, suggests that these were not ordinary shepherds and their sheep. They were shepherds appointed to care for the temple flocks, destined for sacrifices. These flocks stayed in the fields throughout the year, even during the winter.

The Messiah, whose birth was announced to these shepherds, would someday die at the time of the three o'clock afternoon sacrifice, making it no longer necessary for sheep such as theirs to die for people's sins. The Lamb of God had come to die once and for all, so that lambs such as these would not need to die again. No wonder the angel announced the birth of the Messiah to these shepherds!

Announcement of the Messiah

The angel visit was the first public announcement that the Messiah had come. It could have been made to King Herod's court, or Caesar Augustus' throne room, or even to the high priest and temple dignitaries in Jerusalem. It could have been made to the Pharisees or Sadducees, the religious leaders, or to other high-ranking men. But God chose to make His first announcement to the small band of shepherds caring for the temple sheep which would be sacrificed in the temple. He had already privately announced to Mary and Joseph that this Son

PROPHECIES CONCERNING JESUS' BIRTH

PROPHECY	FULFILMENT
The place of Jesus' birth, Bethlehem, was prophesied in Micah (5:2).	The fulfilment was given in Matthew (2:1) and Luke (2:4–7).
The tribe into which Jesus would be born, Judah, was prophesied in Genesis (49:10).	The fulfilment was given in Luke (3:33) and Matthew (1:2–3).
The fact that Jesus would be born of a virgin mother was prophesied in Isaiah (7:14).	The fulfilment was given in Matthew (1:18) and Luke (1:26–35).
The murder of the babies of Bethlehem was prophesied in Jeremiah (31:15).	The fulfilment was given in Matthew (2:16–18).
The flight into Egypt was prophesied in Hosea (11:1).	The fulfilment was given in Matthew (2:13–15).
The fact that Jesus would be heir to the throne of David was prophesied in Isaiah (9:7).	The fulfilment was given in Matthew (1:1).

The shepherds see Mary wrap her son in swaddling clothes in *Adoration of the Shepherds* by Gerard van Honthorst.

would be the Messiah. Elizabeth and Zacharias knew this. John the Baptist would know it someday, but at this time he was still an infant. Other than these, few at that time had heard the wondrous news that the Messiah, for whom these people had waited so long, had at last come to the world.

Simeon and Anna Honour Jesus

LUKE 2:21–38

On the eighth day after His birth, Jesus was circumcised and named. A little more than three weeks later, Mary and Joseph took Him to the temple in Jerusalem for two ceremonies. The first was to redeem the firstborn. The second, to "purify" the mother ceremonially. While in the temple Anna and Simeon, who lived there and ministered to the Lord, saw Jesus and praised God that they had seen His Son.

Simeon with Infant Jesus by Petr Brandl.

Circumcision

During the time of Jesus, circumcision was an important ceremony, filled with both joy and solemnity. Relatives and neighbours gathered with the family for circumcision and to name the son on the eighth day after his birth. The ceremony was held either in the home or at the temple, and with it, the child entered symbolically into the covenant relationship of his people, to live under the Law of God. In this ceremony the father acted as a sort of high priest, offering his child to God with love and gratitude. Often his father-in-law, the child's maternal grandfather, performed the circumcision itself. Some suppose the ceremony began with a benediction, as it did in later times, and closed with the naming of the child in a prayer over a cup of wine. The prayer may have been much like one of later times: "Our God, and the God of our fathers, raise up this child to his father and mother, and let his name be called in Israel Jesus", and so on. Circumcision set a Jewish male apart from his Gentile neighbours, who were often considered "uncircumcised heathen".

Redemption of the firstborn

The second ceremony which the baby Jesus had took place at least 31 days after His birth. Like all other firstborn sons of a household, He was to be taken to the temple and was to be "redeemed" by the priest at a price of five "shekels of the sanctuary", as specified in Numbers 18:16. In Jesus' time, a shekel was a silver coin.

Purification from childbirth

There were numerous ceremonies of purification. One was to be held after childbirth, which was thought to make a woman unclean. If the baby was a boy, the woman was considered ceremonially unclean or defiled for seven days, and on the eighth day the boy would be circumcised. Then for another 33 days she was still considered unclean and must not touch anything sacred or enter the tabernacle (or temple later). This law was found in Leviticus 12:2–5. If the baby was a girl, the time of uncleanness was twice as long. The law continued (Lev. 12:6–8): when the 40 days were ended, the mother was to bring to the temple a yearling lamb and a young pigeon; present them to the priest to offer for her; and if too poor, bring two turtledoves or two young pigeons instead, which Mary did (Luke 2:24) for she was poor.

Wise Men See a Star

MATTHEW 2:1–8

In a land to the east of Palestine, some wise men, or Magi, saw a star, or arrangement of stars, which told them that the Messiah had been born. Leaving their homes, they travelled to Jerusalem, where they inquired about the newborn king. Naturally King Herod was curious about a new king and jealously called for his own religious leaders, inquiring about the place where this Messiah should be born. When he learned it was Bethlehem, Herod called for the wise men privately and asked when the star appeared. He apparently learned that it had been almost two years earlier, so he sent them on their way, pretending to want to worship this new king also, telling them to let him know when they found Him.

A camel train at sunset. The Magi probably rode on camels.

The Magi or wise men

King Herod's fear of the newborn king was more than personal fear for his own job. It was fear of another serious revolt against himself and Rome, one which could shift the balance of power in Palestine for years to come. The story goes all the way back to the time of Daniel, who was a powerful ruler in the Babylonian Empire. Some think that the Jews at that time helped the Medians overthrow Babylon and place Cyrus in control of the ancient world. This would explain, of course, why Cyrus was so generous in helping the Jewish people rebuild their land and capital city of Jerusalem.

A religious group had great power in the Persian Empire at that time and had held these political powers for years before. They were known as Magi, and while religious leaders, also exerted powerful influence in government. During the time of Christ's birth, they had the power to choose the king over their realm, which was then known as the Parthian Empire.

The rivalry between this Parthian Empire and the Romans had been intense for a number of years. Palestine itself had been the scene of a number of skirmishes between them, including one Parthian invasion when Herod's father, Antipater, was defeated in 40 BC. Three years later, Mark Antony gained control of the land, but then tried to go farther against the Parthians. When he was defeated, the Parthians swept across the land and forced the Romans to retreat. Herod himself had to flee to Rome and could not return until three years later when Rome finally gained control again.

Herod ruled for the next 30 or so years between two competing empires – Rome, whom he served, and the Parthians, who were still unfriendly and could at any time launch another invasion, aided by the Jews under Herod's control.

Thus in 4–5 BC, when the small band of Magi came to

The Magi saw a star (or was it a comet?) which told them that the Messiah had been born.

Herod asking about a newborn king, Herod accepted them in an uneasy peace. They were probably Parthian king-makers, asking about a new Jewish king who had just been born. At this time, Herod was a very sick man, suffering from a disease which would claim his life within a year. He would soon execute his own son Antipater, so it certainly would not trouble him to execute a few Jewish babies in Bethlehem, which he did. By doing this, he hoped to kill that one baby who was "born king of the Jews". If not, that one baby might swing the balance of power from Rome to the Parthians.

How many?
Traditionally three wise men, or Magi, are shown in pictures. This is only a tradition, for the Bible does not say. It could have been two, three, or more.

Camels
The Bible does not say the Magi rode on camels. But this would have been the logical means of transportation for important men of that time. Donkeys or horses were not as suited for long travels through the desert country as camels were.

The star
Strange that Balaam (Num. 24:17) should refer to the coming Messiah as "the Star out of Jacob". Balaam later led Israelites astray, but at this time God must have revealed to him the Messiah, God's Son, who would come some 14 centuries later. Thus, while Christ was a star, so also was the sign in the heavens which led the wise men first to Jerusalem and then to Bethlehem.

Some say this star may have been a conjunction of Jupiter, Saturn, and Mars in 6 BC. Others think it was a nova, or exploding star, which burns with intense heat and light for a short time. But could not the God who made the heavens make one more special star to announce the coming of His Son, the Star of Jacob?

The wise men may have travelled for as long as two and a half years, covering over 14,500 km (9,000 miles), to see Jesus.

Wise Men Visit Jesus

MATTHEW 2:9–12

From the East, in the Parthian Empire, came a group of Magi to seek the newborn king of the Jews. When they arrived in Jerusalem, they inquired about Him. This attracted the nervous attention of King Herod, who feared that this new king might not only take his throne from him, but might swing the control of Palestine from Rome to the Parthians. Herod quickly inquired of his own religious leaders where the Messiah would be born and learned that it would be Bethlehem. Then he privately talked with the wise men and asked when the star had first appeared, which had been almost two years earlier. When Herod learned these things, he sent the Magi to Bethlehem, pretending to also seek the new king so that he might worship Him. The star that had brought the Magi from the East led them to Bethlehem and stood over the house where the child Jesus now lived. They worshipped Him and presented to Him gifts of gold, frankincense, and myrrh. Then, warned by God in a dream not to return to Herod, they went home another way, over 1,500 km (1,000 or so miles) back to their homeland. The Magi, powerful men in their own empire who helped put kings on their thrones, had travelled almost 3,200 km (2,000 miles) through the desert country to worship a newborn baby!

The gifts of the Magi

The Magi brought three types of gifts to young Jesus – gold, frankincense, and myrrh. How much of each we are not told. Nor are we told what these men expected the Infant Jesus to do with these treasures. But we may guess that these financed the flight to Egypt for a family so poor that they could not afford a lamb for an offering in the temple.

THE MAGI'S GIFTS

GOLD was the gift of royalty. Most people in Jesus' time, other than royalty and the very wealthy, could not afford to own gold. As far back as the patriarchs, gold and silver were standards of money, as they still are throughout the world today. Of all the standards of wealth, gold is perhaps supreme, a gift fit for any king.

FRANKINCENSE mingled with the offerings of priests. It was the gift of worship, for in the many references to frankincense in the Bible, it is almost always associated with worship (see Lev. 2:1–16; 6:15; Ex. 30:34–38; Num. 5:15; and Neh. 13:5, 9). It is also a perfume of love, the adoration of a king for his bride (Song 3:6; 4:6, 14). Frankincense was a gum exuded from a tree in Arabia.

MYRRH was a gift of suffering. Myrrh was mixed with vinegar and offered to Christ on the cross (Mark 15:23) and brought to anoint his body after He had died (John 19:39–40). The process of obtaining myrrh suggests suffering, for the skin or bark of the plant is pierced so that the plant will "bleed" a white gum which turns red on contact with the air.

A bowl of frankincense, a chalice of myrrh, and nuggets of gold.

The Flight to Egypt

MATTHEW 2:13–18

Warned by God in a dream, the Magi returned home secretly, instead of returning to Jerusalem to tell Herod the Great where the child Jesus could be found. Herod was angry when he learned that he had been avoided. He had hoped to murder this newborn King. Now all he knew was that this King was under two years old and had been born in Bethlehem. Taking no chances, he planned to murder all baby boys in Bethlehem and the surrounding countryside who were two years or less. But before he could put his plan into effect, an angel of the Lord appeared to Joseph in a dream and warned him, ordering him to take Mary and Jesus to Egypt. Joseph obeyed immediately, leaving by night, and remained in Egypt until Herod the Great died. After they were gone, Herod put his plan into effect, murdering the baby boys of Bethlehem. This fulfilled the prophecy in Jeremiah 31:15, as the flight into Egypt fulfilled the prophecy in Hosea 11:1.

The Flight into Egypt by Carlo Dolci.

The angel of the Lord
The Bible does not name the angel, but it may well have been Gabriel, for it was he who seemed to be entrusted with the care of the baby Jesus. Gabriel had announced the birth of John the Baptist, the forerunner of the Messiah, and had announced the birth of Jesus to Mary. He probably was also the angel of the Lord who announced to Joseph that Mary's Child was God's Son.

Jesus' home in Egypt
For a year or perhaps slightly more, Jesus lived in Egypt with Joseph and Mary. The Bible does not tell where in Egypt, but tradition says it was at On, or Heliopolis. If so, the father-in-law of Joseph (Jacob's son) served there as a "priest of On" (Gen. 41:45, 50; 46:20) many centuries earlier. Heliopolis was located only 16 km (10 miles) from the place where modern Cairo, Egypt, is built. It was the centre of the worship of the sun god Re, or Ra, and thus took its name "City of the Sun" from this.

The road to Egypt
When Joseph and Mary left Bethlehem for Egypt, how did they travel? There were no numbered highways as we have today. Nor were there paved roads, except in certain places where the Roman Empire had built roads with large stones.

Usually people joined a caravan which was travelling on one of the many caravan routes through the land. Joseph and

The word *angel* is Greek for messenger, and the Bible frequently speaks of angels as those who run God's errands between heaven and earth. Sometimes they appear in heavenly form (Luke 2:9–13) and sometimes in human guise (Gen. 19:1–2). Cherubim and seraphim are special kinds of angels and belong to the hosts of angels who surround God. Some angels we know by name: **Gabriel** (Luke 1:19), **Michael** (Daniel 12:1), **Raphael** (Tobit 3:17*) and **Uriel** (2 Esdras 5:20*).   *These books are considered apocryphal by many Christians.

Mary left Bethlehem by night, so they probably risked the dangers of the road to join a caravan in another town.

A caravan route which went north and south from Bethlehem was the way to Ephrath. The next stop to the south was Hebron and the next Beersheba. They may have joined a caravan at one of these places.

Travel conditions

Travelling with a caravan was hot, dirty, and tiring. But at least it was much safer than travelling alone, for bandits lurked along the way to steal from anyone foolish enough to travel without the safety of large numbers. Joseph and Mary had to be especially careful, for they had the rich gifts which the wise men had brought, which probably financed their trip to Egypt and back up to Nazareth.

Caravan leaders often paid local rulers or sheikhs for protection through their territory, who provided armed guards to go with the caravan. At night, a caravan stopped at an inn, a crude structure with a well in a central courtyard, a place to keep the animals safely, and a second floor where the people slept and traded goods with one another.

Merchants were the nucleus of a caravan, carrying goods from place to place, including spices, incense, gold, silver, wine, oil, food, cloth, jewellery, and slaves. Since they carried many valuable items, they were, of course, always subject to bandits or raiding parties, so even a caravan was not a completely safe place to be.

The distance between Bethlehem and Heliopolis, Egypt was between 480 and 640 km (300 and 400 miles), a trip of some two to three weeks. During this time, Jesus' family was taken to a very different type of lifestyle in Egypt.

The route from Bethlehem to Egypt.

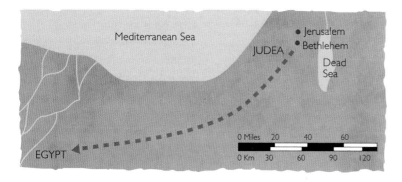

The Return to Nazareth

MATTHEW 2:19–23; LUKE 2:39

The family's return from Egypt.

When Magi came from the East seeking a newborn king, Herod the Great was frightened. He believed a truly Jewish king would cause a revolt against Rome. The Parthians to the east would join the Jewish people, and the balance of power would be upset. Herod knew he would surely be deposed and executed. Thus Herod killed all the baby boys of Bethlehem two years old and younger, hoping to kill that one Baby. But an angel of the Lord had warned Joseph to take Mary and Jesus to Egypt, where they lived during the year or two while Herod the Great still reigned. When Herod died, the angel returned, instructing Joseph to take Jesus and Mary back to Israel.

Herod's death is said to be around 4 BC. If so, Jesus' birth, trip to Egypt, and return from Egypt took place within a year, or slightly more. However, these dates are still not known for certain.

Archelaus

The Bible tells us that Joseph learned Archelaus ruled over Judea in place of his father, Herod the Great. Joseph was therefore afraid to return to Judea, but God told him to take Mary and Jesus to Galilee, to the town of Nazareth.

Before Herod the Great died, he changed his will a number of times. Altogether, he made six wills. In the last, he made his son Archelaus king, his brother Antipas tetrarch of Galilee and Perea, and his other brother Philip tetrarch of four other areas.

As soon as Herod the Great died, Archelaus took charge, but was reluctant to be crowned king, for his brother Antipas had challenged Herod's will. When Passover came Archelaus was overly anxious to keep a revolution from starting, so he killed 3,000 of the Jewish people.

Antipas and Archelaus travelled to Rome to settle their dispute over the will. Caesar Augustus settled it by making Archelaus ethnarch with a promise that he would become king if he proved a good ruler. Antipas and Philip remained in the position their father had chosen for them.

But Archelaus was brutal with the Jews and Samaritans. Perhaps this is why Joseph was afraid to settle once more in Bethlehem, under Archelaus' rule, but went back home to Nazareth, under Antipas' rule. Some 30 years later this same Antipas would murder John the Baptist and judge Jesus.

In AD 6, 10 years after he began to rule, Archelaus was deposed and banished. His brothers Antipas and Philip had gone to Rome to complain about his leadership, along with a delegation of Jews and Samaritans who complained about his cruelty. Rome recognized that when the Jews and Samaritans, bitter enemies, sent a joint delegation, something was seriously wrong. After Archelaus was banished, his territory was placed under the control of procurators. Pontius Pilate was the procurator during the time of Jesus' judgement, while Herod Antipas was still tetrarch of Galilee.

The trip home to Nazareth

Normally a traveller from Egypt to Nazareth would follow the caravan route called the Via Maris, a direct route from Egypt through Nazareth to the north. But Jews tried not to travel through Samaria, so Joseph and Mary may have crossed the Jordan River east of Jerusalem, then travelled north through Perea, then back westward into Galilee, as shown on the map. For safety reasons, they may also have avoided the main highway.

The Carpenter's Shop

LUKE 2:40; MATTHEW 13:55; MARK 6:3

When Joseph and Mary returned to Nazareth, Joseph set up his carpenter's shop again. Through the years, he trained Jesus to be a carpenter, as all good Jewish men trained their sons for a trade, usually their own. Thus Jesus' neighbours knew Him as "the carpenter the son of Mary". Joseph must have died somewhere between the time when Jesus was 12 and the time He began his ministry around the age of 30. Jesus evidently took over Joseph's work as a carpenter until the time for His ministry to begin.

Almost nothing more is known about Jesus' childhood except His visit to the temple at age 12. The timetable seems to be this:

6–5 BC Jesus was born;

4 BC Jesus was brought from Egypt to Nazareth;

4 BC–AD 26 Jesus grew up in Nazareth, learned Joseph's trade as a carpenter, and after Joseph's death, took over the carpenter's shop. Jesus' public ministry began in AD 26.

An adze (with a bronze blade bound to a wooden handle with leather thongs), along with other ancient carpentry tools.

What a carpenter made

Many things in Bible times were made of wood, including carts, wagons, wheels, bowls and other utensils, some tools and tool handles, and furniture. Houses were usually made of stone, which was plentiful, so carpenters were not primarily house builders and cabinetmakers. Jesus must have made many of the items listed above.

The Church of Joseph, near the Church of the Annunciation, is built over the site where some believe Joseph's carpentry shop was once located.

Jesus and the Teachers

LUKE 2:41–52

After Jesus returned from Egypt with Joseph and Mary, He grew up in Nazareth, learning Joseph's trade as a carpenter. At the age of 12, He went with Joseph and Mary to the temple to celebrate the Passover feast, as most Jewish men did every year. On this occasion, however, He entered into a discussion with the teachers in the temple, astounding them with His knowledge. Mary and Joseph left for Nazareth, thinking He was among their friends and relatives, but when they discovered that He was not, they returned to find Him teaching the teachers.

Christ Among the Teachers by Vasily Polenov.

Who were the teachers?

During the time of Jesus there were few remaining authorities on the Law of Moses, but those who remained were apparently there in the temple. Jesus may have found them teaching in the sacred enclosure and began to ask them questions.

A Jewish boy's education

In Jesus' time, a Jewish boy was taught the Law at age five, including catechetical instruction in synagogue schools. By the age of 12, he was expected to obey the Law, and at 13 wore the phylacteries as he recited his daily prayers. At the age of 12, Jesus was on the threshold of manhood, more like a boy of 18 today.

The Passover

At the time of the Exodus, the angel of the Lord struck down the firstborn of Egypt, while passing over the firstborn of Israel. To commemorate this, the Israelites set up the Passover feast. A lamb was slain, and its blood was sprinkled with hyssop on the doorposts of the house, as it was the night before the Exodus. The whole lamb was roasted and eaten by the family, without breaking a bone of its body. The time when the lamb was killed was between 3–6 P.M., the exact time of the day when Jesus, the Lamb of God, died for the sins of the world.

Every male Israelite was expected to travel to Jerusalem three times each year to the great festivals, of which one was the Passover. When Jesus, or any Jewish boy, reached the age of 13, He became "of age", and was expected to begin these pilgrimages. Jesus began His a year early.

About 21 years later, Jesus would eat another Passover feast, this time with His disciples in an upper room. This Passover feast has come to be known as "the Last Supper". The Passover was considered the most important of the three great annual festivals of Israel.

John Preaches in the Wilderness

MATTHEW 3:1–12; MARK 1:1–8; LUKE 3:1–18

A locust.

Eighteen years had passed since the boy Jesus amazed the teachers in the temple. Now He and His cousin, John the Baptist, were 30. John had already begun to preach in the wilderness and was attracting crowds from the cities and villages of Judea. John's message was a call for repentance, to turn from sin to a God who could forgive and would forgive. John's message was not the Gospel of Jesus Christ, but was a stepping stone to that Gospel. John told the people that he was not the Messiah, but was there to point to the Messiah, who was coming.

The Judean wilderness, a bleak country.

The rulers over John and Jesus

During the ministry of John and Jesus, the Mediterranean world, that is, the lands surrounding the Mediterranean Sea, were part of the Roman Empire, ruled by Tiberius Caesar, the Roman emperor. The land that had once been part of the nation Israel, under King David, formed several small territories – Idumea, Judea, Samaria, Galilee, Perea, and others. Herod the Great had ruled over all of this, and more, in the years before Christ was born. Then, a year or so after Christ came, Herod died and his kingdom was divided among his sons, Herod Antipas (Galilee and Perea); Herod Philip (lands northeast of the Sea of Galilee); and Archelaus (Judea, Samaria, and Idumea, the largest and most important part of the kingdom, with Jerusalem toward the centre).

Archelaus proved to be a poor ruler, so he was deposed and banished. His territory was placed under a series of procurators. Pontius Pilate was the procurator when Jesus was crucified.

The kingdom of heaven

John and Jesus each used the term "kingdom of heaven" and "kingdom of God" to mean the same thing – the kingdom over which Jesus, the Messiah, would rule. It was not limited to heaven, or a specific time or place, but to that over which King Jesus rules.

Camel's hair, locusts, and wild honey

John wore rough hairy clothing, like that of Elijah (2 Kings 1:8). This seemed to be appropriate for prophets with strong messages (see Zech. 13:4). The "girdle" mentioned in some versions was a wide leather belt. Locusts were acceptable food, eaten by the poor (Lev. 11:21). Wild honey was found in hollowed trees. John could never be accused of living a worldly life!

Jesus Is Baptized

MATTHEW 3:13–17; MARK 1:9–11; LUKE 3:21–23

The location of Jesus' baptism and temptation.

When John and Jesus were about 30, it was time for their public ministries. John preached in the wilderness of Judea, calling on people to repent from their sin and to recognize that the Messiah was coming soon. One day, while John was at the Jordan River, probably baptizing those who believed in his message, Jesus came along and insisted that John baptize Him also.

The Jordan is the most frequently mentioned river in the Bible, occurring about 200 times in all. The river is about 380 km (240 miles) in length and meanders in its course from its source near Mount Hermon in the north of Palestine. It flows south in a valley through the Sea of Galilee to the salt-saturated Dead Sea in the great Rift Valley. Its banks are covered with dense vegetation, which in the past provided cover for many wild animals. The river is at its highest in spring, between April and May, when the snows in the northern hills melt. Some modern spirituals and hymns use the image of crossing the Jordan as a picture of passing from earth to the promised land of heaven. Shown above is Betania, considered to be the site of the baptism of Jesus.

John the Baptist
He was called "the Baptist" as another way of saying "the baptizer", or "the one who baptizes". Denominations came many centuries later, so the term did not refer to a denomination or people today who are called Baptists. Nor was his given name "the Baptist", but merely John (Luke 1:13, 63).

The Jordan River
Jesus came from Nazareth, in Galilee, to the Jordan River, where John had been baptizing, so that John might baptize Him also. This river was rich in Israelite history. Fourteen centuries earlier, the Israelites who had come from Egypt in the Exodus yearned to cross this river to enter the Promised Land. Because of their disobedience, they died in the wilderness, and the next generation finally crossed to form the new nation Israel.

Four centuries later, David fled across this river to escape his son Absalom, who had seized David's throne, and then returned back across it victorious. Elijah ministered in the Jordan River area some years later.

The voice from heaven
Time after time throughout the Gospels, God clearly revealed to the people around Jesus that He was God's Son. Thus far in the Gospel narrative, this has happened: (1) when the angel announced to Mary that her Son would be God's Son (Luke 1:32, 35); (2) when Elizabeth, filled with the Holy Spirit, recognized that Mary's baby was the Son of God (Luke 1:43); (3) when the angel announced to Joseph that Mary's baby was the Son of God (Matt. 1:20–23); (4) when the angel of the Lord announced to the shepherds that God's Son had been born in Bethlehem (Luke 2:11); (5) when Simeon took the Child Jesus into his arms in the temple (Luke 2:28–32); (6) when Anna talked of Jesus (Luke 2:38–39); (7) when the Magi visited Jesus (Matt. 2:2, 11); and (8) when Jesus spoke of the temple as His Father's house (Luke 2:49).

Jesus Is Tempted

MATTHEW 4:1–11

Jesus and His cousin John were 30 when they began to preach. John preached in the wilderness of Judea, calling people to repent of their sins, baptizing those who did. Jesus came to him one day and insisted that John baptize Him. When Jesus came up out of the water, the heavens opened and the Spirit of God came upon Him in the form of a dove. Then God proclaimed that this was His beloved Son, in whom He was well pleased. Shortly after that, Jesus was led into the wilderness by the Holy Spirit. There Satan came to tempt Jesus.

Satan tempting Jesus.

Three desires

At first glance it would seem that Jesus was tempted with three simple desires: food, fame, and power. But a closer look shows that Satan's temptations were not quite that simple. Instead, they were food without work, fame without accomplishment, and power without effort. Satan still tempts us today in these three ways. Beware when he offers something for nothing!

The Monastery of the Temptation is located on the slopes of the Mount of Temptation – the traditional location of Christ's meeting with Satan.

The Bible records numerous temptations, but two stand out above all others. They also stand in stark contrast to each other. Satan tempted Adam in the paradise called Eden. He also tempted Jesus in the wilderness. He tempted Adam through his helper, Eve, but he tempted Jesus personally and directly. He tempted Adam in a plentiful garden, where he lacked nothing. He tempted Jesus in a barren wilderness, where there was nothing for Him to eat. Adam was well fed. Jesus was almost at the point of starvation. Adam yielded to Satan's temptation and brought sin into the world. Jesus resisted Satan's temptation and conquered sin. Adam's disobedience forced him out of his paradise home, separating him from God. Jesus' obedience brought Him into a closer relationship with God the Father, who sent angels to minister to Him.

Angels

Angels were closely involved with the life of Jesus on earth. An angel: announced that Jesus would be born; assured Joseph that Jesus was God's Son; named Jesus; announced His birth to shepherds; and made plans for Jesus to be taken to Egypt for safety. In His last days, they would minister to Him in Gethsemane.

The Wedding at Cana

JOHN 2:1–11

After Jesus was tempted by Satan, He returned to the place where John had baptized Him. John told those around him that Jesus was the "Lamb of God" who would take away the sin of the world. Andrew quickly became a disciple of Jesus, then brought his brother, Simon Peter, and encouraged him to follow Jesus also. The next day Philip became a disciple and immediately brought Nathanael to meet Jesus. Shortly after that, Jesus visited Cana in Galilee and attended a wedding there.

home. Wedding guests joined the party along the way.

A feast was prepared at the home of the bridegroom, or his father, and all the friends and neighbours were invited. It was this kind of feast that Jesus attended at Cana. It lasted seven days, sometimes 14, and was filled with eating, drinking, and festivities. At the end the bridegroom took his bride to the wedding chamber and their marriage was completed.

This Roman marble relief shows a merchant receiving a deliveryman carrying a jar over his shoulder. Other sealed jars are stacked behind the man to the left.

Weddings

In Jesus' time a couple who planned to marry was usually first "betrothed". This was similar to engagement in our times, for two people promised to marry, but as yet did not live together. However, to be betrothed was more binding than our engagement, for the two were considered to belong to one another. Gifts were given and oaths were exchanged.

The wedding came later. Unlike weddings today, these were not religious ceremonies, but a ceremony of taking the bride from her father's house to the bridegroom's house.

The bridegroom dressed in his best, then with groomsmen left his house for that of the bride, who was waiting for him with her bridesmaids. With shouting and singing, and often musical instruments playing, the bridegroom escorted the bride back to his

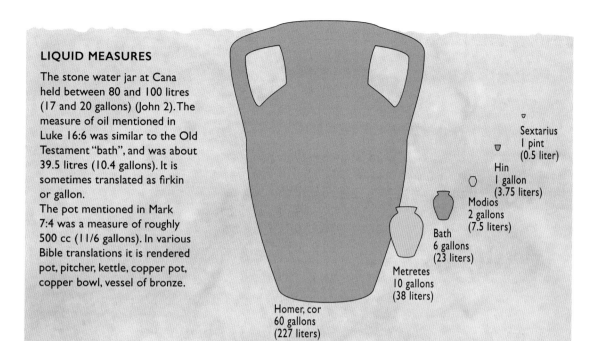

LIQUID MEASURES

The stone water jar at Cana held between 80 and 100 litres (17 and 20 gallons) (John 2). The measure of oil mentioned in Luke 16:6 was similar to the Old Testament "bath", and was about 39.5 litres (10.4 gallons). It is sometimes translated as firkin or gallon.

The pot mentioned in Mark 7:4 was a measure of roughly 500 cc (11/6 gallons). In various Bible translations it is rendered pot, pitcher, kettle, copper pot, copper bowl, vessel of bronze.

Sextarius
1 pint
(0.5 liter)

Hin
1 gallon
(3.75 liters)

Modios
2 gallons
(7.5 liters)

Bath
6 gallons
(23 liters)

Metretes
10 gallons
(38 liters)

Homer, cor
60 gallons
(227 liters)

Cana

Nobody knows for sure where the Cana of Jesus' time was located. Four places have been thought to be the location of Cana, two of them likely. Kafr Kanna, pictured below, is the traditional site of Cana.

Kafr Kanna is the traditional site of Cana.

Jesus Cleanses the Temple

JOHN 2:13–22

After Jesus turned water to wine at the wedding in Cana, He went to Capernaum with His mother and brothers and disciples. Then when the Passover time came, He went to Jerusalem. While at Jerusalem, Jesus overturned the tables of the money changers in the temple and talked with Nicodemus about being born again.

The cleansing of the temple took place in the Court of the Gentiles, the large outer courtyard in the temple, probably in AD 27. Anyone could enter this courtyard, but no Gentile dared go farther, into a more sacred courtyard.

Money changers

Each Jewish man was expected to attend the Passover, the annual festival being held when Jesus overturned the money changers' tables. They came from all over the ancient world, for Jews were scattered throughout the lands. Arriving in Israel, they made their way to the temple as soon as possible, for that is why they came, to celebrate the Passover there. With them they brought money from their native lands.

But in the temple this foreign money could not be used to buy animals for sacrifices, for it was considered unclean.

In New Testament times, many different coins circulated in Palestine, including Roman denarius, quinarius and sesterce; Greek drachma, didrachma, tetradrachma, and assarion; and Tyrian shekels and half shekels, as well as Herod the Great's own coinage.

So money changers set up little tables in the large outer courtyard, the Court of the Gentiles, where they exchanged acceptable Jewish coins for foreign coins.

There was no standard rate of exchange, so it became a time for bargaining. The money changers usually cheated these visitors as often and as much as they could.

Jesus objected to their cheating. He also objected to His Father's house, a house of prayer, becoming a giant bazaar.

Oxen, sheep, and doves

In the Court of the Gentiles of the temple, merchants sold animals for the sacrifices. Three types of animals used in the sacrifices are named here – oxen, sheep, and doves. There were others, such as bulls, goats, and pigeons. Certain offerings called for certain types of animals. Also, a man's station in life suggested certain types of animals – a bullock for a man on a level with the high priest, a he-goat for a nobleman, a she-goat or sheep for an ordinary person, and a pigeon or dove for a poor person. A very poor person could just offer some fine flour.

Herod's temple building

The people with Jesus said that the temple had been under construction for 46 years. Herod the Great, who ruled from 37 BC to AD 4, was a prolific builder. The temple was one of his most ambitious projects. He began to build it around 20 to 19 BC. But even though the temple had been under construction for 46 years at this time, it would continue under construction for 30 more, to be finished in AD 64. But the

sad ending to all this magnificent work came only six years after it was completed, in AD 70. The Romans destroyed Jerusalem completely, including this beautiful building. It has never been rebuilt. Over the site of the temple today stands a Moslem mosque, called the Dome of the Rock.

A scourge of cords

Jesus wove a whip from rope or cords to punish the merchants. This was quite a mild whip, compared with the scourge which the Romans used against Jesus before His crucifixion. That one had sharp pieces of metal imbedded in the whip to tear the flesh as it beat the victim.

MONEY CHANGING AT THE TEMPLE

Only coins of the Jews or of Tyre – silver didrachmas or tetradrachmas – could be offered as gifts at the Jerusalem temple. Jewish worshippers would visit the money changers, who set up tables in the Court of the Gentiles, to get the necessary coins.

It seems odd that the Jews could use coins of Tyre, but not those of Greece and Rome. Perhaps it was felt they could not use for holy purposes coins of nations by whom the Jews had been conquered, while the Jews did not mint any silver coins themselves.

It is known that the money changers charged anything from four to eight per cent commission and often cheated their clients, sharing their gains with some of the temple priests. Hence Jesus' denunciation of them as thieves.

Nicodemus

JOHN 2:23–3:21

After Jesus turned water to wine at Cana, He, with His mother and brothers, went to Capernaum, where He stayed awhile. Spring came and with it the annual Passover festival. Jesus went to Jerusalem to celebrate, as all Jewish men were expected to do. He visited the temple, where He chased the merchants and money changers from the Court of the Gentiles. During this festival, a high Jewish official named Nicodemus visited Jesus at night, to ask Him more about God.

Nicodemus learned that being born again was the door to God's kingdom.

Nicodemus was a "ruler of the Jews", a Pharisee, and a member of the powerful council called the Sanhedrin. As a Pharisee, he was a member of the most strict and one of the most influential groups of Jewish leaders. As a member of the Sanhedrin, he took part in the council of 70 elders who ruled the Jewish people. This council, with the high priest as president, could try a person for a crime. It could pass the death sentence, but under the Romans, could not actually execute that person.

Jesus was tried before the Sanhedrin and was judged guilty and sent to Pilate for His judgement, which would lead to execution. This council could even judge a high priest, or the king, so it was similar to a supreme court in today's society.

Nicodemus risked losing this high position when he came to Jesus. As a whole, the council hated Jesus, viewing Him as an imposter and certainly not God's Son, as He claimed. So Nicodemus came at night, when superstition kept most people off the streets.

It seems that Nicodemus became a secret believer. He admitted to Jesus immediately that, despite his position, he believed Jesus had come from God. Later, when the Sanhedrin tried to arrest Jesus, Nicodemus asked if their law permitted them to try a person until he first appeared before them and an attempt had been made to find if he was guilty or innocent (John 7:50–52).

Later, when Jesus was crucified, Nicodemus and Joseph of Arimathea placed expensive spices on His body and buried Him in a new tomb. The Bible is silent about Nicodemus after that, but one tradition says that he was baptized by Peter and John, removed from the Sanhedrin, and was supported by a wealthy relative named Gamaliel.

Where Nicodemus met Jesus

Most paintings show Nicodemus on a rooftop with Jesus. Although the Bible does not say this, it was probably the only logical place to meet at night. Some say this was a home that the apostle John owned in Jerusalem, with a guest chamber built on the rooftop, as was often done.

It was a spring evening, with gentle winds blowing through the streets of Jerusalem as Nicodemus made his way up the outside stairway leading to this upper room. The meeting was lighted by oil lamps.

Nicodemus had always thought that his religion was the doorway into the kingdom of God. A person received new life after he entered. This thought was used in Nicodemus' time to express what happened to a bridegroom after his wedding or a king after his coronation.

Jesus told Nicodemus that the new birth, being "born again", was the doorway to God's kingdom. No one could enter heaven without it. The right order was: believe in Jesus as Saviour from sin, turn to God for forgiveness and receive new birth, which leads into His kingdom.

The Woman at the Well

JOHN 4:1–42

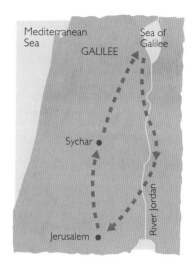

The Passover ended, and Jesus left Jerusalem for the open countryside of Judea. With His disciples He went to a quiet place, probably at the Jordan River near the place where He had been baptized. There His disciples began to baptize those who repented from their sins. Some of the disciples of John the Baptist complained to John about this, but John reminded them again that Jesus was from God. Not long after that, Jesus and His disciples headed back toward Galilee, going through Samaria, where most Jewish people refused to travel. At Sychar, He met "the woman at the well".

The western route from Galilee to Jerusalem passed through Samaria, and the eastern one went through Perea.

Samaria and the Samaritans

In 721 BC King Sargon of Assyria destroyed Samaria, the capital city of Israel's Northern Kingdom. He took the people away to Assyria and brought foreigners into the land to live. In time these foreigners intermarried with the few Jewish people who were left, producing a mixed race. These people became known as Samaritans. The region in which they lived was called Samaria. The Jewish people hated these "mixed" people and

Jacob's Well, under the Saint Photini Church at Bir Ya'qub, Israel.

usually tried to avoid travelling through their territory. Some say the Judeans felt this way even more than the Galileans, and that some Galilean people were not as reluctant to travel through Samaria as their Judean kinsmen. Jesus, of course, seemed to have no problem with this, and even chose to go through Samaria. The route was certainly much shorter than going around through Perea.

The well

After Jacob returned from Paddan Aram, where he had lived for 20 years, and where he had married Leah and Rachel, he settled near Mount Gerizim and bought a parcel of land from Hamor, Shechem's father (Gen. 33:18–20). Jacob's son Joseph was later buried at this place (Josh. 24:32). The well where Jesus talked with the Samaritan woman is thought to be the one which Jacob dug at this place. It is 1.2 m (4 feet) wide. In AD 670 a visitor wrote that it was 73 m

(240 feet) deep. In 1697 another said it was only 32 m (105 feet) deep. By 1861 it was only 23 m (75 feet) deep. The reason for this changing depth is that pilgrims threw pebbles into the well throughout the centuries, gradually filling it in. But water from the well is still pure enough to drink.

Sychar

The village near Jacob's well was on the main road from Jerusalem to Galilee. It was probably on the eastern slope of Mount Ebal, about half a mile north of Jacob's well. A modern village, Askar, is thought to be the site where Sychar was located.

Mounts Ebal and Gerizim

Ebal and Gerizim stand like twins, Ebal slightly more than 915 m (3,000 feet), Gerizim slightly less. The Samaritans worshipped in the open at the top of Mount Gerizim.

The Nobleman's Son Is Healed

JOHN 4:46–54

After leaving the Passover festival in Jerusalem, where He cleansed the temple and talked with Nicodemus, Jesus returned to Galilee after stopping in Samaria to talk with a woman at a well. Back home in Galilee, Jesus returned to Cana, where He had turned water into wine. There He met a nobleman of Capernaum, who begged Jesus to heal his sick son.

The nobleman

During the time of Jesus there were a number of types of leaders in the land. The scribes, Pharisees, Sadducees, high priest, and chief priests were religious leaders. Herod was a tetrarch, or Roman civil leader. Pilate was a procurator, another Roman civil leader with somewhat different status, though he had similar responsibilities.

Centurions were military leaders, over groups of 100 Roman soldiers each. Publicans were tax collectors, appointed by Rome, but many were Jewish men. The nobleman in this story was a courtier, someone appointed to the service of Herod, the tetrarch. He was an official attached to the office of the highest ranking position in the land, and was probably a Jewish man, not a Roman.

A lesson in power

The nobleman or courtier brought out a lesson in contrasting power. He, as an officer in the court of Herod, had power over the people of the land, including Jesus. But he had no power over the sickness of his own son. Jesus alone had that, and he begged Jesus to save his son's life. Great and powerful people are, like others, often weak and helpless in certain personal situations.

A synagogue in Capernaum, on the northwest shore of the Sea of Galilee.

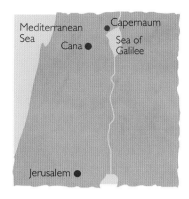

The locations of Cana and Capernaum.

Capernaum to Cana

Cana was located in the highlands of Galilee, contrasting with Capernaum, which was below sea level, on the northwest shores of the Sea of Galilee. Later, Jesus would make His headquarters at Capernaum. Cana was about 30–40km (20–25 miles) from Capernaum. Note their locations on the map.

The seventh hour

Clocks and watches were not developed in Bible times, so people had to tell time in other ways. The sun determined the time during the day, beginning with sunrise and ending with sunset. Between sunrise and sunset were 12 divisions, called hours. When the sun rose at 6:00 in the morning and set at 6:00 in the evening, the hours were exactly 60 minutes each. But when the day shortened, so did the hours.

The seventh hour was 1:00 in the afternoon of a full 12-hour day. The third hour was 9:00 in the morning and the ninth hour was 3:00 in the afternoon.

Sundials were used in some places to measure the progress of the day. But average people could not afford sundials in their yards.

Night was divided into four "watches", two before midnight and two after. With sunrise at 6:00 and sunset at 6:00, the first watch began at sunset and ended at 9:00 P.M. The second began at 9:00 and ended at midnight. The third began at midnight and ended at 3:00 A.M. The fourth went from 3:00 to 6:00 A.M. These watches would be longer or shorter, depending on the length of the day.

Miracles of healing

Thirty-five miracles of Jesus are given in the four Gospels. Of these, 23 are miracles of healing. Three concerned raising someone from the dead.

In His healing miracles, Jesus did many different kinds of work. He drove out demons, stopped a haemorrhage, healed paralysis, cured leprosy, restored a withered hand, removed blindness, caused a dumb person to speak, removed deafness, restored a cut-off ear, and made a lame person walk.

Jesus' miracles showed a power that no mere man possessed. They proved that He had come from God. All who saw them should have realized that He is God's Son. But those who were closest to "religion" seemed to be the most difficult to persuade. They simply refused to believe. Only a few of them ever admitted that this Man who could heal and raise from the dead was more than a mere man!

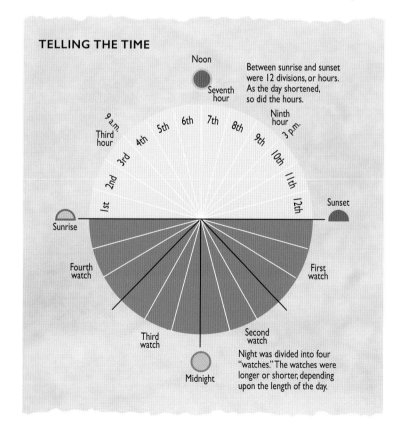

TELLING THE TIME

Noon

Seventh hour

Between sunrise and sunset were 12 divisions, or hours. As the day shortened, so did the hours.

Ninth hour

Third hour

Sunrise

Sunset

Fourth watch

First watch

Third watch

Second watch

Midnight

Night was divided into four "watches." The watches were longer or shorter, depending upon the length of the day.

Jesus at the Synagogue

LUKE 4:16–31

Mount of Precipitation, the place said to be where people tried to kill Jesus.

After talking with the woman at the well, Jesus and His disciples returned to Galilee, stopping first at the village of Cana. A nobleman of Capernaum arrived at Cana, asking Jesus to heal his son, who was at home in Capernaum. Jesus spoke, and the child was healed, even though he was 30–40 km (20–25 miles) away. After that, Jesus returned to His hometown, Nazareth, where He visited the synagogue on the Sabbath.

The synagogue

As the word "church" refers to both the building and the people who gather there, so also does the word "synagogue". It means "to gather together".

Synagogues began during the time of the Exile, when the temple in Jerusalem was destroyed and the Jewish people were carried away to Babylon. Without home or temple, they gathered together to worship and teach the Scriptures. By the time of Jesus, every Jewish community had a synagogue. Ten or more Jewish men could start one. A city the size of Jerusalem had many.

The synagogue was supposed to be built on the highest hill in town, near water, with the entrance toward the east, as was the temple. It was to be built so that the people at prayer faced Jerusalem.

Inside, the synagogue had a Torah shrine, where the scrolls with the Scriptures were kept. Nearby was the *bema*, an elevated platform of wood or stone, where Scriptures were read and benedictions were given.

Two or three rows of stone benches surrounded the room, with a special row for the elders and rulers of the synagogue. A menorah, a large seven-branched lampstand, as well as other lamps and objects of worship, were placed in the room.

People gathered on the Sabbath to worship at the synagogue. Scriptures were read and prayers offered. A visiting rabbi might preach, though preaching was not a vital part of the service.

The synagogue was also a centre of education for the village, for there was no public education at that time.

The Sabbath call to worship

As the sun began to set each Friday evening, the Sabbath began. From the roof of the synagogue minister's house, a double blast of a trumpet signalled the time for work to cease. A second time it sounded, and then a third before the horn-blower quickly laid it aside so that he himself would not break the Sabbath by bearing a burden.

The Sabbath had begun, and the festive Sabbath lamp was lit. This holy day would last until sunset on Saturday evening.

On Saturday morning, people began to gather early at the synagogue service.

Jesus had attended this Nazareth synagogue as a child and young man. He had been known in the last few years as the carpenter.

The people were especially interested when this hometown carpenter stood to read the Scripture this particular Sabbath. He had grown up among the people and was much aware of each person in the room, especially the leaders of the synagogue who eyed Him suspiciously, wondering at the reports they had heard of His miracles and His activities in the temple in Jerusalem.

Nazareth – Jesus' hometown

About 30 years earlier, the angel Gabriel had announced to Mary that she would become the mother of the Messiah, God's Son. Mary and Joseph left Nazareth, where this announcement was made, and moved to Bethlehem, where Jesus was born. After a short time in Egypt, they returned to Nazareth, where Joseph resumed his work as carpenter until he evidently died during Jesus' teen years. Jesus then became the carpenter, supporting Mary, until it was time for His ministry to begin.

The Miracle of Fish

LUKE 5:1–11

After the people of Jesus' hometown, Nazareth, tried to kill Him, He moved to Capernaum, a town on the northwest shores of the Sea of Galilee. There He probably lived with His disciple, Simon Peter, a fisherman. One day Jesus was teaching the multitudes by the seaside but was gradually being pushed towards the water. He stepped into one of the two boats used by Peter, his brother Andrew, and their fishing partners, James and John, also brothers. A short distance from shore, Jesus taught the people. Then He called to Peter to go fishing again. Peter said that he and his partners had fished all night without a catch. But when the fishermen did as Jesus suggested, their nets filled with so many fish that they were almost breaking. Peter bowed before Jesus, who told him that these four would be "fishers of men". These four fishermen later became His most important followers. John and Peter authored books included in the New Testament.

The fishing business

Peter and his brother Andrew were apparently involved in a fishing business with James, his brother John, and their father Zebedee. Peter and Andrew lived in Capernaum. James, John, and Zebedee lived a short distance to the east in Bethsaida. Zebedee had hired servants (Mark 1:20), so he must have had a thriving business. It is thought that John may have had a second home in Jerusalem, where Nicodemus visited Jesus by night. John knew the high priest personally, so he was able to go into the courtyard when Jesus was tried. John may have supplied the high priest's household with fish from the Sea of Galilee. If so, he would have become acquainted with the high priest through business dealings.

Many of the villages and cities of the land depended on the Sea of Galilee for fish, which were sold fresh to nearby places but because of the heat had to be dried for distant sales. Josephus, an ancient historian, recorded that there were about 330 fishing boats on the Sea of Galilee during his lifetime, only a few years after Jesus was on earth.

The Sea of Galilee

This "sea" is really a large inland lake about 95 km (60 miles) north of Jerusalem. As the Jordan River tumbles from north to south toward its final destination in the Dead Sea, it passes through this large hole where the Sea of Galilee has accumulated.

The surface of the water is about 210 m (685 feet) below sea level. The water in the sea is as much as 45 m (150 feet) deep.

Since this is a fresh-water body, it provides excellent fishing. There were about 30 fishing towns around this sea in Jesus' time, with perhaps 100,000 people in them.

Capernaum was one of the largest of these fishing villages. Bethsaida, home of James and John and Zebedee, actually means "house of fish".

The four fishermen in this story used nets to catch their fish. These were probably drag nets drawn together into a tightening circle between two boats. There were also cast nets, skilfully thrown by one man.

St Peter's Fish is the variety from which Peter took his tax money when Jesus told him to throw in a hook and pull out the first fish, which had a shekel in its mouth. This also shows that fishing with hook and line was common in Jesus' time.

219

Jesus Calls Four Disciples

MATTHEW 4:18–22; MARK 1:16–20

After Jesus came to live at Capernaum, perhaps at Simon Peter's house, He attracted crowds who came to hear Him teach and preach. One day He taught a crowd while sitting in a boat, speaking to the people on the shore. After He finished, Jesus told Peter, Andrew, James, and John to go fishing again. Even though they had caught nothing all night, they went with Him. As they pulled in their nets, they were so filled with fish that they almost broke. From this miracle, they recognized again that Jesus was more than just a man. Afterward, Jesus would call them to become "fishers of men".

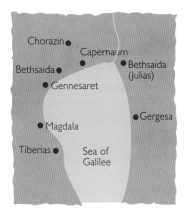

One site of Bethsaida.

Jesus tells Peter and Andrew to cast their net.

We are not quite sure how much time passed from the fishing miracle to the time when Jesus called the four fishermen to become His full-time followers, "fishers of men". Perhaps it was the same day. Mark and Matthew say that Peter and Andrew were casting nets into the sea, while James and John were sitting in a boat, mending their nets.

The nets

Peter and Andrew tossed out a type of net called the cast net, or casting net. It was about 3 m (10 feet) wide, bell-shaped, with lead weights around the edges. A fisherman twirled the net so that it fell flat on the water, with the lead weights causing it to sink over the fish. The fisherman then pulled on a cord attached to the centre, drawing the net around the fish.

James and John were probably mending the large drag nets pulled by their boats. Fishermen constantly had the job of washing weeds and other undesirable things from their nets and mending the places where the nets were torn.

The hired servants

Zebedee and his family had hired servants, a sign of prosperity (Mark 1:20). Evidently, Peter and Andrew's family did not. Some think that Zebedee's real home was in Jerusalem and

that the family fishing business in Bethsaida was "home" only as a convenience. Salome was Zebedee's wife, and mother of James and John. She later followed Jesus and ministered to His need, probably supplying money for His support and the support of her sons. John's acquaintance with the high priest may have been through his parents, who may have marketed fish from the family business in Jerusalem for years. The parents of Simon Peter and Andrew are not mentioned, only those of James and John. The Bible does mention Peter's mother-in-law, but not his parents. The only reference to Peter's father is that Peter was "Simon, son of John [or Jonah]" (John 21:15).

Leaving the family business

A first glance suggests that Jesus walked along the shore of the sea, saw these four men, and told

A pile of fishing nets and ropes today in Israel. James and John were mending their nets when Jesus called them.

them to follow Him. From this, some have been tempted to think that these were strangers, whom Jesus encountered and abruptly caused them to leave their work to be His followers.

Actually James, John, Peter, and Andrew were seen with Jesus shortly after His baptism and temptation. They began to consider themselves His followers at that time, but not enough to leave their profitable business and follow Him full-time.

James and John may have been Jesus' cousins. Three women were at Jesus' cross and at the tomb on Sunday morning (Mark 15:40; 16:1). Two were named Mary and one was Salome. Two women named Mary were at the cross with the mother of Zebedee's sons, James and John (Matt. 27:56). And two women named Mary were with Jesus' mother and His mother's sister (John 19:25). It seems that Salome, mother of James and John, was also the sister of Mary, mother of Jesus. If so, Jesus was a cousin of James and John.

John the Baptist was also related to Jesus. Mary and Elizabeth were either cousins or Elizabeth was Mary's aunt. John was thus either Jesus' first or second cousin.

Bethsaida

The exact location of Bethsaida is not known for sure. The map shows two possible locations. The name Bethsaida-Julias was a new name Philip the Tetrarch gave it, honouring Augustus' daughter Julia.

At the Capernaum Synagogue

MARK 1:21–28; LUKE 4:31–37

After Jesus moved from Nazareth to Capernaum, He performed a miracle for His four fishermen friends. They had fished throughout the night without a catch. After Jesus taught a crowd from one of their boats, He suggested they go out again on the sea. When they did, they caught so many fish that their net almost broke. Later, Jesus called these four fishermen to follow Him, so they left their fishing business to become His full-time disciples. One Sabbath Day, Jesus went into the synagogue at Capernaum, where He healed a man with an evil spirit in him.

Important people at Capernaum

Since Capernaum was at an important checkpoint on two trading routes, a number of important people lived there. Jesus touched the lives of several. He healed the palsied servant of a centurion, the Roman army officer in charge of the garrison there (Matt. 8:5–13). He healed the son of an official in the court of King Herod Antipas (John 4:46–54); He called the customs officer, Levi or Matthew, to become one of His 12 disciples; and He raised from the dead the daughter of Jairus, the ruler of the synagogue at Capernaum.

Four columns and an aisle from the Capernaum synagogue.

Miracles at Capernaum

In addition, Jesus performed other miracles at Capernaum: He caused four disciples to catch fish in a miraculous way (Luke 5:1–11); He drove an evil spirit from a man in the Capernaum synagogue (Mark 1:21–28); He healed Peter's mother-in-law and many others (Mark 1:29–34); He healed a paralyzed man let down through a roof (Mark 2:1–12); He told Peter how to catch a fish that miraculously had a coin in it (Matt. 17:24–27).

The curse on Capernaum

Jesus predicted Capernaum's ruin because its people refused to fully believe in Him, even though He lived among them (Matt. 11:23–24). Capernaum remains in ruins today, as it has for hundreds of years.

Teaching with authority

Why the difference between Jesus' teaching and that

of the scribes, the professional religious leaders? Jesus taught what He had learned firsthand, for He had lived in heaven with His Father, God. He therefore taught what was vital to the lives of His listeners, not merely what had been learned in books. He taught things that would change people's lives and not merely enlighten them. He taught with authority, for He had authority as God's Son, far more authority than the scribes, even though they thought they had more authority than He. He taught what was important for today, and not merely the traditions of the past. He taught truth, God's truth, and not merely human rules and principles. And He taught the way to know God, not merely the way to conform to authority.

Evil spirits and Jesus

Jesus recognized the evil spirit in the man at the Capernaum synagogue. The evil spirit also recognized Him immediately and called him the Holy One of Israel. How strange that the demon knew that He was God's Son, but the religious leaders of the day could not recognize that!

SYNAGOGUE

The most important piece of furniture in a synagogue was the shrine which held the Torah, the sacred roll or scroll on which the Scriptures were written. This roll of course contained nothing of what we know today as the New Testament and only parts of what we know as the Old Testament.

The Torah shrine was often of carved wood, sometimes ornamented with beautiful hangings. It might hold one or more scrolls. There was also a platform called the bema, made of stone or wood, from which the readings and blessings were given.

Around the walls were stone benches where the people sat. The elders and rulers of the synagogue sat apart.

BOOKS OF JESUS' TIME

Books with separate pages did not come into use until more than a hundred years after the time of Jesus. During His time on earth, books were scrolls.

In Jesus' time scrolls were usually made of animal skins, smoothed so that they could be written on. The skins were rolled on two rods so that the beginning was on the right and the ending on the left.

Writing was done in narrow columns, usually with a reed or metal pen and ink. As these columns were read, the scroll was rolled from the left rod onto the right one.

The scroll was actually not one large skin, but several, sewed together. One found at Qumran was made of 17 skins. One place where they were joined was glued while the other places were sewed.

A scroll might be about a foot high, but when unrolled might be as long as 7 m (24 feet). Only the skins of "clean" animals were used.

Jesus Heals Peter's Mother-in-Law

MATTHEW 8:14–17; MARK 1:29–34; LUKE 4:38–41

When the people of Nazareth rejected Jesus and tried to kill Him, He moved to Capernaum, where He probably lived with Peter in his house. Jesus called Peter, Andrew, James, and John to follow Him full time, leaving their profitable fishing business. One Sabbath after that, Jesus created quite a stir in the nearby synagogue in Capernaum when He commanded an evil spirit to come from a man. After this service in the synagogue was over, Jesus returned home with Peter, Andrew, James, and John and found Peter's mother-in-law sick with a fever. Jesus healed her immediately. By evening, crowds of sick people had gathered to ask Jesus to heal them.

PETER AND JESUS

- Peter was a fisherman; Jesus was a carpenter by trade.
- Peter owned a house; Jesus never owned a house (as far as we know).
- Peter was married, for he had a mother-in-law; Jesus was not.
- Peter recognized that Jesus was the Messiah, God's Son, but perhaps not at first.
- Peter followed Jesus and became a dynamic apostle, one of the truly great figures in our Christian heritage.
- Peter wrote two books in the New Testament; he dedicated his life to tell others about Jesus, his Saviour and Lord.

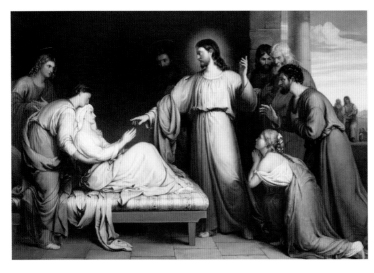

Healing Peter's Mother-in-Law by John Bridges.

Peter's home

The synagogue in Capernaum faced southeast, looking toward the Sea of Galilee, only a few hundred feet away. Between the synagogue and the sea were streets lined with private houses. One of these belonged to Peter, where apparently Jesus and Andrew and Peter's mother-in-law also lived. In the fifth century AD an octagonal church was built over this site and the ruins of this church may still be seen today among the ruins of ancient Capernaum.

Those who excavated here say that the ruins of a home beneath this church show that it existed between the first century BC and the second part of the first century AD. For many years after Peter's time, the house apparently was used for some Christian purpose, for inscriptions were found with the name of Jesus on them. They call Him the Lord, the Most High God. These inscriptions are in four languages including Greek and Aramaic, languages common in Jesus' time and later in Galilee.

This house, which many believe was Peter's house, where his mother-in-law was healed by Jesus, was southeast of the synagogue, toward the Sea of Galilee. It was only about 60–90 m (200–300 feet) from the synagogue.

Houses of Capernaum were made of basalt stones with doorways leading into the street. Doorjambs found on these houses show that they had doors which opened and closed. Doorways inside the houses were open, without doors that opened or closed. They were single-story homes, with roofs of mud mixed

with straw. Nothing was found to indicate drainage or private toilets within the houses.

Homes were very modest, with no touches of luxury. But Peter was a town dweller, not a Bedouin who lived in a tent, so he probably enjoyed a private stone house with enough room to include Jesus, Andrew, and his mother-in-law also. This seems to show that Peter was certainly not a wealthy man, but he was prosperous enough to have his own home in a neighbourhood close to the most important building in town, the synagogue, which was also the highest point in town.

These ruins show part of the foundation of the octagonal church built over Peter's house. Below, a painting of *The Man with the Withered Hand* by James Tissot.

HEALING FROM HIS HANDS

Jesus healed many different types of diseases and injuries. Though the names of some diseases differ, it is thought that these were not different from diseases which still trouble people today. Here are some of the sicknesses and health problems which He healed:
- He drove out demons and evil spirits.
- He gave sight to the blind.
- He gave hearing to the deaf.
- He gave speech to those who could not talk.
- He cured leprosy.
- He helped lame people walk.
- He stopped haemorrhages.
- He removed paralysis.
- He restored a withered hand (illustrated to the left).
- He restored an ear that was cut off.
- He took away a fever.
- He raised people from the dead.

A Healing Tour of Galilee

MATTHEW 4:23–25; MARK 1:35–39; LUKE 4:42–44

While Jesus lived in Capernaum, He called Peter, Andrew, James, and John to become His full-time disciples. Shortly after that, Jesus created a stir in the synagogue at Capernaum by commanding an evil spirit to leave a man. That same day, Jesus healed Peter's mother-in-law at Peter's house. By evening crowds of sick people had gathered for His healing. The next morning Jesus went to a lonely place, but the crowds followed Him there. Then He went with Peter, Andrew, James, and John on a tour of Galilee, preaching and teaching in the synagogues and healing many.

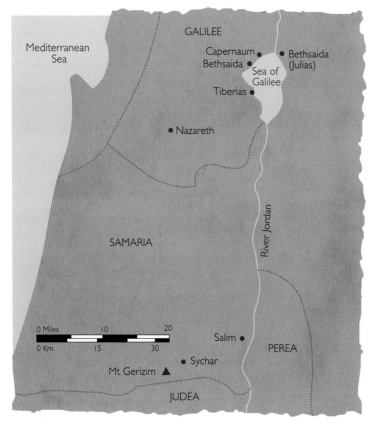

The map shows Galilee in relationship to the other regions.

During New Testament times there were many who were burdened with disease, injury, and other health problems. Sanitation was poor with almost no strict controls over refuse, waste water, or toilets. Flies were abundant and through them and open refuse, disease was easily spread from one person to another. Detection of disease was primitive. Medicine was crude, with little recognition of the causes of sicknesses, and very little knowledge of diseases themselves. Remedies were crude, like home-made medicines. Compared with medicine today and the advances in diagnosis and surgery and drugs for healing, little was known. Doctors were almost powerless to help the sick.

In this setting, one is not surprised to see crowds of hopelessly sick people swarming around Jesus for healing. Once sick, they had little hope and waited till their bodies overcame the disease or succumbed to it.

Blindness was common in Bible lands. The failure to recognize safety in daily life left many with injuries. Those who were blind or lame or dumb were forced to become beggars, for there were hardly enough jobs for the strong and healthy.

Imagine in this setting the thrill of being healed, with sight or hearing or speech restored! Imagine walking again without a crude crutch or using a withered hand again!

Unfortunately it was commonly thought in Jesus' time that sickness was always tied to some sin. Thus those suffering from sickness also suffered with this stigma on them.

Through the Roof to Jesus

MATTHEW 9:1–8; MARK 2:1–12; LUKE 5:17–26

When Jesus arrived home in Capernaum, where He may have been living with Peter, He found Peter's mother-in-law sick with a fever, after a synagogue service. He healed her, and the word of His healing power spread. By evening crowds of sick people were surrounding Him for healing. The next morning He went to a lonely place, but the crowd followed. Jesus then began a tour of Galilee with Peter, Andrew, James, and John, preaching and teaching in the synagogues and healing many. When He returned to Capernaum, crowds surrounded the house so that some men could not bring a paralyzed friend inside for Jesus to heal him. So they lowered the man through the roof, and Jesus healed him.

The friends of the paralyzed man lower him through a hole in the roof.

A hole in the roof

Most people are confused by this incident, for they immediately think of a modern home with a very sturdy wood roof covered by composition shingles or tar and gravel. But the rooftops of Bible-time homes were usually flat, not with a peak as is true of many homes today. Houses of Capernaum, where this story took place, have been excavated.

Archaeologists have found that these homes were simple, with walls made of stone and the flat roofs probably made of mud mixed with straw. It would have been a simple matter to pull apart a section of this sun-baked mud and straw mixture and let the lame friend down through the opening. Most houses in Capernaum, at least those near the synagogue where Peter's home was probably located, had courtyards with outside stairways leading to the roof. Thus the men found it easy to carry their paralyzed friend to the rooftop by way of this stairway.

People often sat on the rooftops of their homes on warm nights. Sometimes they slept on these flat roofs to escape the heat and lack of ventilation in the houses themselves.

Size of houses

The Mishnah, important Jewish writings before the third century AD, contains much information about life in ancient times. It says Bible-time houses were quite small. It says smaller homes were about 2.5 by 3.5 m (9 by 12 feet) and larger homes 3.5 by 4.5 m (12 by 15 feet). However, some think this referred only to the main room. Otherwise it would have been most difficult for a family to live within such a space.

Forgiveness of sins or healing?

Jesus could have told the man that he was healed. Instead He told him that his sins were forgiven. First, Jewish people of Jesus' time thought that sickness was usually the result of sin. Second, in this man's situation, this may well have been true, for as soon as Jesus forgave his sins, the man was healed.

Probably the most important reason for Jesus' statement was to inform the religious leaders there that He could forgive sins, which He proved by healing the man. They were angry at His statement, for it showed that Jesus was from God, for only God could forgive sins. The man and his friends had shown faith by coming to Jesus. Their faith brought healing and forgiveness to the man.

The religious leaders called Jesus' statement "blasphemy", for they did not accept Him as God's Son. If they had accepted Him as God's Son, they would have accepted His statement as truth from God.

Jesus Calls Matthew

MATTHEW 9:9; MARK 2:13–14; LUKE 5:27–28

After Jesus drove out a demon from a man in the Capernaum synagogue and healed Peter's mother-in-law, crowds began to gather, coming to be healed and bringing others to be healed. Jesus toured Galilee, healing and teaching, returning at last to His home in Capernaum. A paralyzed man was healed when he was lowered through a roof where Jesus was speaking. While Jesus was still in Capernaum, He walked to the customs booth, located on the main road that stretched from Egypt to Syria. The customs officer, or tax collector, was at work. Jesus called him to leave his work and become His full-time disciple. Levi, also called Matthew, obeyed and became one of the 12 disciples, later known as the 12 apostles.

The Calling of Saint Matthew by Hendrick Brugghen.

Levi was a Jewish tax collector in Capernaum. His work was to collect customs taxes on the main road that passed through Capernaum from Egypt to Syria. Levi, who took the name Matthew when he became Jesus' follower, was an officer in the service of Herod Antipas, and was thus a nobleman or courtier.

Matthew may have been in touch with Jesus before. It is possible, though there is no way to know for sure, that he was the nobleman who rushed to Jesus at Cana a short while earlier, begging Jesus to heal his son (John 4:46–54). If so, he certainly had experienced the miracle-working power of Jesus and was prepared to follow Him if called.

After he decided to follow Jesus as a full-time disciple, Matthew gave a dinner reception at his home for Jesus, inviting other tax collectors. He undoubtedly was trying to win them to Jesus also.

The hatred for tax collectors comes out at this time. Pharisees and their scribes bitterly denounced Jesus for eating with these tax collectors and sinners.

Matthew is not mentioned again in the Gospels, except in the lists of the 12 apostles.

Taxes and tax collectors
The Romans gathered many different kinds of taxes from their conquered nations. Every five years they put up the job of tax collector at auction. The highest bidder received the job and went about the work of collecting the taxes for which he was responsible. No one could tell him how much to collect, so he often collected far more than he should, as Zaccheus evidently did, cheating the people and often the Roman government.

In Jesus' time, there were taxes on real estate, customs taxes at seaports and city gates for goods shipped through them (which was Matthew's work), a tax on the produce of the land, usually 10 per cent, or even 20 per cent in some instances, income taxes, road taxes, taxes on animals and vehicles, sales taxes, and even taxes on the sale of slaves and other property. In addition to all of these taxes which the Romans gathered, the religious leaders collected a tax for their own support and the support of the temple.

Chief tax collectors were often Romans, but not always. Zacchaeus was a chief tax collector and apparently he was Jewish. These officials were in overall charge of collecting taxes. People such as Matthew may have been a step lower, doing the actual work.

A census was taken from time to time to make sure all the people were on the tax rolls. It was such a census that took Mary and Joseph from Nazareth to Bethlehem, where Jesus was born.

Tax collecting was often a family profession, passed from father to son, as was the work of carpenter or farmer. The Jewish people hated the tax collectors, for they gathered money from their own people to support the Gentiles, the Romans, and collected enough so that the people of Rome did not have to work, but spent their days at the games and easy living. Also many of the tax collectors made themselves rich at the expense of the poor.

The Jewish leaders tried to trick Jesus by asking if it was right to pay taxes to Caesar. If He answered yes, the people would hate Him. If He answered no, then Rome would hate Him.

ROMAN POWER

When Augustus took power as Roman emperor, it was agreed that in those parts of the empire where there was civil unrest, or threat of invasion, the emperor should rule direct, through his army commanders. The emperor had sole command of the army. The commanders, or legates, were given five-year periods in office, during which they ruled their assigned region. We read in Luke's Gospel of the legate Quirinius (Luke 2:1). In the case of smaller areas, procurators, answerable to the legate, were appointed.

The province of Syria, which included Judea, was on the borders of the empire and experienced considerable unrest; for this reason it was governed by a legate. Stable provinces were governed by a proconsul appointed by the Roman senate.

Sometimes "vassal" kings were allowed to rule, provided they followed Roman policies and were loyal to the emperor. Herod the Great ruled as such a vassal king from 40 BC to AD 4. On his death, his kingdom was divided among his sons, but when it was seen that Archelaus, king of Samaria, Judea and Idumea, was ineffective, he was replaced by the Roman procurator Pontius Pilate.

PEOPLE PAID TAXES IN JESUS' TIME, TOO

Taxes are as old as government, for government is usually supported by the working people who are governed. In Jesus' time, the land where He lived was under the control of the Roman Empire. Under the Roman Emperor were officials in charge of specific lands. Galilee was under the direct control of Herod Antipas (one of Herod's coins is shown to the left), whereas that part of the land where Jerusalem was located was under the control of Pontius Pilate (the coins to the right). These rulers were given various names, such as governor, tetrarch, king, and others. The title usually referred to the amount of power or authority given by the emperor and the amount of land governed. These rulers collected taxes to support their local governments and to support a part of the Roman government as a whole. Taxes were also levied to support the temple and the religious leaders. Matthew, or Levi, was part of that hated group in charge of collecting these taxes.

A Dinner at Matthew's House

MATTHEW 9:10–13; MARK 2:15–17; LUKE 5:29–32

After a tour of Galilee, healing and teaching, Jesus returned to Capernaum, where He was probably living with Peter. After healing a paralytic who had been let down through a roof, He went out to the customs booth along the trade route through Capernaum. Matthew, or Levi, was collecting tolls, or customs taxes from merchants who passed that way. Jesus told him to follow Him as a full-time disciple. Matthew gave up his business and followed Jesus. His first act was to give a dinner at his home, where he invited other tax collectors to meet Jesus. But this angered the religious leaders, who rebuked Jesus for eating with tax collectors and sinners.

Two views of sinners

This story points out the conflict between two views of sinners. The Pharisees looked on sinful people as tainted, to be avoided. They did not approve of a rabbi or any other important religious person mingling or eating with sinful people, especially with sinners such as tax collectors, who were hated by the people.

Jesus took the other view. He did not hate sinners, but their sins. He did not want to separate Himself from them, but mingled with them and taught and preached the Word to them so that they might be sorry about their sins and come to God.

The distinction is important today for those of us who follow Jesus. None of us is perfect. We are not to hate any sinner, but his or her sin. We are not to isolate ourselves from sinners, but mingle with them (not with their sin!), so that we might help them come to God through Jesus.

Jesus summed it up by telling the Pharisees that sick people (sinners) needed a physician (Himself). People who were well (without sin) did not. Of course, since there are no people without sin, even the self-righteous Pharisees needed Him more than they realized.

The Pharisees

The Pharisees were the "separated ones" or separatists, for they set themselves apart from others by the way they dressed and believed. Like other Jewish religious groups, they believed in the Old Testament Law. But the Pharisees thought that the oral law, the rules made up by the religious leaders, was equally inspired and was thus to be followed as much as God's Law.

The Pharisees and Jesus often opposed each other on this. Jesus taught that the Scriptures were the Law and were to be followed.

The Pharisees were middle-class people, not the wealthy aristocrats, as were the Sadducees. Many Pharisees were businessmen, merchants, and tradesmen. But even though they were part of these daily trades, they separated themselves from others by the strict way they adhered to both the Law and to human rules.

Because they were separatists, and thus separated themselves from others, they also gathered together into a close-knit group. There were about 6,000 during the time of Jesus. The Pharisees believed that they were being so righteous that they were helping to bring the Messiah.

Pharisees held conservative religious views and were committed to keeping the Law.

Wineskins and Patched Garments

MATTHEW 9:14–17; MARK 2:18–22; LUKE 5:33–39

After Jesus called Levi, or Matthew, the tax collector, to follow Him full time, Matthew invited Jesus to a reception at his house, where a number of other tax collectors were guests. This angered the Pharisees and other religious leaders. They openly criticized Jesus for eating with tax collectors and others of bad reputation. Jesus was also criticized by the disciples of John the Baptist for permitting His disciples to feast while they were fasting. Jesus responded with three parables – a parable about a bridegroom, one about patched cloth, and a third about wineskins.

Meanings

The first parable about the bridegroom meant that Jesus' disciples had no reason to fast while they were with Him, the Bridegroom. But after He was gone from them, they might wish to mourn by fasting. The second parable meant that His teaching was not merely a patch on the old religion of the day. It was a new garment to clothe His people. The third parable meant about the same. It was a new "bottle" or wineskin, not a new infilling of an old container, the religion of the day. To patch the dynamic new Gospel to the old religion would not work.

John and his disciples

Andrew was one of John the Baptist's disciples before he began to follow Jesus. When Andrew recognized Jesus as the Messiah, he found his brother, Simon Peter, and brought him to Jesus also. Some of John's disciples began to follow Jesus instead of John. Others remained with John, and in this incident, even criticized Jesus and His disciples. John himself had said that he must become less important and Jesus become more important. Apparently John never complained when a disciple stopped following him so that he might follow Jesus. John saw his work as God saw it – to point others to Jesus, the Son of God.

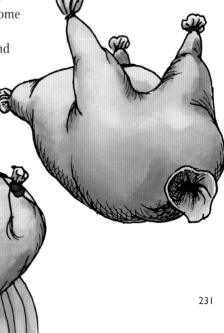

At the Pool of Bethesda

JOHN 5:1–47

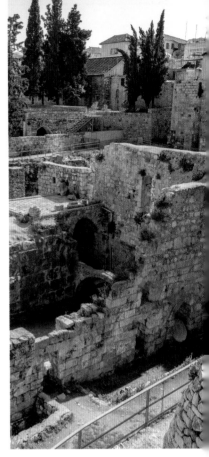

After Jesus called Levi, or Matthew, to become His full-time disciple, Matthew gave a reception for Jesus and invited many tax collectors. The Pharisees criticized Jesus for eating with such sinful people. Not long after that the disciples of John the Baptist criticized Jesus for letting His disciples feast while John's disciples and the Pharisees were fasting. Later, Jesus left Galilee, and went to a great festival in Jerusalem, probably the Passover, where He healed a man at the Pool of Bethesda.

Water for the city

Jerusalem in Bible times required enormous amounts of water, especially for the sacrifices at the temple. Water from rainfall was never enough. To bring water into the city, conduits were laid from large pools near Bethlehem, called Solomon's Pools. Inside the city, pools and cisterns held water until needed. One pool, called the Towers Pool, was just north of Herod's palace. A second was the Siloam Pool, south of the temple. A third was Israel Pool, joining the wall of the temple enclosure along the north. A fourth was the Sheep Pool, where the sheep were washed before being sacrificed in the temple. It was north of the Israel Pool. Farther north was another pool, the Pool of Bethesda.

The Pool of Bethesda. The ruins built over the pool are from a church that was destroyed in AD 614.

The temple mount itself was filled with cisterns, many quite large. These served the water needs of the temple.

The Pool of Bethesda

This pool was located near the sheep gate of Jerusalem, the gate farthest east on the northern wall. It had five porches, and its water was traditionally thought to cure people when an angel stirred it.

Bethesda was also called Bethzetha or Beth-zatha. It is mentioned only once in the Bible, in connection with this story. The name means "house of the olive". The Pool of Bethesda was actually twin pools, separated by a 6 m (20 foot) rock partition.

Jerusalem in New Testament times.

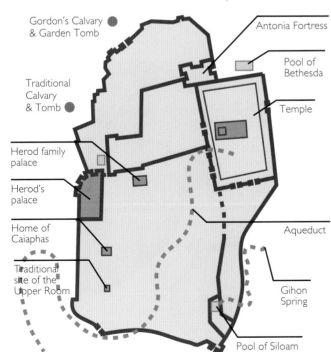

- Gordon's Calvary & Garden Tomb
- Traditional Calvary & Tomb
- Herod family palace
- Herod's palace
- Home of Caiaphas
- Traditional site of the Upper Room
- Antonia Fortress
- Pool of Bethesda
- Temple
- Aqueduct
- Gihon Spring
- Pool of Siloam

Sabbath in a Wheat Field

MATTHEW 12:1–8; MARK 2:23–28; LUKE 6:1–5

After Jesus visited Jerusalem, attending a great festival where He healed a man at the Pool of Bethesda, He returned to Galilee. Along the way, His disciples gathered a little wheat in a field and began to eat it. This angered the Pharisees, who accused the disciples of harvesting, or working, on the Sabbath.

Sabbath rules

The Law of Moses set apart the Sabbath as a day unto the Lord (Ex. 20:10; Deut. 5:14). It was to be a day of rest. But the Pharisees and others added to the Law, spelling out far more specifically than it did, what this meant. Harvesting was work, they said, so it should not be done on the Sabbath. Any form of plucking grain was harvesting. Therefore, even taking a few heads of wheat into one's hands and removing the grain was harvesting, which was breaking the Sabbath.

Jesus knew this was adding too much to the Law. When the Pharisees criticized His disciples for "breaking the Sabbath", Jesus told them that He was Lord of the Sabbath.

Were the disciples stealing?

The disciples were hungry, so they walked into a field and gathered some wheat to eat. Was this stealing? Today it would be thought to be stealing, for our laws do not arrange for hungry people to eat their neighbours' crops.

But the Law of Moses, which guided the people of Israel, did provide for such things. A hungry person could go into a neighbour's field or vineyard and eat his fill (Deut. 23:24–25). But he could not carry grapes away in a vessel or harvest his neighbour's wheat with a sickle.

The disciples were doing exactly what was right. They were taking food that the Law provided, and they were not "harvesting" on the Sabbath, but merely gathering some food to eat.

One tradition locates the wheat field where the disciples plucked the grain near a small village called Turan. It is about 10 km (6 miles) north of Kefar-Kana, the traditional location of Cana. In Arabic it is called Merj es-Sunbul – meadow of the ears of corn. This lovely meadow is immediately south of the little village of Turan.

Sabbath day's journey

Some people think Jesus was on the way to the synagogue referred to in the next story, for that healing took place on the Sabbath. There is nothing to confirm this, of course. But wherever He was travelling, it was within 2,000 cubits (1.2 km or 0.75 miles), as that was the limit a Jew was to travel on the Sabbath.

Wheat harvest was in June. Barley harvest was in May.

The Withered Hand

While returning to Galilee, after attending a great festival in Jerusalem, Jesus and His disciples stopped in a grain field to eat. The Pharisees criticized Jesus for letting His disciples gather some grain to eat on the Sabbath. They criticized Him again when He reached a synagogue, possibly the one in Capernaum, and healed a man with a withered hand. The Pharisees then plotted with the Herodians to kill Jesus.

The Herodians

Who were they? Nobody is quite sure. Some say they were Herod's soldiers, or courtiers, or some other group related to the rule of the Herod family. They were political, not religious. Undoubtedly in some way they supported the rule of the Herods over the land.

The rule of the Herods began with Antipater, father of Herod the Great. When the Roman general, Pompey, captured Jerusalem and Roman rule began, Antipater rose in power. This was in 67 BC. Later, in 48 BC, he risked his life for Julius Caesar in Caesar's struggle with Pompey. For this, Caesar rewarded him with Roman citizenship and appointed him procurator of Judea.

Antipater appointed his son, Phasael, as governor of Jerusalem and his son, Herod, as governor of Galilee. At this time, Herod was only 25 years old. In the numerous struggles that took place, Herod's power increased until in 40 BC Caesar and the Roman senate made him king of Judea.

Herod the Great, as he was called later, ruled until AD 4. During his rule, Jesus was born, and the babies of Bethlehem were massacred in an attempt to kill Jesus. When he died, his son, Archelaus, ruled Judea, Idumea, and Samaria until AD 6, when he was deposed because of his brutality. His brother, Herod Antipas, ruled Galilee and Perea; and his brother, Herod Philip, ruled a kingdom east of the Sea of Galilee. Antipas still ruled Galilee during Jesus' ministry.

During Jesus' time, Herodians were a group that wanted to keep the Herod family in power. Normally the Pharisees would have been their enemies, for loyal Jewish leaders hoped the Jews would regain their independence. But a common hatred for Jesus, plus fear that Rome would remove their power, caused the Pharisees and Herodians to join forces against Jesus.

Teaching by the Sea

MATTHEW 12:15–21; MARK 3:7–12

While returning from a great festival in Jerusalem, Jesus and His disciples stopped in a grain field to eat. The Pharisees criticized Him for letting the disciples pluck grain on the Sabbath. They said it was work and should not be done on the Sabbath. They criticized Him again when He healed a man with a withered hand on the Sabbath. After that, Jesus taught a great crowd by the shore of the Sea of Galilee.

Around the Sea of Galilee

Most of Jesus' ministry was focused on the small band of land surrounding the Sea of Galilee. Names such as Capernaum Bethsaida, Chorazin, Gergesa, Magdala, Gennesaret, and Tiberias bring to mind a number of important events in His ministry. One is reminded also of a miraculous catch of fish, Jesus walking on the water, and Jesus stilling a storm on the sea itself.

The home of Mary Magdalene was thought to be at Magadan, or Magdala. This is also mentioned as a place where Jesus landed on one of His journeys around the sea.

Tiberias was the capital of Herod Antipas, whom Jesus called "that fox". Herod ruled the region of Galilee and Perea and would later question Jesus when He was being judged for crucifixion. There is no mention that Jesus ever visited Tiberias, even though it was only just across the sea from His home in Capernaum.

Near Gergesa, Jesus healed a man possessed with many demons, causing the demons to enter some pigs who rushed into the sea. Somewhere, not far from the sea, Jesus multiplied loaves and fish so that He could feed 5,000 men, plus women and children.

Boats on the Sea of Galilee, that is, Lake Kinneret, near Capernaum.

The Jordan River enters the sea at the north and leaves it at the south, pausing to fill this deep basin with water. Surrounding the sea are gently rolling hills, sometimes called "mountains", with an occasional plain along the shore. The Plain of Gennesaret is a rather large, fertile plain along the western side of the sea, one of the few rich agricultural areas adjoining it.

Names of the Sea of Galilee

This sea, which is actually a large inland fresh-water lake, has had four names. Often in the Gospels it is called the Sea of Galilee, named for the region in which it was located. It is also called the Lake of Gennesaret (Luke 5:1), the Sea of Tiberias (John 6:1; 21:1), and the Sea of Kinnereth, or Chinnereth in some versions of the Bible (Num. 34:11). Gennesaret and Kinnereth, or Chinnereth, were areas near the sea. Tiberias was a town near it. Today it is called Lake Kinneret, but the name Sea of Galilee often appears as a second name.

Choosing the Twelve

MARK 3:13–19; LUKE 6:12–16

On one occasion, Jesus spent all night in prayer. In the morning He chose the 12 men who became known later as the 12 Apostles. These 12 would be His closest followers.

SIMON PETER
With his brother Andrew, Peter was active in a fishing business, probably in partnership with James, John, and their father Zebedee.

Originally Peter was from Bethsaida but moved to Capernaum, where Jesus probably lived in his home. Peter was a strong leader among the Twelve, though impetuous at times. His name originally was Simon, but Jesus changed it to Peter. He authored 1 and 2 Peter, two epistles of the New Testament.

JAMES, ZEBEDEE'S SON
Like his brother John, James was in the fishing business. He was probably in partnership with Peter and Andrew, and with his father Zebedee. The family was probably wealthy, for Zebedee had hired servants. James was the first of the Twelve to be martyred.

JOHN
Author of the Gospel according to John, and the three epistles of John, this apostle was among the "inner circle", those closest to Jesus. With his brother James, he was called a son of thunder, perhaps because of an emotional nature. He, with Peter and James, was with Jesus when He went apart from the others to pray in Gethsemane. After Jesus' crucifixion, John took care of Jesus' mother.

ANDREW
Simon Peter's brother, Andrew, was at first a disciple of John the Baptist. When he came to believe in Jesus as Messiah, he quickly became Jesus' disciple and led Peter to Jesus, also. Andrew and Peter were both sons of a fisherman named John, or Jonah, also probably of Bethsaida. At the feeding of the 5,000, Andrew told Jesus about the boy with the loaves and fish.

PHILIP
Like Peter and Andrew, Philip came from Bethsaida. When Philip believed in Jesus, he also brought Nathanael. He was present at the feeding of the 5,000, and Jesus asked him how they might buy bread for all of the people who were present.

THOMAS

Thomas was also called Didymus in some Bible versions, which meant "twin". Nobody is quite sure why he was called "twin". Thomas is often remembered as the doubter, the one who could not believe in Jesus' resurrection unless he felt Jesus' wounds.

The illustration of the disciples above is from Gerona Beatus, an illuminated manuscript in the Girona Cathedral. The portraits on this and the previous page are all paintings by Peter Paul Rubens.

BARTHOLOMEW (NATHANAEL)

Little is known about Bartholomew. It seems likely that he was also known as Nathanael. If so, Philip found him and brought him to Jesus not long after Philip had believed in Him. Nathanael was the one who asked if any good thing came from Nazareth; but when Jesus told about him sitting under a fig tree, he believed on Him.

MATTHEW

Levi was a tax collector, manning a booth along the busy trade route that led through Capernaum. Jesus called him to follow Him full time. After that, it seems that his name changed to Matthew, which meant "true". Matthew is the author of the first Gospel.

JAMES, SON OF ALPHAEUS

James was also known as James the Less or James the Younger. He may have been shorter or younger than James, brother of John.

SIMON THE ZEALOT

He was also called a Cananean (Matt. 10:4 in some Bible versions). Zealots belonged to a political party which wanted to overthrow Roman rule.

THADDAEUS

In the Gospels two lists of the Twelve name Thaddaeus. Another two lists name Judas (not Iscariot). He has also been called Lebbaeus.

JUDAS ISCARIOT

For 30 pieces of silver, Judas betrayed Jesus into the hands of His enemies. Later, he threw the money back at them and hanged himself.

The Sermon on the Mount

MATTHEW 5:1–8:1; LUKE 6:17–49

After Jesus returned from a great festival in Jerusalem, He was criticized by the Pharisees when His disciples gathered some grain to eat on the Sabbath. He was criticized again when He healed a man with a withered hand on the Sabbath. But Jesus continued to teach great crowds of people. After one night of prayer, He chose the Twelve, who would be His closest followers. Then His disciples followed as He led them into a high mountain not far from Capernaum, where He presented what we know as the Sermon on the Mount.

A beautiful view of the Sea of Galilee from the Mount of Beatitudes, a possible location of the Sermon on the Mount.

No one is sure about the exact location for the Sermon on the Mount. However, two locations are traditionally accepted – the Horns of Hattin, a short distance south of the Sea of Galilee, and a hilly region not far from Capernaum, toward the west. This second location is now called the Mount of Beatitudes, and a graceful church is erected on the highest "mountain" or hill in the region to commemorate the Sermon on the Mount, and especially the Beatitudes.

Since the thirteenth century AD the mountain known as the Horns of Hattin has been accepted by some as the location for the Sermon on the Mount. This mountain has twin peaks, separated by a crater-like formation.

The Mount of Beatitudes is much nearer to Capernaum. But there is as much reason to think that Jesus wanted to go to a lonelier mountain further away. So the mystery remains as to where the Sermon on the Mount was given.

Karnei Hitin (Horns of Hattin), also considered a possible location of the Sermon on the Mount. Below, a painting by Carl Bloch, *Sermon on the Mount*.

Beatitudes

As God gave the Law to Moses on Mount Sinai to guide His people's conduct and service, so Jesus gave His disciples the Sermon on the Mount to guide their conduct and service to Him and His Father.

The Beatitudes state simply some guidelines to happiness. "Blessed" in some Bible versions could as easily be translated "happy". Both the Ten Commandments and the Beatitudes say, "Accept the Lord as King and obey Him, for that is the way to happiness".

A Centurion's Servant

MATTHEW 8:5–13; LUKE 7:1–10

After a night of prayer, Jesus chose the 12 men who would be His apostles. Then, on a hill in Galilee, He gave a beautiful discourse which we have come to know as the "Sermon on the Mount". Jesus returned to Capernaum and was met by a centurion who pleaded with Jesus to heal his servant.

Roman legionary re-enactors.

Centurions who saved Paul from being beaten to death. Some Jews who hated Paul formed a mob and began to beat him. The Roman commander immediately sent centurions to restore order (Acts 21:27–40). Later, Paul was about to be whipped, but when he told a centurion that he was a Roman citizen he was quickly released (Acts 22:24–29).

Centurions who looked after Paul's safety. A plot against Paul's life was uncovered by his nephew. Escorted by two centurions, Paul slipped out of the city to a safer place (Acts 23:11–24).

Julius. This centurion guarded Paul on his voyage to Rome (Acts 27).

Centurions in the New Testament

The centurion in charge of Jesus' crucifixion. When Jesus was sentenced to death, it was the job of this centurion and his men to nail Jesus to the cross. Later, Pilate called the same centurion in to confirm Jesus' death (Mark 15:39, 43–45).

Cornelius. This centurion was a devout Gentile who respected God and prayed often. He and his family were baptized by Peter (Acts 10).

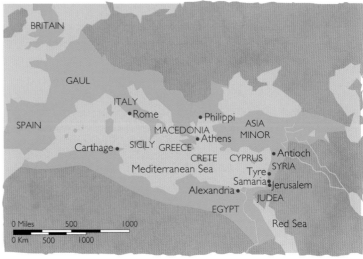

The Roman Empire at its greatest extent.

The Widow of Nain

LUKE 7:11–17

After Jesus' famous discourse, now known as the "Sermon on the Mount", He returned to Capernaum. A centurion came to Jesus, pleading for Him to heal a servant. Jesus spoke the word, and the servant was healed. Soon after this, Jesus entered Nain as a funeral procession was leaving, preparing to bury a widow's only son. Jesus spoke, and the son was raised to life again.

Nain today.

Capernaum to Nain, which Jesus would have travelled, enters the town from the northeast. Along this road, only a short distance from Nain, is a small burial ground where others believe the funeral procession was heading.

Nain and Nazareth.

Nain
The small town where Jesus raised the widow's son is reached from the west by travelling up a steep road with rock tombs on either side. Many believe that it was in one of these tombs that the widow's son was about to be buried. The road leading from

Funerals in Jesus' day
Failing to honour the dead was perhaps the greatest lack of respect a Jew could display. Bystanders were obligated to follow a funeral procession, with hired mourners adding to the wails of friends. The body was wrapped in cloth and carried on a bier. After the funeral, mourning continued for 30 days.

241

The Sower and Other Parables

MATTHEW 13:1–52; MARK 4:1–34; LUKE 8:4–18

Jesus taught and healed in Galilee, giving a long discourse known as the "Sermon on the Mount", healing a centurion's servant, and raising a widow's son from the dead at Nain. Jesus also warned of the coming destruction and desolation of three unbelieving towns – Capernaum, Chorazin, and Bethsaida. One day His mother and brothers came to take Him back to Nazareth, but He refused to go. Then He taught using parables, including a parable about a sower.

THE SOWER

After the soil had been ploughed with a crude wooden plough, pulled by oxen or other animals, the farmer "sowed the seed" on the ground and then used some method to get it under the soil. One easy method was to have animals walk over the planted soil until they had trampled the seed beneath.

Sowing followed one of two widely used methods. The first was to toss the seed by hand. The second method was to attach the bags of seed to animals, with holes in the bags large enough for the seeds to trickle out. As the animal walked over the ploughed field, the seeds were distributed.

Jesus' parable seemed to suggest the first method, with the seeds distributed by hand, as in the picture. Thorns and stones were common problems for Bible-time farmers, familiar to those who heard Jesus.

For centuries, people have told stories, or parables. A parable is a special type of story that teaches people something they do not know, by comparing it to something they do know. Jesus was a master storyteller. He used parables to help people understand things they did not know about God, by comparing them to things they did know on earth. For example, Jesus compared the kingdom of God to a mustard seed. God's kingdom was not easy to understand, but most knew about the tiny mustard seed. Jesus showed how the gospel is like a little seed. When planted in someone's life, it grows and matures until it becomes great and useful.

Jesus Stills a Storm

MATTHEW 8:18, 23–27; MARK 4:35–41;
LUKE 8:22–25

One day in Galilee Pharisees and their scribes came to Jesus, demanding a sign which would prove who He was. He refused. That same day, Jesus' mother and brothers came to take Him home to Nazareth. Again He refused. Then He taught His disciples by the Sea of Galilee, using parables to communicate His message. Also on that same important day, Jesus and His disciples crossed the Sea of Galilee. When a storm arose, Jesus stilled the storm, showing His disciples, and all others, that He is truly the Messiah, God's Son.

with a spoon. Within a very short time a storm can arise. These storms do not always have rain and dark clouds but can occur simply from the violent winds. Some waves have been reported as high as 6 m (20 feet) in recent years. These storms have caught fishermen off guard and can become very dangerous.

Boats on the Sea of Galilee

In Jesus' day, the Galilean fishing boat was probably the most common. It had to be sturdy, built to stand up to the sudden storms that rushed down on the sea. The historian, Josephus, thought there might have been as many as 330 fishing boats on the Sea of Galilee in his day.

Now held together by a steel frame, the "Jesus Boat" was revealed to archaeologists in 1986 when the water level in the Sea of Galilee receded. Although unlikely that Jesus actually used this boat, it dates from Jesus' time and was located near those cities of Galilee where He lived and travelled.

Christ on the Sea of Galilee by Eugène Delacroix.

Like a giant bowl of water among the hills of Galilee lies the Sea of Galilee. This is no ordinary lake , at 5.5 km (3.5 miles) long and 3 km (2.5 miles) wide, but an inland sea capable of quick and violent storms. At the surface, the Sea of Galilee is 210 m (680 feet) below sea level. This makes it easy for the winds blowing across the land of Galilee to come rushing down the hillsides and stir up the sea, as if someone was stirring a large bowl of water

243

Jesus Heals a Man with Demons

MATTHEW 8:28–34; MARK 5:1–20; LUKE 8:26–39

One day in Galilee was especially busy for Jesus. He had just returned from a teaching and healing tour when some religious leaders accused Him of working for Satan. Some of them demanded that He show them a miracle to prove that He was God's Son. Jesus refused, for He knew that even a miracle would not convince them. That same day, Jesus' mother and brothers came from Nazareth to take Him home. But He refused to go with them. Instead, He taught the people with parables. As soon as He finished, Jesus and His disciples crossed the Sea of Galilee in a boat. A storm arose, and Jesus showed His miracle-working power by stilling the storm. When He arrived on the other side of the sea, or lake, he healed a man who was possessed with demons.

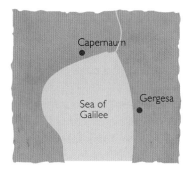

Capernaum and Gergesa (present day Ein Gev), approximately at the location where Jesus healed the demon-possessed man.

Demons

Was the man Jesus healed insane? If not, why would he hide in tombs and rush out at people? At first glance, it would seem to people today that this must have been insanity. It was clearly not that, but that the man was inhabited by demons, evil personalities which controlled him.

Demons were (and still are) spiritual beings with intelligence and personality. Jesus spoke to demons which inhabited people, and they spoke to Jesus through the inhabited persons. Demons often left the persons they inhabited deranged mentally or sick in other ways and robbed them of their own personalities. Demons are on Satan's side in the great struggle between good and evil, God and Satan.

Demons apparently had unusual strength and caused that strength to pass on to the persons they inhabited. They often caused blindness (Matt. 12:22), dumbness (Matt. 9:32–33), defects and deformities (Luke 13:11–13), and suicidal tendencies (Mark 9:22).

Demons are thought to be fallen angels, once like other angels, but who wilfully cast their lot with Satan instead of God. They are still at work in the world today, though in the time of Jesus they seemed to be more evident as personalities, perhaps because God's Son was there, and Satan sent his powerful forces to fight Him. Jesus had complete power over demons. When He spoke they had to obey Him.

Legion

When Jesus asked the evil spirit his name, he replied that it was Legion, for there were many demons present in the man. A Roman legion had 6,000 men in it, so the word legion meant "many", probably a large undetermined number in this case. When the demons went into the herd of pigs, however, they did inhabit 2,000 of them. This suggests that many demons were present.

The Fringe of His Garment

MATTHEW 9:20–22; MARK 5:25–34; LUKE 8:43–48

Across the Sea of Galilee from Capernaum, Jesus healed a man with many demons in him. As He returned home, Jairus, ruler of the synagogue, sent for Him to heal his daughter. On the way to Jairus' house a woman touched Jesus' cloak and was healed.

The issue of blood

The woman had a chronic haemorrage. She was not only physically sick, but ceremonially unclean according to the Law of Moses (Lev. 15:25–27). Luke, a physician, says she spent all her money on physicians, but none could heal her. The Talmud says physicians had at least 11 remedies for chronic haemorrage, and she had evidently tried them all, but not one worked. The woman tried to be healed secretly by touching Jesus' cloak, but He wanted her to tell her story publicly.

Men's clothing in Jesus' time

How did Jesus and the other men of His time dress? Jesus had to be more careful than His neighbours for He was accepted as a rabbi, and rabbis were expected to dress well, even above their means. A man was expected to cover his head as a sign of respect to those he met. A man also wore an inner garment close to the skin, called a coat or tunic. The outer garment, his cloak, was wrapped at the waist with a wide cloth or leather belt called a girdle.

An upper garment, a goltha or tallith, was worn, with fringes or tassels at each corner. On the feet, he wore sandals.

Thus, Jesus was probably clothed with the close-fitting undergarments which went down to His feet, as teachers were supposed to do, plus the tallith with the four fringes as an upper and outer cloak or covering. On His feet were sandals. A cloth belt secured the clothing at His waist. His head was covered with the outer cloak, brought up over His head, or by a separate cloth wound around His head.

According to the Law of Moses, every Jewish man was supposed to wear a fringe or tassel at each of the four corners of his tallith, the rectangular or square outer garment worn over the upper part of the body. Two fringes hung at the bottom of the cloak and two hung over the shoulders where the cloak folded over him. Even today, some Jews wear fringes.

The woman in the story probably touched one of these fringes of Jesus' cloak as he passed through the crowds. The Law of Moses requiring these fringes is found in Numbers 15:37–40 and Deuteronomy 22:12.

The harbour of Ein Gev on the Sea of Galilee.

245

Jairus' Daughter

MATTHEW 9:18–19, 23–26; MARK 5:21–24, 35–43;
LUKE 8:40–42, 49–56

One day in Galilee, some of the religious leaders demanded a miracle from Jesus. He refused. Later that day, Jesus stilled a great storm on the Sea of Galilee, healed a man possessed with demons, and healed a woman at Capernaum who merely touched His cloak. Then He went to the home of the synagogue ruler, Jairus, and raised his daughter from the dead.

The synagogue ruler

Jairus was one of three synagogue rulers mentioned in the New Testament. The other two were Crispus (Acts 18:8) and Sosthenes (Acts 18:17).

The synagogue ruler was also called president of the synagogue. He was in charge of the service, including the reading of the Torah, the Scriptures, and the people who led the service. He also was responsible for the synagogue building, including maintenance and repair, and even the cleaning chores. As an official, he kept order during the service and made sure that people did not become unruly or do anything they should not do in a synagogue.

The synagogue was one of the most important places in town, the centre of Jewish religious life in that community. This placed the synagogue ruler in a place of prominence, a civic leader as well as a religious leader. He was also an elder of the synagogue, so he sat in one of the seats reserved for important people at the services.

Paid mourners

By the time Jesus reached Jairus' house, the paid mourners were there with the mournful cries of their profession. Paid mourners developed as a profession in Old Testament times but continued into the time of Jesus. They did this as a career which usually passed from mother to daughter. Their mourning was with dirges and eulogies, sometimes accompanied by flutes. (See Jer. 9:17–20, Amos 5:16; 2 Chron. 35:25.)

Palestinian ointment jar.

BURYING THE DEAD

When a Jewish person died, the funeral took place very soon afterwards, partly because decomposition occurs rapidly in a hot climate.

First the body was washed, anointed with oil and wrapped in a linen cloth, or shroud. The hands and feet were wrapped in bandages and the face covered with cloth. (We read of these wrappings in the story of the raising of Lazarus.) Although the body was not usually embalmed, it would often be scented with natural perfumes, such as aloes and myrrh.

The body was carried to the grave in an open coffin or bier, with mourners walking in procession behind, wailing and lamenting. To express their sorrow, members of the bereaved family would often fast, tear open their clothes, put ashes on their heads, shave their heads and even wear clothes made of rough sack-cloth.

The poor often buried their dead in caves in the hillsides; however, the rich could afford to have special tombs built in the soft natural limestone.

JESUS' MIRACLES

Resurrection of Jairus' Daughter by Vasily Polenov.

Through His miracles, Jesus showed that He had power beyond that of an ordinary man. The laws of the natural world, which He had helped His Father create, were not boundaries for Him, only for mortal men.

Jesus' miracles prove that He is the Messiah, God's Son. Who else could raise the dead, cause instant healing of leprosy and injury, still a storm, and give sight to the blind?

It is strange that the very people who should have recognized that these miracles prove He is the Messiah failed to do so. Those closest to Him, even His own family in the early years, could not bring themselves to see these things. His hometown, Nazareth, rejected Him as Messiah, as did most of the religious leaders of His time.

Even when many of these people saw Him raise Lazarus from the dead after four days in the grave, they refused to see Him as God's Son. It seems that they never stopped to ask how He did these things. They only worried that, by doing them, He put them and their jobs in danger with the Romans.

1. THE BLIND SEE
Jesus gave sight to blind people on four occasions (Matt. 9:27–31; 12:22; 20:29–34; Mark 8:22–26; John 9:1–8).

2. THE DEAF HEAR
Jesus healed a deaf mute (Mark 7:31–37).

3. THE SPEECHLESS SPEAK
Twice He caused those without speech to speak again (Matt. 9:32–33; Mark 7:31–37).

4. THE LAME WALK
Jesus raised a paralyzed invalid at Bethesda (John 5:1–1).

5. THE MAIMED ARE WHOLE AGAIN
Jesus restored Malchus' ear, which Peter had cut off (Luke 22:49–51); restored a withered hand (Matt. 12:9–13) and stopped chronic haemorrage (Mark 5:25–34).

6. LEPERS ARE CLEANSED
Lepers had no hope until Jesus came (Matt. 8:1–4; Luke 17:11–19).

7. THE DEAD ARE RAISED TO NEW LIFE
Jesus raised Jairus' daughter (Matt. 9:18–19, 23–26); the widow's son at Nain (Luke 7: 11–16); and Lazarus (John 11: 1–4). He also cast out demons and did many other things that only God's Son could do.

Two by Two

Within a single day, Jesus performed a series of dramatic miracles – stilling a great storm on the Sea of Galilee, healing a demon-possessed man and a woman who had suffered for 12 years, raising a dead girl to life, giving sight to 2 blind men, and healing a speechless man with a demon. The jealous Pharisees had an answer – He did it all by Satan's power! After this, Jesus showed His miracle-working power in another way, by sending His disciples to teach and heal as He had done.

THE SCRIP

When the disciples went out two by two, Jesus told them not to take a "scrip", as some versions call it, or "bag", as others call it.

This little leather bag was simply a small travel bag for personal effects. Farmers, shepherds, pilgrims, and even beggars carried one, almost as someone might carry a handbag today. They kept small personal effects in it.

When David fought Goliath, he carried his five stones in one of these little bags. It was made from the skin of an animal, such as a goat, tanned by a simple process.

Jesus was simply telling His disciples that they were to carry nothing with them, to depend on others for their needs.

The drawing below, taken from an ancient monument, shows a scrip. The material is unknown, possibly woven strips of leather, papyrus, or other fiber.

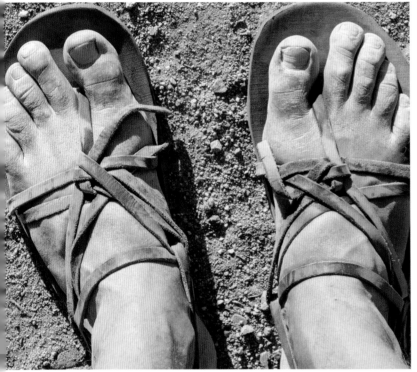

Shaking the dust off one's feet
When the Jews returned to Palestine from despised Gentile lands, they shook the dust from their feet. This symbolized breaking off all ties with the Gentiles they had been in contact with. Jesus' disciples shook the dust from their feet whenever a Jewish or Gentile city rejected them.

The staff

A staff was used by both rich and poor, slave and master. It was one of the most common instruments in Bible times. It supported the poorest beggar, yet in the hands of a shepherd or a king, it represented the power over life and death.

Moses' staff, for example, was probably a crude shepherd's rod cut from the branch of a tree. But as shepherd of the people of Israel, Moses represented the power and authority of God, and his staff was his sceptre, more powerful than Pharaoh's sceptre.

A shepherd always carried a staff. He used it not only as a walking stick, but also as a rod to beat down the bushes where the flocks strayed, checking for snakes and lizards. When wild animals attacked, his staff became a weapon to protect the sheep.

Travelling in Bible times involved walking long distances on difficult roads. Most travellers carried a staff. It supported and protected them while they walked or rested.

Christ with His Disciples
by A. N. Mironov.

A staff could be something as crude as a rod cut from the branch of a tree.

John Is Beheaded

MATTHEW 14:1–12; MARK 6:14–29;
LUKE 3:19–20; 9:7–9

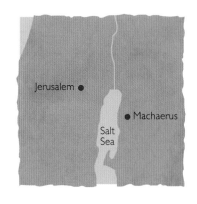

Herod Antipas, ruler of Galilee, soon heard the news of Jesus' miracles. His first thought was that John the Baptist, whom he had beheaded, had risen from the dead!

What remains of Machaerus, the fortified hilltop palace where John the Baptist was imprisoned and beheaded.

The ruins of the fortress of Machaerus may still be seen on a high mountain east of the Dead Sea. Many believe this is the place where John the Baptist was imprisoned and beheaded by Herod Antipas. Herod probably placed John at Machaerus because it was far from Herod's capital at Tiberias and therefore far from Herod's wife, Herodias. She hated John and wanted him killed because John had criticized her for divorcing her husband, Herod Philip, and marrying her husband's brother, Herod Antipas. Because of John's popularity, Antipas did not want to kill him and feared a riot if John was executed. But because

of Antipas' foolish oath, no distance was far enough to save John's life.

Intermarriage of the Herods

The family of Herod the Great certainly did not follow the teachings of Jesus. Marriages took place within the family and brother fought against brother. Herod the Great had many wives. One of his sons, Herod Philip, married his own niece, Herodias. Herodias then left Philip and married his brother, Herod Antipas. Herod Philip II, another brother of Herod Philip, married his great-niece, Salome, who was the daughter of Herodias. It was Herodias and Salome who tricked Herod Antipas and forced the execution of John the Baptist. Bernice, daughter of Herod Agrippa I, married her uncle, Herod Chalcis. These intermarriages caused nothing but grief and strife to a family already riddled with greed and selfish pride.

Herod Antipas

As a son of Herod the Great, Herod Antipas played an important role in New Testament events. He inherited a portion of his father's kingdom and became tetrarch, ruler of Galilee and

Perea. It was Herod Antipas who imprisoned and beheaded John the Baptist and judged Jesus before He was crucified. And it was because of Jesus' trial that Antipas and Pilate, previously enemies, became fast friends.

In AD 6, Rome gave Antipas the distinguished title of Herod, impressive in the political and social society of the Roman world. He then married the daughter of Aretas, king of Arabia, probably for political reasons. But he soon left her for Herodias, the wife of his brother Herod Philip. Herodias had a brother, Herod Agrippa I, who had earned the title of king.

Herodias persuaded Antipas to go to Rome and ask for the title of king as well. Agrippa quickly brought charges against

Coin of Herod Philip II, brother of Herod Antipas and son of Herod the Great. Philip's coins were struck at Caesarea and carried the portraits of the Roman emperors Augustus and Tiberius. Philip is mentioned in Luke 3:1.

HERODIAS AND HER FAMILY

Herodias was one of the Bible's evil women. Like Jezebel, in the time of the kings of Israel, she was an influential wife of a powerful and ruthless king. Herodias came from a long line of evil relatives. This chart shows her relationships to the various members of the Herod family.

Various members of Herodias' family were involved with people of the New Testament. They were the rulers of the land in which Jesus lived and kept that rule from the time of Herod the Great's father, Antipater, in 48 BC until the death of Herod Agrippa II, who died around AD 100.

Uncle/1st husband

HEROD PHILIP I
Father of Salome, whose dance brought about the death of John the Baptist (Mark 6:14–29)

Grandfather

HEROD THE GREAT
Murdered the babies of Bethlehem, hoping to kill the child Jesus (Matt. 2:1–18)

Father

ARISTOBULUS
Also grandfather of "King Agrippa", Herod Agrippa II, before whom Paul went (Acts 25:13–26:32)

Uncle/2nd husband

HEROD ANTIPAS
Ruled during Jesus' lifetime. Judged Jesus before His crucifixion (Luke 23:7–12)

Brother

HEROD CHALCIS
Married Bernice, his niece

Uncle/son-in-law

HEROD PHILIP II
Married Salome, even though he was her great-uncle

Nieces

BERNICE and DRUSILLA
Bernice married Chalcis, but was with Agrippa when Paul was before him (Acts 25:13); Drusilla married Felix (Acts 24:24)

Daughter

SALOME
The girl who danced before Antipas. Married her great-uncle, Herod Philip II

Brother

HEROD AGRIPPA I
Father of "King Agrippa", Bernice, and Drusilla. Murdered the apostle James (Acts 12:1–2), imprisoned Peter (Acts 12:3–11)

Nephew

HEROD AGRIPPA II
Paul appeared before "King" Agrippa (Acts 25:13–26:32)

Antipas, and Antipas was exiled to what is France today. Agrippa, a friend of the emperor Caligula, was then given all the territories of Antipas.

Salome's dance

After Moses led the Israelites out of Egypt, the people celebrated with a dance of joy and thanksgiving to the Lord. Salome's dance was completely opposite to a dance of worship. Prompted by her mother, Herodias, Salome's purpose was to entice Herod Antipas. An evil dance for evil reasons ended with his foolish vow that could not be broken. Herod Antipas was deceived by Salome's dance, a dance of death.

Jesus Feeds 5,000

MATTHEW 14:13–21, MARK 6:30–44;
LUKE 9:10–17; JOHN 6:1–13

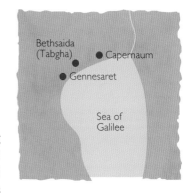

After Jesus performed a number of miracles in Galilee – stilling a storm, driving demons from a man, and even raising a girl from the dead – His fame spread everywhere. Even Herod Antipas, ruler of Galilee, was startled. He felt certain that Jesus was John the Baptist, risen from the dead. Now Jesus was about to perform a different sort of miracle – feeding a multitude with one boy's small lunch.

Bethsaida, west of Capernaum, one possible site of the miracle.

The crowd was really many more than 5,000. Only the men were numbered (Matt. 14:21). The total number may have been more than double that number, if there were more women and children than men. Thus the feeding of the 5,000 may actually have been the feeding of more than 10,000.

Bethsaida
Where was Bethsaida? Nobody knows for sure. Some point to a place just east of the Jordan

The coast of the Sea of Galilee near Ein Eyov Waterfall in Tabgha, Israel – a traditional place for this miracle.

River, and others point to a place west of Capernaum. The eastern location was in the territory ruled by Herod Philip. The western location was in the territory ruled by Herod Antipas, in Galilee.

We read in Luke 9:10 that the feeding of the 5,000 took place near Bethsaida. It was in a desert (lonely) place (Matt. 14:13). Then we read that Jesus and His disciples left this place and sailed across the Sea of Galilee to Capernaum (John 6:17).

It would seem that there were in Jesus' time two towns named Bethsaida. The one west of Capernaum, in Galilee, was located at the place shown on

the map. The other, just east of the place where the Jordan River enters the Sea of Galilee, also went by the name Bethsaida Julias.

One tradition locates the feeding of the 5,000 at a place known today as Tabgha, the western Bethsaida. However, some scholars believe it happened at the eastern location. As was said earlier, nobody knows for sure.

When?
From John 6:4 we learn that this was just before the time of the Passover, almost exactly one year before Jesus was crucified.

Jesus Walks on the Sea

MATTHEW 14:24–33; MARK 6:47–52;
JOHN 6:16–21

Only recently Jesus had healed a demon-possessed man, raised a girl from the dead, and fed more than 5,000 with one boy's small lunch. All Galilee was astir because of these miracles. What would He do next? The people did not have long to wait. On the same day that He fed the multitude, He walked on the waters of the sea. No one had ever done that before!

His disciples were awed by seeing Jesus walk on the water and witnessing the high winds die down as He stepped into their boat. *Walking on Water* by Ivan Aivazovsky.

From the place where the more than 5,000 were fed, the disciples rowed toward Capernaum, about 10 km (6 miles) away. Some Bible versions say the disciples had rowed only 25–30 furlongs by early morning, probably rowing since sunset (John 6:19). A furlong was about 185 m (607 feet), so they had rowed only a little over 5 km (3 miles), slightly more than half of the way back home to Capernaum. Their progress was slow because they were going against the wind and waves.

The fourth watch
It seems likely that the disciples started across the sea, or lake, about sunset. They rowed until the fourth watch of the night (Matt. 14:25; Mark 6:48). The Romans, who ruled the land where Jesus lived at that time, divided the night into four "watches" of three hours each. Starting with 6 o'clock in the evening, the end of the first watch would have been 9 o'clock. The end of the second watch would have been midnight, the end of the third watch 3 o'clock in the morning, and the end of the fourth watch 6 o'clock in the morning. Using this system, one realizes that the disciples were still trying to row back to Capernaum sometime between 3 and 6 o'clock in the morning. Still they were only a little more than halfway home.

The ship
A better translation is "boat". The Galilean fishing boats had both oars and sails. The wind on this particular night was too strong to use sails, or perhaps too uncertain. The Bible says "the wind was contrary" (Matt. 14:24, KJV). The boat was apparently large enough for at least 13 people, for it seems that all 12 disciples were in this boat (Matt. 14:22), and there was still room for Jesus to board (Mark 6:51).

Matthew and John
The story of Jesus walking on the water appears in three Gospels – Matthew, Mark, and John. Matthew and John were in the boat that night and saw it happen. Matthew had been a tax collector for the Romans while John had spent his life fishing on the sea. Mark would hear the story from others later and record it, primarily for Gentile readers.

Healing at Gennesaret

MATTHEW 14:34–36; MARK 6:53–56

Crowds followed Jesus everywhere, hoping that He would heal, feed, teach, or give them something He had given others. When He walked along the road, they followed. When He climbed into the hills, they went with Him. And even when He crossed the sea to Gennesaret, they would not let Him go alone.

The mound behind the field shown above is Tel Kinrot, the remains of Gennesaret, on the northwestern shore of the Sea of Galilee.

In Jesus' time Gennesaret was the name of the fertile plain on the west side of the Sea of Galilee, as well as the name of a village in that region. The sea itself was sometimes called the Sea of Gennesaret or the Lake of Gennesaret (Luke 5:1).

The plain lies between Capernaum and Magdala, running north and south along the western coast of the Sea of Galilee. It is about 6.5 km (4 miles) long and 3 km (2 miles) wide.

In Jesus' time this plain was the garden spot of the land. Streams from the surrounding hills watered the rich land. With the warm climate, it was an ideal agricultural area, where trees and flowers added beauty to the grapes, olives, wheat, melons, figs, rice, and vegetables. Some called the area a paradise, the Garden of God.

Jesus' reputation

When Jesus landed in Gennesaret, the people who saw Him knew that He had the power to heal. His reputation as a miracle healer had gone before Him to this place. It is interesting to notice that

the people did not run to Jesus themselves, but sent word immediately to the sick people of the area, so that all of the sick might come for healing. This was an unselfish act on their part.

The border of His garment

These people must have heard about the woman who was healed by touching the fringe of Jesus' cloak (Matt. 9:20–21). Somehow they knew that they would be healed if only they touched this fringe, instead of touching Jesus Himself.

Beds

The people carried their sick to Jesus on their "beds". When we think of modern beds with mattresses, as well as headboards and footboards, this seems strange. But the beds of Jesus' time were not like ours at all.

The beds on which these people carried their sick were more like mats of woven fabric or other type of cloth. It was easier to carry a person on this mat than without it.

Marketplaces

The people of Gennesaret laid their sick in the marketplaces, the bazaars of that time where people brought their goods to sell, came to hire labourers, and to talk together.

The Syro-Phoenician Woman

MATTHEW 15:21–28; MARK 7:24–30

This Phoenician coin depicts the goddess Astarte.

The crowds had seen Jesus perform miracles that no mere man could perform. He had healed the sick, given sight to the blind, and even raised the dead. They had heard of other miracles from His disciples – stilling a storm and walking on water. Of all the miracles, feeding over 5,000 with a small lunch caught their attention the most. Food was scarce, and here was a man who could feed them with almost nothing. He must become their king, not because He was the Messiah, but because He supplied food. Jesus would have none of this. He left Galilee and travelled north to the region of Tyre and Sidon.

In Jesus' time, the territory surrounding the cities of Tyre and Sidon was inhabited mostly by Phoenician people, though a number of Jewish communities were scattered throughout. The home where Jesus stayed was probably Jewish (Mark 7:24). But the woman who came for Jesus' help was a Gentile .

Galilee in Jesus' time was ruled by Herod Antipas, under the control of the Roman emperor. Herod at this time was involved in the execution of John the Baptist and the problems that surrounded that execution. The territory around Tyre and Sidon was under the rule of the proconsul of Syria, who was governed by the Roman emperor.

Jesus left Galilee at this time for several reasons. His public miracles had created quite a stir, so much that the people wanted to make Him king, not because of the miracles, but because He had fed them. Crowds were swarming around Jesus daily. He needed to take His disciples away to a lonely place, where He could train them. Also, it was important to show them that He reached out to include Gentiles in His love and help, too.

The Syro-Phoenician woman

The woman who came to Jesus for help was called Syro-Phoenician (Mark 7:26), Greek (Mark 7:26), and Canaanite (Matt. 15:22, GNB). "Greek" was a way of saying she was a Gentile, not a Jew. "Syro-Phoenician" meant she was Phoenician by race, living in the region of Syria. "Canaanite" was an Old Testament term for the people who lived here.

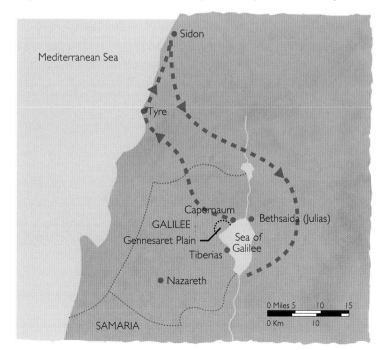

Mediterranean Sea

Sidon

Tyre

Capernaum

GALILEE

Bethsaida (Julias)

Gennesaret Plain

Sea of Galilee

Tiberias

Nazareth

SAMARIA

0 Miles 5   10   15
0 Km   10

The possible route Jesus followed through the regions of Tyre and Sidon and then to the north and east of the Sea of Galilee. Jesus may not have actually visited the cities of Tyre and Sidon, but the countryside nearby. Note the relationship of Capernaum and the plain of Gennesaret.

Jesus Heals a Deaf and Dumb Man

MATTHEW 15:29–31; MARK 7:31–37

With a small lunch Jesus fed a great multitude in Galilee. They wanted to make Him king, not because of the miracle, but because of the food! But Jesus left Galilee and went to the region of Tyre and Sidon, where He healed the daughter of a Gentile woman, then on to the north and east of the Sea of Galilee, where He healed a man who was deaf and dumb.

Throughout the life of Jesus, a number of geographical names appear – territories through which He walked. His hometowns, Nazareth and Capernaum, were in Galilee. The regions of Tyre and Sidon are mentioned in the preceding story. This one speaks of the Decapolis. In other places in the life of Jesus, Judea, Perea, Samaria, and Idumea are mentioned.

When Jesus was born, Herod the Great ruled the land. His kingdom included territories such as Judea, Idumea, Samaria, Perea, Galilee, and the region east of the Sea of Galilee. But when Herod the Great died, his kingdom was divided.

Herod Antipas ruled Galilee and Perea. Herod Philip ruled a territory east of the Sea of Galilee. Archelaus ruled Judea and Idumea. These three sons quarrelled, and Archelaus was sent into exile. His territory, Judea and Idumea, was placed under the control of a procurator. When Jesus died, Pontius Pilate was procurator of these territories.

Galilee and Judea

Most of Jesus' early ministry was in Galilee. It included such towns as Cana, Nazareth, Capernaum, Magdala, Korazin, and Herod's capital, Tiberias. Galilee was part of the territory ruled by Herod Antipas, whom Jesus called "that fox". He was the son of Herod the Great. Herod Antipas beheaded John the Baptist and later took part in judging Jesus.

Galilee is a region of rolling hills, plus some large plains. The Sea of Galilee is the focal point of the region.

Joseph and Mary lived in Galilee before Jesus was born. Then they went to Bethlehem, in Judea, to enrol in Caesar's census. Next they moved to Egypt, then back to their hometown Nazareth, in Galilee. Here Jesus lived till He was rejected. Then He moved to Capernaum, also in Galilee.

Jerusalem and Bethlehem were in Judea, a region of hills high enough to be called "mountains". Jerusalem, for example, is in mountains about 915 m (3,000 feet) above sea level, compared with Jesus' home in Capernaum, below sea level. When Jesus was born, Judea was ruled by Herod the Great, who killed the babies of Bethlehem in an effort to kill the baby Jesus. After this Herod died, his son Archelaus ruled a while; then came a line of procurators, including Pontius Pilate.

Perea and Samaria

Perea was the territory east of the Jordan River, across from Samaria and Judea. It was also ruled by Herod Antipas. Jesus worked here before His last week in Jerusalem.

Between Galilee and Judea was a region with "mixed people", part Jewish and part foreigners, brought in during the Exile. It was also ruled by procurators during Jesus' life on earth. Most Jews did not travel through Samaria, for they hated these "foreigners".

Jesus Heals at Bethsaida

MATTHEW 16:5–12; MARK 8:13–26

Who can heal the sick, raise the dead, still a storm, walk on water, and perform amazing miracles of many sorts? Who else but God and His Son! But the Pharisees and Sadducees could not accept Jesus as God's Son. They had seen and heard of His miracles, but still they would not believe. It seemed that no miracle could be great enough to convince them that He was God's Son, not even healing a blind man at Bethsaida.

The ruins of Bethsaida.

This seems to be Bethsaida Julias, on the eastern side of the Jordan River as it enters the Sea of Galilee, not the Bethsaida west of Capernaum.

Bread and leaven

Loaves of bread were flat, like extra-thick pancakes. They were also of a thicker consistency than modern bread, more like that of pancakes.

Whenever bread was made, a piece of the sour or fermented dough was kept apart. This leaven, as it was called, was placed in the next batch of dough to cause it to ferment and rise. Leaven served the same purpose as yeast does today.

The Bible also uses the word leaven to mean an influence which something has on people. For example, in this incident, Jesus warned the disciples to beware of the leaven of the Pharisees and Sadducees. By this, He meant to beware of their teachings, which may have seemed religious, but did not honour God.

The blind

In Jesus' time blind people lived hopeless lives. Not only were they handicapped by their blindness but were unable to find work to support themselves. A blind person was forced to become a beggar, depending on donations to feed himself and his family.

Blindness was common in Jesus' time, from many causes, including unsanitary conditions, bright sunlight, fly-carried disease from person to person and from waste to people, blowing sand, venereal diseases, accidents, and war injuries.

Jobs were scarce for strong, healthy men, and almost completely unavailable to the blind. Blindness was also viewed as a result of sin, either by the blind person or by his or her parents. Sometimes this was true, as in the case of blindness from venereal diseases.

Many people had more than one handicap, such as being both blind and deaf, or deaf and speechless, or blind and crippled.

A Visit to Caesarea Philippi

MATTHEW 16:13–20; MARK 8:27–30; LUKE 9:18–21

For some time Jesus had performed numerous miracles in Galilee, His home territory. But now He was travelling to other places – the regions of Tyre and Sidon, into the cities of the Decapolis, including Caesarea Philippi.

Ruins of the city of Caesarea Philippi.

Jesus and His disciples as He went apart from the crowds for a time of training, something like an original summer Bible conference, with Jesus as the teacher!

Caesarea Philippi – the place
After the death of Herod the Great, who killed all male babies of Bethlehem in an effort to kill the baby Jesus, Herod's son Philip was made "tetrarch" and placed over the territory in which Caesarea Philippi was located. Philip named the city Caesarea to honour his emperor, Caesar, but added the name Philippi to distinguish

Caesarea Philippi – location

The map below shows the location and approximate distance from Capernaum, where Jesus lived, to Caesarea Philippi, northeast of Capernaum. The distance was about 40–65 km (30–40 miles), depending on the route travelled, but it lay in much different land than Capernaum.

Capernaum, on the shore of the Sea of Galilee, was about 210 m (680 feet) below sea level. Caesarea Philippi was built in the high foothills of Mount Hermon, at a height of about 350 m (1,150 feet) above sea level. Rising to the north and east, Mount Hermon reached an elevation of about 2,800 m (9,100 feet). When the heat of summer baked Capernaum, Caesarea Philippi enjoyed a much lower temperature plus mountain breezes which came down from snow-capped Mount Hermon. It must have been a lovely retreat for

SON OF MAN

Jesus spoke often of Himself as the "Son of Man". What did He mean? No one is completely certain, but it seems that He meant:

1. The Son of God in human form, not merely anyone descended from man;
2. Thus, He was unique, the only One who was both God and man, God in heaven and man on earth;
3. As God and man both, He was the bridge between the two, God redeeming man through His Son; and
4. He is Lord over humankind, who must ultimately bow before Him and confess Him as Lord.

Caesarea Philippi was near a grotto dedicated to the Greek god Pan. Later it was called Caesarea Paneas, and is now known as Banias. This might also be the city in the Old Testament known as Baal Gad.

the city from the Caesarea on the western coast.

Caesarea Philippi was one of the 10 towns known as the Decapolis.

The Decapolis

The 10 towns of the Decapolis formed an alliance, probably for mutual protection, for they were quite scattered in a territory which bordered on hostile country to the east. Under Alexander the

Great, Greek influence moved into the area, and with it, political independence for cities such as these. Thus, the cities and their surrounding territories were like small kingdoms, but allied for their protection.

In the time of Jesus, the Decapolis was flourishing, with temples and amphitheatres, art, literature, and games. It was a Gentile world on the doorstep of Galilee. The prodigal son may have gone into such a Gentile world for his taste of loose living, breaking with his Jewish heritage. This is seen in the fact that he took care of pigs, which were eaten only by Gentiles.

Time

Jesus' visit to Caesarea may have been in the heat of summer. The training of the 12 disciples began before Passover (John 6:4), in the spring, and continued till the feast of Tabernacles (John 7:2) in the autumn. This incident took place somewhere in the centre of that training period.

Mediterranean Sea

Caesarea Philippi

GALILEE

Capernaum
Bethsaida •   • Bethsaida (Julias)
Sea of
Tiberias • Galilee

Nazareth •
▲ Mt Tabor

River Jordan

SAMARIA

0 Miles   10   20
0 Km   15   30

The Transfiguration

MATTHEW 17:1–8; MARK 9:2–8; LUKE 9:28–36

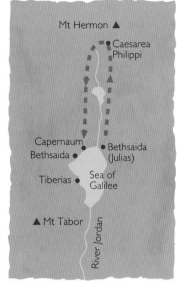

After performing many miracles in Galilee, Jesus went into the surrounding territories – the region of Tyre and Sidon, the territory where the 10 cities known as the Decapolis were located, and specifically into the area of Caesarea Philippi. On a high mountain one day, He was transfigured, changed in appearance, as the glory of God shone through Him.

Titian's painting of the Transfiguration from the Church of San Salvador in Venice shows Moses on the left with the tablets of the Law and Elijah visiting Jesus as Peter (bottom left) and James (centre) try to shield themselves from the great light while John raises his hands in prayer.

Transfiguration – meaning

What happened when Jesus was transfigured? What did this term mean? Three things happened as part of the transfiguration of Jesus:

1. Jesus' appearance changed, so that for a short time He looked different;

2. Moses and Elijah talked with Jesus, as God brought personalities back from the dead to communicate with someone on earth; and

3. God's voice spoke from heaven, stating that Jesus is His Son.

All three of these signs indicated that Jesus is the Messiah, God's Son. God used many ways to

Mount Tabor, one of two places the Transfiguration might have occurred.

show us that Jesus is His Son –
His spoken word at Jesus' baptism
and transfiguration; His written
Word, the Bible; Jesus' own
words; the testimony of those who
walked with Him for three years;
His miracles; His resurrection.

Booths were built of tree branches,
usually from palm, myrtle, willow, or
olive. They were temporary shelters
from the scorching sun for those who
camped for a few days. People built
them on their houses for the feast of
Booths or Tabernacles. This modern
booth has table, chairs and decorations.

Where?

Where was Jesus transfigured?
Some say on Mount Tabor;
others say on Mount Hermon. He
was near Mount Hermon when
Peter gave his "great confession"
that Jesus is the Messiah. But as
early as the fourth century AD,
a tradition pointed to Mount
Tabor, and within the next 200
years, three churches were built
on its summit to commemorate
the Transfiguration.

However, it has since been
learned that a fortified city

Mount Hermon, as seen from the
Hula Valley.

occupied the top of Mount Tabor
in Jesus' time, so this would not
have been a likely place for this
event. Scholars think Mount
Hermon, near Caesarea Philippi,
was where this event took place.

When?

Jesus' transfiguration was about
six days after the incident at
Caesarea Philippi. Thus it was
still summer or early autumn.

A Fish with Tax Money

MATTHEW 17:24–27

Jesus had returned to Capernaum at last after travelling through a number of regions surrounding Galilee. It must have been time to pay taxes, for Jesus sent Peter on an unusual mission to get the money.

Many of these sound quite modern!

In addition, Jewish people were taxed to keep up the temple. This was the tax to which Jesus referred. The temple tax, which every Jewish male in the world was supposed to pay, was one-half shekel per year.

The shekel was coined during the time when the Jewish people revolted against Rome in AD 66–70, several years after the crucifixion, and a short time after Paul's final journey to Rome. Such Jewish coins were not available for temple taxes in Jesus' time. The coins which were probably used during the time of Jesus were the tetradrachms of Tyre, or of other places, the coins which Judas received when he betrayed Jesus.

Fishing in Jesus' time
Jesus told Peter to fish with a hook (Matt. 17:27). In addition to fishing with hook, line, and pole, fishermen in Jesus' time also used three types of nets, including these two:

1. The cast net was a circular one which a fisherman skilfully threw on the water. Around the edges were weights which quickly sank into the water, taking the net over the fish below. A line, attached to the centre of the net, was drawn by the

Taxes in Bible times
Taxes are not new. They are as old as governments, for kings and their officials have long used a system of taxes to gather the money for their support while they run the affairs of the land. In Bible times there were many kinds of taxes. Here are a few:

- Taxes on land
- Customs taxes on goods

which went through a country on a trade route
- Export and import taxes at seaports
- Taxes on crops grown in fields
- Income taxes
- Road taxes
- Taxes on vehicles
- Taxes on animals
- Salt tax
- Taxes on the sale or transfer of property

FISHING IN NEW TESTAMENT TIMES

Fishing did not develop in Palestine until New Testament times, when it was carried out on the Sea of Galilee (as shown above). One centre of fishing was Magdala, whose name means "fish-salting".

ROD FISHING

Jesus told Peter to go to the lake and throw out his line (Matt. 17:24–27); he would have used a rod and line to catch the fish with the shekel coin in its mouth.

CAST NET FISHING

Another type of fishing was using the cast net, a circular net about 15 feet (5 metres) across, with weights at the edges. The net was thrown or dropped over a school of fishes when they were seen swimming through shallow water; the weights would pull the net down, trapping the fish

beneath it. Cast nets could be used both from the shore or from a boat; Peter and Andrew were using cast nets when Jesus called them (Mark 1:16–17).

When the cast net was drawn in, it brought with it all sorts of things from the bed of the lake, and the good fish had to be separated out from the garbage (see Matt. 13:47–48).

SEINE NET FISHING

The seine net, or drag net, was about 8 feet (3 metres) wide, but hundreds of feet long, and was hung from corks in the water, like a submerged fence.

The net could be hung between two boats, or from a single boat, which made a great circle with the net. The net would be drawn into a tight circle, the lower rope pulled in, and the net would form a great bag from which the fish could not escape (Luke 5:4).

FISHING BOATS

The fishing boats on Galilee were not very big, normally built to hold about four men. They would have a single, triangular sail on a central mast, and would be steered with a large oar acting as a rudder.

---

fisherman, so that the net closed tightly around the fish. With that, he could draw the netted fish to him.

2. The draw net was a long rectangular net, with weights along the bottom. It was pulled between two boats, with the bottom of the net

below the water and the top floating on top of the water. As the two ends of the net were drawn together the fish were trapped in the closing circle made by the net. At last the net closed in on the fish, trapping them for the catch.

Where?

Jesus told Peter to fish in the sea. This was obviously the Sea of Galilee, for they were at Capernaum. Actually this "sea" was, and is, a large lake fed by the Jordan River.

Who Is Greatest?

MATTHEW 18:1–6; MARK 9:33–37; LUKE 9:46–48

Jesus had performed miracles that no one had ever done before – stilling a storm, healing blind people, driving out demons, feeding a multitude with a small lunch, and walking on water. He had taken the gospel to regions surrounding Galilee. The disciples had seen all these things. But suddenly miracles were not uppermost in their minds. This day they were more concerned about who would be first in Jesus' new kingdom.

These castle walls in old Jerusalem represent what the followers of Jesus thought the "kingdom of Heaven" should look like, in contrast to what Jesus was teaching about.

Jesus' kingdom is more than heaven. It is wherever He is. Thus His kingdom reaches into earth, and even into our hearts, minds, and souls. Many who followed Jesus thought His kingdom would be Israel, and He would be the new king who would free the people from the Romans.

The Romans

Many years before, the people of Israel were free, ruling their own land. Under King David and King Solomon, almost a thousand years before the time of Jesus, Israel was at its peak, one of the most powerful nations of the Middle East.

But during the latter part of Solomon's reign, he let his foreign wives build altars to pagan gods. Israel's people began to worship these gods, turning from the true God who had freed them from slavery in Egypt and had given them this Promised Land.

The centuries passed, with Israel growing weaker with each evil king who ruled. The nation divided shortly after Solomon's death and never united again before it was carried at last into exile in Assyria and Babylon. This happened between 722–586 BC.

During this time the Assyrians grew weaker and the Babylonians took over as the world power. During the time of Daniel they were conquered by the Persians, so the land became part of the Persian Empire. In 334–331 BC it became part of the Greek (Macedonian) Empire. (Greek kings called Ptolemies ruled the land then from about 323-198 BC, and another group of Greeks, called Seleucids, ruled from 198-165 BC.) Then the Jews ruled their land again, from 165-63 BC, after which it became part of the Roman Empire, as it was in Jesus' time.

Millstones

Jesus said that whoever would offend a little child (cause him or her to be led astray) would be better off if they had a millstone tied about their neck and were thrown into the deep sea. Millstones were commonly used in Jesus' time, and were very heavy.

The millstone was powered by two people, one pushing against each side of the pole, moving the millstone around the centre pole and grinding as it moved.

The Two Debtors

MATTHEW 18:15–35

Jesus' ministry in Galilee had proved beyond a doubt that He is God's Son. He had healed the sick, given sight to the blind, and even raised the dead. Transfigured before His three closest disciples, Jesus was proclaimed God's Son by a voice from heaven. Now that the disciples knew that He would someday set up a kingdom, they quarrelled about who would be the greatest in that kingdom. Not only that, Jesus' disciples had forbidden another man from casting out demons in Jesus' name because he was not part of their group. Jesus responded to the disciples with some parables, including one about two debtors. This parable told of forgiving both great and small things.

A jail in Jerusalem from the time of Jesus.

In Bible times, a person was in serious trouble if he could not pay back money that he owed. The creditor, the person lending the money, was allowed to seize the debtor and force him to work until the debt was paid off. He could keep the debtor in chains and even throw him into prison. The creditor also had the option of selling the debtor as a slave, taking away his house and personal belongings, or selling his wife and children into slavery.

A debtor was thrown into prison with the hope that he might have some secret property he would sell to pay off the debt. If he did not, the creditor hoped that friends or relatives would quickly pay off the debt. If they could not, the debtor might have to spend the rest of his life in prison.

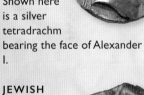
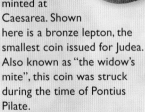

The Pool of Siloam

JOHN 9:1–41

In Galilee, where He had lived since a child, Jesus performed many miracles to show that He is truly God's Son. He healed the sick, gave sight to the blind, drove out demons, fed over 5,000 with a small lunch, walked on water, and stilled a storm. He had been transfigured before three of His disciples, with God's voice confirming that He is indeed the Messiah, His Son. Now Jesus was leaving Galilee. From this time on, His ministry would focus in Jerusalem and in the surrounding regions of Judea and Perea. Before long, He would face the Cross. In the meantime, people from Jerusalem, Judea, and Perea would see His miracles, such as the one near the Pool of Siloam.

Christ Healng the Blind Man by El Greco.

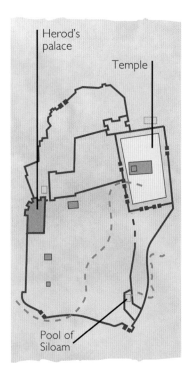

The Pool of Siloam in relationship to the temple and other important sites in the Jerusalem of Jesus' time.

The Pool of Siloam

Just south of Jerusalem lies the Gihon Spring. Seven hundred years before the time of Christ, King Hezekiah was being threatened by the invasion of King Sennacherib and the Assyrians. To prepare for the attack, Hezekiah built a water tunnel which travelled from the Gihon Spring, beneath the city walls, and into Jerusalem. In this way, the city would have plenty of water even if Sennacherib surrounded the city for months. The place where the water tunnel emptied into the city was called the Pool of Siloam.

Here, within the safety of the city walls, the people came to draw water with their pots and animal skins. In Jesus' time, the pool must have been a bathing place as well, for Jesus told a blind man to wash there in order to receive his sight.

Other pools of Jerusalem

Before the age of modern plumbing, the city of Jerusalem had a big water problem. There was little rainfall, and the city was far from the salty Mediterranean Sea to the west and the Jordan River to the east.

However, there were springs in the area, and the Israelites solved their problem by building tunnels or aqueducts to channel this water into Jerusalem, where large pools were built to collect the water.

One of these pools is known as the Towers' Pool, because it is located just outside the towers of Herod's citadel. Built by Herod the Great, it is fed by a spring located just south of Bethlehem. The aqueduct first carried the water through Herod's palace and then emptied into the pool.

The Pool of Israel was also constructed by Herod the Great when he built the temple. The walls of the temple platform served as a dam, blocking the path of the Bezetha Brook. As a result, a pool of water collected just outside of the temple. It was still used into the twentieth century when it was found to be contaminated and had to be filled.

The Pool of Bethesda is said to have been near the Jerusalem sheep market. It was used to wash the sheep that were to be sacrificed at the temple. It was also the place where Jesus healed a man who had been sick for 38 years (John 5:1–10).

The historic pool of Siloam today (where Hezekiah's tunnel ends). and opposite, the steps leading down to it.

The Good Shepherd

JOHN 10:1–21

For about two years, Jesus had ministered in Galilee, healing and performing other miracles which no mere man could do. Now He moved on to Judea and Perea, regions surrounding Jerusalem, where other people would see His miracles. A man who was born blind was healed at the Pool of Siloam. The religious leaders were angered by this, for it was another reason for people to recognize Jesus as the Messiah, God's Son. With their anger and hostility toward Him as a backdrop, Jesus told how He, the Good Shepherd, would die for His sheep.

Qualities of a good shepherd

A good shepherd is familiar with each one of his sheep. He knows which ones may wander and which ones need special care. Day and night the shepherd watches over his flock and will risk his own life to protect them. If a single sheep gets lost, the shepherd will ask someone else to watch over the flock while he searches for it.

A good shepherd always leads his sheep and never drives them. Every day he finds food and water and every night he leads them back to the safety of the sheepfold. Knowing this, it is easy to see why Jesus is called the Good Shepherd.

The sheepfold

Sheep are helpless animals. They may wander aimlessly about the countryside, unable to defend themselves. For this reason, shepherds built sheepfolds.

A sheepfold was a place of shelter for the sheep. A simple sheepfold was built of four walls made of stones gathered from the fields. The walls were just high enough to keep wild animals out. Some walls had thorns laid along the top, to discourage thieves.

PARABLES OF THE KINGDOM

	MATTHEW	MARK	LUKE
The sower	13:3–9,18–23	4:3–9,13–21	8:5–8,11–15
The seed		4:26–29	
The weeds	13:24–30,36–43		
Leaven	13:33		13:20–21
The pearl	13:45–46		
Hidden treasure	13:44		
Drag net	13:47–50		
Unwilling children	11:16–19		12:31–35
Fig tree			13:6–9
Vineyard workers	20:1–16		
Two brothers	21:28–32		
Marriage feast	22:1–14		
Great banquet			14:16–24
Wicked workers	21:33–46	12:1–2	20:9–19
Lost sheep	18:12–14		15:3–7
Lost coin			15:8–10
Lost son			15:11–32
Two creditors			7:41–47
Pharisee and the Tax Collector			18:9–14
Rich man and Lazarus			16:19–31
Vigilant servants	13:33–37		12:19–38
Ten bridesmaids	25:1–13		
Unreliable servant	24:45–51		12:41–46
Five Talents	25:14–30		
Ten gold coins			19:11–27
Rich fool			12:16–21
Good Samaritan		10:30–37	
Unforgiving servant	18:23–35		
Troublesome friend			11:5–8
Unjust judge			16:1–13
Dishonest steward			18:1–8

A single entrance led into the fold, and a shepherd could be found there guarding his sheep. Often many shepherds used the same sheepfold and took turns guarding the entrance. The shepherds did not worry about mixing their sheep together, because each sheep knew its own shepherd's call, usually a loud piercing cry.

Early Christian image from Rome of Jesus as the Good Shepherd.

The Good Samaritan

LUKE 10:25–37

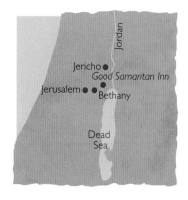

After about two years of ministry in Galilee, Jesus began to teach and work miracles in Judea and Perea, territories near Jerusalem. After healing a blind man near the Pool of Siloam, Jesus taught how He, the Good Shepherd, would be killed for His sheep. An expert on the Law of Moses asked Jesus about eternal life, and He answered with a parable about a Samaritan who helped an injured traveller.

An "inn" traditionally called the Inn of the Good Samaritan, on the road from Jerusalem to Jericho.

Samaria and the Samaritans

Who were the Samaritans? Little is known about their origin, and there is much confusion about their history. Most, including the Israelites, believe that the Samaritans began when King Sargon and the Assyrians captured the city of Samaria in 721 BC and deported the inhabitants, including thousands of Israelites. Assyria then repopulated the region of Samaria with captured foreigners from other lands. These foreigners intermarried with the Israelites who were left in Samaria. Years later, when the exiled Israelites returned to Samaria, they could not accept this mixed race as true Israelites. They called them Cuthim or Samaritans. As a result, an intense hatred developed between the Samaritans and the Jews.

But the Samaritans claimed that their race had never intermarried with foreigners. They insisted that they began when Joshua gathered the 12 tribes together at Mount Gerizim and Mount Ebal, and that Moses hoped the tabernacle would be built on Mount Gerizim. The Jews, of course, considered this remark as heresy because they believed the temple at Jerusalem was the sanctuary of God. These opposing beliefs served only to deepen their hatred for each other.

Bible-time inns

The inn where the Good Samaritan stopped with the wounded man was by no means luxurious. The only thing it offered was protection from the dangers of travelling by night. In most cases, travellers had to supply their own food and sleeping pads. Some inns did not even have innkeepers, but were simply empty buildings surrounded by high walls with a well in the courtyard. The inn where the Good Samaritan stopped may have been a Greek type of inn. Here a traveller felt a bit closer to home, for the innkeeper acted more as a host, offering both food and entertainment.

The Jericho road

Known as "the Way of Blood", the Jericho road winds its way down from Jerusalem to Jericho. The steep descent is a rugged and rocky pass, well suited to the wiles of criminals and thieves. The road was a busy one, especially in the winter when travellers came from the cold hills of Jerusalem (760 m – 2,500 feet above sea level) to the warm climate and beautiful springs of Jericho (240 m – 800 feet below sea level). Why did Jesus mention a priest and a Levite in His parable of the Good Samaritan? A large number of them lived in Jericho and travelled to Jerusalem for their service in the temple.

Mary and Martha

LUKE 10:38–42

Bethany and the Dead Sea.

After two years of ministering in Galilee, Jesus returned to Judea and Perea, territories near Jerusalem, to minister there. In Jerusalem, He healed a man by the Pool of Siloam and told a parable about Himself as the Good Shepherd who would give His life for His sheep. Somewhere in Judea, He answered the question, "Who is my neighbour?" with a parable about a good-hearted Samaritan who helped a fellow traveller. After that, He went to Bethany, to visit Mary and Martha's home.

The small town of Bethany was the home of Mary, Martha, and Lazarus, close friends of Jesus. It still exists today, about 3km (2 miles) east of Jerusalem on the Jericho Road.

When in the area, Jesus often stayed in the home of these friends. In Bethany, He raised Lazarus from the dead (John 11), ate dinner with Simon the Leper, and was anointed by Mary (Matt. 26:6–13; Mark 14:3–9; John 12:28).

On this occasion, Jesus probably visited Mary and Martha because the Feast of Tabernacles was being held at Jerusalem. But it is likely that Jesus did not stay in the house itself, for it was during this feast that Jewish people lived in booths made of the branches of living trees. According to Jewish law, it was their duty to eat, sleep, and live in these booths during the festive week.

Mary, Martha, and Lazarus were sisters and brother. Martha was the older sister and mistress of the house. This put her in charge of the household duties, which included going to the market and preparing meals. During the Feast of Tabernacles, Martha was especially busy making sure that everything was just right for her special Guest. Martha showed her love for Jesus through hospitality.

Mary showed her love for Jesus in a different way. She chose to sit and listen to Jesus. When Jesus visited Bethany for the last time, Mary anointed Jesus' feet with a most expensive perfume. Some of His disciples were irritated, but Jesus recognized this was a token of her love.

Lazarus was probably celebrating the Feast of Tabernacles in Jerusalem when Jesus came to visit Mary and Martha. Later, after Lazarus died, Jesus wept with Mary and Martha, but knew that Lazarus' death would reveal the glory of God. When Jesus raised Lazarus from the dead, many of Jesus' sceptics believed in Him.

Entertaining guests

Hospitality to guests was one of the most important social functions of the ancient East. A guest was highly honoured even if he was a stranger passing by.

Though there were inns in Jesus' day, most travellers looked for a home where they could spend the night. When a stranger knocked on someone's door or passed by close to evening, the head of the household almost always let him in and asked him to spend the night. If he refused to be hospitable, he could be snubbed by friends and neighbours. A host always kept in mind that someday he too might be a weary traveller looking for shelter and company.

Once inside, the host brought water to wash the guest's feet. If he had no servant, the host would do the washing himself. Since the roads were always dusty and most people walked, washing was an important step in making one's guest feel at home.

When a guest was in the home, a large meal was prepared. Often the guest would be served first, and the host waited until he was finished. Other customs included anointing the guest with oil, which they used as soap, or even providing clothing for the mealtime.

According to custom, a guest should stay no longer than three days in his host's home. While there, he was protected by his host. On leaving, the host was to escort his guest a short distance, sending him on his way.

Tears for Jerusalem

LUKE 13:31–35

Herod was a fox! Jesus said so Himself. Herod was a member of the crafty family who had ruled the land since before Jesus was born. But Jesus would certainly not run away from Herod. He taught openly throughout Jerusalem, Judea, and Perea, giving parables and working miracles which must have startled Herod. Herod was in charge of Jesus' home territory of Galilee, but not over Judea and Jerusalem. That was under the rule of Pilate, who represented the Romans. In a few years the Romans would completely destroy Jerusalem. Jesus wept for the city, which would reject its Messiah and fall to its enemies.

A detail from the Arch of Titus, depicting treasures plundered from the temple.

Jerusalem continued to be a thriving city after Jesus left the earth. Herod Agrippa I initiated many building projects, indicating more growth and activity in this city that had already become important in the eyes of the world. Christianity had spread rapidly as well, despite rising persecution (Acts 21:20).

But in AD 66, the Jews began to revolt against Roman control. This revolt began nearly 30 years after Jesus was crucified. Jesus' prediction about Jerusalem's destruction was about to unfold (Mark 13:2).

For three years the Romans tried unsuccessfully to put down the Jewish rebellion in Jerusalem. The Roman emperor, Vespasian, finally became angry and sent his son Titus, a Roman general, to crush the rebellion.

Jerusalem was a difficult city to attack, with its strong walls and strategic hilltop location. Titus and his Roman legions first attacked the city walls from the north. The Jews were ready and threw large rocks from the battlements. Fierce fighting lasted for two weeks until the Romans finally broke through the northern wall. But Titus' 80,000 Roman soldiers could not enter the city and were driven back.

Titus now realized that Jerusalem would not be taken by force. But he had another plan. He ordered his soldiers to allow no one in or out of Jerusalem. Any Jews caught trying to escape would be crucified.

After a year of starvation, the Jews could no longer withstand the Roman siege. In AD 70, Titus attacked the city walls once again. The Jews' strength was gone. They could no longer defend themselves, and the Romans stormed through the city. The Antonia fortress was the first to fall. Many of the Jews fled to the temple but could not hold it. Titus had wanted the building spared, but during the fighting a soldier threw a flaming torch into the sanctuary. The temple

THE MIGHT OF THE ROMAN EMPIRE

The Roman army was all too familiar to the Jews of Jesus' time. We find many references to Roman soldiers in the Gospels, and Paul uses illustrations from military life, for instance in Ephesians 6:13–17; Colossians 2:15; and 2 Timothy 2:3–4.

The main base for the Roman army in Palestine was Caesarea, though there was also a garrison in Jerusalem at the Antonia Fortress. The Jews were excused military service; the Roman army in Judaea consisted mainly of Italians and Syrians.

Each Roman legion consisted of about 6,000 men, commanded by a legate. The legion was divided into 10 divisions, or cohorts, of 600 men, each commanded by a military tribune. The division was in turn divided into three units called maniples, each divided into two centuries, commanded by a centurion.

During Jesus' time, four legions were based in the region: the Third, Sixth, Tenth and Twelfth. In addition to the infantry, each legion had its quota of specialist troops: engineers, bowmen, horsemen and medical officers. Each century also had a trumpeter, orderly, and standard-bearer.

The Roman Empire stretched from Spain in the west to the Caspian Sea.

The bust of Tiberius Caesar.

was soon in flames, and the fire spread across the city. The entire city of Jerusalem was destroyed. Only the towers of Herod's palace and a part of the western wall of the temple platform were left standing among the smouldering ruins. Six hundred thousand Jews had been killed. Survivors were taken to Rome to become slaves or be thrown to beasts.

Masada is an ancient fortress overlooking the Dead Sea. Herod the Great built it between 37 and 31 BC, and the historian Josephus tells us that in 73 Roman troops laid siege to Masada, and in the end, over 900 Jewish patriots chose to die there rather than surrender.

The Lost Sheep

LUKE 15:1–7

In Judea and Perea, Jesus spoke to people in parables, short stories which taught spiritual truths. To those who understood His teaching, the parable would be clear. To others, it would be only a story. This way, He could keep on teaching His followers while His enemies would not know His message.

A shepherd's work has seen little change over the centuries. In Israel, shepherding was a respected occupation. Such men as Jacob, Moses, and David were shepherds.

Shepherding was an important occupation because sheep were such important animals. As a source of food, sheep provided both meat and cheese. Their thick wool and tanned skins were used to make clothing and tent materials. Sheep were also offered as sacrifices to God till the Romans destroyed the temple.

But sheep are helpless animals, unable to find their own food and water, while wandering aimlessly about the countryside. A shepherd is essential for the care and protection of the flock.

Each day a shepherd must look for a pasture where his sheep may graze. There is no need to drive them, for the sheep willingly follow wherever he leads. At noon, the sheep are led to the nearest stream, which may be miles away. In the evening, the sheep are taken into the sheepfold, a fenced pen which keeps them from wandering. Only one door leads into the sheepfold, and the shepherd sleeps in front of it. If there is no sheepfold, a shepherd might have to stay up all night watching his sheep.

The shepherd always carried a staff and a sling. Both were used to protect his flock from snakes and wild animals. Many times he was forced to fight jackals, wolves, and even bears. Each day the shepherd lived with his flock, cared for them, and protected them. Out of this grew a tremendous bond of affection. If a single sheep wandered, the shepherd risked his life to bring it back safely.

The shepherd was careful to make sure that each member of his flock was well cared for. An injured sheep was carried on his shoulders until it was able to walk again. And a newborn lamb was sometimes carried in the shepherd's cloak, till it was strong enough to move along with the rest of the flock.

Two kinds of shepherds were found in Bible lands. One is the settled type, who led his sheep out to pasture each day and brought them home at night. The other was the nomad, who travelled the countryside looking for good pasture, while living in a tent.

Why Jesus taught in parables

Jesus taught much about Himself, His home in heaven, and His Heavenly Father in parables, short stories from everyday life. Why? Why not just tell these truths in plain language instead of hidden in stories?

Jesus' enemies heard the parables as stories, little more. But those who earnestly sought Him and believed in Him saw the hidden meanings. So it also is today.

The Lost Coin

LUKE 15:8–10

Jesus said that He came to seek and save what was lost. But the Pharisees and teachers of the Law criticized Him for welcoming sinners. Jesus told this story to show how important they were.

Coins of Jesus' time

When Jesus was on earth, there were numerous coins available. People came to the temple from all parts of the known world. There they exchanged their foreign coins with the money changers so they could buy birds or animals to sacrifice. Foreign coins were not accepted, so visitors had to exchange their money for the specific coins accepted in the temple.

Several events in Jesus' life are also associated with the coins of His time. In some cases these were coins He mentioned or which were mentioned as part of the background of the story in which He was involved. Some of these coins bore images of people associated with the life of Jesus.

During Old Testament times, coins were not widely used. Gold and silver were the medium of exchange, but these metals were in the form of jewellery or broken pieces which were weighed. Numerous references throughout the Old Testament refer to men or women of wealth as those who possessed large amounts of gold, silver, or bronze. Animals were also a measure of a person's wealth, especially among the Bedouin.

Coinage began with the Lydians during the seventh century BC. They were captured by the Persians in the fifth century BC, and coinage spread. Athenians issued silver coins known as tetradrachms. This same term later was used among other nations to represent their silver coins. The tetradrachms of Tyre were probably the "30 pieces of silver" Judas got for betraying Jesus. Antioch, Rhodes, and other places minted silver tetradrachms.

No gold coin is mentioned by name in the New Testament. The Jewish people did not mint a gold coin. The reference in Matthew 10:9 may be to gold and silver coins. So also may other references to silver and gold (Acts 3:6;1 Cor. 3:12; James 5:3;1 Peter 1:18).

It is hard to assign present-day values to these coins except by comparing the values of their metal. Purchasing power of silver and gold has varied greatly since Bible times.

The Prodigal Son

LUKE 15:11–32

Travelling throughout Judea and Perea, Jesus taught that He was the Good Shepherd, searching for lost sheep. He taught with many parables, making truths clear to those who wanted to learn and confusing to those who did not. The disciples would understand much more later, after the Holy Spirit came. They would recognize that God was like a loving father, welcoming home a wandering son.

The Return of the Prodigal Son, an oil painting by Rembrandt completed a few years before his death.

Carob pods

The prodigal son became so hungry that he was forced to eat the "pods" or "husks" that were the pigs' food. These were probably carob pods which come from the carob or locust tree. This tree is an evergreen and can grow as tall as 15 m (50 feet). The pods which grow on the tree are usually 15–25 cm (6–10 inches) long and very bitter when still green. But as they ripen, they take on a darker colour, and a sweet syrup forms inside. Today this syrup is extracted as a gum and is used in the food, textile, and cosmetic industries.

In Jesus' time, these pods were used as food for pigs and cattle. Poor people also ate them because they were cheap. A few scholars think that these pods may have been the "locusts" John the Baptist ate, since they came from carob or locust trees.

Swine

Swine, or pigs, were forbidden food in Israel, considered the most unclean and sinful of animals. As a Jew, the prodigal son must have detested these swine. But now in a foreign country and at the brink of starvation, the only available job was feeding and tending these animals. To make matters worse, he was forced to eat the swine's food in order to survive. In the eyes of any Jew, including himself, he could stoop no lower.

The fattened calf

The Israelites were always ready for hospitality, so many homes kept a fattened calf on hand for special events. Meat was often hard to come by and killing the fattened calf was a sign of honour and respect. The arrival of a special guest meant that a great feast was on hand.

The Rich Man and Lazarus

LUKE 16:19–31

Jesus taught hidden lessons in one parable after another. With a story about a lost sheep, He told how He, the Good Shepherd, searched for His own. In another story, about a lost son, He told how His Father in heaven welcomed a lost but repentant sinner home. In this parable He told of a poor man who loved God and a rich man who did not. The poor man was rich, and the rich man was poor.

Rich people

Middle-class society was rare in Israel during New Testament times. A few families lived with great wealth; most had almost nothing. A tremendous gap existed between rich and poor, and as a result the poor were exploited.

A man usually acquired wealth because he was born into the right family. Most wealthy men rode in chariots drawn by their own horses and owned much land and many slaves. Their houses

A Babylonian plaque featuring a mastiff, c. 2000–1600 BC.

were filled with expensive furniture and beautiful oriental rugs in a variety of colours. They wore white wool or silk robes, and their wives wore embroidered linen and bracelets, necklaces, and armbands of gold and silver.

Poor people

A poor man struggled to make ends meet, but he was not necessarily a beggar. He hoped to earn a denarius each day (a day's wages). This was just enough to buy food and keep up with the oppressive Roman taxes. For some, slavery was preferred to poverty. A man might sell himself or his children into slavery, giving him some security when it came to food and shelter.

DOGS OF BIBLE HOMES

In Bible homes dogs had a different role than they do today. Modern people think of dogs most often as "man's best friend", warm spirited pets, or household animals. Bible-time people did not usually keep dogs as pets, especially as affectionate animals. Israelites thought of dogs as unclean, for they were scavengers, living off refuse and dead animals. So dogs were one source of diseases.

Wild dogs that roamed the streets ate the flesh of Jezebel almost as soon as she had died. Dead bodies were often thrown to dogs to eat, so Jezebel's case was not so unusual (see 2 Kings 9).

But in Egypt, the dog was esteemed and often associated with a god, such as Anubis. In Mesopotamia also dogs were valued, and many were used for hunting and guarding a person's property. Assyrians, for example, had hunting dogs.

When Jesus spoke to the Syrophoenician woman about "dogs", He was undoubtedly referring to those so common in Israel, the scavenger dogs. The dogs which licked the sores of poor Lazarus were held in contempt, as Lazarus was. They were mentioned to show the low estate to which Lazarus had sunk.

Jesus Raises Lazarus

JOHN 11:1–44

In His travels around Judea and Perea, Jesus had visited the home of Mary, Martha, and Lazarus before, probably many times. These people were like a family to Him, with a bond of affection. But Jesus deliberately let Lazarus die, so that he might live again.

A detail from *The Raising of Lazarus* by Jean Jouvenet.

Jesus raised Lazarus from the dead sometime between the Feast of Dedication, which took place in December, and the Passover, when He was crucified. It was probably on a brisk winter day in January or February when Jesus arrived in Bethany. The town is just 3 km (2 miles) from Jerusalem and only slightly higher in elevation. Both experience much the same weather, and in Jerusalem at that time of year the average temperature is 9°C (49°F), with mild afternoons but very cool nights.

Lazarus

As brother of Mary and Martha, Lazarus must have known Jesus quite well. In fact, Jesus had a deep love for Lazarus and his sisters (John 11:5, 36). But little is known about the personality of Lazarus. In the Bible he does not speak a word. When he was raised, it caused many Jews to believe in Jesus (11:45), but it also prompted the Sanhedrin to lay plans for Jesus' death (11:47–53). And because Lazarus was a key witness to the authority of Christ, the chief priests and elders plotted his death as well (12:10).

A tomb in a cave

The Bible tells us that Lazarus was buried in a cave. This could have been a natural cave or a tomb or vault cut into the rock. A large round stone was often rolled across the entrance of such a tomb after burial. Some of these tombs had a "court" cut into the rock just in front of the tomb entrance. It was only large enough for the bier and its bearers.

Upon death, the body was sealed inside the tomb. After the flesh had decayed and only the skeleton remained, the bones were placed in a box called an ossuary. This small box was then placed on a shelf which had been carved out of the tomb wall. In this way, a whole family could be buried in the same tomb.

Some wealthy people preferred to be buried in large stone coffins called sarcophaguses. Special niches were carved in the tomb wall for

Bethany and Jerusalem.

The so-called "St Lazarus' Tomb", from which traditionally Lazarus was raised in al-Eizariya.

Preparing the body for burial

Because of the warm climate in Palestine, burial usually took place the same day as death. But before the funeral, the body was prepared for burial.

Rarely did the immediate family become involved in preparing the body for burial. Friends and other family members took the body, washed it, and clipped the hair and nails. Strips of linen were then wrapped around the body. Spices, such as hyssop, rose oil, and rose water were placed in between these strips. Finally, a linen napkin was placed over the face and the body laid on an open bier.

these coffins. Such tombs had to be much bigger to accommodate the large-size sarcophaguses.

Soon catacombs developed, which were large underground mazes of tombs.

What happened to Lazarus? According to some traditions he ended up in Cyprus, where the apostle Paul made him the first bishop of present-day Larnaca, where he served for thirty more years, here, at what is now called the Church of Saint Lazarus.

Ten Lepers

LUKE 17:11–19

The time was approaching when Jesus would enter Jerusalem for His last week before the crucifixion. He was travelling throughout Judea and Perea, teaching through many parables about His Father and His heavenly home. In certain places He paused to perform miracles on some needy persons, such as healing the 10 lepers.

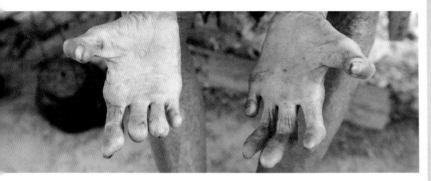

This leprosy patient's hands have been affected by the disease.

Shortly after the raising of Lazarus, Jesus went from Ephraim (John 11:54) north into southern Galilee to join the pilgrims to Jerusalem. The border between Samaria and Galilee ran roughly from Mount Carmel southeast through the Plain of Esdraelon and the intervening hills to Mount Gilboa and the Jordan River. There were two main roads through Samaria, one along the coast, the other along the high ridge. On their way to Jerusalem for the Passover, Jesus and the pilgrims took the high road.

It is impossible to determine exactly which village is intended. Luke may not have known. But possible villages include Capercotnei, Agrippina, and Scythopolis.

"Show yourselves to the priests"

The Old Testament gives detailed regulations for the ceremonial cleansing of those cured of infectious skin diseases such as leprosy. Moses, for example, mentions the offerings and rites involved (Lev. 14). The offerings included live clean birds, one to be killed over fresh water in a clay pot, the other dipped in its blood. On the eighth day two male lambs and a ewe, flour, and oil were taken to the temple, with the individual cured from the disease. If the person was too poor, a substitute offering was possible. The ceremonies could be performed by any local priest, not just those in Jerusalem.

Note that Luke, in his concern for "minorities", focuses on a grateful Samaritan.

LEPROSY

One of the most feared diseases of the ancient world was leprosy, especially among the Israelites. The disease itself was frightening, but the Israelites added an even more terrifying note – complete isolation. A person with leprosy could not live among family and friends but had to go away to live by himself or with other people with leprosy.

Leprosy came in two types. The tuberculoid type started with a change in skin colour, to a white or pink spot. Sometimes it went away by itself. In any case it did not cause the severe problems caused by the other type.

Lepromatous leprosy also started with a change in skin colour, such as a white or pink spot. But this type spread rapidly, with swellings appearing. In time the hands and feet became deformed, bones deteriorated, and nerves were destroyed.

The person with leprosy in Bible times faced a tragic future, for there was no known cure. He or she was condemned to be an outcast and suffer alone.

A Pharisee and a Tax Collector

LUKE 18:9–14

As Jesus travelled through Judea and Perea, territories near Jerusalem, He often faced the proud Pharisees. These people separated themselves from many ordinary things of life, pretending to be holier than others. But in their pretended holiness, they were blind to their one hope for heaven – the Messiah, God's Son, who had come to show them the way to His home. One day Jesus told a story about a Pharisee, who thought he was holy, and a tax collector, who did not.

An orthodox Jew praying in an Israeli synagogue. He is reading the Torah and wears tefillin, tzitzit, and tallit.

Josephus, the famous Jewish historian, knew that three Jewish parties (Pharisees, Sadducees, and Essenes) existed as early as 145 BC. As Judaism's legalistic branch, Pharisees separated themselves from those who neglected the Law. Their piety made them popular. Jesus condemned their self-righteousness and hypocrisy, not their basic beliefs.

There were two kinds of tax collectors in Jesus' day: the tax gatherer who collected land, income, and poll taxes; the more hated customs men, who collected tolls on everything from bridges to food.

Fasting and tithing

Fasting means not eating, and sometimes also not drinking, from sunrise to sunset. Jews were expected to fast on the Day of Atonement and in times of crisis. A second-century document called the Didache notes that while Jews fasted on Monday and Thursday, the Christians fasted on Wednesday and Friday. Tithing is giving one-tenth of one's income. Egyptians gave even more to their Pharaohs.

SADDUCEES & PHARISEES

The Sadducees were Jews from the wealthy, ruling class and were connected with the high priesthood. The name "Sadducee" may be linked with the name Zadok, an early high priest. In general, they took in a lot of Greek thinking; they believed the world to be a good place to live in and did not believe in a resurrection, judgement, or afterlife. Instead of physical resurrection, they believed in the immortality of the soul. They believed Scripture consisted solely of the five books of Moses and rejected any belief in angels or spirits.

In Jesus' time, the Sadducees formed the majority in the Sanhedrin, the Jewish court; they argued vehemently over the resurrection with the Pharisees.

The name Pharisees means "those who separate themselves". In Jesus' time, there were about 6,000 Pharisees. They aimed to be pure, undefiled in ritual. They believed that the Jewish Law divided very clearly between being "clean" and "unclean"; "unclean" meant disobeying the Law.

Because they were so anxious to obey the Law, often they had to make new regulations which defined the Law of Moses more precisely, or applied it to contemporary situations.

However, ordinary Jews were not interested in detailed interpretations of the Law and would not join the Pharisees. There was much bitterness between the two parties.

In general, the Pharisees believed all the historic doctrines of their faith: the resurrection of the dead, the final judgement, the importance of leading a moral life, and the election of Israel.

Jesus and the Children

MATTHEW 19:13–15; MARK 10:13–16;
LUKE 18:15–17

When Jesus raised His friend Lazarus from the dead, He startled the people of that part of the land. Some believed on Him as God's Son. Others wanted all the more to kill Him. For a time, Jesus returned to Galilee, then made His way to Perea, east of the Jordan River. One day some parents brought their young children to Jesus, so that He might bless them. The disciples rebuked the parents. Why did these people think that Jesus had time for children?

Perea is the region on the east side of the Jordan River (Matt. 19:1). Luke's account follows the story of the healing of the 10 lepers on the west side of the Jordan, so all three accounts harmonize. If Perea is used in a general geographical sense, this moving narrative may have taken place in or near Pella; if it is used in the stricter, more political sense, the site may have been Gedor or Philadelphia. If it took place in the same house in which Jesus so strongly supported the marriage bonds, no wonder the mothers brought their children to Jesus to bless them!

Little children
There are several words in Greek that refer to children. The word used by Matthew and Mark refers to very small children. Luke reveals that they were babies in the arms of their mothers. That this is the age of the little children to which Matthew and Mark refer is confirmed by Mark's reference to the fact that Jesus took them in His arms (Mark 10:16).

Jesus blesses the children.

As was so often true, Jesus once again upset traditional values, as the reaction of the disciples suggested. Rabbis did not lower their dignity by associating with little children. Jesus, on the contrary, used children to illustrate some of His most basic teachings.

The laying on of hands
The act of laying one's hands on another person is an ancient tradition with many meanings. The mothers who brought their children to Jesus undoubtedly were seeking His blessing, much as Jacob blessed Joseph's children (Gen. 48:14). The words used in a blessing were considered full of power, so the mothers of the children clearly recognized that Jesus' blessing and touch had special significance.

Children and God's kingdom
What did Jesus mean when He said the kingdom of God belongs to those who are like children, and that anyone who does not receive the kingdom like a little child will never enter it? Some have suggested such qualities as humility, receptiveness, meekness, simple trust, innocence, simplicity, and directness. Probably the best answer is that Jesus was not thinking of any such qualities, since the children were just babies. He probably referred to their absolute dependence on their parents. Christians too depend totally on God for salvation and life.

What a beautiful picture of Jesus this story contains! Though busy and important, Jesus still had time for the tiniest baby.

The Rich Young Ruler

MATTHEW 19:16–30; MARK 10:17–31;
LUKE 18:18–30

After He had raised Lazarus from the dead, Jesus returned for a while to Galilee. Later He went to Perea, east of the Jordan River, to minister. Some mothers brought their young children to Jesus, and He blessed them. Then a rich young man came to see Jesus, asking what good thing he had to do to get eternal life.

Who was this man? The word "young" means that he would have been between 24 and 40 years old. To say that he was a ruler probably meant that he was a member of the Sanhedrin. The Sanhedrin, which literally means "sitting together", was the highest Jewish authority in all of Palestine. The man must have been unusually devout in his faith if he was a member of this important council at such a young age.

Nobody is perfect. For a perfect person would never do anything wrong. In Bible times the word meant something a bit different. When Jesus said to the young man, "If you want to be perfect", He meant, "If you want to be fully developed in a moral sense". The word was a synonym for "complete" or "mature". It sometimes meant "adult" or "full-grown". The word was also used of a person who had been fully initiated into one of the "mystery" religions of New Testament times.

Sell your possessions

Some people have wondered if all Christians are supposed to sell everything they own and give the proceeds to the poor. Most of us probably need to give more to help others than we do. But Jesus' command was given specifically to a rich young ruler because he had a problem with covetousness. For some people, like St Francis of Assisi, following Christ does mean selling everything. But for other wealthy men, such as Philemon, wealth should be used in a Christian way. The danger is that our concern for keeping too much for ourselves can keep us from following Christ.

The rich and the poor

Why were the disciples "greatly astonished" at Jesus' words about the difficulty of rich people getting into heaven? Because it was the popular view that riches were God's reward for a good life. Sometimes that is true. A good life makes a man richer than a wasteful life.

But the New Testament is full of reminders that riches can distort life too.

EYE OF THE NEEDLE

What did Jesus mean when He said it was easier for a camel to go through a needle's eye than for a rich man to enter the kingdom of God? It is impossible for a camel to go through the eye of a sewing needle. Does this mean that it is impossible for a rich man to enter the kingdom of God That certainly cannot be true, for many rich men have been devout Christians using their wealth to serve God. What then did Jesus mean?

There were two types of needle's eyes in Jesus' time. One was a sewing needle, almost like those we use today, except larger and made of bronze or iron. It had an eye through which thread was passed as with modern needles. Some people believe Jesus spoke literally about this kind of needle. Perhaps, but it seems more likely that He spoke of the other type.

This second type of needle's eye was a small door within a larger door, usually in the large wooden door that was a city gate. Humans could walk through these small gates, but large animals such as camels could not.

When the large door was closed, such as late in the evening, people could still go through the "needle's eye", the smaller door. But if a camel came, burdened with a heavy load on its back, it became necessary for the load to be removed and for the camel to almost crawl through the "needle's eye" on its knees. It suggests that Jesus was saying a rich man must lay aside his burdensome "things" and kneel to enter God's kingdom.

The Labourers in the Vineyard

MATTHEW 20:1–16

After raising Lazarus from the dead, Jesus returned to Galilee for a while. Then He went to Perea, east of the Jordan River, where He blessed some young children who were brought to Him and talked with a rich young man about eternal life. Then Jesus told a parable about some labourers in a vineyard.

A vineyard in rural Israel.

Vineyards
The vineyards the landowner hired labourers to work in would have been quite different from today's vineyards. The vines would most likely have been trailing along the ground, though in some cases Jews allowed them to grow up trees or on trellises. Most vineyards were on the south side of hills so the vines would mature in the sun. They were surrounded by walls to keep out wild animals, such as foxes and boars, with a watchtower from which thieves could be seen.

Raising grapes is one of the hardest forms of farming because the grapes require constant attention.

The marketplace
Greek and Jewish marketplaces differed. Greek marketplaces were for trials and disputes; they were surrounded by statues and temples. Jewish marketplaces were more like bazaars, busy with buying and selling, children playing, and men hiring workers.

Time
In ancient times people did not divide time the way we do. The Old Testament speaks only of morning, afternoon, evening, and night. The Babylonians were the first to divide daylight into 12 equal parts, and everyone else followed them. The day began at 6:00 in the morning. So the third hour was 9 A.M.; the sixth, noon; and so on.

Denarius
A denarius or "penny" was a full day's pay. About the size of our dime, it had Caesar's head on the front and another image on the back.

A denarius, c. 118 BC.

A vineyard in Israel at sunset.

A winepress, with men trampling the grapes with their feet, while hanging onto ropes above them. The juice of the grapes ran into containers sitting beside the large basin in which the men stood.

Blind Bartimaeus

MATTHEW 20:29–34; MARK 10:46–52;
LUKE 18:35–43

Jesus had left Galilee to minister in Judea and Perea. In Judea, at the village of Bethany, He had raised Lazarus from the dead. In Perea, He had welcomed little children and blessed them. Now He was on His way to Jerusalem, where He would be crucified. The way to Jerusalem led through Jericho.

Jericho as it appears today.

The pilgrims on their way to Jerusalem from Galilee crossed over the Jordan from Perea, into Jericho, the last major stop on their journey. The town of Jericho is tied in the minds of Bible-readers with Joshua, Zaccheus, and the Good Samaritan. It may have received its name from Yarih, an ancient Semitic moon goddess. The town is located near a spring, which makes it an attractive place to dwell. Built by Herod the Great as his winter capital because it was much warmer and drier than Jerusalem, the Jericho of New Testament times was built partly of cut stone and partly of a distinctive construction of small rectangular stones set in mortar. Herod probably saw a building in this style when he was on a trip to Rome. The modern city of Jericho is about a mile east of the New Testament town.

Beggars and Cloaks

One writer has said that beggars existed in the Middle East wherever wealth was found.

People became beggars for many reasons. Sometimes, as in the case of Bartimaeus, blindness or some other illness made them incapable of working. Sometimes robbers, heavy taxes, or even laziness left people so poor they became beggars.

Mark alone tells us that Bartimaeus threw his cloak aside when Jesus called him. This might have been the outer of three garments he was wearing. But a poor beggar would probably have only one, a garment like a nightgown with openings only at the neck, arms, and hemmed bottom. Jesus' seamless robe would have been this garment.

The garment most people wore over this undergarment would be the tallith, a shirt almost as long as the undergarment, but made of wool, flax, or even leather. It was a close-fitting, sleeved garment that was fastened around the waist by a belt.

The outer garment Bartimaeus threw aside would have been a light coat or jacket of a coarser material, which came in various shapes. This long jacket had white knots (fringes) attached with a blue cord at each of its corners.

In addition to these three pieces of clothing, the Jew would wear a turban or some other type of headgear on his head and sandals on his feet.

The outer garment was the garment people in mourning would tear; it was also the garment that was removed before a person was flogged.

Blindness

Blindness was common in Egypt, Israel, and the other countries of the neighbouring Near East. It had numerous causes, including poverty and inadequate food, unsanitary conditions at home, overexposure to the sun, excessive heat, blowing sand, accidents, and war injuries. Blindness is mentioned no less than 34 times in the Gospels alone.

JESUS' LAST JOURNEY TO JERUSALEM

1. After Peter confesses Christ as Lord, Jesus explains to His disciples that He will go to Jerusalem to suffer, be killed, and rise again on the third day.
2. Jesus is transfigured on the mountain top. States again He will suffer at the hands of the murderers of John the Baptist.
3. Ministry around Capernaum.
4. While in Galilee He resolutely sets Himself to go to Jerusalem.
5. Travels through the towns and villages of Galilee on the way to Jerusalem. Large crowds follow Him.
6. Leaves Galilee for the regions of Judea and Perea. Teaches and heals.
7. On the road between Samaria and Galilee meets ten men with leprosy.
8. In Perea – takes the Twelve aside and explains again that He is going to Jerusalem to fulfil prophecies about Himself. The disciples still do not understand.
9. Approaches Jericho. Restores a blind beggar's sight.
10. In Jericho – meets Zaccheus.
11. To Bethphage and Bethany. On to the Mount of Olives. Weeps over Jerusalem before entering the city on a donkey, with the crowds cheering.
12. Enters the temple area, drives out the traders.
13. He teaches in the temple precinct every day until Passover time
14. Six days before Passover – in Bethany a woman breaks a jar of perfume over Jesus' feet.
15. With Passover two days away He tells disciples again that He is about to be handed over to be crucified.
16. Passover week – Jesus' final week – the Last Supper, arrest, trial, Crucifixion, and Resurrection.

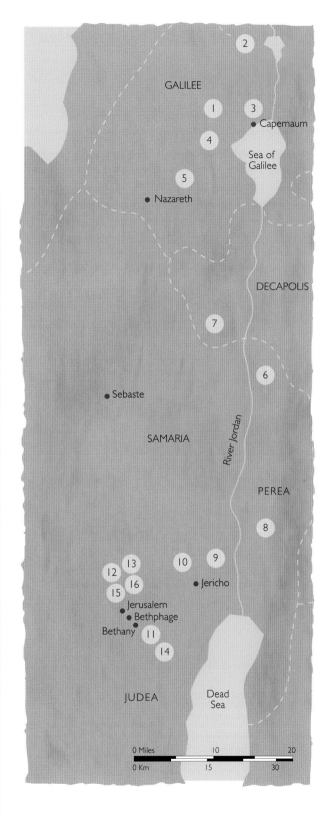

Zaccheus and the Parable of the Three Servants

LUKE 19:1–27

Throughout the early part of His ministry, Jesus spent most of His time around the Sea of Galilee, ministering in villages such as Capernaum and Bethsaida. Now He had left that region and was heading toward Jerusalem, ministering in both Judea and Perea. On the way to Jerusalem, He stopped in Jericho where He healed a blind man and met a tax collector named Zaccheus.

This tree stands at a major intersection in Jericho and is called the Zaccheus Tree. Testing on the tree has shown that it is over 2,000 years old, so it is possible that this is the very one a tax collector climbed to get to see Jesus.

Chief tax collector

Zaccheus was the chief tax collector, the head of the regional taxation division of the Roman government. Usually such men were Romans. But Zaccheus probably represented the Jews in Jericho, which was the central station for collecting taxes for the whole region. He would have been the equivalent of the Roman censor, the one who sold the privilege of collecting taxes to the highest bidder. This man,

the *publicanus*, could then add as much of a commission as he could collect. One's right to collect taxes usually lasted for five years. Tax collectors were notorious for cheating both the government and the people. Sons of tax collectors often continued their fathers' work. In Jesus' day taxes were levied on everything the Romans could think of, so tax rebellions were common and people were often reduced to poverty by the numerous taxes. A drawing on an Egyptian tomb shows a man being beaten because he failed to pay his taxes. It is little wonder the common people hated tax collectors. That Jesus could love them is one more example of His love for the unlovely.

The sycamore tree

A sycamore tree was a type of fig tree, often called the fig-mulberry. It had many strong, wide-spreading branches, so it was easy for a person to climb. The sycamore-fig bore fruit several times a year, in clusters. People did not often eat it, however, because it was not as tasty as ordinary figs. To make

Although a type of fig tree, sycamore trees were more important for their timber in Bible times.

them ripen properly, workers would puncture the fruit with the point of a knife.

The sycamore-fig was just one of many trees that grew in the warm climate of Jericho. So many palm trees grew there that Jericho was known as "the City of Palms". The perfume of the sweet-scented balsam, carried for miles by the wind, may even have given the city its name, which may mean "the Perfumed".

Mina

To the crowds who welcomed Him in Jericho, Jesus told the Parable of the Minas/Talents. The mina was a Greek rather than a Roman coin. Coins were first introduced by the Lydians in the seventh century BC. The mina was 100 drachmas. The drachma was the equivalent of a day's wages, similar to the value of a Roman denarius.

It is extremely difficult to put values on money from Bible times, for even in our times the value of gold and silver has increased more than 20 times, then decreased, then increased again until within a few years values become difficult to fix.

Jesus' Triumphal Entry into Jerusalem

MATTHEW 21:1–9; MARK 11:1–10; LUKE 19:29–44;
JOHN 12:12–19

Jesus had left His native region, Galilee, to minister in Judea and Perea on His way to Jerusalem. On this visit to Jerusalem, He would be crucified and would rise from the dead. As He entered the city triumphantly, He fulfiled an old prophecy which pointed to Him as the Messiah, God's Son. But many failed to recognize Him.

The Kidron Valley, looking up toward the walls of Jerusalem.

Bethphage and Bethany

Both of these villages are on the Mount of Olives. Bethphage, meaning "the place of unripened figs", is nearer the top of the mount. Since it is only about 3 km (2 miles) from Jerusalem, it is not surprising that it is often mentioned in Jewish literature as part of the capital. Scholars differ as to whether ancient Bethphage was on the site of present-day Abu-Dis, near the top of the Mount of Olives, or Kefr et Tûr, on the very top.

Bethany, meaning "house of dates" or "house of figs", is farther down the slope of the Mount of Olives. Identified today with the Arab village of el-Azariyeh, it now has about 1,000 inhabitants. Over the ruins of the traditional site of the home of Mary, Martha, and Lazarus is the modern Church of St Lazarus, Mary, and Martha.

The Mount of Olives

The Mount of Olives, from which Jesus could see the Holy City, is a two-mile rise with three peaks. The modern road from Jericho to Jerusalem still passes along its southern slopes. Rising about 30 m (100 feet) above Jerusalem, it gives an unforgettable view of the city, which is to the west.

Colt and donkey

The donkey was the usual animal for travelling in Palestine because it could travel the steep, narrow, rocky roads. Kings usually rode in wheeled vehicles. But according to Zechariah 9:9, the Messiah, the King of kings, would arrive on a lowly donkey.

Temple and Eastern Gate

Jesus would have had a magnificent view of the gleaming white marble and gold of the temple as He rode into Jerusalem. Herod's temple, completed later, just six years before Jerusalem was destroyed (AD 70), was almost an exact replica of Solomon's temple, built 1,000 years before. Jesus would have crossed the Xystus bridge, 135 m (450 feet) above the Kidron Valley, and entered the Susa Gate (now the Golden Gate).

Jesus at the Temple

MATTHEW 21:10-17; MARK 11:11-19;
LUKE 19:45-48

As He came to Jerusalem from Perea, Jesus stopped in Jericho, where He healed a blind man and brought new life to the tax collector, Zaccheus. From there, Jesus came to the village of Bethany, east of Jerusalem, where He frequently stayed at the home of Mary, Martha, and Lazarus. As the Passover drew near, Jesus rode triumphantly into Jerusalem as the prophets of old had said the Messiah would do. There He taught in the temple.

The Greeks
To us today the word "Greek" means someone from Greece. The Greeks who came to Jerusalem to worship, however, were a special type of Greek. They were proselytes. That means they accepted the beliefs and practices of the Jewish religion. Some proselytes were called "God-fearers"; they accepted the Jewish faith but rejected circumcision, a practice not popular outside Judaism.

The temple porches
All around the outer courts of the temple were covered walkways, called "porches" or "porticoes". The walkway on the east side was called "Solomon's Porch", perhaps because a tradition said Solomon had built a similar wall. It was 476 m (1,562 feet) long and was built over a retaining wall above the Kidron Valley. People were free to meet, talk, and even teach in this area. Jesus loved to walk and talk here, and so did His disciples after His death and resurrection.

HEROD'S TEMPLE

The rebuilding of the temple and its courtyards was the greatest building achievement of Herod the Great. So extensive were his plans for it that it was doubted the work could ever be completed. The people refused to start work until all the necessary materials and workmen had been brought together.

| Royal Portico | The Holy of Holies — The Holy Place | Court of Priests with altar — Court of Israel | Pinnacle of the Temple — Treasury (Women's Court) |

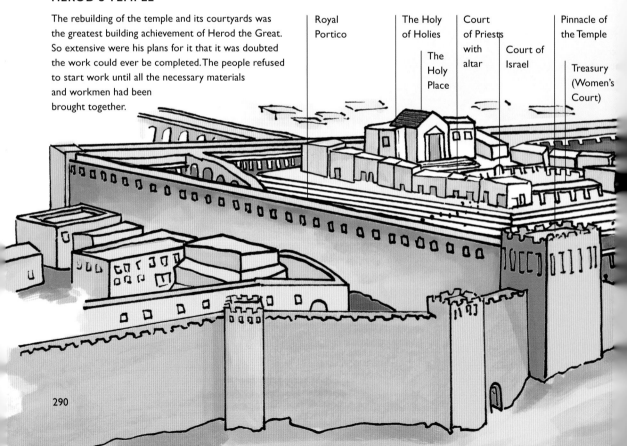

The Royal Portico was the walkway that went along the south wall of the temple courts. It was a magnificent structure with 160 ornate columns gracing its 281 m (921 feet). This is the area in which the money changers and other businessmen conducted their business. Close to the centre were the two Huldah Gates through which pilgrims entered the temple. This area has been the site of many excavations since 1968. As a result many no longer believe Robinson's Arch led to a bridge over the Tyropoean Valley that led to the upper city. There was probably a stairway, which led down to a street 10 m (32 feet) wide, that went along the west wall.

The large area in the foreground of this model of Herod's temple was called the Court of the Women. Behind it, the temple proper stood as high as a 15-story building.

The money changers

Money changers were in the Royal Portico to change unacceptable foreign currency into acceptable half-shekels (didrachms), shekels (tetradrachms), and other forms of offering. How surprising that the shekel, a coin from Tyre that had the picture of Tyre's god, Baal Melcarth, on it, was acceptable!

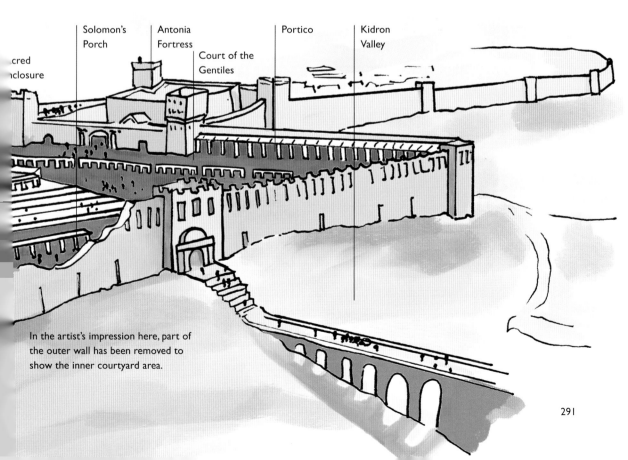

In the artist's impression here, part of the outer wall has been removed to show the inner courtyard area.

Give to Caesar

MATTHEW 22:15–22; MARK 12:13–17;
LUKE 20:20–26

After Jesus rode triumphantly into Jerusalem, He taught in the temple. The religious leaders tried to trap Him, for they wanted Him out of the way. He was a threat to them. In one of their efforts they tried to get Jesus to take sides – the Roman emperor Caesar, or the people.

Pharisees and Herodians

It is surprising to find these two groups linked together. The Pharisees originally stood against evil in society and in personal lives, though by Jesus' day many had often become narrow and petty, more concerned with rules than with God. Pharisees were middle class and more religious than the Sadducees, who often were willing to compromise with the political leaders of the country and tended to be more upper class. It has been estimated that in Jerusalem alone there were more than 20,000 associated with the Sadducees.

The Herodians, on the other hand, were probably more political than religious. While they in some sense supported the dynasty of Herod the Great, opinion differs widely as to whether they were soldiers,

Tiberius

courtiers, Jews from regions ruled by Herod's sons, or those who favoured direct rule by Herod rather than by Rome. The most widely held view is that they were supporters of Herod Antipas.

Both of these groups, religious and political, united in an effort to trap Jesus.

Caesar

Originally "Caesar" was the last name of the family of Julius Caesar. His successors adopted it as a title, so that it came to mean something like "king".

The Caesar who ruled the Roman Empire when Jesus was born was Julius Caesar's grandnephew, but Julius Caesar adopted him. He took the name Caesar Augustus. "Augustus" means "revered". He was the emperor who defeated Antony and Cleopatra at the Battle of Actium in 31 BC and made Egypt a Roman province.

The Caesar mentioned most often in the New Testament, however, is Tiberius, who was emperor from 14–37. Tiberius was the stepson of Augustus and also, by marrying his daughter, his son-in-law! The denarius mentioned in Jesus' comments about paying taxes to Caesar probably had the head of Tiberius on it.

Tribute to Caesar

The tribute was a tax that was required to support the Roman government. Jews hated it because it went directly to the emperor's treasury. This proved that the Jews were subject to Rome. Note that neither Jesus nor His questioners had the required silver money in their possession. They had to ask someone for it. The coin would have been a denarius, not the shekel that was used to pay the temple tax. The wording on the coin probably said that the emperor, Tiberius, was the divine son of Caesar Augustus. No wonder Jews didn't like it!

The coin which was shown to Jesus was probably a denarius with the image of Tiberius on it.

The Widow's Mite

MARK 12:41–44; LUKE 21:1–4

Jesus rode triumphantly into Jerusalem on Sunday, with crowds cheering Him. That night He stayed in Bethany, probably at the home of Mary, Martha, and Lazarus. On Monday morning, He pronounced a curse on a barren fig tree as He returned to Jerusalem, where at the temple, He drove out the money changers and merchants. On that same day, while the religious leaders tried to trap Him, Gentiles came to seek Him. On Tuesday, as Jesus made His way back to Jerusalem from Bethany, He and His disciples noted that the fig tree He had cursed was now withered. That same Tuesday afternoon, while Jesus and His disciples were in the treasury, or Women's Court of the temple, Jesus pointed out the great value of a gift which a widow was giving.

Mite

What was the gift the widow was giving? The word "mite" does not help us much because it is a seventeenth-century English word used to translate the Greek word *lepton* and the Roman word *quadrans*. The tiny lepton (mite) was the smallest bronze or copper coin made. There were many different *lepta*. On the front and back they may have had pictures of open flowers, anchors, grape clusters, helmets, fringed umbrellas, ears of corn, a wine jug, or a palm tree with two date clusters. Most had inscriptions referring to the emperor or some other ruler.

A bronze mite, minted by Alexander Jannaeus, King of Judea, 103–76 BC.

The *quadrans* was a large bronze or copper Roman coin. At the time of this story the quadrans probably had the head of Tiberius Caesar on one side and a wreath enclosing the letters "SC". on the other. The letters were short for *Senatus consulto*, meaning "by decree of the senate". A *quadrans* would buy two sparrows, the only meat the poor could afford .

The temple treasury

Where was the temple treasury? The answer is that we don't exactly know! Since the widow was able to put her small copper coins into the treasury, it was probably in the part of the temple called the Court of the Women, but where in that room we do not know.

In this area there were 13 boxes or urns with trumpet-shaped tubes called "trumpets" on the top to receive money offerings. Seven of these trumpets were for men to deposit their half-shekel temple tax; the other six were for free-will offerings such as the one the widow gave.

In the Old Testament the "tithe" or a tenth of one's goods was to be given to God. Jesus used the widow to teach that Christians should give more than they can easily afford. The purpose of giving is to support God's work and help those who are physically and spiritually needy.

Widows

It was not easy to be a widow in New Testament times. People grouped widows with orphans and foreigners as the most to be pitied. Though she might live with her children or her deceased husband's parents, she really belonged nowhere until she remarried. To make a widow's life more tolerable, a custom called "levirate marriage" required the husband's brother or other member of the family to marry her, if she was childless, and have children so the dead man would not be forgotten. The church made special provision for widows (see 1 Tim. 5:3–16).

Figs, Lamps, and Sheep

MATTHEW 24:32–25:46; MARK 13:28–37;
LUKE 21:29–36

As Jesus left Jerusalem on Tuesday afternoon to return to Bethany for the night, He and His disciples stopped on the Mount of Olives. He taught them many things, among which were important truths presented in parables. Some parables were about simple, everyday things such as figs, lamps, and sheep. But they taught eternal truths.

opening through which a fig wasp crawls to pollinate the plant. The pear-shaped, hollow fruit is, strictly speaking, not the fruit at all. The real fruit is the tiny little seeds inside.

The fig has many uses. Ancient peoples made it into cakes (1 Sam. 25:18). A poultice to cure boils was made from pressed figs (2 Kings 20:7). And the large, hand-shaped leaves were used by Adam and Eve as clothing (Gen. 3:7).

Lamps

It is strange that the Bible nowhere describes the ordinary, domestic lamp. It does mention, however, the twisted flax-thread wick and the jar of olive oil that was stored as lamp fuel.

Archaeologists have discovered lamps from all periods of ancient history and can trace the changes in

Jesus used the fig tree in several of His teachings.

Figs

The fig tree exists in both wild and cultivated forms. It can, under proper conditions, grow to a height of 9 m (30 feet) or more. It bears its fruit twice a year, a winter crop in May or June and a summer crop in late August or September. The fruit buds appear in February, some two months before the leaves appear. A tree can live for as long as 400 years. Figs often grow in the corners of vineyards in Palestine.

The fruit has some interesting characteristics. The flower grows inside what we think of as the fruit of the tree. At the tip there is an

lamps through the centuries. The earliest Palestinian lamps were made of clay pottery, though they may have been copied from the metal lamps of other cultures. Early lamps had four, or even seven, spouts for wicks. Later lamps in Canaan had a single spout. But these lamps tipped easily and caused fires, so a base was added, and under Greek influence Jews learned how to close in their lamps and fill them through a nozzle or filling hole. Because lamps were fed by oil, women got up a couple of times each night to "trim their lamps", i.e., raise the wick so the flame wouldn't go out.

Sheep and goats

Sheep and goats are among the earliest of man's domesticated animals, as early as 6000 or 7000 BC. Sheep are gentle, dependent; goats are not. The earliest evidence suggests that they may have been domesticated that early in northern Iran. Dogs have been used to herd sheep from 5000 BC on. These sheep were probably brown and reddish in colour, not the white colour we expect. They were first valued for their meat, then later for their wool, milk

Sheep and goats graze together in the countryside.

and cheese, skins, and manure. The broad-tailed sheep is most common, its 4.5–7 kg (10–15 lb) tail being considered a delicacy.

Though the skeleton of a goat is almost indistinguishable from that of a sheep, the goat has quite distinct habits. It was first valued for its milk, but with the development of the cow it declined in popularity. The goat can strip land rapidly in quest of food. Ancient peoples normally ate only kid meat. Goats' skin was used to make water bottles, and its hair was valued for making cloth.

This terracotta oil lamp was made in the first century, likely during the period when Jesus was working as a carpenter. It depicts the Greek goddess Nike.

295

Mary Anoints Jesus' Feet

MATTHEW 26:6–13; MARK 14:3–9; JOHN 12:2–11

The last week before Jesus' crucifixion had come. On Sunday, Jesus had entered Jerusalem triumphantly, riding on a donkey. On Monday, He pronounced a curse on a barren fig tree and drove out the merchants and money changers from the temple. On Tuesday, He answered a question about paying taxes to Caesar and pointed out a widow giving her small coins in the temple. That evening, He taught His disciples on the Mount of Olives. Tuesday evening, Jesus was a guest at the home of Simon the Leper. While there, Mary of Bethany anointed His feet.

The alabaster box

There is only one word for this in Greek; it should probably be translated "an alabaster jar". Alabaster is a soft marble common in the area of Alabastron in Egypt, from which the word may come. It is very fine-grained and pure white or translucent when no impurities are present, but the presence of iron oxide and other impurities produces beautiful combinations of yellow, pale and dark brown, and red. This soft marble was so often used for ointment containers that the word came to mean an ointment jar. Alabaster is formed by water dripping in limestone caves to form stalactites and stalagmites.

Alabaster flasks, like this early first century BC example with stopper, held ointments such as nard.

Spikenard

What an interesting history this word has! The word resulted from the fact that the Greek adjective describing the nard is very rare and very difficult to translate.

Wycliffe seems to be the first to coin the word; he speaks of "spikanard". Today we believe the word means "pure", though a good case can be made for the conclusion that the adjective is a technical word for a specific kind of nard, or even that the phrase should be translated "Indian nard".

Nard comes from the Himalayan Mountains and other high altitude places in northern India. Cheaper varieties come from other countries. It is a fragrant ointment made from the shaggy roots and lower stems of an Indian plant. It is used to anoint royalty. John may have seen Mary's act as a symbol of the anointing of Jesus as king of the Holy City. One historian tells us nard was very expensive.

JESUS' LAST WEEK IN JERUSALEM

Jesus often told His followers that eventually He would have to go up to Jerusalem to die. They did not understand Him. Finally, after preaching and travelling for some three years, Jesus came to Jerusalem for the Passover.

SUNDAY

Jesus enters Jerusalem from the Mount of Olives, riding on a donkey. The crowds welcome Him as Messiah, throwing down palm branches in the roadway (Mark 11).

MONDAY

Jesus overturns the money-changers' tables in the temple courts and expels the merchants from the temple (Mark 11).

TUESDAY

Jesus teaches in the temple (John 12). Judas Iscariot makes an agreement with the Jewish leaders to betray Jesus.

WEDNESDAY

Jesus spends a quiet day in Bethany.

THURSDAY

Jesus eats the Last Supper with His disciples in an Upper Room in Jerusalem. Afterwards they leave the city and go to Gethsemane, where Jesus is arrested (Matt. 26).

FRIDAY

Jesus is tried before Annas, Caiaphas, and the Sanhedrin, the Jewish Council (Matt. 26; Mark 14). Then Jesus is taken before Pontius Pilate in Herod's palace (Luke 23). After sentence, Jesus is taken through the streets of Jerusalem to Golgotha, the place of the skull, to be crucified (Mark 15). Before the beginning of the Sabbath, he is buried in the new tomb belonging to Joseph of Arimathea (Luke 23).

SUNDAY

Jesus' disciples see the risen Christ (Luke 24).

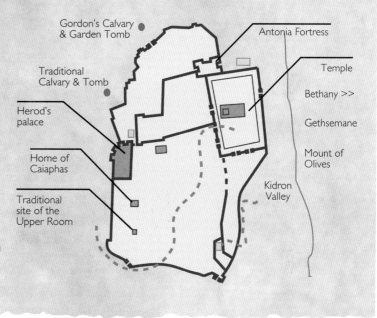

Gordon's Calvary & Garden Tomb

Traditional Calvary & Tomb

Herod's palace

Home of Caiaphas

Traditional site of the Upper Room

Antonia Fortress

Temple

Bethany >>

Gethsemane

Mount of Olives

Kidron Valley

The bag

Mark says simply that some complained about the waste of the ointment. Matthew adds that they were disciples. John singles out Judas Iscariot and mentions that he had the bag. What was this bag? The word John uses refers to a money box or chest made of wood or some other hard material such as tortoiseshell. Originally it referred to the small case in which reeds and mouthpieces for woodwind instruments were kept. Then it came to mean the money box in which some people kept money to help the poor.

Thirty Pieces of Silver

MATTHEW 26:14–16; MARK 14:10–11; LUKE 22:3–6

Tuesday had been a busy day for Jesus. He had taught in the temple and answered questions about paying taxes to Caesar. He also pointed out a widow who had given her all – two small coins. He entered into discussions with the religious leaders, who questioned His role as a teacher. That evening, on the way back to Bethany, He stopped at the Mount of Olives to teach His disciples there. In Bethany, while eating dinner at the home of Simon the Leper, Mary of Bethany anointed His feet with expensive ointment. After this happened, Judas Iscariot went into Jerusalem and sold his loyalty to Jesus for 30 pieces of silver.

Matthew and Mark both tell us that immediately after Judas complained about Mary's "extravagance" in anointing Jesus' feet with nard, he went to the chief priests to betray Him. Why did he choose this moment? Perhaps he finally decided Jesus wasn't going to overthrow Rome. Perhaps he could not appreciate the lavish attention Mary paid to Jesus. But the best answer is perhaps that Jesus' rebuke (John 12:7–8) made Judas so furious he finally decided to do what he had been thinking about for some time. Or he may have felt he would get more money by betraying Jesus than by being His treasurer.

Judas was paid 30 silver coins to betray Jesus.

Judas Iscariot
Iscariot seems to be a surname, since his father Simon also had it (John 6:71). The name may mean "from Kerioth," a small town in southern Judea. But it may also refer to the Sicarii, or "dagger men", who were the most radical of the Jewish nationalistic groups. Jewish historian Josephus said that they did not hesitate to put their opponents to death with Roman sicas, or daggers.

The chief priests
The chief priests would have been the current high priest, all former high priests, members of a few select families from whom the high priests were selected, and the treasurer and captain of police. The office of high priest was no longer hereditary or for

A silver half-shekel used in Palestine around AD 67.

While going back and forth from Bethany to Jerusalem, Jesus often passed by the Mount of Olives. In this photograph of the Mount of Olives today, the Church of All Nations is in the foreground, and the gold-topped Church of Mary Magdalene can be seen among the trees.

life. It had become a political plum. Members were always Sadducees. Though they are always mentioned in the New Testament before scribes and Pharisees, they no longer were respected by the common people.

Field of Blood, where it's thought that Judas killed himself.

Thirty pieces of silver

The same Greek word is translated "silver" in Matthew and "money" in Mark and Luke. In all cases the reference is probably to the silver shekel pictured here. About the size of an American half dollar, the usual shekel used in Palestine to pay the temple tax was from Tyre in Syria. It was the equivalent of the Greek tetradrachm.

The Last Supper

MATTHEW 26:17–29; MARK 14:12–25;
LUKE 22:7–20, 24-30; JOHN 13:1–20

The week prior to the crucifixion was quickly drawing to a close. Wednesday of that last week before the crucifixion was a day of silence. The Bible says nothing about it. Jesus probably rested in Bethany with His disciples. But on Thursday, preparations were made for the Passover, which we remember as the Last Supper. In an upper room in Jerusalem, Jesus ate with His disciples.

The Passover meal
According to the Talmud, a commentary on the laws of Moses by the rabbis, four or five cups of red wine were drunk at various times during the paschal supper. The wine was mixed with water, one part to three of the wine. The first cup (see Luke 22:17) introduced a blessing on the day and the wine. This was followed by ritual washings. Bitter herbs, unleavened bread, roast lamb, a special feast called "the Chagigah of the fourteenth day", and a spicy sauce were then brought in. The ritual in which the son was instructed in the meaning of the Passover was followed by the singing of Psalms 113–114 (the Hallel). After the second cup of wine, a blessing was made on each item of food. Guests ate in a reclining position, with the lamb eaten last. The ceremony was completed with thanks, a third cup of wine called "the cup of thanksgiving" (see 1 Cor. 10:16), Psalms 115–118 (the remainder of the Hallel), and a final cup of wine. Sometimes the Great Hallel (Pss. 120–136) and a fifth wine cup were added.

Jesus probably introduced the "Lord's Supper" after the meal and before the cup.

Passover bread.

The Upper Room

An upstairs room is mentioned in connection with the Last Supper, the post-Resurrection meetings of the apostles, and Pentecost. Luke, however, uses two different words, so two different places may have been meant.

Large upstairs rooms with both inside and outside stairs are known in Old Testament times (see 2 Kings 1:2 for an example). The room in which the Last Supper took place could have been such an enclosed room; it could also have been an open room, or *medhafeh*, above a clay-covered roof, on which Arab families in the main house of the village still spend a lot of time.

It is probably impossible to locate the site exactly today. Some identify it with the house of Mary, John Mark's mother. Epiphanius tells us the Emperor Hadrian visited it in AD 135. What is now called the "Cenacle", a traditional upper room, is located in a church that was until recently the En Neby Daud Mosque.

Benefactor

Gods, kings, and outstanding citizens were called benefactors for some special act they had performed. They received a title, and their names were recorded in a register. Even cruel despots, like Ptolemy VII of Egypt (147–117 BC), nicknamed "Big Belly" and "Malefactor", were given the title of Benefactor.

Couches on which people in Roman times reclined to eat. The Last Supper may have been eaten from couches like this.

A Greek octadrachm issued by Ptolemy VII (the "Malefactor").

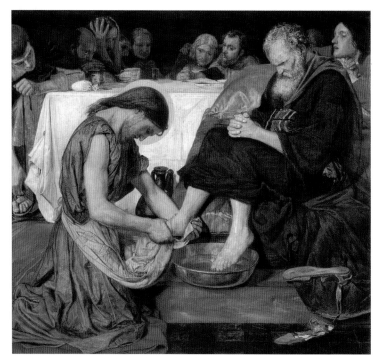

Jesus Washing Peter's Feet by Ford Madox Brown.

Foot washing

Moses wrote of a ritual washing for priests (Ex. 30:17–21). The wife or a servant usually washed the feet of house guests, though the host might do it for a special guest.

The cup

Cups were made of pottery or metal in ancient times. There were two basic types. Some had handles. The more common cup was a shallow bowl without handles, which came in a variety of shapes and sizes. Many materials were used to make cups. Gold, silver, bronze, pottery, wood, horn, and, somewhat later, lead and pewter were used. Zephyrinus of Rome, a contemporary of Tertullian, and Jerome both spoke of glass cups for communion (Jerome also spoke of baskets for bread).

Numerous rituals and ceremonies came to be associated with cups. The Jewish Talmud, for example, prescribes ritual cleansing for seven types of containers, including earthenware, metal, bone, and wooden vessels. Strict Jews, as the Pharisees, washed all cups that had in any way come into contact with sinners and the "people of the land", the average citizen. This special washing ceremony did not only include cups, but also pitchers and kettles (Mark 7:4). Its purpose was to distinguish Jews from their Gentile counterparts.

Much symbolism is also connected with cups. In the Old Testament a cup is a symbol of blessing for a good man; for an evil man it symbolizes punishment. In the New Testament a cup is always a symbol of suffering or trouble. Yet it also symbolizes fellowship with the Lord Himself.

Luke mentions two cups at the Last Supper. This may reflect

This terracotta cup with Barbotine decoration was made in the mid-first century AD. The cup used by Christ to institute the sacrament of the New Covenant might have looked like this.

The entrance (lower left) to the "Cenacle" – the traditional location of the Last Supper.

the influence of the paschal meal or a local tradition in the church.

Bread

Along with water, bread has long been considered the staff of life. If someone ate bread and drank wine with another, it was a sign of intimate friendship.

In biblical times bread could be made from wheat, barley, bean, lentil, millet, or spelt meal or flour (see Ezek. 4:9), though the first two were the most common. The grain would be ground with a mortar and pestle or taken to a mill. The ground meal or flour was then mixed with water. In 1941 at ez-Zeb the clay figure of a woman kneading bread was discovered in a cemetery; it dated back prior to 600 BC. After kneading, the bread was baked in one of four ways:

1. On heated flat rocks,
2. On a flat clay griddle or saucepan,
3. Around a heated earthenware cylinder,
4. In a portable firepot or cooking jar.

The fuel consisted of twigs, sticks, stubble, or grass. The bread was round, flat, spherical, or heart-shaped. It was usually about 45 cm (18 inches) in diameter and was sometimes punctured with holes.

The New Testament

A testament can be either a will or a covenant. When after the supper Jesus took the third cup of the paschal meal and spoke of the New Covenant in His blood (Luke 22:20), He combined the truths in Exodus 24:8 and Jeremiah 31:31. A covenant is God's declaration of His will. Jesus was perhaps talking about His will, since He was about to die. Both meanings are possible.

303

Gethsemane

MATTHEW 26:36–56; MARK 14:32–52;
LUKE 22:39–53; JOHN 18:2–12

Early that Thursday before the crucifixion, the disciples prepared the Passover meal in an Upper Room in Jerusalem. After sunset, when the time of the Passover began, they ate with Jesus, celebrating what we have come to know as the Last Supper. As the supper ended, they made their way to a lonely garden on the Mount of Olives, a place known as the Garden of Gethsemane. There, in Gethsemane, He prayed. But as Thursday night wore on into the very early hours before dawn on Friday, Judas came to betray Jesus.

The great olive trees in Gethsemane. Though some say these date from the time of Christ, this is not likely, for all trees were destroyed in AD 70.

Gethsemane

The Upper Room is, according to tradition, close to David's tomb, south of the house of Caiaphas and Herod's palace in what was then the wealthy Upper City in Old Jerusalem. Today it is easy to go from this spot directly to Gethsemane on the Ophel Road just south of the Zion and Dung Gates. But the western portion of the Ophel Road

was built very recently. And in New Testament times the wall went south of the Cenacle, the traditional site of the Upper Room, and enclosed it, whereas today the wall is on the north and excludes half of Mount Zion. The Bible says simply that Jesus and His disciples went out into the Mount of Olives as was their custom. John tells us they crossed the Kidron Valley, through which a winter stream flows (St Mary's Spring). Thus, the exact route Jesus followed is not known today.

Gethsemane was a garden, field, or enclosure in an olive grove on the southwestern slopes of the Mount of Olives. The word "Gethsemane" means "olive vat" or "olive press", so there probably was a stone structure of that type there, as there still are in many places in Israel today. Matthew and Mark both suggest that Gethsemane was some distance inside the area called the Mount of Olives.

Two of the sites in present-day Jerusalem identified with Gethsemane are: east of the modern road from Jerusalem to Bethany, where the Church of the Tomb of the Virgin and the Franciscan Basilica of the Agony are located; and higher up the Mount of Olives where the Russian Church of Magdalene and the Franciscan Basilica are located.

Torches and weapons

The detachment of soldiers and officials from the chief priests and Pharisees came to arrest Jesus with torches, lanterns, and weapons. What did these lights look like?

Lanterns and torches are so much alike it is difficult to distinguish them in Hebrew and Greek. When the lamps used in houses were inadequate, as they would be outdoors at night, torches were often used, but the Romans also had lanterns made of various kinds of translucent material.

Weapons were basically of two kinds, offensive and defensive. Some of the common offensive weapons were: swords and shorter daggers (double-edged and worn in a leather sheath at the side, the sword on the right, the dagger on the left); spears (long wooden shafts tipped with stone or metal heads); javelins (spears used for hurling – all Roman legionnaires had them); lances (spears with longer shafts used for thrusting in the front lines of battle); and mauls (war clubs made with stones, balls of metal, or wood).

Defensive weapons included shields and armour. Archaeologists have never discovered a shield in Israel. This is because, contrary to what we might think, they were made of perishable materials such as skins, wood, leather, and wickerwork – usually not metal. Two exceptions are King Solomon's gold-plated and King Rehoboam's bronze shields. Two shapes were common: those round at the top and square on

Jesus prays in this detail from *Agony in the Garden* by Andrea Mantegna.

the bottom, and smaller, round ones. The ordinary soldier had a leather shield over a wooden frame, reinforced with a metal stud in the centre. It had a handle on the inside.

The ordinary soldier did not have the coat of mail the medieval knight wore. His armour was made of leather cut in strips, wrapped with metal, and wired together. To this body armour a heart guard of bronze and shoulder pieces were added. The whole suit was tied in the back. To this body armour were added a helmet (usually a leather cap, then metal lined with felt or sponge) and greaves (leg armour made of bronze moulded to the shape of the leg; Greek greaves wrapped their legs, but Roman

greaves covered only the fronts of their legs).

Olive trees

Olive trees are so important in the life of Israel they have been called the tree of life! This small, grey, twisted evergreen with its pale olive undersides will grow where no other tree will grow. Its oil has many uses: cooking, lighting lamps, treating wounds, anointing kings. Its wood was used for furniture. Olives were eaten as a relish, much as they are today. One tree can produce as much as 90 l (20 gallons) of olive oil in a year. To get the fruit from the trees, the trees are shaken. So many blossoms are produced in the spring they thickly blanket the ground. They are so hardy only locusts can destroy them. Gethsemane probably had an olive vat. This was an upright stone with a wooden handle which was rolled over olives on a flat round stone with grooves, which let the oil flow out.

Judas' kiss

In the Near East kissing is more of a ceremony than it is for us. Children in Jewish families would normally kiss older people on the hand or beard. Fathers and husbands would kiss their children and wives on the forehead. Disciples would not normally kiss their masters on the face first, as Judas did to Jesus.

Jesus on Trial – Annas, Caiaphas, and the Council

MATTHEW 26:57–68; MARK 14:53–65; LUKE 22:54, 63–65; JOHN 18:12–14, 19–24

The Passover meal, which we remember as the Last Supper, began after sunset on Thursday evening. When it ended, Jesus went with His disciples to Gethsemane, a garden in an olive grove on the Mount of Olives. There He prayed and waited until Judas led a band of men to capture Him. As night wore on into early morning, Jesus was led to Annas, then Caiaphas, and the council for trial.

Annas the high priest

Annas, or Ananos, was high priest from 6 to 15. So powerful and influential was he, however, that even after he was deposed by Valerius Gratus he was able to control the selection of his successors. Five of his sons, his son-in-law Caiaphas, and his grandson Matthias became high priests after him! Appointed by the Quirinius who is mentioned in Luke 2 as governor of Syria, he seems to have controlled the priestly party in Jerusalem for the rest of his life. This conclusion is supported by John's insistence that Jesus appeared before Annas before He went to Caiaphas (John 18:13).

Visitors to Jerusalem today may see the house of Annas, just outside the present wall. An olive tree at the northeast corner of the chapel of the Convent of the Olive Tree is said to be the tree to which Jesus was chained while awaiting Annas' examination, but this is very unlikely.

Caiaphas the high priest

Joseph Caiaphas (or Caiaphas) was made high priest by Valerius Gratus in 18 and was deposed by the Roman Procurator Vitelius in 36. He was succeeded, however, by Annas' son Jonathan. The Roman government controlled its Jewish citizens by appointing both civil and religious leaders. The fact that Caiaphas held office for so long while all the others had such short tenures suggests that he was shrewd and flexible. A Sadducee, Caiaphas first suggested the idea of Jesus' death to save the nation. He continued to persecute the church after Jesus' death.

In Jerusalem today a ruined Armenian shrine that is being rebuilt is claimed to be the house of Caiaphas. That claim goes back to the fourth century. The shrine contains the prison in which Jesus is supposed to have been imprisoned and has an excellent view overlooking the temple.

A statue in Portugal of Annas the High Priest.

ANNAS

Annas had been high priest from 6–15, until deposed by the Romans. Five of his sons and his son-in-law, Caiaphas, kept the high priesthood in the family. It was to Annas that Jesus was taken first, and he who tried to silence the disciples when they started talking about the resurrection (Acts 4:5).

CAIAPHAS

Joseph Caiaphas was appointed high priest by the Romans in 18 and deposed in 36. Caiaphas took the lead in the trial of Jesus and made the crafty proposal to sacrifice one man, Jesus – to save the nation from rebellion and consequent destruction by Rome.

PONTIUS PILATE

Although the Jews regarded Pilate as a harsh and insensitive governor, he had an extended term of office. He was reluctant to order Jesus' crucifixion, aware that He had done no wrong, and knew that He claimed to be the Son of God (John 19:7).

HEROD ANTIPAS

Pilate sent Jesus to be examined by Herod the Tetrarch – a privilege rather than a right – which helped reconcile the two leaders following a previous quarrel. Herod seems to have hoped to see Jesus perform a miracle, and in this was disappointed (Luke 23:6–16).

The Christ and the Son of man

When the high priest asked Jesus if He was "the Christ", he was asking if Jesus was the Messiah. The first word is Greek, the second Hebrew. The word, meaning "the anointed one", has a very special meaning in Jewish history. Kings were anointed to indicate the special role God wanted them to play. Jesus preferred to be called "Son of man", however (Dan. 7:13).

From the south wall of Old Jerusalem one may see the area where the house of Caiaphas was thought to have been.

Peter Denies Jesus

MATTHEW 26:58, 69–75; MARK 14:54, 66–72;
LUKE 22:54–62; JOHN 18:15–18, 25–27

After the Last Supper, the Thursday evening Passover meal, Jesus left Jerusalem with His disciples and went to Gethsemane, on the Mount of Olives. In the early morning hours, Judas came with a band of men to betray Jesus and take Him prisoner. Jesus was taken for trial first to Annas, then to Caiaphas and the high council. During these trials, Peter waited in the courtyard of the high priest. But when Peter was recognized as a disciple, he cursed and denied that he knew Jesus.

Peter denied knowing Jesus three times.

To understand the scene of Peter's denial, the reader of the New Testament needs to have a general idea of what the high priest's palace or house looked like. Otherwise it is hard to understand why someone would build a fire in the midst of "the hall".

First of all, "hall" (Luke 22:55) is better translated "courtyard" (per NIV), what we sometimes call a "quadrangle". This is a space surrounded on four sides, usually by buildings. Today it may be covered with grass, but most often in the Near East a courtyard would be paved or covered with

flagstones. To enter this "hall" a person first opened either a heavy folding gate or, in the case of one or two individuals arriving on foot, a small door. That gate or door opened onto a passageway that led to the courtyard, which was open to the sky and in which a fire could be built on colder nights.

The passageway, called a "porch" in the King James Version (Matt. 26:71), that led from the street to the courtyard was probably selected by Peter for an easy escape, should his identification as Jesus' disciple become so dangerous it might lead to arrest.

While Peter was out in the courtyard with the temple guards and the high priest's servants and maids, Jesus was probably in one of the open rooms that faced the courtyard, since He could both see and hear Peter. Mark suggests that the rooms were raised somewhat above the level of the courtyard (Mark 14:66). Rooms that were open on the courtyard side were common in houses of this type.

It is possible that Peter made more than three denials of his close association with Jesus. At least the four Gospel writers list more than three people who asked Peter about his association with Jesus. Mark mentions that the servant girl, probably a female porter, questioned him twice, followed by those who were standing near Peter. Matthew mentions this "damsel" only once; then another servant girl and those standing near Peter question him. Luke tells of a servant girl, someone else (a man), and another man. John mentions the girl at the door, an unspecified person, and Malchus, the high priest's servant who was a relative of Annas and whose ear Peter had cut off.

Judas Hangs Himself

MATTHEW 27:3–10; ACTS 1:18–19

After the Passover meal, the Last Supper, ended, Jesus went with His disciples to Gethsemane, a garden among olive trees on the Mount of Olives. While He prayed until the early morning hours, Judas came with a band of men to capture Him. Jesus was taken before the high priests Annas and Caiaphas, and the council, for trial. During the trial Peter, waiting in the courtyard of the high priest's home, denied that he knew Jesus. By dawn the council had condemned Jesus to death. When Judas learned this, he was suddenly filled with remorse, tossed the 30 pieces of silver at the chief priests, and hanged himself.

The Potter's Field

Today the phrase "potter's field" means a cemetery, usually in a large city, in which the poor, criminals, and the unknown are buried. But how did it get such an unusual name? The answer is found in Matthew 27:8. The chief priests apparently needed a burial place for "strangers", people from other towns and cities. When Judas threw at them the 30 Tyrian shekels they had given him to betray Jesus, they agreed to buy the much-needed field from a potter who had offered to sell it to them. It is interesting that they had had enough money to pay Judas to betray Christ, but not enough to provide a place to bury foreigners. Sin distorts priorities in unbelievable ways!

Akeldama, the Field of Blood

Two traditions tell us that what Matthew calls the "potter's field" came to be known as the Field of Blood. Matthew tells us that the name was based on the fact that Judas said he had betrayed innocent blood, namely that of Jesus.

Acts, however, gives a slightly different tradition. It says that Judas bought a field with "the reward for his wickedness" (Acts 1:18) and poured out his life's blood as a result of a fall in the field.

Some argue that Matthew's account may in some way reflect the influence of Zechariah 11:12–13. But an easier answer is that Luke, in Acts, is reporting a local tradition that differs from the tradition Matthew heard.

Akeldama (Haceldama or Hakeldema), "the Field of Blood", has traditionally, and perhaps correctly, been identified with Hakk ed-Dumm, near the Greek Orthodox Church and Convent of St Oniprius, at the point where the Valley of Hinnom joins the Kidron Valley, south of Gethsemane. Another tradition says the apostles hid here when Jesus was on trial.

An archway at the burial site of Hakeldama in the Gehenna valley, near the monastery of St Onuphrius.

Jesus Is Sent to Pilate

MATTHEW 27:2, 11–14; MARK 15:1–5;
LUKE 23:1–5; JOHN 18:28–38

The week before Jesus' crucifixion was filled with activity in and around Jerusalem. Jesus rode triumphantly into Jerusalem on Sunday. On Monday He drove out the merchants and money changers from the temple. On Tuesday He taught in the temple, answered questions about paying taxes to Caesar, and pointed out a widow giving her two small coins in the temple treasury. Wednesday appears to have been a day of rest. On Thursday the disciples prepared the Upper Room for the Passover supper, the Last Supper, which they ate with Jesus Thursday evening after sunset. That night, after the supper was ended, they went to Gethsemane, where Jesus prayed until the early morning hours, when Judas came with a band of men to capture Him. Jesus was then taken to the high priests Annas and Caiaphas, and before the council, for trial. When the council condemned Jesus to death, Judas was filled with remorse and hanged himself. Jesus was then taken before Pilate, procurator of Judea, to be sentenced.

The Hall of Judgement
Where was Pilate when Caiaphas sent Jesus to him? Scholars suggest two possible places: The palace of Herod, a magnificent building with three towers straight north of Caiaphas' palace. One of these three towers is still standing. It is known as "the Tower of David". Jesus could have appeared before Pilate in the "barracks", which was part of Herod's palace; or The Tower of Antonia, on the northwest corner of the temple and connected to it by both stairs and underground passages. Herod the Great

Christ before Pilate by Mihály Munkácsy.

JESUS' TRIALS

Jesus was arrested at night in Gethsemane by a mob, including temple guards.

I. ILLEGAL TRIAL BY SANHEDRIN

He was first taken to Annas, the deposed high priest, who called an illegal assembly of the Jewish Sanhedrin court in his house. False witnesses gave conflicting evidence. Jesus was convicted of blasphemy when He agreed with Annas' inquiry whether He was the Son of God.

2. DAWN MEETING OF SANHEDRIN

At dawn, the Sanhedrin reconvened to confirm their verdict officially. They condemned Jesus to death – but had no power to execute the sentence. They therefore sent Jesus to Pilate.

3. JESUS BEFORE PILATE

Since it was no crime by Roman law to claim to be God, the Jews now accused Jesus of subverting the nation, forbidding the Jews to pay Roman taxes, and claiming to be king. Pilate recognized Jesus was innocent of the charges, but, when the Jews clamoured for the death sentence, he examined Jesus a second time. Hoping to avoid the dilemma, Pilate now sent Jesus to Herod, who ruled Jesus' homeland of Galilee.

4. JESUS BEFORE HEROD

Jesus refused to perform a miracle, as Herod desired; the tetrarch sent Him back to Pilate.

5. BEFORE PILATE AGAIN

Once again, Pilate attempted to release Jesus, offering the Jews to free either the innocent Jesus or the notorious criminal Barabbas. The crowd, led on by the priests, chose Barabbas. When the Jews threatened to report Pilate to Caesar for releasing a man "who claimed to be king", the governor finally complied and ordered Jesus' crucifixion.

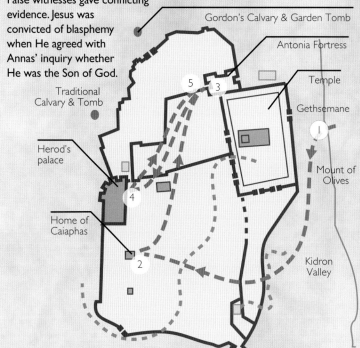

Gordon's Calvary & Garden Tomb

Antonia Fortress

Traditional Calvary & Tomb

Temple

Gethsemane

Herod's palace

Mount of Olives

Home of Caiaphas

Kidron Valley

had used this fortress as his praetorium before his palace was built.

The word "praetorium", which the Bible uses for the place where Pilate was, originally meant the place where the military general's headquarters were during a military campaign. Then it came to refer to the governor's official residence. In its atrium or open court was the *bema* or judgement seat, where Pilate would have condemned Jesus to death.

Pontius Pilate

We don't know much about Pontius Pilate. We don't know anything about where or when he was born (perhaps Italy before AD 1). We know nothing about his family, beyond the fact that he was married. He must have been an equestrian, a member of the second highest class in Rome, to have become a procurator or governor. We do know he was appointed by the emperor Tiberius in AD 26 to

succeed Valerius Gratus and that he held this post until AD 36.

At least three times Pilate handled the Jews badly. The third time led Vitellius, governor of Syria, to depose him and send him to Rome, where he may have committed suicide.

Jesus is Sentenced to Death

MATTHEW 27:15–30; MARK 15:6–19;
LUKE 23:6–25; JOHN 18:39–19:5

While Jesus prayed in the Garden of Gethsemane on Thursday night and into the early hours of Friday morning, Judas led a band of men to capture Him. They led Him back into Jerusalem before dawn, where He was tried – first by the retired high priest Annas, then by the acting high priest Caiaphas, then by the council, and after that by Pontius Pilate, the Roman procurator. Pilate was frightened, so he sent Jesus to Herod Antipas, who was visiting Jerusalem from Galilee. Herod sent Jesus back to Pilate, where the leaders of the people pressured Pilate into sentencing Jesus to die by crucifixion. In one last effort to free Jesus, Pilate had Him scourged, hoping the religious leaders would pity Him.

Herod's palace

Just as Pilate could have been at one of two different places, so could Herod have been at either the old Maccabean or Hasmonean palace, about halfway between the temple and what is now the Citadel, or at the Citadel itself, formerly Herod's palace.

If Pilate were at Herod's palace, Herod Antipas must have been at the old Maccabean palace. Built by an unknown Hasmonean ruler, this palace is higher up the hill of Zion than Caiaphas' house and not far from the temple. Herod would have been in Jerusalem on a visit for the Passover feast. His normal residence was in Tiberias in Galilee.

If Pilate were at the Tower of Antonia , however, Herod could have been at his luxurious palace just inside the Jaffa Gate. Built by his father, Herod the Great, in 24 BC on the site of a Hasmonean city wall, this palace was surrounded by walls that were protected even further on the north by three enormous towers.

Herod Antipas

The son of Herod the Great by one of his several wives, Herod Antipas became tetrarch of Galilee and Perea. He is the Herod mentioned most often in the New Testament. His capital, Sepphoris, was only 6.5 km (4 miles) from Nazareth, so Joseph may have worked on it. Around AD 25 he built a new capital, Tiberias, on the Sea of Galilee. His half nephew

Coins
of Herod
Antipas

Herod Agrippa denounced him to Caligula, the Roman emperor, and he was banished to Gaul in AD 39.

The Tower of Antonia

The Tower of Antonia, called the "barracks" or "castle" in the New Testament, was a great square fortress built by Herod the Great to protect the temple. The Roman procurators who succeeded him used it more as part of their surveillance system against the Jews.

Named in honour of Mark Antony, Herod's friend and patron from army days, and built on Zion, the highest hill in the area, the Tower of Antonia was located on a cliff that towers 23 m (75 feet) above the valley below. Its walls rose 18 m (60 feet) above the cliff. The building was 150 m (490 feet) by 80 m (260 feet) and served both as a royal residence and as a military barracks. It probably had a large courtyard in the centre where the judgement seat (*bema*), from which Pilate may have delivered his verdict, was located. Titus destroyed the structure in AD 70 by setting fire to it. As many as 500–600 soldiers (a cohort) were stationed in the castle.

Barabbas

Not much is known of Barabbas. Mark and Luke tell us he was in prison with a group of revolutionaries who had

murdered people during an uprising. Matthew says only that he was a notorious prisoner, and John says he had taken part in a rebellion. His father may have been a rabbi.

Scourges

The ancients used many kinds of scourges to punish those convicted of criminal or religious offences. The number of lashes was determined by the severity of the crime, up to a total of 40. More than that was considered "degrading".

Roman citizens could not be scourged, but freemen, slaves, and foreigners could be beaten with elm or birch rods or whipped.

The Citadel, built on the ruins of Herod's palace – a possible site where Jesus met Herod Antipas.

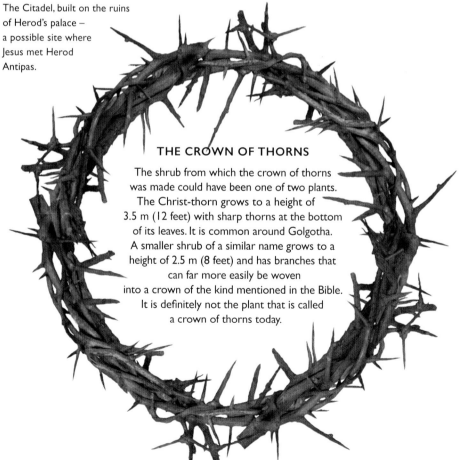

THE CROWN OF THORNS

The shrub from which the crown of thorns was made could have been one of two plants. The Christ-thorn grows to a height of 3.5 m (12 feet) with sharp thorns at the bottom of its leaves. It is common around Golgotha. A smaller shrub of a similar name grows to a height of 2.5 m (8 feet) and has branches that can far more easily be woven into a crown of the kind mentioned in the Bible. It is definitely not the plant that is called a crown of thorns today.

The Way of the Cross

MATTHEW 27:31–34; MARK 15:20–23;
LUKE 23:26–33; JOHN 19:16–17

After Jesus was taken prisoner by the mob which Judas brought to Gethsemane, He was brought before the high priests Annas and Caiaphas for trial and then was condemned by the Sanhedrin, the high council. But this group had no authority to sentence Jesus to death, so they sent Him to the Roman procurator, Pontius Pilate. Pilate didn't want to sentence Jesus, so he sent Him to Herod, who in turn sent Jesus back to Pilate. Pressured by the religious leaders, Pilate at last condemned Jesus and had Him scourged, beaten with whips. Then Jesus was forced to carry His cross on the way to Golgotha, a path which has become known as Via Dolorosa, the Way of the Cross.

The black metal disc on the wall in the lower right corner of this photo marks the ninth Station of the Cross.

The Via Dolorosa

The Via Dolorosa is the traditional route by which Jesus went from Pilate's hall of judgement to Calvary. The words are Latin for "Way of Sorrows". Every Friday some Christians in Jerusalem walk along the 14 "stations" associated with Jesus' sad final journey. These 14 stations are listed here in an effort to make you feel part of those taking that walk. Remember, these are only traditions, not known facts.

The stairs on the Via Dolorosa lead to the Christian quarter in Jerusalem.

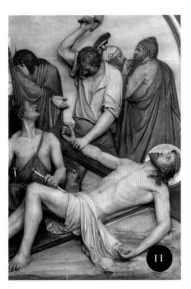

FOURTEEN STATIONS

1. JESUS WAS CONDEMNED
As you stand on St Mary's Street looking west, you can see an arch, the first of three. On the left side of the street is the Al Omariya School. Some say the part of the Antonia Tower courtyard where Pilate sentenced Jesus was under the present yard of this school.

2. JESUS TOOK THE CROSS
Across the street on the wall of a building owned by Franciscan monks is a Roman "II" that marks this site. The wall is part of the Condemnation Chapel.

3. JESUS FELL
A pillar in the wall of a small Polish chapel marks this spot, not part of the biblical story.

4. MARY MET JESUS
In the crypt of a small chapel of an Armenian church, "Our Lady of the Spasm", are mosaic footprints to mark the spot where Mary supposedly stood.

5. SIMON THE CYRENIAN TOOK THE CROSS
At the intersection of El Wad Road and El Khanqa Street, just south of the last two sites, is a Franciscan chapel that marks this spot.

6. JESUS' FACE WIPED
Also on the left as you go west along El Khanqa is the Church of St Veronica. Tradition says she wiped the blood, sweat, and dust off Jesus' face at this spot.

7. JESUS FELL AGAIN
The spot is at the corner of El Khanqa and Suq Khan Ez-Zeit, marked on the doorway in the Khan Ez-Zeit Market.

8. JESUS SPOKE TO THE WOMEN OF JERUSALEM
A cross in the wall of the Greek Orthodox monastery of Charalambos, across the street from the market, marks the spot where Jesus foretold Jerusalem's destruction.

9. JESUS' THIRD FALL
Going south on Suq Khan Ez-Zeit you come to a column built into the door of the Abyssinian Coptic Church that marks this spot.

10-14. JESUS WAS STRIPPED OF HIS CLOTHES, NAILED TO THE CROSS, DIED, WAS REMOVED FROM THE CROSS, AND WAS BURIED
Touching the Abyssinian Coptic monastery is the Church of the Holy Sepulchre, the traditional site of Jesus' death at Calvary. As you enter the church from the south, Calvary is on the right up a steep flight of stairs over the Rock of Golgotha. The church was built by the emperor Constantine in 336. This traditional place of Jesus' death is marked by a silver disc on an altar.

Three depictions of the Stations of the Cross from the Basilica of the Sacred Heart of Jesus in Zagreb, Croatia.

The Day Jesus Died

MATTHEW 27:27–56; MARK 15:16–41;
LUKE 23:26–49; JOHN 19:14–30

After the Lord's Supper ended, Jesus went with His disciples to Gethsemane, where He prayed. But while Jesus prayed, Judas led a band of soldiers and a mob to arrest Jesus. In the darkness they led Him back to Jerusalem to the high priest and Sanhedrin, the Jewish high court, for trial. The council then sent Him to Pilate, who was afraid to try Him and sent Him to Herod. But Herod would not condemn Jesus either and sent Him back to Pilate. While Jesus was with Pilate, the crowd and religious leaders forced Pilate to condemn Jesus to death. When Jesus had been "scourged", or beaten, He was forced to carry His cross toward Golgotha.

Gordon's Calvary, one of the traditional sites for Golgotha.

the Damascus Gate, north of the city. It is also a short distance from the Garden Tomb, thought by many to be the burial place for Jesus. Golgotha was called "the Place of a Skull" (John 19:17).

In the time of Jesus, the wall went westward for a short distance from the Damascus Gate, then south, then west again. It was north of this last section that the place on which the Church of the Holy Sepulchre is located. There is no hill on the site today. Some say it was cut down in the years that followed the crucifixion.

Both places were "outside the gate" (Heb. 13:12) and "near the city" (John 19:20). The two places are only a few hundred feet apart.

The name Golgotha is Hebrew and means a skull-like mound or hill which is barren. The name Calvary is Latin and means about the same thing.

Golgotha was a place where criminals were executed and was located near the public highway so that all could see the criminal put to death.

Golgotha – where was it?

Two places have been suggested for Golgotha. The traditional place is the Church of the Holy Sepulchre. The other place is sometimes known as Gordon's Calvary.

Gordon's Calvary looks like a human skull and is just outside

Pilate, the Roman governor

Pilate had no reason to kill Jesus except that he was afraid that he might get into trouble if he did not kill Him. Pilate had made two political mistakes already. A third mistake would have caused Caesar to bring him back to Rome and account for the problems.

The Church of the Holy Sepulchre – a major pilgrimage centre for Christians all around the world – is said to contain both Golgotha and the tomb of Jesus.

Pilate was afraid that a riot might break out if he did not crucify Jesus, and that would be his third mistake.

The Roman soldiers

The Roman soldiers were acting on orders from Pilate. They were forced to crucify Jesus. But they were not forced to show as much cruelty to Him as they did, making Him carry His own cross, mocking Him, forcing a crown of thorns over His head, and insulting Him. However, when Jesus died, the Roman centurion and "those with him" confessed that He was the Son of God (Matt. 27:54). The religious leaders did not.

The religious leaders

The Pharisees and other religious leaders of the Jews were afraid that Jesus would gather a large following who would depart from their control. They were angered that He was accepted by many as the Messiah, God's Son. Unable to cope with His growing popularity among the people, the only way out seemed to be to have Him killed.

The other two crucified

The other men died the same day in the same way that Jesus died. They, like Jesus, were crucified and died on a cross, for that was the Roman method of capital punishment. Stoning was the Jewish method. These two were criminals and were being punished for their crimes. Jesus was God's Son, being sacrificed for the sins of the world.

Daughters of Jerusalem

Among the women of Jerusalem whom Jesus addressed as "daughters of Jerusalem", there was a group who provided strong wine mixed with myrrh at crucifixions. It was a mixture which deadened pain and consciousness. Jesus refused this mixture when it was offered to Him, choosing to die fully alert.

THE DAY JESUS DIED

The events of Jesus' crucifixion are divided into three-hour periods of time:

6–9 A.M.

Jesus before Pilate, then Herod, then Pilate, where He is condemned. He is taken to Golgotha to be crucified.

9 A.M.–NOON

Jesus is crucified. He is nailed to the cross, where He speaks His first three sayings. The Roman soldiers gamble for His clothing.

NOON–3 P.M.

As Jesus dies, darkness covers the land. Jesus gives His fourth through seventh sayings on the cross.

3–6 P.M.

After Jesus dies at 3:00 in the afternoon, Joseph of Arimathea and Nicodemus wrap His body, putting spices with it and lay it in a tomb.

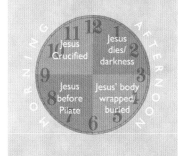

Women Visit Jesus' Tomb

MATTHEW 27:57–68; MARK 15:42–16:8;
LUKE 23:50–24:3; JOHN 19:31–20:8

After Jesus was taken prisoner in the Garden of Gethsemane, He was tried before Annas and Caiaphas, the high priests; the Sanhedrin, Jewish high council; Pilate, the Roman procurator; Herod Antipas, ruler of Galilee; and was finally condemned to die by Pilate. Through the streets of Jerusalem, He carried His cross to Golgotha, where He was crucified. The soldiers divided His clothing but cast lots for His seamless robe. After Jesus died, Joseph of Arimathea asked Pilate for His body and, with the help of Nicodemus, embalmed it with spices and buried it in his own new tomb. On Sunday morning after the crucifixion, some of the women who had followed Him came to the tomb.

Joseph of Arimathea

Who was Joseph of Arimathea? The New Testament tells us he was a member of the Jewish council or Sanhedrin who had not agreed with the decision to condemn Jesus to death and that he went to Pilate to get Jesus' body so he could put it in his new, rock-hewn tomb.

Some believe that the town of Arimathea is today called Ramla, about 32 km (20 miles) northwest of Jerusalem. It was one of three prefectures in Samaria that Demetrius II Nicanor of Syria gave to Jonathan the Maccabee in 145 BC, when it was called Ramatha. Samuel the prophet is buried here (1 Sam. 25:1). Today it is a large village that sits on two hills at the edge of the Ephraim Mountains. To the west there is a beautiful panoramic view of the Mediterranean Sea. The remains of a Crusader Abbey of St Joseph of Arimathea can still be seen.

A sculpture of Joseph of Arimathea.

Despite his humble origins, Joseph had reached the peak both socially and financially. Only the very wealthy could afford to have a rock tomb, and if as has been suggested this was an extra tomb because executed criminals could not be buried in family tombs, he was especially wealthy.

Why would he ask for Jesus' body? Two factors might be involved. First, it is not too surprising that one or two religious leaders might be attracted to Jesus' teaching about the kingdom. But more important is the fact that Joseph seems to have taken the rabbinic tradition about bodies being buried on the day of death more seriously than the others (see Deut. 21:22–23).

Ancient burial practices
People have buried their dead through the years in everything from a hole in the ground to elaborate burial caves, mausoleums, and pyramids. One practice that has greatly aided our understanding of ancient times, including biblical times, was the burial of cherished objects with a deceased person.

The earliest graves discovered date about 8000 BC. At Mount Carmel, for example, a communal grave for about 60 people in Natufian times has been excavated. But as late as 5000 BC in Jericho dead bodies seem

to have been buried with no ceremony at all.

The next stage included stone pit tombs, called "cists", and dolmens, house-shaped tombs constructed of two upright stone slabs topped by a flat stone slab. A dolmen, for example, has been found across the Jordan from Jericho.

Caves, both natural and man-made, became popular sites for tombs. The limestone hills of Israel today are still honeycombed with these ancient tombs. Sometimes hundreds of bodies in containers have been discovered in a cave sealed with a large stone. The cave at Machpelah that Abraham purchased for Sarah may be an example. Man-made caves were dug from the top down 1–4.5 m (3–15 feet) by a shaft 1–3 m (3–10 feet) in diameter. To prevent thieves from entering, the shaft would be filled with debris after burial. Several such shafts mark family tombs. When bones accumulated, they were gathered into a common pit or thrown out to make room for new bodies. Skulls, however, were respected and retained.

No tombs, however, match the Egyptian flat-topped mastabas and their even more elabourate pyramids. Mummification involved drying a body, placing internal organs in alabaster and marble jars, and wrapping the body in linen sheets as long as 24 yards.

In Jesus' day Jews washed the body, dressed it in linen sheets sprinkled with a mixture of aromatic spices (calamus, myrrh, cassia, aloes, cinnamon) and pure olive oil that made an ointment, and laid it on a bier or pallet for burial. From Roman times, every kind of tomb has been found in excavations. Pliny, Roman first-century historian, criticized the extravagant cost of the embalming spices.

This large rock is rolled over the entrance to seal the tomb.

Myrrh and aloes

Myrrh is the fragrant resinous gum of certain trees in Arabia. It was used to anoint kings. When branches are cut, they produce abundant quantities of an oily substance that quickly solidifies.

Myrrh is mixed with aloes and sprinkled over the embalming cloths of the dead. The aloe is the pure aloe plant, not the tree mentioned elsewhere in the Bible. It is bitter.

An aloe plant.

Peter and John Visit Jesus' Tomb

LUKE 24:11–12; JOHN 20:2–10

After Jesus was crucified, Joseph of Arimathea asked Pilate for Jesus' body and, with the help of Nicodemus, embalmed it with spices and buried it in Joseph's new tomb. This was Friday afternoon, shortly before sundown and the beginning of the Sabbath. When the Sabbath ended at dawn on Sunday morning, some of the women who had followed Jesus came to visit this tomb. But they found the stone rolled from the entrance, and Jesus' body gone. They quickly reported this to the disciples, and Peter and John rushed to see for themselves.

John and Peter rush to the tomb.

What happened to Jesus' tomb in the years that followed His death? Some say His tomb is near Gordon's Calvary. Others say its location is where the Church of the Holy Sepulchre (*right*) now stands. The following tells what happened to that location.

1. Hadrian's Aelia Capitolina
In AD 135 the Roman Emperor Hadrian, seeing Christianity as nothing more than a sect of Judaism, destroyed all its holy places along with those of the Jews and erected a Roman city, the Aelia Capitolina, in place of Jerusalem. Over this traditional site of Jesus' tomb he built a Temple of Venus.

2. The Visit of Queen Helena, Constantine's Mother
The godly Queen Helena visited the Holy Land in AD 326 to locate all the sites connected with Jesus' life. Because she knew that Hadrian had built the Temple of Venus over what was thought to be Calvary, she was able to locate the place. In an unused cistern she found many objects that today are associated with the death of Jesus. She did what she could to restore this and other places connected with the Christian faith.

3. Constantine's Church of the Holy Sepulchre
Constantine removed Hadrian's temple and erected in its place a huge, magnificent basilica. He cut away the rock from three sides of the cavern and levelled and paved the area so he could erect columns and a cupola to form a rotunda called the Anastasis (Resurrection). He made lavish use of gold, silver, precious stones, marble, mosaics, and stone carvings.

4. Subsequent history
In AD 614 the Persians destroyed this magnificent structure. But two years later the patriarch of the Greek Orthodox Church, Abbot Modestus, rebuilt it on a modest scale. The mad Egyptian caliph, El Hakim, destroyed that, and it was hastily rebuilt in AD 1037. The church built by the Crusaders in the twelfth century was partially destroyed in AD 1240 by Tartan invaders. Today the sepulchre is located behind the Chapel of the Angel and is marked by a white marble slab.

The Church of the Holy Sepulchre – could this be the location of Jesus' tomb?

Mary Magdalene

MARK 16:9–11; JOHN 20:11–18

Joseph of Arimathea and Nicodemus prepared Jesus' body for burial and laid it in Joseph's new tomb not far from Golgotha. The Sabbath passed, and some women who had followed Jesus came to visit the tomb. But they found the stone rolled from the entrance and the body of Jesus gone. Quickly, they returned to Jerusalem and told the disciples. Peter and John came to see for themselves. Later, alone, Mary Magdalene was startled when Jesus appeared to her.

The Magdala Stone was discovered during a 2009 excavation of Magdala's Migdal Synagogue – one of the oldest synagogues in Israel. Carved into its surface is the earliest known representation of the Temple Menorah found in a synagogue.

Mary Magdalene

Mary Magdalene was as prominent among the women as Peter was among the apostles. She came from the city of Magdala. She should not be confused with Mary of Bethany or the woman who anointed Jesus' feet. The expulsion of seven demons from her suggests that she had been "mentally ill", not morally dissolute. She appears to have been a person of some means and to have possessed leadership abilities, for she is always listed first when grouped with others. Some say she had aroused public indignation by divorcing her Jewish husband, Pappus ben Juda, to marry Panther, an officer of Herod Antipas' entourage, but this is probably not historically correct. When she first met Jesus we do not know, but it was probably on one of His visits to Gennesaret, near Magdala. Present at Jesus' crucifixion, she was the first to see the risen Lord, who she thought was the gardener.

Today the Mary Magdalene Church, named in her honour, stands halfway up the Mount of Olives.

Magdala

Some ruins of Magdala may be found along the shores of the Sea of Galilee today. Located just north of Herod Antipas' capital of Tiberias, it was called Tarichea by the Greeks, who caught a small fish of that name, still used as a relish, in its lakes. Once famous for its fine woollens and dyed products (the dye came from shellfish caught in its waters), the area is today near the village of Mejdel or Majgal, a modern name which preserves both its ancient name and its locality. Josephus, who once lived here, said it had 4,000 inhabitants and 230 boats. The Talmud tells us it had 80 weavers' shops and 300 shops that sold pigeons for sacrifices. The word "Magdala" is Hebrew for "watchtower". In Jesus' day it was primarily a Gentile city, as its horse and chariot race track indicates. A human skull from early history was found not far from Magdala in 1925.

Mary Magdalene's early home was at Magdala. Shown here are the ruins of Magdala.

The Road to Emmaus

MARK 16:12–13; LUKE 24:13–35

After Jesus was crucified, Joseph of Arimathea and Nicodemus prepared His body for burial and laid it in Joseph's new tomb. On Sunday morning, when some women visited the tomb, they discovered the stone rolled from the entrance and His body missing. They reported this to the disciples, and Peter and John came to see. Then Jesus appeared personally to Mary Magdalene. Later that day, He appeared to two people walking on the Road to Emmaus.

Road sign to Emmaus-Nicopolis.

may be Luke himself, since the account has all the reality of personal experience.

The two disciples may have belonged to the 70 (Luke 10:1–24).

Emmaus

Where is Emmaus? Once again, we do not know exactly. But at least we have some clues. First, the name means "hot springs", and Bible students have tried to locate the village by locating wells, springs, or baths near Jerusalem. Second, Luke says it was 60 stadia, or 12 km (7.5 miles), from Jerusalem, though he does not indicate in which direction. The two most likely sites are:

Who were these two disciples? No one knows for sure. Cleopas may be a variant of the name Cleopatros or Alphaeus. There is no evidence either for or against the identification of Cleopas with the Clopas of John 19:25.

Because the other disciple is not named, he has fascinated biblical scholars. Traditionally, he is called Simon. Several modern interpreters have been fascinated by the idea that he

1. El Kubeibeh (Qubeibeh)
This village, 11 km (7 miles) northwest of Jerusalem, has a number of things to suggest it was Emmaus. Crusaders in 1099 discovered an ancient Roman fort called Castellum Emmaus near here. In 1878 the Franciscans built the Church of St Cleophas here and discovered the remains of a basilica that dates from either Crusader or Byzantine times.

2. Imwas or Amwas
This city preserves the name and has two hot springs. It also has the earliest support, since two pilgrims in about AD 333 accepted Imwas as Emmaus, and Jerome, the great biblical scholar, agreed. But it was a city, not a village, and it is 32 km (20 miles), not 12km (7.5 miles), from Jerusalem.

The remains of the Basilica of the holy place of Emmaus-Nicopolis, Israel.

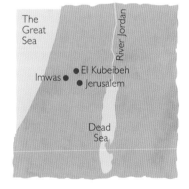

The Supper at Emmaus by Caravaggio.

Doubting Thomas

MARK 16:14; LUKE 24:36–43; JOHN 20:19–31

On the Sunday after Jesus' crucifixion, some women visited His tomb, only to find the stone rolled from the entrance and His body missing. Then Peter and John rushed to the tomb to see for themselves. Later, Jesus appeared alive to Mary Magdalene, to some other women, and that afternoon to two people walking on the road to Emmaus. That night Jesus appeared to His disciples in a closed room, but Thomas was not there. When Thomas heard about this, he doubted. He would not be satisfied until he had touched the wounds of the risen Christ. A week later, again on Sunday night, Jesus appeared to the disciples again. As Jesus invited Thomas to check out His wounds, Thomas believed!

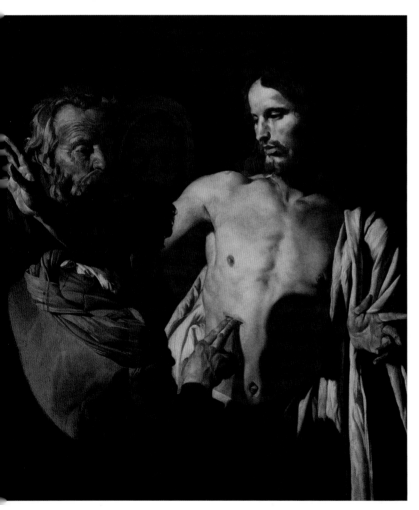

The Incredulity of Saint Thomas
by Matthias Stom.

The fact of the resurrection

Many believe that Jesus never rose from the dead. In fact, ever since the Resurrection, some have claimed that Jesus' resurrection was a lie and a conspiracy. But the real conspiracy involved the chief priests.

When the Roman guards noticed the empty tomb on Sunday morning, they reported it to the chief priests. Matthew says that the guards were given a large amount of money by the chief priests as a bribe. They were then told to spread the news that the disciples had stolen Jesus' body (Matt. 28:11–15).

This might be a believable story had the disciples never been heard from again. But why would these disciples spend the rest of their lives risking death and preaching about something that wasn't true? And if Jesus' enemies had stolen His body, they would have produced it as proof that Jesus did not rise from the dead. So the facts are clear. Jesus Christ and His followers are very much alive in the world today!

Thomas

Thomas was one of Jesus' 12 Apostles. He is always listed in the second of the three groups of four apostles when the Gospel lists the Twelve. This may suggest that he

40 DAYS – FROM RESURRECTION TO ASCENSION

SUNDAY MORNING

1. Matthew 28:2–4
   Early on Sunday morning, before sunrise, an angel of the Lord rolls away the stone from the tomb.
2. Matthew 28:5–8; Mark 1:2–8; Luke 24:1–8; John 20:1
   Women who followed Jesus visit His tomb and discover He is missing.
3. Luke 24:9–12; John 20:2–10
   When the women tell about the empty tomb, Peter and John rush to the tomb to see.
4. Mark 16:9–11; John 20:11–18
   While Mary Magdalene is alone in the garden by His tomb, Jesus appears to her, and then to other women.
5. Matthew 28:11–15
   The guards who were at Jesus' tomb report to the religious rulers that an angel rolled away the stone and are bribed to keep quiet.

SUNDAY AFTERNOON

6. Mark 1:12–13; Luke 24:13–32
   Jesus appears to two men who are walking to the village of Emmaus, outside Jerusalem.

SUNDAY EVENING

7. Luke 24:33–35
   The two disciples from Emmaus tell the others that they have seen Jesus.
8. Mark 16:14; Luke 24:36–43; John 20:19–25
   Jesus appears to 10 disciples in the Upper Room, when Thomas is absent.

THE FOLLOWING SUNDAY

9. John 20:26–31
   Jesus appears to His disciples, including Thomas. When Jesus asks Thomas to touch him, he believes.

THE NEXT 32 DAYS

10. John 21
    Jesus appears to seven disciples by the Sea of Galilee and performs a miracle of fish.
11. Matthew 28:16–20; Mark 16:15–18; 1 Corinthians 15:6
    Jesus appears to 500 at a mountain in Galilee.
12. 1 Corinthians 15:7
    Jesus appears to His half brother, James.
13. Luke 24:44–49; Acts 1:3–8
    At Jerusalem, Jesus appears again to His disciples.
14. Mark 16:19–20; Luke 24:50–53; Acts 1:9–12
    On the Mount of Olives, Jesus ascends into heaven while the disciples watch.

was neither the most important nor the least important of the Twelve.

Pessimistic, loyal, honest, dull, disillusioned, sceptical – all these characteristics spring from the New Testament and give us one of the most precise portraits of an apostle available.

But this same man utters a climactic confession of faith in Jesus in John's Gospel, a confession unequalled in all literature – "My Lord and My God!" This confession may have come after Thomas touched Jesus' wounds. Whether Thomas did or not, he was in awe over the fact that Jesus had truly risen from the dead and is therefore God's Son.

Greetings and salutations

As the apostles gathered in the Upper Room, Jesus appeared in their midst and greeted them by saying "Peace be unto you". This was one of the common greetings of the day, as ordinary as if we said "Good morning" today.

The Upper Room

The traditional site of the Upper Room can be seen in Jerusalem today. But if this was the room where Jesus gathered with His disciples, no one knows just how it looked in their day.

Some think the Upper Room was simply a room built on the top of a roof, quite common in Bible times. Others believe this was a most important room. In many expensive homes, a special room was built facing the courtyard. This room was expensively decorated and used for special occasions or for business.

The Miracle of Fish

After Jesus arose from the dead, He appeared to many people. On the Sunday after His crucifixion, He appeared to Mary Magdalene, some other women, and then to two disciples walking on the road to Emmaus. That night He appeared to the disciples in a closed room, but Thomas was not present. A week later, on the following Sunday night, He appeared to the disciples again, with Thomas there. When Jesus asked him to touch His wounds, Thomas believed that He had truly risen from the dead.

The Sea of Tiberias

The Sea of Tiberias is the same as the Sea of Galilee. Strictly speaking it is not a sea at all, but a freshwater inland lake.

Various names have been given to the lake through the years. The earliest name, the Sea of Chinnereth, possibly comes from the Hebrew word for "harp", the shape of the lake.

The Gospels, however, usually speak of the Sea of Galilee, so named because of the region to the northwest and west. The word means "ring" or "circle", probably because the region was known as the "district" of the Gentiles. The Gospels also occasionally speak of the Sea of Gennesaret (Gennesar), so named for the fertile, thickly populated plain southwest of the city of Capernaum. Following New Testament times it came to be known as the Sea of Tiberias, after the capital city of Galilee, and today's Arabic name, Tabariyeh, preserves that designation. Located about 95 km (60 miles) north of Jerusalem, the limestone formations that underlie the mountains, valleys, and lake resulted from volcanic eruptions. The mountains of Galilee on the north side of the lake rise some 1,220 m (4,000 feet) above sea level. The hills to the east and west rise only about 600 m (2,000 feet), but because they drop so sharply

Early morning fishing on Kinneret.

FISHING ON THE SEA OF GALILEE

Three different types of fishing nets were known in Bible times:

THE CASTING NET

Standing on shore a fisherman could throw this cone-shaped net weighted with lead on the outside over a school of fish. This type of net was not used commercially.

THE GILL NET

Used for catching medium-sized fish, this was a long net fitted with floats that would stay in the water all night and be hauled in by boat the next day. Its openings were large enough for small fish to escape but small enough to trap the big fish! The seven apostles were probably using this type of net.

THE DRAG NET

Boats would lower this long net in a semicircle and pull the ends to shore together with everything they caught. In addition to the use of nets, a Galilean fisherman also used a simple hook and line. Jesus told Peter to use this method (Matt. 17:27).

Peter, Andrew, James, and John, as well as Zebedee, father of James and John, were fishermen on the Sea of Galilee, operating a fishing business. It appears that they sold their fish as far away as Jerusalem, and that the high priest may have been a customer (John 18:15).

Fish were sold fresh or dried and were an important source of meat at this time. In Jesus' time a large fleet of fishing boats operated on the Sea of Galilee.

Christ greets His disciples on the shore of the Sea of Galilee.

The Sea of Galilee.

(7.5 miles) at its widest. It is 51 km (32 miles) around and 48 m (160 feet) deep in some spots. Though the shore is made up of pebbles and small shells, the fertile plains surrounding the lake produce an abundance of wheat, barley, figs, grapes, and other fruits and vegetables. In biblical times nine cities with populations over 15,000 surrounded the lake, and as many as 22 varieties of fish have been caught in its waters. At one time the whole Jordan Valley may have been one big lake.

and the lake is 210 m (685 feet) below sea level, abrupt drops of as much as 810 m (2,650 feet) occur. Standing on the southern shores of the lake, one can see Mount Hermon in the north. The Sea of Galilee is 21 km (13 miles) at its longest and 12 km

Jesus Ascends into Heaven

MARK 16:19–20; LUKE 24:50–53; ACTS 1:9–12

Jesus appeared to many after He arose from the dead. On Sunday morning, He talked personally with Mary Magdalene and appeared to other women. On Sunday afternoon, He talked with two disciples on the road to Emmaus. That night, He appeared to the disciples in a closed room. On the following Sunday night, He appeared to them again, and Thomas saw His wounds and believed. In Galilee, Jesus appeared to His disciples by the Sea of Galilee and then to 500 on a mountain in Galilee. He appeared to James and again to His disciples. Then on the Mount of Olives, His disciples clearly saw Him go up into heaven.

rebuilt at least twice through the centuries. The present structure was built some 900 years ago, during the time of the Crusaders. It covers a rock from which some say Jesus ascended into heaven.

Jesus' ascension

Jesus' ascension was the time when He bodily left this earth to

The Chapel of the Ascension

Jesus ascended into heaven from a place somewhere on the Mount of Olives. Today there are two places on the Mount of Olives marked with shrines, each claiming to mark the spot where Jesus ascended.

Of course, no one knows for sure where the exact spot was located. Shrines such as these usually mark a traditional place claimed by people through several centuries.

The Russian Orthodox Church and Bell Tower of the Ascension is one of the two shrines, chosen by Russian Christians. The Chapel of the Ascension is the other. It stands at the top of the Mount of Olives. This shrine was first built by Queen Helena, mother of the Roman Emperor Constantine. She lived from 248 to 327. Her shrine was destroyed and

The Chapel of the Ascension surrounds a rock said to hold the last mark left by Jesus as he ascended into Heaven.

return to heaven. As He came in Bethlehem, in the form of a baby, so He ascended as a full-grown man. Jesus ascended visibly so there would be no doubt. A large number of disciples saw Him go and recorded this as eyewitnesses.

When?

Jesus' ascension was 40 days after His resurrection. During these 40 days, He showed Himself alive to many of His disciples, who recorded these appearances as eyewitnesses.

The Ascension, part of Rembrandt's five paintings of the Passion of Christ made from 1628–1633 for the Prince of Orange.

The bell tower of the Russian Monastery of Ascension on the Mount of Olives.

Pentecost

ACTS 2

After Jesus was crucified, many of His disciples saw Him, the risen Christ, alive again. He walked among them and touched them, both in Jerusalem and in Galilee. One day Jesus ascended into heaven while the disciples watched. Then they returned to Jerusalem to wait, as He had told them to do. While waiting in the Upper Room, they chose Matthias to take the place of Judas as one of the Twelve. When the Day of Pentecost came, while they were waiting in the Upper Room, the Holy Spirit came on them as tongues of fire and gave them power. He appeared as had been prophesied in the Old Testament, yet was a surprise to all who were there.

Pentecost is the Greek word for "50". To Christians it means 50 days after the Resurrection, but to Jews it speaks of the 50 days of harvest that follow the offering of the barley sheaf at the Passover. Together with Passover and the Feast of Tabernacles or Booths, it was one of the three great pilgrim festivals of Judaism. Since AD 70 it has commemorated the giving of the Law at Mt Sinai, though originally it began the seven-week period called "first fruits". It appears to have played a far less important role in Judaism than the other two festivals, since it is not mentioned nearly as often in the literature of the Jews.

The same Greek word was used to refer to a harbour tax in ancient Greece, the Pentecost tax.

Originally Pentecost (Shavuot) fell on a Sunday 50 days after the barley sheaf Sabbath. But after AD 70 the practice of the Pharisees prevailed: 50 days after the first day of Passover.

To Christians it celebrates the beginning of the church.

WHERE DID EVERYONE COME FROM?

At Pentecost, one of the Jewish festivals, Jerusalem was crowded with Jewish pilgrims who had come from many parts of the Middle East where Jews had been scattered in the "Diaspora". They came from the region of the Caspian Sea, from what is now Turkey, from north Africa and from Rome and Arabia.

The building now housing David's Tomb and the Upper Room. During Jesus' time, the house with the Upper Room would have been next to David's Tomb, a separate structure. Today one building covers both pieces of ground.

Some early Christians stood to pray instead of kneeling, and candidates for baptism were baptized on this day.

The "nations" of Pentecost

In general the "nations" are listed in a circle from east to west. These "nations" were Jews of the Diaspora, living in nations other than Israel. Parthians, Medes, and Elamites came from present-day Iran; the Mesopotamians from Iraq; the Cappadocians, residents of Pontus, Asians, Phrygians, and Pamphylians from Turkey; the Egyptians from Egypt; the Libyans from Cyrenaica west of Egypt on the African coast; the Romans from Italy; and the Cretans from Crete. "Judeans" may perhaps refer to Armenians and "Arabs" to Cilicians. Pentecost temporarily ended the confusion of Babel.

David's Tomb

David's Tomb is below the traditional Upper Room. Peter referred to it (Acts 2:29). In 1948 it became a synagogue; Jews still flock to it on Pentecost, David's traditional death date.

A detail from a small egg tempera on wood painting about Pentecost by Giotto di Bondone.

Peter and John Heal a Lame Man

ACTS 3

After Jesus ascended into heaven, the disciples returned to Jerusalem, where they waited in the Upper Room. On the day of Pentecost, the Holy Spirit came on them, and they were filled with power. Peter preached a great sermon, and thousands turned to Christ Believers united, shared their possessions, and provided for the needs of others. One day, at the hour of prayer, Peter and John went to the temple. As they entered, a lame man begged them for coins.

A possible site for the Beautiful Gate, traditionally accepted by many Christians. This is called the Golden Gate and faces the Mount of Olives. It is the only eastern gate of the Temple Mount. Its Hebrew name is Gate of Mercy, and some claim it is the Shushan Gate, which would make it the oldest of the gates in the city.

There is no reference to this gate in Jewish writings. Josephus, however, refers to a gate that was made of solid Corinthian bronze and greatly excelled the other nine gates that were merely covered with silver and gold, without bronze. The gate could be the Nicanor Gate, named after the man who contributed its cost. It led from the Court of the Gentiles to the Court of the Women. Josephus also tells us that whereas the other gates had two doors 30 cubits high and 15 cubits wide, this gate was 15 m (50 feet) high and each of its two doors was 12 m (40 feet) wide. The gold and silver on this gate, contributed by Alexander, the father of Tiberius, was much thicker than on the others.

Christian tradition identifies it with the Susa or Golden Gate, however.

Solomon's Porch

The temple built by Herod the Great was surrounded on all four sides by a roofed colonnade or walkway. The colonnade on the east side leading into the Court of the Women, was called Solomon's Colonnade because of a tradition that Solomon had a similar portico in about the same area. Zerubbabel may also have had a similar walkway around the second temple.

Built on a platform or high retaining wall, Solomon's Colonnade was a place for people to walk and talk and for teachers to share their learning. It was about 15 m (50 feet) wide and had three separate rows of columns made of white marble. The columns were about 12 m (40 feet) high. Carved cedar beams formed the roof, and on the floors were mosaic stones, all in the latest Hellenistic architectural style.

Prayer times

Though people also prayed when they needed to, certain times came to be traditional. At first morning and evening prayer were customary, but then three different times became common. The most commonly observed were those at "the sixth hour" and "the ninth hour" (see Acts 10:9, 30; 3:1). Since the day began officially at 6 A.M., the sixth hour was noon and the ninth hour was 3 P.M.

Based on Psalm 119:164, monks said prayers seven times a day.

Peter and John before the Council

ACTS 4:1–31

After Jesus ascended into heaven, the believers returned to the Upper Room, where they waited. On the day of Pentecost, the Holy Spirit came and gave them power. At the temple, Peter and John healed a lame man, which brought much excitement and caused Peter to preach again to the people who gathered. The religious leaders were angry about this and arrested the two men and took them before the Sanhedrin, the high council.

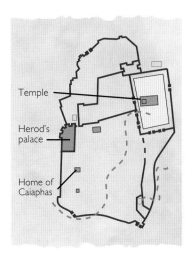

The temple guard
The ones who actually arrested Peter and John were probably members of the temple guard. We know little of this body beyond the fact that its head was called a "captain". Jeremiah (20:1–2) mentions a priest named Pashhur the son of Immer who had the power to arrest prophets who did not conform and put them in the stocks at the Upper Gate of Benjamin in the temple. Other references reinforce the fact that priests had police powers.

Though the highest officials in the Roman colony at Philippi were also called "captains", the captain of the temple guard seems rather to be related to the "*sagan*", a priestly official who ranked next to the high priest and was responsible for guarding some 24 posts in and around the temple. This included three chambers in the temple, and 21 other sites, including the temple gates, guarded by Levites.

The Sadducees
The Sadducees were not a distinct group like the priests. Rather they were a party, like the Pharisees and Essenes. They consisted of both priests and laymen, especially wealthy, aristocratic rural landlords. They had a reputation for being far less polished and refined than the more cultured urban Pharisees.

The origin of the three parties is shrouded in the unrecorded pages of history. Some suggest that the Sadducees owe their origin to Zadok, a leading priest during the reigns of David and Solomon. The problem with this theory is that not all Sadducees were priests.

Another theory is that the Sadducees originated with the "syndics" or judges in the days of the Maccabees, with whom they were close until 76.

The common people tended to hate the Sadducees because as politicians they compromised with Rome and adopted some of the influences of Hellenization (Greek customs). They were, nevertheless, conservative Jews who did their best to avoid any disturbance of the delicate peace they had worked out and were ready to stamp out popular

movements like the one Peter and John represented. They rejected the oral traditions of the Pharisees and accepted only the Torah.

The Sanhedrin
The Sanhedrin, the supreme administrative and legal body of the Jews, consisted of 71 members. Jerusalem also had two lower tribunals, each with 23 members, to whom the name was given. Tradition traced its origin back to the 70 elders who assisted Moses. Most of its members, including the high priest, were Sadducees; hence the Sanhedrin was an aristocratic body. It could not meet at night, so Peter and John were questioned the morning after their arrest.

The high priest and president of the Sanhedrin was at this time Caiaphas. His house is marked on the map. The Sanhedrin, or council, probably met in the temple, in the large outer courtyard called the Court of the Gentiles.

333

The Believers

Exciting things happened in Jerusalem after the Holy Spirit came on the disciples. People shared what they had with other believers and told what Jesus had done for them. Peter preached a sermon which brought thousands to Christ for forgiveness. At the temple Peter and John healed a lame man, but this and their teaching angered the religious leaders, who brought them before the council. Meanwhile, more people believed in Jesus, and the mighty works continued.

The Death of Ananias and Sapphira by Aubin Vouet.

Ananias and Sapphira

We know nothing about this Christian couple other than what is recorded in Acts. The name "Ananias" means "God is gracious". "Sapphira" means "beautiful". Yet Ananias did not appreciate God's graciousness, and Sapphira's moral integrity was certainly not beautiful. The two of them were apparently impressed by the high regard their fellow Christians held for those who sold their land and gave the money to the church.

When?

About AD 61: Some 30 years earlier, Jesus had planted the seed of the gospel. The disciples watered that seed, first preaching the gospel in Jerusalem and eventually throughout all the Bible world. At the time of this story, the church was growing almost overnight. Men, women, and children were believing in Jesus as Christianity spread.

Time frame

The Old Testament, from beginning to end, covers a period of thousands of years. But the events of the New Testament scarcely take up 100 years.

In the Old Testament we read about the lives of Noah, Abraham, Samson, Ruth, David, Isaiah, Daniel, Esther, and many, many more. But the New Testament focuses in only on Jesus, the apostles, and Paul.

Because the events of the Old Testament lasted many more years than the New, archaeologists have found a greater number of artefacts, or ancient objects, from the time of the Old Testament.

SPREAD OF THE GOSPEL

After the Day of Pentecost, and with the beginning of the persecution of followers of The Way, the Christian faith spread rapidly – to Samaria, Galilee, Damascus, Ethiopia, and across the Mediterranean to Asia Minor, Greece, and Rome itself.

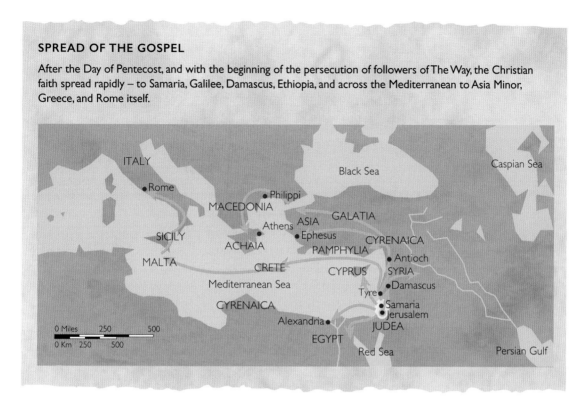

Barnabas

This is the first time we meet Barnabas. Later he comes to play an important role in the history of the early church by singling out Paul and encouraging his leadership abilities. In fact, Barnabas' name means, "son of encouragement".

We do not know how Barnabas came to believe in Jesus, but it is interesting to note that more than one member of his family became a member of the early Christian community. John Mark, his cousin, wrote the Gospel of Mark and joined Paul and Barnabas on their first missionary journey (see Col. 4:10).

Barnabas seems to have been trained in the Christian community as a Levite. Levites were assistants to priests in the temple and performed more minor priestly functions than priests did. But Barnabas does not seem to have had the gifts needed to become a great leader. After he became a Christian, it appears that his talent was not one of preaching, but rather of discovering and encouraging someone as talented as Paul.

A resident of Cyprus

Barnabas came from the island of Cyprus. This is a large island, the nearest island of any size to Antioch and Jerusalem (about 95 km – 60 miles west). When Barnabas became one of the leaders of the Christian community at Antioch, he returned to Cyprus on a missionary journey with Paul and John Mark. This might reveal that he had many relatives and acquaintances on the island.

Cyprus is 260 m (160 miles) wide and 95 km (60 miles) from north to south. This island was probably evangelized from Antioch, but Barnabas probably became a Christian through contact with Christians while he lived in Jerusalem.

Christianity did not become a major force on the island until the days of Constantine. Though Barnabas and John Mark returned to Cyprus on a second missionary tour, Paul probably did not return to the island, though he did pass near it on two occasions.

It is interesting that, though Barnabas was a Levite, he owned land. Perhaps the Old Testament rule against Levites owning property was no longer observed, or perhaps it did not apply outside Israel.

The Seven Deacons

After healing a lame man in the temple, Peter and John were taken before the high council, warned, and released. But they continued to preach, heal, and teach, which angered the high priest. He brought them before the council again and would have killed them had not Gamaliel, a member of the council, cautioned his fellow members to be careful. The numbers of believers grew, until some tension arose because there were not enough apostles to take care of the distribution of food. To solve the problem, seven deacons were chosen to do this work, so that the apostles could have time to teach and preach.

A medieval statue of Stephen at the Cathedral of Notre Dame in Paris.

The seven

Who were the seven men selected to "serve tables"? They have traditionally been called deacons.

This is because the Greek word for "serve" and the Greek word for "deacon" have the same root. The seven men mentioned in Acts 6 should not be seen as deacons in the later sense of church officers, though there are some similarities. The deacons were assistants of the elders in local leadership in the churches. Similarly, the seven were assistants of the apostles in the sense that they freed them for preaching the Word of God. Yet the seven probably only *supervised* the serving of food to the widows, since it is not likely that men would actually wait on the tables when the widows could do that for themselves.

The fact that Stephen and Philip are better known for their preaching and evangelism also indicates that in no sense were they or their colleagues limited to the supervision of food distribution and other charitable activities in the local Christian community.

All seven have Greek names. This indicates that they may have been Gentile converts to Christianity. Though the complaint is made by Greek-speaking Jews against Aramaic-speaking Jews, nothing in the text suggests that the seven were Jewish – though they could have been.

What do we know about the seven men who were selected to be in charge of food distribution? From the New Testament we know that Stephen was martyred. Eusebius the historian tells us that Philip and his prophesying daughters later settled in Hierapolis in Asia Minor. According to tradition Procurus was John's secretary when he wrote the fourth Gospel. Clement of Alexandria, an early church father, tells us that Nicolas from Antioch, a convert to Judaism before he became a Christian, was very jealous of his beautiful wife. Other church fathers identify him as the founder of an unorthodox Christian sect called the Nicolaitans. This sect is mentioned by John (Rev. 2:6, 15). Tradition tells us that Parmenas was at one time bishop of Soli, a town west of Tarsus in Cilicia, and that he suffered martyrdom at Philippi under Emperor Trajan. Procurus is said to have been consecrated bishop of Nicomedia, a city east of present-day Istanbul in Turkey now called Izmir, by Peter. Dorotheus of Tyre tells

THE NUMBER SEVEN

Some have gone to great lengths to find a mystical or symbolic meaning behind numbers in the Bible. This has led to abuse, for it can be carried to ridiculous conclusions. But it is worthwhile to note the similarity between certain uses of a certain number, such as the number 7. Other numbers used in many circumstances are: 3, 12, and 40.

FLOOD	JERICHO	JACOB	SAMSON	NAAMAN	MIRACLE	REVELATION
7 pairs of animals and birds (Gen. 7:1–2)	7 times around the city (Josh. 6:6–16)	7 years for Rachel (Gen. 29: 16–30)	7 locks of hair (Jud. 16:19)	Dipped 7 times in the Jordan River (2 Kings 5:10–14)	Jesus fed 4,000 with 7 loaves and had 7 baskets of scraps left (Mark 8:6–9)	John wrote to 7 churches in Asia Minor (Rev. 1:4)

us that Timon was one of the 70 disciples and that he later became bishop of Bostia, a town east of Samaria, where he was later burned as a martyr.

It has been suggested that just as 12 represents the 12 tribes of Israel to Luke, so too the numbers 7 and 70 represent the world. Hebrew tradition does say there were 70 nations in the world. Luke is saying that just as the 12 apostles represent the 12 tribes of Israel, so the seven in a sense represent the rest of the world.

It has also been suggested that the underlying reason for the complaint that resulted in the appointment of the seven men was that some of the Aramaic-speaking widows still had difficulty eating with those who did not observe their strict kosher eating habits. Later the Jews accused Stephen of laxity in keeping the Law and temple attendance, so the suggestion may have some truth to it.

The Aramaic language

Who were the "Hebrews" who were apparently overlooking the "Grecian" widows in the daily distribution of food?

The Christian community was growing so quickly that, Luke tells us, Greek-speaking Jewish Christians and those who spoke "Hebrew", i.e., a Palestinian version of Aramaic, were forming distinct subgroups.

The Aramaic language has a very interesting history. Originally the language spoken by the people of Syria, a land once known as Aram and called that sometimes in the Old Testament though it is generally translated Syria or Mesopotamia, Aramaic was based on an alphabet rather than on cuneiform syllables. When the Persians looked for a language that could be used throughout their vast empire, they liked the alphabetical foundation and adopted Aramaic for use from

India to Egypt. It thus completely superseded the earlier Akkadian cuneiform language.

After their exile in Babylonia and Persia, Jews who spoke Aramaic had such difficulty with the Hebrew Bible that it was regularly translated orally into Aramaic. Those translations have been preserved in the Mishnah portions of the Talmud. The New Testament indicates that Jesus knew Aramaic. Among the many Aramaic works that have been discovered are the Elephantine Papyri, the Dead Sea Genesis Apocryphon, the Targum of Onkelos on the Pentateuch, and that portion of the Talmud called the Gemara.

Stephen Is Killed

ACTS 6:8–7:60

The apostles taught and preached about the risen Christ. As they did, thousands of new believers were added to their already large number. Peter and John were taken before the council and warned not to preach about Jesus, but they continued. The high priest got angry and took the apostles before the council. But Gamaliel, a member of the council, warned against killing them. So the apostles were beaten and released. The number of believers continued to grow. Seven deacons were chosen to minister to those who needed food. One of these seven, a man named Stephen, was accused of wrongdoing and stoned to death.

A detail from *The Stoning of Saint Stephen* by Charles Thévenin.

Where Stephen was stoned

Two churches stand as memorials to Stephen today. The first, the Church of St Stephen, is a modern Greek Orthodox church. It is said to stand on the spot where Stephen met his death. Located at the foot of the southern tip of the western slope of the Mount of Olives, it lies north of Gethsemane on the Jericho Road. In AD 415 a priest named Lucian discovered what he believed to be Stephen's skeleton at a place he called Caphar Gamala. In 1916 at Beit Jimal, about 32 km (20 miles) south of Jerusalem on the way to Beersheba, a small church with mosaics dating back to the fifth or sixth century was discovered. Under it was a tomb believed to be the spot of which Lucian wrote. (A new church, built according to the plan of the original one, has been built here in Stephen's honour.) In AD 460 the Empress Eudoxia built the second memorial to Stephen, the Basilica or Cathedral of St Stephen, her patron saint. It was built to house the relics of the martyred saint. Today one of the most important biblical and archaeological schools in the world is located near this cathedral, just north of the city.

St Stephen's Gate

Christians have called this gate, the first one north of the Golden Gate and the Temple Mount, St Stephen's Gate because it is located near the traditional site of Stephen's martyrdom. It is located a few blocks east of the Via Dolorosa and just north of the temple. The Pool of Bethesda, to the right of the gate, was once used to wash the sheep to be sacrificed in the temple. This gate is also known as the Lion Gate.

Philip and the Ethiopian

ACTS 8:26–40

After Stephen was stoned to death, Saul began to persecute the Christians in Jerusalem. Though it may have seemed as if the Christians were being punished, it was God's way of sending the Christians into surrounding areas with the gospel. Philip took the Good News of Jesus to Samaria, where many believed.

In the midst of Philip's successful work at Samaria, an angel of the Lord ordered him to leave and go to a lonely place on the road that led from Jerusalem to Gaza.

It must have been difficult for Philip to leave a place where dozens or perhaps hundreds were coming to Christ. But his faithfulness in going opened the way for Ethiopia to hear the gospel through one of the nation's own people, a high-ranking government official.

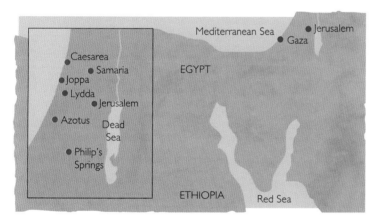

The map shows Philip's Springs, on the road from Jerusalem to Gaza.

Between Bethlehem and Hebron there is a spring of water known as Ain ed Dirweh, or Fountain of St Philip. According to tradition, this is the place where Philip stopped to baptize the Ethiopian. Philip's Springs is only a short distance north of Mamre, where Abraham lived for some time. If this was the place, it was certainly not a desert area, as we often think, but rather a deserted area.

The land in this region is very fertile, not far from the Valley of Eshcol, from which the Hebrew spies brought enormous bunches of grapes when they reported to Moses and the people at Kadesh Barnea. The road led on to Gaza, which was sandy desert.

The chariot
A two-wheeled cart drawn by horses, the chariot was used both as transportation for officials and as an instrument of war. Chariots are mentioned many times in the Bible (Joseph, Gen. 41:43; Jacob's funeral, Gen. 50:9; Philistines, 1 Sam. 13:5; Solomon, 1 Kings 9:19). But they are seldom mentioned in the New Testament.

Philip
There were two Philips who lived at this time and who were prominent in the Book of Acts. One was Philip, the apostle. The other was Philip, the evangelist or deacon, who is the Philip of this story. Paul stayed later at his home (Acts 21:8–9). Philip preached to the Gentiles long before Peter or Paul did. Luke also tells us that Philip had four unmarried daughters who were prophets (Acts 21). Of course this was much later than this story.

The Ethiopian
He was an African, Treasurer of Ethiopia under Queen Candace. He was a nobleman, a man of great importance who would have much influence for Christ when he returned to his own country. He was already a devout man, for he was reading from the Scriptures when Philip met him, and wanted to know more about what he was reading. The Scripture from which he was reading was Isaiah 53, which told about Christ.

Saul Becomes Paul

ACTS 9:1–22

As more people became believers in Jesus, the council and other religious leaders became more angry. Persecution of the believers began, causing many to leave Jerusalem for other places, not only in Israel, but in Samaria, and even beyond. Saul hated these believers and persecuted them bitterly. In one great effort to track them down, he headed toward Damascus to persecute the believers there. But on the way, he fell to the ground, and Jesus spoke to him. Saul became a new person – a believer, like those he had persecuted.

Saul's likely route from Jerusalem to Damascus.

Damascus
The city of Damascus was situated on an oasis about 280 km (175 miles) northeast of Jerusalem in the Roman province of Syria. The Amana River flows north of its north wall. The walls of the city form a rectangle, with two parallel streets going from the west to the east wall. Politically it was often considered part of the Decapolis, and it is close enough to Palestine that Mt Hermon can be seen from there on the western horizon. At the time of Paul's conversion, it appears that Tiberius may have allowed King Aretas of the Nabateans to have a representative ("ethnarch" or "governor") in Damascus to protect the interests of its many Nabatean residents.

Saul was travelling to persecute believers in Damascus. Here is an ancient colonnade in the ruins of ancient Damascus.

Straight Street

One of the two parallel streets that ran from the western to the eastern wall was called Straight Street (sometimes known as the *Via Recta*, its Latin name). Today the street goes only from the eastern gate to the middle of the city. It is really more of an alley than a street, since it is very narrow and so covered over with archways that even in the daytime parts of it are dark. In Paul's day the theatre was at its western extremity, and the king's palace was near its centre. Today tourists are shown what is reputed to be the same window in the wall where Paul was lowered in a basket, the spot where Paul received his vision, and even the house of Ananias.

Tarsus

Paul's original name was Saul. He came from Tarsus, a city on the southern coast of present-day Turkey. In Paul's time it was in the Roman province of Cilicia. Lying 16 km (10 miles) inland from the Mediterranean coast, it was proud of its reputation as a port. The Cydnus River, up which Cleopatra once sailed to meet Mark Antony, was a major highway through the Taurus Mountains. It helped make Tarsus a cultural crossroads, an ideal background for Paul's future role.

Jesus appears to Saul on the Damascus road, from *The Conversion of Saint Paul* by Benjamin West

Saul Escapes

ACTS 9:23–31

Believers multiplied rapidly in Jerusalem, and as they did, the high priest and the council began to persecute them for their beliefs. Many moved out of Jerusalem and took the gospel with them. But Saul, a Jewish religious leader, headed for Damascus to persecute believers there. On the way, Jesus spoke to him, and he became a believer. Now others who persecuted the believers wanted to kill Saul, but some fellow believers helped him escape from Damascus in a basket.

Cleopatra's Gate is one of the only remains of the ancient city of Tarsus.

Caesarea

After Saul left Damascus, he returned to Jerusalem and was introduced to the Christian community there by Barnabas. But Grecian Jews tried to kill him when he boldly witnessed to his newfound faith in Christ. So members of the church took him down to Caesarea and put him on a boat.

Caesarea was a very important city at the time. It had, under the Roman procurators of Palestine, become the capital of the country. Though first called Straton or Strato's Tower after the Phoenician king who first occupied it, the city as Saul saw it was the result of a major building project of the master builder Herod the Great, started in 22 BC. A gift from Caesar Augustus, it was pounded by the gale-swept waves of the Mediterranean, so Herod's first task was to fill the harbour with enormous blocks of limestone, some 15 m by 3 m by 2.9 m (50 feet by 10 feet by 9 feet) thick. After 12 years the city was a model of Hellenistic culture with its own hippodrome, theatre, temple to Caesar (after whom Herod named it), and exposed brick aqueduct. A small garrison of 3,000 soldiers was stationed there. Though Caesarea later became one of the seven major centres of the Christian church, with its own very influential bishop, it otherwise fell into relative oblivion and was captured by Muslim invaders near the end of the Roman Empire. The Crusaders did some restoration, and Israeli archaeologists are currently excavating in that area.

Tarsus

With over 6,000 years of continuous existence, Tarsus may well be the oldest city in the world still in existence, even older than Damascus, its chief rival for the title. A walled town as early as the third millennium BC, its name is at least as old as the Hittite empire that made it the capital of an area called Kizzuwatna. It was destroyed around 2000 BC, but then after the Trojan War it was resettled by Greeks. The city began minting its own coins in the fifth century BC. During his stay in Tarsus, Alexander the Great took a bath in the chilly waters of the Cydnus River and became seriously ill. The notorious Seleucid (Syrian) king Antiochus IV Epiphanes changed the city's name to Antioch on the Cydnus, but the change did not last. The Romans made Tarsus the capital of the Roman province of Cilicia in 67 BC. Shortly afterward Cicero, the famous Roman orator, became its governor. After the murder of Julius Caesar, Cassius levied a gargantuan fine against the city for opposing him, but Mark Antony redressed the fine by exempting the city from taxes. Dressed as Aphrodite, Cleopatra sailed up the Cydnus to meet him during his stay in Tarsus. Tarsus became an intellectual centre of some half million people, with its schools rivalling those of Alexandria. It was indeed "no mean city", an ideal place of preparation for the one who transformed Christianity from a Jewish sect into a world faith.

Dorcas

ACTS 9:36–42

As the believers scattered from Jerusalem because of the persecution, Peter went to Lydda to visit. There he healed a sick man named Aeneas. At Joppa, he raised Dorcas from the dead. This brought much excitement in those parts, and many believed in Jesus because of it.

Jaffa, a suburb of Tel Aviv.

Sharon

Peter's fame travelled from Lydda to Joppa, apparently because Aeneas travelled to Joppa and "Sharon". "Sharon" is the Hebrew word for "plain". It refers to the great plain that stretches from Joppa all the way to Haifa and Mt Carmel to the north, 80 km (50 miles) away. The largest of the coastal plains of Israel, it is about 16 km (10 miles) wide. Its swampy dunes have a reddish hue, especially in the north. Once densely covered with oaks and other vegetation, and then denuded, it is once again, thanks to irrigation, covered with lemon groves and even banana fields. Five streams and countless springs water its surface. It was not heavily populated in Old Testament times. David's shepherd chief, Shitrai, pastured his flocks in the area when the hill regions were dry.

Joppa

The city of Joppa is today Jaffa, a suburb of Tel Aviv. With about 800,000 inhabitants, the greater Tel Aviv area today has roughly one third of Israel's population. Set on a rock that rises about 38 m (125 feet) above sea level and juts out into the Mediterranean, Jaffa has an excellent location for defence. Its sandy beaches hide treacherous reefs offshore, but ships can enter from the north. In ancient times it was the only natural harbour from Egypt to Ptolemais, north of Mt Carmel.

First mentioned in the list of cities captured by Thutmose III in the fifteenth century BC, it long remained a key Egyptian governmental centre. Under the Philistines it became the nation's northern seaport. David recaptured it, and Solomon used it to receive the cedar logs he floated down from Lebanon and transported overland to Jerusalem to be used in his temple. Jonah fled from Joppa by ship to avoid going to Nineveh. In 701 BC Sennacherib destroyed the city, but by Ezra's time it was once again available to Zerubbabel for transporting cedar logs to his temple in Jerusalem. Alexander the Great changed its name from Yapho to Joppa in honour of Jope, the daughter of Aeolus, god of the winds. Under Rome it became part of Herod the Great's territory. Because the people of Joppa hated Herod, he built Caesarea some 65 km (40 miles) to the north, and Joppa declined in importance.

Tabitha – burial place

Near the Russian monastery in Tel Aviv is a tomb said to be that of Tabitha (Dorcas). The monastery's tall, pointed tower is surrounded by palms.

Cornelius

ACTS 9:43–10:48

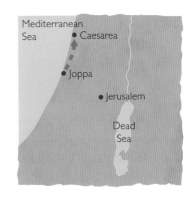

Peter visited Lydda, where he healed a man named Aeneas. Then he went on to Joppa, where he raised Dorcas from the dead. While staying at Joppa, he saw a vision from the Lord, a sheet filled with unclean animals. This was followed by a visit by some men from Caesarea, who took him to Cornelius' home. There Peter told this Roman centurion about Jesus, and he too became a believer.

To reach Jerusalem from Damascus, Paul travelled south about 280 km (175 miles). To go on to Tarsus, he first had to go to the seaport of Caesarea, then sail northward to his hometown Tarsus, near the coast of Cilicia.

Peter's Vision of a Sheet with Animals, painted by Domenico Fetti.

Caesarea

Caesarea is sometimes known as Palestinian Caesarea to distinguish it from the Caesarea Philippi in the Decapolis. From Joppa to Caesarea, Peter and Cornelius' three messengers travelled 50 km (32 miles) up the coast, a long journey by foot. Caesarea is 40 km (25 miles) south of Mt Carmel and 120 km (75 miles) northwest of Jerusalem. The city is important in the history of Christianity as the first city ever to have Gentile Christians and a non-Jewish church.

In New Testament times Caesarea was capital of the Roman province of Judea, the place from which the Roman procurators governed the nation. Though the city was built in the typical Hellenistic Greek fashion with amphitheatres, temples, and palaces, its population was a mixture of Greeks and Jews. An aqueduct on the north brought water from Mt Carmel and the Crocodile River.

In the third century AD the great theologian Origen taught here. When Arabians conquered the area, however, Caesarea lost its prestige. Most of the stones of the old city were transported north to Acre, just north of Mt Carmel and present-day Haifa.

Roman re-enactors demonstrate the tortoise formation. The soldiers arrange their shields into a wall resembling the shell of a tortoise. This approach was particularly useful during sieges.

ROMAN CIVILIZATION

Some three centuries before the birth of Christ, Alexander the Great established a huge Greek-speaking empire, stretching from Macedonia to the borders of India. Greek became the common language, and Greek ideas and customs were often adopted.

Some benefits of Roman civilization were: Roman roads, efficient government, and aqueducts, like this one still standing in Spain.

After years of struggle, the Romans established their own empire. Inaugurated by Caesar Augustus, the Romans brought peace to the region, with fair, but tough, government. Hard-working and highly organized, the Romans built a vast network of long-distance roads across the empire, promoting trade and allowing the Roman army swift access to all parts.

The Romans also built towns throughout the empire, which acted as centres of trade and administration. They often had stadia and amphitheatres for races and contests, and public baths, as well as government buildings and temples.

The Romans were very eclectic in their religious ideas. The belief of both Romans and Greeks in a number of rather quarrelsome and fickle deities had become formalized. At the same time superstition, astrology, and magic practices were commonplace.

The Greek language, in an everyday spoken version, in which the New Testament was written, was used across the empire and was another strong bonding agent.

Simon the tanner

Simon lived by the seashore outside the walls of Joppa because tanning, which required contact with dead bodies, was regarded as unclean in Jewish eyes (see Lev. 11:40). Christians, however, readily accepted tanners. That Peter would stay with someone like Simon suggests that already he did not share the strict attitudes of more traditional Jews.

What was probably the only tannery in Joppa has been unearthed. It has three oval-shaped tanners' vats hewn out of rock and lined with Roman cement.

Cornelius, the Roman centurion

Cornelius was probably a descendant of the slaves who took the name of Cornelius Sulla when he freed them.

Centurions, in command of a "century", technically 100 men, were the backbone of the Roman army. Six centuries formed a cohort. Centurions carried vine staffs.

Christians at Antioch

ACTS 11

Something new was happening in the circle of believers. When Peter was in Joppa, he saw a vision of unclean animals. Soon some men took him to the home of Cornelius, a Roman centurion who with his household became believers. Now Gentiles were added to the growing number of believers. Barnabas went to Antioch, saw a need, and travelled to Tarsus to bring Saul back to help him. There in Antioch, in a growing church, believers were first called Christians.

Antioch

Often called Syrian Antioch to distinguish it from the Antioch in Pisidia in Asia Minor, this city became part of Turkey in 1939 after centuries of existence as part of Syria. It is now called Antakya, a name that suggests its ancient name, and is a town of about 30,000 people.

In ancient times, Antioch had periods of great splendour and at the time of Herod the Great may have been a city of half a million people. Located 24 km (15 miles) inland from the Mediterranean Sea on the Orontes River and vulnerable to earthquakes, flooding, and enemy attack from the east, it was nevertheless happily situated on major land routes and became a major trade centre.

Antioch was founded in 300 BC, shortly after the death of Alexander the Great. Seleucus, head of the Seleucid (Syrian) empire, named it after his father, Antiochus and modelled it after Alexandria in Egypt. Located at the foot of Mt Sulpius and Mt Staurin, it depended for its water supply on an aqueduct from Daphne, a hillside resort 6.5 km (4 miles) to the west known for its temple to Apollo and the lax morals that also tarnished Antioch the Golden. Under Antiochus IV Epiphanes (175–163 BC) the city flourished

This ancient Roman road in Syria connected Antioch and Chalcis.

The emperor Claudius

Claudius was emperor of Rome from AD 41 to 54. Affected as a young man by both physical and mental problems, his position as Tiberius' nephew did not prevent him from being regarded as stupid and inconsequential. Caligula was amused by his handicaps and, perhaps in jest, gave him important leadership posts. As a result the Roman guard made him emperor at Caligula's death. His early reign was efficient, quite the contrast to his later reign, and to the reigns of his predecessor and successor, which were marred by suspicion and intrigue.

as the capital of a great empire. After Pompey's conquest in 64 BC, Antioch was settled by Roman businessmen and once again became a major trade centre. Various emperors contributed a temple, theatre, circus, bath, and aqueduct and expanded its walls to make it more secure. Herod the Great added its still-famous 3 km (2 mile) long, 27 m (90-foot)wide boulevard. Under Tiberius Caesar magnificent columns, gates, and statues were added. Then at the height of its glory, it became the eastern hub of the Roman Empire.

Relations between its heavy Greek population and its Jewish population were never particularly good. The coming of Christianity only aggravated the problem. We know from Acts 6 that one of the seven deacons, Nicolaus, a convert from Judaism, came from Antioch.

Whether he returned and founded the Christian community there or not, Antioch became a strong Christian centre. The word "Christian" was first used here. Only after a great deal of conflict between Jewish and Greek Christians did Paul's gospel finally triumph free from the burdens of the Law. When Jerusalem fell in AD 70, Antioch became the centre of Christianity. The names of great men, such as Peter and Ignatius, are listed as bishops of Antioch. But Simon Magus' descendants also made it a strong centre of the Gnostic heresy.

Bronze head of Claudius.

Some cities associated with Bible events in the early life of Paul.

Peter in Prison

ACTS 12:1–23

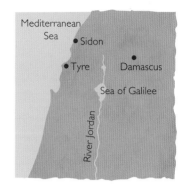

Mediterranean Sea

Sidon

Tyre

Damascus

Sea of Galilee

River Jordan

Peter had left Jerusalem to visit Lydda, where he healed Aeneas, then Joppa, where he raised Dorcas from the dead. While at Joppa, Peter saw a vision of unclean animals and received visitors who took him to see Cornelius, a Gentile Roman centurion. Cornelius became a believer in Jesus. The door was open for the Gentiles to receive the gospel also, and before long a strong church appeared at Antioch, with many of its members Gentiles. Barnabas went to Tarsus to find Saul and bring him back to work with him there. About that time, Herod Agrippa began persecuting the believers, killing James, John's brother, and putting Peter into prison. But an angel of the Lord set Peter free.

Herod Agrippa I

The Herod referred to in Acts 12 is Herod Agrippa I, one of many people to bear the name "Herod", which had come to be synonymous with "king". Agrippa was the grandson of Herod the Great; the half nephew of Herod Antipas, Archelaus, and Philip; the brother of Herodias; and the father of Bernice, Drusilla, and Herod Agrippa II, all mentioned later in Acts.

Born in 10 BC, this Herod was one of the worst. His mother took him to Rome when he was six, but he neglected his studies to lead a spendthrift existence that made him run out of money and into debt. When the Emperor Tiberius' only son Drusus was

poisoned in AD 23, Agrippa fell out of imperial favour and sometime later retired to a small fortress town in Idumea called Maltha. He left Rome without paying his debts. Depressed at his humiliation, he contemplated suicide, but his sister Herodias got her husband and half uncle, Herod Antipas, to make him a civil servant in Tiberias. He quarrelled with Antipas and with his friend Flaccus, the Roman governor of Syria. Back in Rome he became the friend of Caligula, and on Tiberius' death Caligula made him a king over two Palestinian tetrarchies and, later, Antipas' territories as well. He also was rewarded for helping make Claudius emperor. He died in Caesarea in AD 44.

Coin featuring the image of King Agrippa I.

Four squads of soldiers

Greeks and Hebrews divided the night into three watches. Romans, however, broke the night into four three-hour periods from 6 P.M. to 6 A.M., the evening, midnight, cockcrowing, and dawn watches. Each detachment or squad of soldiers would have had one watch.

The Feast of Unleavened Bread

The seven days following the Passover meal were observed by eating unleavened bread, baked without yeast, to remind Jews that their ancestors left Egypt so quickly they took dough and baked it on the way.

The house of John Mark's mother

In the south-central section of Old Jerusalem, only a short distance south of the Church of the Holy Sepulchre on St Mark's Road, is a Syrian Orthodox monastery called St Mark's House. It is said to be the site of the house of Mary, the mother of John Mark, to which Peter headed when he was released from the prison in Herod's palace. The monks, who speak and pray in Syriac or Aramaic, the language most people in Jerusalem spoke

Re-enactment of a legion of Roman soldiers marching through a city.

in Jesus' day, claim that the Last Supper was celebrated in the upper room of the house, that Peter founded the first church here, and that Mary, the mother of Jesus, was baptized in the church's little baptistry.

Under the lectern of the church are the tombs of the Armenian patriarchs and archbishops, buried seated on their elabourate thrones according to Syrian custom. An ancient painting of the Virgin and Child is said to have been painted by Luke.

The death of Herod Agrippa I

Josephus, the Jewish historian, gives an interpretation of Agrippa's death that differs from that given by Luke in Acts 12. He relates that on the second day of a festival in honour of Caesar in Caesarea, Agrippa dressed in spectacular robes made wholly of silver. They reflected the sun's rays and led certain people to call him a god. Agrippa did not rebuke them, but he immediately saw an owl sitting on a rope on the awning of a theatre, an omen that his death was imminent. Seized with violent abdominal pains, he was carried to his palace where he died five days later. Though he received 12 million drachmas a year, he nevertheless still owed others huge sums because his expenses were even greater.

Luke says Agrippa was addressing ambassadors from Tyre and Sidon when he was smitten by the Lord's angel and died of worms.

Some interpreters have rejected the biblical account as legendary. It seems, however, that we have several accounts of the same event because each historian looked at the event from a different perspective.

Tyre and Sidon

Tyre and Sidon were two port cities in Phoenicia, north of Israel. They were located about 50 km (30 miles) apart on the Mediterranean coast.

Tyre, located on a 140-acre island rock, was forced to build "up", and constructed buildings with more stories than even Rome had. In 333 BC Alexander the Great connected the island to the mainland by means of a "mole" half a mile long. Today shifting sand has shortened that distance to one-third of a mile. Tyre was a commercial city but insignificant politically.

Sidon to the north is situated on a hill that juts into the Mediterranean. Millions of murex shells produced the dye for which Sidon was famous. Its eastern wall protected it from enemy attack.

Although King Herod put Peter in prison, an angel of the Lord set Peter free, as seen in the painting called *The Liberation of St Peter*.

349

Paul's First Missionary Journey

ACTS 13: 1–3

Saul had been one of the most violent men who persecuted the believers, pursuing them to Damascus to kill or imprison them. But Jesus talked to him on the Damascus Road, and Saul became a believer himself. Later, he returned to Jerusalem with Barnabas to work with believers there and in time was back at his hometown Tarsus. There Barnabas found him and brought him back to Antioch, to work in the church. This church set Saul and Barnabas apart and sent them on their first missionary journey.

The Tombs of the Kings, near Paphos harbour in Cyprus. The tombs predate the visit of Paul by over four hundred years.

Between AD 46 and 48 Paul and Barnabas visited the following nine cities mentioned in the New Testament:

1. Antioch
A splendidly "modern" city of half a million people with a spectacular boulevard constructed by Herod the Great, Antioch in Syria lay about 25 km (15 miles) inland from the Mediterranean Sea. Located on a major trade route, its colonnaded 27 m (90 foot) wide main street was busy with commerce. After the fall of Jerusalem in AD 70, Antioch became the centre of Christianity, and by AD 400 as many as 100,000 Christians lived here.

2. Seleucia
Seleucia was for a brief time capital of Syria after the death of Alexander the Great. It lay 25 km (15 miles) west of Antioch. Founded by Seleucus I in 300 BC and busy with naval activity during Roman times, the city declined when the harbour filled with silt. After a day's journey from Antioch, Paul and Barnabas sailed for Cyprus from here.

3. Salamis
Tradition tells us that the city was named after the island in Greece from which Teucer, its founder, came. In Greek and Roman times Salamis was prosperous as a result of an excellent harbour. The New Testament reveals that many Jews lived here and that Salamis had its own synagogue. How long Paul and Barnabas stayed here we do not know, but Barnabas made a second visit with John Mark and, according to tradition, was martyred here under Nero.

4. Paphos
Located across the island on the west, Paphos was the capital of Cyprus. Barnabas and Paul visited New Paphos, a Roman city which had only recently been rebuilt by Caesar Augustus. The old city with its temple to Aphrodite lay about 16 km (10 miles) southeast.

5. Perga

Located in the Roman province of Pamphylia, Perga was northwest of Cyprus in Asia Minor. It lay 20 km (12 miles) east of Attalia (the important modern port of Antalya) on the River Cestris and some 13 km (8 miles) in land to avoid Cilician pirates. It had a famous temple dedicated to Artemis (Diana). The ruins of a theatre that could have held 13,000 people and dates back to the first century can still be seen.

6. Antioch in Pisidia

Seleucus, founder of the Syrian dynasty that took his name, founded this Antioch, too. Strictly speaking not part of Pisidia, Antioch became part of the Roman province of Galatia in 25 BC and could therefore justifiably be called Galatian Antioch. A fortified Roman colony and capital of southern Galatia, it controlled the area's barbarian tribes.

Paul's first missionary journey took him and Barnabas first to the island of Cyprus and then into the heart of modern-day Turkey.

Paul and Barnabas Taken for Gods, from the basilica of Saint Paul Outside the Walls, Rome, Italy.

7. Iconium

A two- or three-day trip from Antioch along the Via Sebaste, Iconium was an oasis entrance to an enormous plain after crossing through a mountain pass. On the trade route leading west to Ephesus and Rome, it became a Roman colony under Hadrian.

8. Lystra

Lystra was founded by Caesar Augustus. It lies 32 km (20 miles) southwest of Iconium through the cool Galatian plateau. A statue to Zeus and Hermes (Jupiter and Mercury to the Romans) has been discovered here. Ovid tells us that Philemon and Baucis entertained the two gods when other Lystrans ignored them.

9. Derbe

Today an uninhabited sheep land, Derbe was about 40 km (25 miles) southeast of Lystra. On the borders of the Roman province of Galatia, it was a frontier town of no special significance. To have gone further east would have taken Paul and Barnabas into Cappadocia .

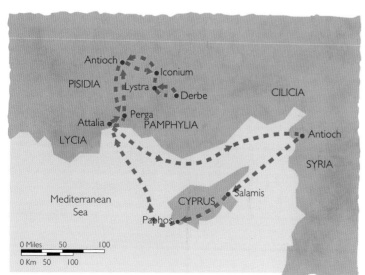

Paul's Journey Begins

ACTS 13:4–52

Saul, who became known as Paul, was commissioned with Barnabas by the church at Antioch and sent forth on a missionary journey. The journey took them first to Cyprus, then to the mainland where John Mark deserted them and went home. Paul and Barnabas went inland to Antioch of Pisidia, where many believed because of Paul's preaching.

The ruins of Antioch of Pisidia, an ancient city in Asia Minor where many believe Paul and Barnabas travelled to preach.

Ships and sailing

Ships were nothing new to the people of Paul's day. The vessels were used mainly for trade, travel, and war. Due to the great number of shipping routes on the Mediterranean Sea, pirate ships grew confident attacking unarmed vessels and stealing their goods. But the Romans built a large fleet of navy ships which put an end to this piracy.

Paul frequently sailed on ships during his missionary journeys (Acts 13:4, 13; 14:26; 16:11; 18:21; 27; 28:11–13). There were no ocean liners or cruise ships in that day, so those who wanted to travel by sea rode on merchant or trade ships. Paul began his voyage to Rome on a ship carrying wheat (27:38).

Saint Paul by Bartolomeo Montagna.

The shipping season lasted from April to October. During the winter months, the weather was rough and unpredictable. Since this was also the rainy time of the year, the sky was usually cloudy, and the stars, the compass of ancient times, could not be seen.

Jealous Jews

Many Jews did not accept Jesus as the Messiah, so they continued to follow the Old Testament laws as well as their own laws very carefully, believing this would bring them salvation.

Paul, however, entered the Jewish synagogues and claimed that Jesus' death had given people freedom from these strict laws. Naturally many people were very interested and wanted to hear more. This left many important Jews, usually prominent speakers on the Sabbath Day, no longer the centre of attention. Of course this made these Jews jealous of Paul, who was becoming quite popular. Jealousy often buds into hatred, and soon these leaders began plotting Paul's death, much as they had plotted Jesus' death.

Preaching to Jews or Gentiles?

Most Jews were familiar with the laws, lessons, and prophecies of the Old Testament. But the Gentiles were not Jews, and often were called "pagans". They were men and women who usually had no knowledge of the Scriptures. In preaching the gospel to these two diverse groups of people, the message was always the same, but the method of telling it was different, so that each group could understand.

Both Jews and Gentiles needed to know that Jesus' death meant a new life for all and that accepting this new life meant rejecting sin. To the Jews, Paul showed Jesus as the Messiah, the fulfilment of Old Testament prophecy. Jesus rescued people from the old laws which they could not keep.

But to the Gentiles, Jesus is portrayed as the conqueror of all evil. He is still the same Lord, but He is shown as One who can bring sense and meaning into an evil world because He knows sin will someday be destroyed.

Ruins in Cyprus, the first place Paul visited on his journey.

A notable convert

To Paul, no person was too great or too small to hear the message of Christ. On the island of Cyprus lived a most important man named Sergius Paulus, the Roman proconsul. He was in charge of the entire island, for though Cyprus was far from Rome, it was under the control of the Roman government. As Paul spoke, this man became a Christian believer (Acts 13:4–12).

Mistaken for Gods

ACTS 14

Paul and Barnabas worked together in the church at Antioch, which in time sent them out on a missionary journey. Their first stop was the island of Cyprus, and then on to the mainland, where John Mark deserted them and returned home. Paul and Barnabas continued on to Antioch of Pisidia, where many believed because of Paul's preaching. From there they travelled to Iconium, where, as at Antioch of Pisidia, local Jewish people stirred others against them. Moving on, the two went to Lystra and Derbe. At Lystra, after Paul healed a lame man, the people thought that he and Barnabas were gods. Shortly after this, some people came from Antioch of Pisidia and Iconium and accused Paul of certain things. Paul was stoned and left for dead. Then, after recovering, Paul and Barnabas retraced their steps to the home church at Antioch. This ended their first missionary journey.

Iconium

Though the other towns of Paul's first missionary journey have all but disappeared, Iconium, the modern Konya, is today a Turkish provincial capital, on the major crossroads south of Ankara.

In Greek and Roman times it was the leading city and capital of a region known as Lycaonia, though it still identified itself with Phrygia. About 130 km (80 miles) from Pisidian Antioch (Antiochea on today's maps) along the Via Sebaste, the great Roman road leading from Ephesus to the Euphrates, it is still today a city of beautiful scenery, fertile land, comfortable climate, and 50,000 people. The name may have come from the images Prometheus and Athena, who were made after a great flood destroyed many people.

Archaeologists have uncovered a first-century building beneath the ruins of a church here in ancient Antioch which may be the synagogue where Paul preached.

St Paul and St Barnabas at Lystra,
by Michel Corneille the Elder.

Zeus and Hermes

There was at this time a myth
that Zeus and Hermes had once
come to the area disguised as
human beings seeking lodging.
After a thousand people rejected
them, a poor, elderly man
named Philemon and his wife
Baucis fed them lavishly and
housed them. They destroyed
the inhospitable people but
made Philemon and Baucis
priest and priestess of their
straw-roofed reed cottage, which
they transformed into a gold
and marble temple. No wonder
Lystrans welcomed Paul and
Barnabas so enthusiastically!

Zeus (Jupiter) was the chief of
the Greek gods. Hermes, son of
Zeus and spokesman of the gods,
was called Mercury by Romans.

Lystra

Lystra has been identified with
an unexcavated mound near
Hatunsaray in modern Turkey,
30 km (20 miles) southwest
of Iconium (Konya). It has
been a relatively insignificant
rural settlement throughout
its long existence. Little
is known about it. In 6 BC
Caesar Augustus made it a
Roman colony and renamed
it Julia Felix Gemina Lustra.
Perhaps he chose it because
he needed an eastern frontier
fortress. He built a branch of the
Via Sebaste to it.

Head of Zeus (AD 69–96), the chief of the
Greek gods, for whom Paul was mistaken,
from the Ephesus Archaeological Museum.

Paul's Second Missionary Journey

ACTS 15:36–41

After Paul and Barnabas returned from their first missionary journey, they reported to the people at Antioch, remaining there for some time. A controversy arose concerning circumcision, for some said a man could not be saved without it. The church at Antioch sent Paul and Barnabas to Jerusalem to confer with the apostles, who determined that Gentiles did not need circumcision in order to become believers. After returning to Antioch, Paul and Barnabas decided to go on a second missionary journey, but when Barnabas wanted to take John Mark, he and Paul disagreed so sharply that Paul took Silas and Barnabas took John Mark, and they parted ways.

These ancient columns at Ephesus still retain their ornate capitals.

The cities of Paul's second journey

In addition to the cities Paul revisited, the New Testament mentions 12 other places Paul visited on his second missionary trip:

1. Troas
The name sounds like Troy and is only 16 km (10 miles) from that famous city of ancient Greek history (today it is Hisarlik in modern Turkey). An important city in northwest Asia Minor in Paul's day, it was a port on the major trade route to Macedonia.

2. Neapolis
The first city that Paul visited in what is now called Europe, this town was Philippi's seaport. Located on the coast of Macedonia in northern Greece, it is believed to be near modern Kavalla.

3. Philippi
Located about 16 km (10 miles) north of the Mediterranean Sea and Neapolis, Philippi was founded by Philip II of Macedon, the father of Alexander the Great. Here, in 42 BC, Mark Antony defeated Brutus and Cassius, the murderers of Julius Caesar. Augustus made Philippi a Roman colony. The tradition that this was Luke's birthplace is supported by the fact that an important physicians' guild was located here. Though there is no significant settlement here today, Philippi was the first European city in which Paul preached the gospel.

4. Amphipolis
Located 53 km (33 miles) southwest of Philippi, Amphipolis was its rival and the capital of the region.

5. Apollonia
Like Philippi and Amphipolis, Apollonia was located on the famous Roman road called the Via Egnatia. It was 45 km (28 miles) west of Amphipolis and 61 km (38 miles) east of Thessalonica.

6. Thessalonica
The most important city in this part of Greece today, Thessalonica was founded by Cassander, the military officer

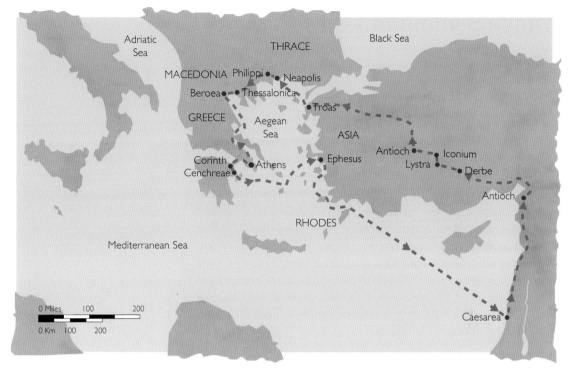

The route of Paul's second missionary journey.

who took control of Greece after the death of Alexander the Great in 323 BC. A consolidation of several small towns, it lay on both sea and land trade routes. Its sheltered harbour made it Macedonia's major seaport. Coins that have been excavated reveal it to have been a very prosperous city.

7. Berea

The origins of this small town on a branch of the Aliakmon River are unknown. It surrendered to the Romans after the battle of Pynda in 168 BC.

8. Athens

The well-known capital of Attica and educational centre of all of ancient Greece, Athens was named after the goddess Athene. According to tradition, Cecrops of Egypt founded the city in 1556 BC.

Many of its best-known buildings were built during the days of its most famous leader, Pericles (461–429 BC). With a population of over a quarter of a million in Paul's day, Athens was situated on and around the Acropolis, a large, rocky hill 6.5 km (4 miles) in from the Saronikos Bay. It was connected to its seaport, Peiraeus, by a street 76 m (250 feet) wide, with high walls on both sides.

9. Corinth

Because Corinth is located on a narrow neck of land that joins the southern part of Greece, called the Peloponnesus, to the northern mainland, it became the most important city in the region. In addition, sailing around the south of the Peloponnesus was treacherous, so most sea traffic between Rome and the East passed through Corinth.

10. Cenchrea

Located east of Corinth, Cenchrea was its seaport.

11. Ephesus

The most important seaport along the west coast of Asia Minor in Paul's day, Ephesus was the centre of the Artemis cult.

12. Rhodes

A city and island off the Asia Minor coast, Rhodes once rivalled Rome in wealth.

The Macedonian Call

After Paul and Bamabas returned to Antioch from their first missionary journey, they remained there for some time. A controversy over circumcision took them to Jerusalem to confer with the apostles, who determined that Gentiles need not be circumcised to be saved. Back in Antioch, Paul and Barnabas decided to go on another missionary journey, but they disagreed about taking John Mark, so they separated. Paul took Silas, and Barnabas took John Mark. Paul and Silas went through Syria and Cilicia, retracing some of the steps Paul had taken earlier. But at Troas, Paul saw a vision of a man of Macedonia, asking Paul to come and help his people. Paul and Silas immediately left for Macedonia, arriving at last in Philippi.

Roman provinces of Asia Minor

Asia Minor in Paul's day was divided up into provinces. There were three basic types: senatorial provinces, imperial provinces governed by consuls or praetors, and imperial provinces governed by procurators.

1. Senatorial provinces
Ten older, more stable provinces remained under senatorial control as they had been during the republic. Macedonia was one of these.

2. Consular or praetorial provinces
Twelve old provinces and all provinces added after 271 BC, when Augustus reorganized the empire's political structure, were governed by the emperor's appointees, called legates, for one-year terms. Large frontier provinces requiring a military presence were given a consul, smaller ones a praetor.

Ancient remains of the Via Egnatia in Greece. This road was built by the Romans after they conquered Macedonia, helping them tame a once turbulent region.

A detail from a fresco in the basilica of Saint Paul Outside the Wall, showing Paul and Silas being whipped in Philippi.

Macedonia

United by Philip II and head of an empire that stretched from India to Egypt under Alexander the Great, Macedonia then became a maelstrom of political struggle until Rome conquered it and built the Via Egnatia, an impressive road that went from west coast to east coast.

Silas

Greek writers often abbreviated names. Silas is probably short for Silvanus, from the Latin word for "wood". His name suggests he was a Roman citizen, probably with Hellenistic Jewish roots. Tradition says a Silas and a Silvanus became bishops of Corinth and Thessalonica.

3. Provinces governed by procurators

Provinces that were problematical were ruled by procurators, members of a military elite called equites, who were responsible both to the emperor and to the legate of the neighbouring province.

Some ancient territories, such as the old kingdoms of Pergamum, Mysia, and most of Phrygia, were absorbed in larger units such as the province of Asia.

Timothy's Family and Home

ACTS 16:1-4; 2 TIMOTHY 1:5

While Paul and Silas were on their second missionary journey, they met Timothy at his home in Lystra. He was the son of a Jewish mother, a devout woman, and a Greek father. Timothy joined Paul and Silas as they went on their way.

Timothy's name means "one who honours God". He was raised in Lystra by his Christian mother and grandmother. Probably both Lois and Eunice became believers in Jesus as a result of Paul's preaching on his first missionary journey, when Timothy was in his teens. By the time Paul made his second visit to the towns of Lycaonia, Timothy may have already been functioning as a prophet or elder (see 1 Tim. 4:14), though the existence of a group of elders suggests a more well-organized church than might have existed in AD 48. His natural talents and spiritual gifts appear to have been recognized by a prophet in the Christian community in Lystra or Iconium (see 1 Tim. 1:18) and he was enthusiastically approved by the Christians in both churches (Acts 16:2). His familiarity with the Old Testament from his childhood (2 Tim. 3:15), combined with his abilities and acceptance by the Christian community, made him an ideal choice for Paul's companion in his ministry for Christ, despite his youth.

He is not mentioned in the stories of Paul's imprisonment in Philippi or Paul's work in Thessalonica. Perhaps Timothy was using his talents in other

This marble grave marker of a Greek youth from the fourth century BC reminds us of Timothy and his mother.

It is believed that Lystra was south of Iconium (the city of Konya today). There is a present-day village called Kilistra to the southweSt Among its ruins (shown above) is a church with a big cross on the wall, a winery, and house-like buildings.

places such as Amphipolis and Apollonia, since he was known in Thessalonica (1 Thes. 3:1–2). The fact that he remained Paul's companion until his death, whereas Silas disappeared after the end of the second journey, suggests that Timothy's gifts as a preacher and leader were greater. Timothy took Paul's place in Corinth when Paul was in Ephesus and sent his greetings to Rome when Paul wrote to the church there (1 Cor. 4:17; Rom. 16:21). As Paul faced death, he passed his responsibilities on to Timothy, his successor and "dear son" (2 Tim. 1:2), who had spent 20 years as his associate. The writer of Hebrews (13:23) mentioned Timothy's release from prison.

Later tradition tells us that Timothy became the bishop of Ephesus. Liberal scholars in the nineteenth century saw him as the author of Acts. Other Bible scholars suggest that he was the "angel" of Revelation 2:1–7.

Eunice and Lois

Both names, Eunice ("good victory") and Lois ("more desirable") are Greek. Tradition says both were widows.

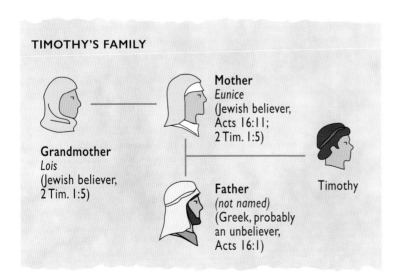

TIMOTHY'S FAMILY

Grandmother
Lois
(Jewish believer, 2 Tim. 1:5)

Mother
Eunice
(Jewish believer, Acts 16:11; 2 Tim. 1:5)

Father
(not named)
(Greek, probably an unbeliever, Acts 16:1)

Timothy

Lydia Becomes a Believer

ACTS 16:11–15

On his second missionary journey, Paul travelled through many of the same places he had visited on his first journey. But when he came to Troas, he saw a vision of a man of Macedonia, asking Paul to come over there to help. Paul and Silas went, arriving at Philippi. There they joined a group of women who met together for prayer. Lydia, one of these women, accepted Jesus as her Saviour.

The women's prayer group Paul found probably gathered on the banks of the Ganga or Gangites River, a mile west of Philippi. Flanked on the west by the Strimon River and on the east by the Nestos-Mesta River and surrounded on all sides by mountains, Philippi looked out over a broad plain. The Via Egnatia ran down its main street. On the south side in the centre of the city was the forum or marketplace in which Paul and Silas appeared before the city's two magistrates, called praetors or, more exactly, *duumviri*. This forum was excavated in the 1920s, when other buildings, temples, houses, and a theatre were also found.

Settlers first arrived in Philippi from the off-coast island of Thasos to mine gold. Philip II of Macedon named the city after himself, built a wall, and colonized it in 356 BC. At the Battle of Philippi in 42 BC Cassius committed suicide here after Mark Antony defeated his army. Luke may have grown up and attended medical school here. The church at Philippi was Paul's favourite church.

Paul and Lydia from an edition of
John Brown's Self Interpreting Bible
first published in 1778.

362

This contemporary Greek Orthodox chapel was built on a possible site of Lydia's baptism.

Purple cloth

The purple or crimson cloth so valued by the ancients as a sign of nobility and distinction came from either a shellfish called the murex, or "turkey red", a dye taken from the madder root. A dyers' guild was located in Thyatira.

Lydia's purple goods may have been dyed in Thyatira with a substance made from *bolinus brandaris* – a predatory sea snail.

Thyatira

Thyatira was a busy commercial centre. Lydia probably learned her trade in one of its many guilds.

The Philippian Prison

ACTS 16:16–40

While travelling on his second missionary journey, Paul saw a vision of a Macedonian man, asking Paul and Silas for help. They went immediately, arriving in Philippi. There they joined a group of women who met for prayer, and Lydia, one of them, accepted Jesus as Saviour. But in that same city there was a girl who was used for sorcery. Paul commanded the evil spirit to leave the girl, and for that he and Silas were beaten and thrown into prison. But when the magistrates in town learned that Paul was a Roman citizen, they were frightened, for they had beaten him and imprisoned him without a trial. They begged Paul and Silas to leave town.

FORTUNE-TELLING
The girl at Philippi with the sprit of divination is the only reference to this form of fortune-telling in the New Testament. The word for "divination" derives from the Greek region of Pytho, where the famous Delphic oracle was found. Telling the future, or fortune-telling, was done by various means, including the interpretation of dreams, astrology, the examination of animals' entrails, consulting mediums, and casting lots. The Bible condemns all such means of trying to foretell the future.

The remains of a prison at Philippi, presented today as the jail cell where Paul and Silas stayed.

Roman citizenship
Citizenship was a coveted honour in ancient Rome. The better emperors tried to expand the number of citizens, so that by the time of Claudius (AD 41–54) there were almost six million citizens, one of whom was Paul. Emperor Pompey may have granted Paul's Jewish ancestors their citizenship, over half a century earlier.

To be a Roman citizen involved certain rights and imposed certain duties. If a citizen felt he had been unjustly imprisoned, for example, as Paul did later on in his career, he had the right to appeal directly to Caesar. At one time a citizen had the duty of serving in the army and the right to vote, but both of these rights had gradually

disappeared. Paul saw Christians as citizens of God's kingdom ("conversation" or "conduct" in Phil. 1:27; 3:20).

Fortune-telling
Can you imagine anyone thinking he could tell his future by looking at the liver of an animal? Perhaps not, but that method of determining an individual's future was once as popular as the horoscope is today – and just as foolish!

The slave girl who earned money for her owners by fortune-telling is an example of the age-old superstition that by natural or supernatural omens we can learn specific facts

The Temple of Apollo at Delphi.

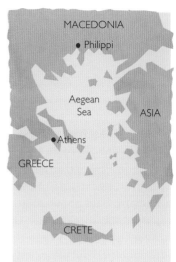

about our futures. The Greek text says she had "a python spirit". The slave girl's owners saw her as an instrument of Python, whose spirit was thought to live in her belly.

Whatever its name, an evil spirit lived in her.

There were many other superstitious methods in the ancient world by which people thought they could foretell events.

Soothsayers used omens from nature, such as earthquakes, a sneeze, and the flight of birds; and signs, such as dreams, star patterns, and casting lots. Diviners communicated with the gods through oracles. Mediums consulted the spirits of the dead. The reason Babylonians consulted animals' livers was that they believed the liver was the seat of life. Whenever God is abandoned, as He was in ancient Rome, astrology seems to become popular. The Bible opposes such practices (Lev. 19:26, 31; Deut. 18:9–14).

Stocks

Stocks are mentioned a number of times in the Old Testament, but only in Acts 16:24 in the New. In Paul's day they were iron bolts attached to wooden posts, through which the prisoner's hands and feet were attached.

SOME OF THE PEOPLE WHO BELIEVED IN JESUS

FISHERMEN
Peter and Andrew: Brothers, fishermen on Galilee, sons of Zebedee and later apostles (Matt. 4:18–20; 16:15–19; Acts 2).

DOCTOR
Luke: Evangelist, physician and writer of the third Gospel (Col. 4:14; 2 Tim. 4:11; Phile. 24).

TAX-COLLECTOR
Matthew (Levi): One of the 12 apostles and writer of the first Gospel (Matt. 9:9, 10:3; Mark 2:14).

SLAVE
Onesimus: Paul wrote to his master pleading his case (Col. 4:9; Phile. 10, 15).

SLAVE-OWNER
Philemon: Convert at Colossae; Paul wrote to him about his slave, Onesimus (Phile. 1, 5–7).

RICH MERCHANT
Lydia: Dealer in fine cloth from Thyatira (Acts 16:14–15).

ROYAL AMBASSADOR
In charge of the Treasury of Queen Candace of the Ethiopians (Acts 8:5–13).

TENT-MAKERS
Aquila and Priscilla: Husband and wife Jewish-Christian team who worked alongside and helped Paul (Acts 18:2, 18, 26; Rom. 16:3; 1 Cor. 16:3, 19).

PHARISEE
Paul: Pharisee who studied the Jewish law under Gamaliel and became the apostle to the Gentiles (Acts 26:12–20).

JAILER
Was about to kill himself because he thought his prisoners had escaped (Acts 16:16–36).

CENTURION
Cornelius: A Roman Gentile converted after Peter's vision (Acts 10:1–31).

Paul at Thessalonica

ACTS 17:1–9

While at Troas, Paul had a vision of a man of Macedonia, begging Paul to come there to help. Paul and Silas went immediately, arriving in Philippi, where they joined some women who met for prayer. Lydia, one of the women, became a believer. While in Philippi, Paul commanded an evil spirit to leave a girl who was used for sorcery. For this her masters had Paul and Silas thrown into prison. When they were released, they went on to Thessalonica. Paul preached in the synagogue there, but jealous men stirred up trouble, and Paul had to leave town.

The ancient ruins of the Roman forum in Thessalonica.

Still the largest city in the region once known as the capital of the Roman province of Macedonia, Thessalonica (today's Thessaloniki) is located on the Gulf of Salonika.

Coming from Apollonia to the east, Paul entered the city through the southeastern gate, called the Arch of Galerius. The famous Roman road, the Via Egnatia, went through the city.

Known as the leading seaport of Macedonia, Thessalonica assumed that reputation only after Pella, a short distance to the west, filled up with silt. When it was conquered by Rome in 167 BC, it became the capital of one of four districts. Then in 148 BC, when it was made a province, it became the capital of the whole area. Octavian and Mark Antony made it a free city as a reward for its support against Brutus and Cassius. Its five or six governors, called "politarchs" (see Acts 17:6), formed the city council.

Jason

Jason of Thessalonica was a Jewish Christian who may have been one of the three relatives of Paul mentioned in Romans 16:21. His name, meaning "healing", was often used by Greek-speaking Jews instead of the names Jesus and Joshua. Paul and Silas probably stayed at his house during their stay in Thessalonica. After his trial in the marketplace Jason was freed, but six years later he may have accompanied Paul to Corinth. Tradition says he became bishop of Tarsus.

The marketplace

The marketplace in Thessalonica was probably in the centre of the city, north of the Via Egnatia. Unlike the ancient Near Eastern marketplace with its open bazaars and shops, the agora of the typical Greek city was like the Roman forum. A large square surrounded by beautiful columned buildings, statues, and temples, the agora was far more than just a place where slaves purchased food for their masters. It was also a political and social centre. Here the aristocracy met to discuss current topics of interest, students and philosophers exchanged ideas, and the small group of politarchs sat to try people such as Paul and Silas. But when Paul preached in the agora in Athens he appeared more in the role of a philosopher who was presenting his view of life.

The Bereans Accept Paul

ACTS 17:10–14

In a vision, Paul saw a man of Macedonia begging him to come over and help. Paul and Silas went, stopping first at Philippi, where they joined a women's prayer group. One of the women, Lydia, became a believer. But Paul and Silas were imprisoned in Philippi for driving an evil spirit from a girl. When they were released, they went to Thessalonica, where jealous men stirred up trouble and Paul and Silas had to leave town, stopping next at Berea.

Berea

Berea lives in the minds of Christians as a town where believers searched the Scriptures. With a population today of about 30,000, the small city, called Verria, is a ski resort. Berea is located 74 km (46 miles) southwest of Thessalonica and 30 km (20 miles) from the Thermaic Gulf on the Mediterranean coast.

In New Testament times Berea was one of the largest cities in Macedonia, perhaps because it was just south of the famous Roman commercial and military road called the Via Egnatia. In normal circumstances Paul's next stop after Thessalonica would have been Edessa, but perhaps for safety reasons he chose a city off the beaten path. It is interesting that Cicero also mentions that a century earlier an unpopular Roman governor named Piso crept into Thessalonica at night but withdrew to Berea when the citizens rose up in protest. On the eastern slopes of a mountain in the Olympian range, the city gave Paul a beautiful view to the north, east, and west, including Dium, the seaport to which he probably fled to reach Athens. Today only a few ruins of the ancient city remain. Near a mosque is a platform from which Paul is said to have preached to the Bereans. Sopater, one of Paul's associates, came from Berea, and Onesimus is said to have been Berea's first bishop.

The Jewish diaspora

The word "diaspora" means "scattering". It refers to the voluntary settling of Jews outside Palestine. Large groups of Jews settled in Egypt, Syria, Mesopotamia, Asia Minor, Greece, and even Italy. Such Jews usually became enterprising merchants. Though Judaism was officially recognized by Rome, emperors such as Tiberius and Claudius persecuted the Jews. Many Gentiles were attracted to Judaism because of its high ethical standards and one God.

The Bereans examined the Scriptures to see if what Paul said was true, and as a result, many of them believed. *Saint Paul* (c. 1468) by Marco Zoppo.

The translation of the Old Testament into Greek, called the Septuagint, made it even easier for Gentiles to convert to Judaism, and probably many did so.

Diaspora Judaism (Jews scattered in other lands) was also a bridge for infant Christianity to cross into the Gentile world.

Many diaspora Jews made trips to Jerusalem at the time of the Passover, as Luke (Acts 2) indicates. Those who could not contributed to the annual collection for the temple.

Paul at Mars Hill

ACTS 17:16–34

When Paul saw a vision of a man from Macedonia calling for help, he crossed over and began his work at Philippi. There a woman named Lydia became a believer. There also Paul and Silas were thrown into prison after they drove an evil spirit from a girl. When they were released, they went to Thessalonica, but troublemakers forced them to leave. Next stop was Berea, where people searched the Scriptures to check out what Paul said. From Berea, Paul went to Athens.

Athens

Draw a circle and imagine it to be the walls of ancient Athens. Now draw an upside-down T inside the circle. The tip of the stem is where the *agora* or marketplace was. The left arm of the T is where the Areopagus was, and the right arm is where the Acropolis was.

At one time, Athens was the cultural centre of the world. Religion, philosophy, and education thrived. Magnificent buildings seemed to spring up overnight. By Paul's day however, the elegant city had lost much of its importance.

The Areopagus

Mars Hill, or Areopagus, originally referred to the large limestone hill, 115 m (375 feet) high, that overlooked the *agora* (marketplace) from the south. Over time, the name also came to mean the court that met there. Earlier, this court had the power to judge all

When Paul preached on Mars Hill, he would have seen the Parthenon. Its modern-day ruins are shown here.

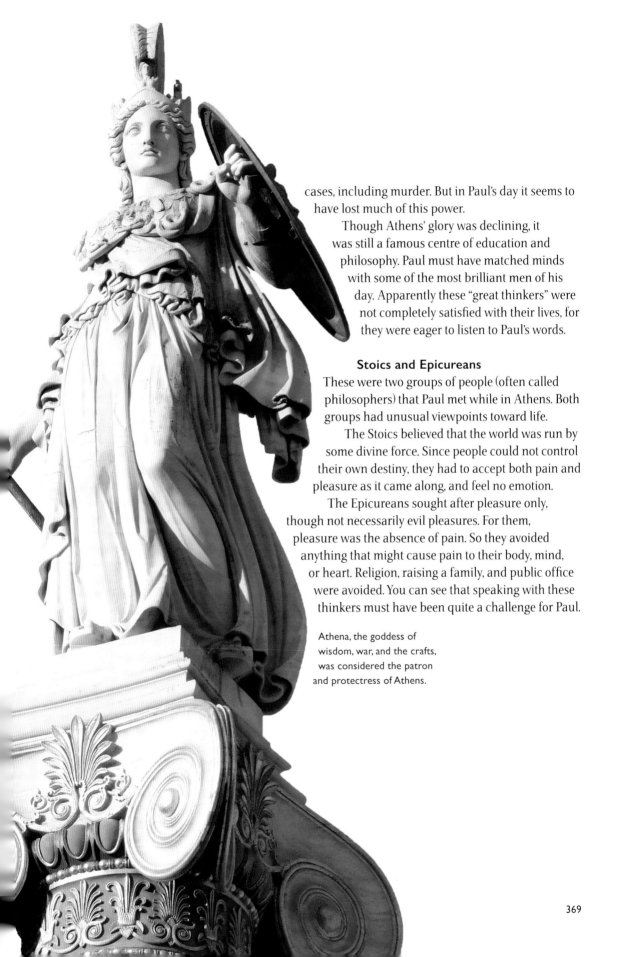

cases, including murder. But in Paul's day it seems to have lost much of this power.

Though Athens' glory was declining, it was still a famous centre of education and philosophy. Paul must have matched minds with some of the most brilliant men of his day. Apparently these "great thinkers" were not completely satisfied with their lives, for they were eager to listen to Paul's words.

Stoics and Epicureans

These were two groups of people (often called philosophers) that Paul met while in Athens. Both groups had unusual viewpoints toward life.

The Stoics believed that the world was run by some divine force. Since people could not control their own destiny, they had to accept both pain and pleasure as it came along, and feel no emotion.

The Epicureans sought after pleasure only, though not necessarily evil pleasures. For them, pleasure was the absence of pain. So they avoided anything that might cause pain to their body, mind, or heart. Religion, raising a family, and public office were avoided. You can see that speaking with these thinkers must have been quite a challenge for Paul.

Athena, the goddess of wisdom, war, and the crafts, was considered the patron and protectress of Athens.

Paul at Corinth

ACTS 18:1–4

When Paul saw a vision of a man of Macedonia, he went there to minister. His first stop was at Philippi, where he helped Lydia and a jailer become believers. From there Paul and Silas went to Thessalonica but were forced by troublemakers to leave. At Berea, the people searched the Scriptures to test what Paul said. Paul went on to Athens and then to Corinth, where he, Priscilla, and Aquila worked as tentmakers.

The old city of Corinth was located 5.5 km (3.5 miles) southwest of the present city. With the Corinthian Gulf 3km (2 miles) to the north and Cenchrea (Kenchreai) 11 km (7 miles) to the east on the Saronic Gulf, Corinth was a very important trade centre because ships preferred to use the paved stone passageway that linked the two gulfs rather than risk the treacherous waters around the Peloponnesus. The Acrocorinth Mountain to the south of the city was a steep, rocky fortress that was all but impregnable. Long walls joined the mountain and the city to the Corinthian coast. The Isthmian Games were held here every two years and further enhanced Corinth's reputation. At the peak of its glory it may have had 300,000 to 450,000 inhabitants. In an age of moral decadence, Corinth had a reputation for its excesses, connected with the worship of Aphrodite, goddess of love and beauty.

The strategic location of this city is underlined by the fact that it has been settled since the fifth millennium BC. A battle with

The ruins of the temple of Apollo may be seen at Corinth today.

The view from the summit of Acrocorinth of Corinth today, and the Gulf of Corinth.

one of its colonies led to the Peloponnesian War (431–404 BC). Some two centuries earlier Periander built the *diolkos*, or paved stone slipway, that carved out Corinth's future. (Today there is a canal about 8km (5 miles) northeast of Old Corinth). After Philip of Macedon became its leader it experienced two centuries of prosperity, but in 146 BC Rome razed it to the ground for siding with rebels, and it was not rebuilt until Julius Caesar made it the capital of Achaia, in 44 BC.

Tentmaking

This is the only place in the Bible that mentions tentmaking. It could mean the weaving of tent cloth from goats' hair, or it could mean the cutting and sewing of tents. The latter is probably what Paul, Priscilla, and Aquila did. Paul's province of Cilicia was noted for the goats'-hair cloth, called *cilicium*, used in making tents.

But some have asked, could the word mean "leatherworker"? The earliest Latin translators thought that the Greek word used by the author of Acts meant someone who made beds and the leather cushions to go on them. So many of the Latin and Greek church fathers call Paul a leatherworker.

But it is not likely that Paul's father, a strict Pharisee, would have allowed his son to work in a trade that Jews disapproved of. Thus, Paul probably was a tentmaker, not a leatherworker.

Gallio Judges Paul at Corinth

ACTS 18:5–17

After entering Macedonia, Paul visited Philippi, where Lydia and a jailer became believers. From there he went to Thessalonica but was forced by troublemakers to leave. At Berea, the people searched the Scriptures to see if what Paul said was true. Paul travelled on to Corinth, where he worked as a tentmaker with Aquila and Priscilla. He remained at Corinth for a year and a half, during which time the synagogue ruler, Crispus, and many other Corinthians believed in Jesus. Many of the Jewish people of Corinth brought Paul to court, but Gallio, the proconsul, threw them out and refused to stop a crowd from beating Sosthenes, the synagogue ruler.

Gallio, proconsul of Achaia
Lucius Junius Gallio Annaeus was proconsul, or governor, of the Roman province of Achaia in Greece during AD 52 and part of the year before or after. The son of a rhetorician named Marcus Annaeus Seneca and brother of Seneca, the millionaire tutor of Nero and well-known philosopher, he was born in Cordova, Spain, as Marcus Annaeus Novatus. A wealthy friend, Lucius Junius Gallio, adopted him and trained him for political leadership.

Archaeologists have discovered an inscription that reveals that Gallio was proconsul *after* the 26th year of the acclamation of Claudius as emperor of Rome. That date is important for fixing the dates of Paul's ministry.

An unusually agreeable man, Gallio became ill in Corinth's climate and retired to Egypt when his one-year term of office was over to seek a cure for a lung haemorrhage. After returning to Rome, he joined his brother in a conspiracy to overthrow Nero. His brother was killed and, though he was pardoned, he shortly after committed suicide or was executed by Nero's orders.

The ruins of the ancient Acrocorinth – the acropolis of Corinth.

earliest references to synagogues. Pharisees early became their leaders, and by New Testament times the tradition had emerged that synagogues went back to the time of Moses (see Acts 15:21).

Everywhere Paul went in the Hellenistic world there were synagogues. Several have been excavated. The seven-pillared synagogue in Capernaum, where Jesus taught, has been discovered at Tell Hum and partially restored. The synagogue in Rome's seaport town of Ostia may date back to the first century.

Though worship played an important part in synagogue life, teaching was equally important. Had it not been for synagogues, it is questionable that Judaism could have survived, especially in the diaspora. The two leaders of each synagogue, the "ruler" and the *hazzan* (minister, attendant) who was his helper, supervised the worship, which included 18 prayers, readings from the Law and Prophets, and a sermon.

Gallio's judgement seat has been discovered on the south side of Corinth's agora. Surrounded on the left and right by shops, the monumental platform, called a *bema*, was the place on which Roman officials stood and may have been the place where Paul appeared before Gallio. A Christian church was built over its ruins.

feast days and Sabbaths arose to preserve the faith. The New Testament contains some of the

Synagogues

Though the exact origins of synagogue buildings are unknown, they probably began during the Jewish exile in Babylon after 586 BC. The temple of Solomon had been destroyed, so local gatherings on

The Roman coins show lictors, officers who cleared the way in public for the magistrates. These may have been the people referred to in Acts 16:38.

Books of Evil Are Burned

ACTS 19:17–20

Paul visited Macedonia after he saw a vision of a man there, calling for help. In Macedonia, he visited Philippi, where Lydia and a jailer became believers. He moved on to Thessalonica, but troublemakers forced him out. Next he went to Berea, where people searched the Scriptures to test what he was saying. After that, Paul visited Athens and then moved to Corinth, where he stayed for a year and a half, working as a tentmaker with Aquila and Priscilla. From Corinth, Paul travelled to Ephesus and then concluded his second missionary journey, returning to Caesarea and back to the home church at Antioch. Later Paul began his third missionary journey, travelling back to Ephesus. Mighty works happened this time as Paul remained there.

Ephesus

Ephesus is located along the west coast of Turkey, though today it exists only as a historical site. Located about 11 km (7 miles) inland because of the silt that has filled the ancient harbour, it sits on the plain of the Cayster (Kuçuk) River. The ancient town was located on the slopes of the Coressus and Prion hills. The temple to the goddess Artemis (Diana to the Romans) was located a mile lower on the plain itself. The region is southeast of the present town of Selçuk. In biblical times Ephesus was a terminal of the great trade route from the east and linked it with the great western trade routes.

Settled by colonists from Athens, Ephesus was developed to replace Miletus, its rival to the south, which had silted up. The kingdom of Pergamum developed the harbour, and Rome made Ephesus the seat of its proconsul. Coins call Ephesus "the Landing Place".

By New Testament times Ephesus too had begun to fade as a harbour. Silting is indicated even on some coins, which depict shallow-bottomed boats, not the deep-hulled merchant ships of the days of the city's glory.

Devotion to Artemis the Great and her temple produced a replacement for the city's declining naval importance,

The Sermon of Saint Paul at Ephesus by Eustache Le Sueur.

The Library of Celsus in Ephesus was the empire's third-largest library. It is said to have stored around 12,000 scrolls.

however. Founded by the son of the last king of Athens, Ephesus already had a shrine to an ancient Anatolian goddess whom the Greeks renamed Artemis. The fertility goddess was kept "alive", however, in the sexual orgies and prostitution connected with her rites. Through the years the temple became one of the wonders of the ancient world. It was once four times the size of the Parthenon in Athens. Today its ruins have been located in a marsh northeast of the ancient city. Paul was thus attacking a major fortress of paganism.

Scrolls

Paul's Ephesian converts who had been sorcerers burned their scrolls. A scroll was the ancient form of our modern book. Made of papyrus, leather, or parchment, sheets were joined together to form a sheet usually not more than 9 m (30 feet) long and 30 cm (1 foot) high. A scroll was rolled up on wooden rollers and wound off the left and onto the right roller. Occasionally, though, enormous scrolls were made. One in Egypt was 40 m (133 feet) long and 43 cm (17 inches) high. Written in capital letters with no breaks

between words and with a very durable ink, scrolls contained columns with only narrow spaces between them. Writing at first went from right to left. Then the *boustrophedon*, rows alternating from right to left and then left to right, was introduced. But it was soon replaced by the practice we use, from left to right.

Diana of the Ephesians

ACTS 19:23–41

On his third missionary journey, Paul visited Ephesus, where he performed a number of miracles. While he was there, seven sons of a Jewish chief priest, Sceva, tried to drive out a demon in Jesus' name, but the man possessed by the demon jumped on them and beat them. As a result, fear spread among the believers, and many burned their books of sorcery. About this time, the silversmiths of Ephesus started a riot against Paul, angry because his ministry was hurting their sales of Diana's shrines. But the city clerk quieted the riot and sent the people home.

Artemis the Great

The Artemis of Ephesus (Diana of the Ephesians) was quite different from the goddess of classical antiquity. That is not surprising, perhaps, because Artemis was the most widely worshipped and popular of all the Greek deities, especially among women. Homer portrays her as a virgin hunter, but she is also portrayed as a moon goddess, patron of maidens, and female fertility deity associated with childbirth. Ancient myths said she had given her mother, Leto, no pain at her birth. The daughter of Zeus, she assisted at the birth of her twin brother, Apollo! In Greece little girls would "play the bear" in front of her image, suggesting that she originally may have had an animal form. At Halae, south of Athens, blood was taken by sword from a man's neck, a vestige, perhaps, of

A detail from a statue of Artemis of Ephesus.

human sacrifice connected with the worship of Artemis. This rite was brought by Orestes from the Tauric Chersonese of Crimea.

But in Ephesus Artemis was nothing like the gentle moon goddess. Here she was the lusty female fertility goddess said to have been worshipped by the warrior maidens of Asia Minor called

the Amazons. Like them, the female slaves dressed in short skirts and bared one breast when they served in the magnificent temple to Artemis in Ephesus, one of the seven wonders of the world. The temple also had eunuch priests, called *megabuzoi*, and other chaste male attendants. Prostitution may not have been part of the rites of this temple, though it was of all other Anatolian fertility goddess temples.

The city clerk

The Ephesian "city clerk" was more of a mayor than what we think of as a town clerk. The word, which appears in the Bible only in Acts 19, is difficult to translate exactly, since the functions and status of offices changed from place to place. However, Apollonius of Tyana around AD 100 refers to a high official in Ephesus and used the same word Luke used here in Acts. An important, wealthy Roman official of noble birth, he was president of the assembly, chaired meetings, and eventually became the chief executive.

The goddess Artemis was the most popular of all the Greek deities. Here we see a ruined archway of the Temple of Artemis in Ephesus.

MACEDONIA

Aegean Sea

ASIA

GREECE

Ephesus ●

CRETE

Eutychus

ACTS 20:6–12

On his third missionary journey, Paul went through Galatia and Phrygia, encouraging the believers in the churches there. When he arrived in Ephesus, he stayed for some time, performing miracles and teaching. Seven sons of a Jewish chief priest tried to drive out an evil spirit in Jesus' name, but the spirit-possessed man jumped on them and beat them. This brought a fear to the believers in Ephesus, and many burned their books of sorcery. About this time the silversmiths of Ephesus stirred a riot against Paul, whose preaching was hurting the sales of Diana's shrines. When the riot died down, Paul left Ephesus and travelled through Macedonia and Achaia, arriving at last at Troas.

Eutychus

The name Eutychus means "fortunate" or "lucky". It was common among slaves. Josephus mentions two people by that name. One, interestingly enough, was the charioteer who overheard Herod Agrippa tell Caligula he thought the latter would make a better emperor than Tiberius and told Tiberius. The other, also a charioteer "of the green band faction", was a close friend of Caligula, who said he would, after Caligula's murder, bring Claudius – or at least his head – to the soldiers.

Eutychus of Troas was probably an exhausted slave, hot from the oil lamps and sleepy from all the talk and warm bodies in the room. William Jowett described a room where he stayed in 1818 that may have been similar to the room in Troas. The lower level was a storage area for olive oil. The second level was the family living quarters. But the third level, the area for guests and their company, was large and had projecting windows. Divans went around the three sides of the window area. A second row of people could be placed behind and above those on the divan by placing cushions there, level with the windows that could be

A detail of a vintage print showing Paul bringing the young Eutychus back to life.

opened to let in air. A fall from such a window could be fatal. In such a large room Paul might have addressed the Christians of Troas, when Eutychus fell asleep.

Troas

Troas is 16 km (10 miles) south of Troy. Near the present-day town of Hisarlik on the northwest coast of Turkey on the Aegean Sea, it lies at the mouth of the Dardenelles. A port opposite the Bozca Ada (Tenedos) Island, it was originally called Sigia. Renamed Antigonia Troas (Troas means "area around Troy") by Antigonus, one of the generals of Alexander the Great who took over parts of his empire on his death in 323 BC, the city became Alexandria Troas, in 300 BC. Troas stayed independent even during the height of power of the kingdoms of Pergamum and Rome. Julius Caesar, Augustus, and Constantine all thought of making Troas the capital of the empire. It was a large, important city in its day, but is now in ruins.

Heredos Atticus Bath ruins in Troas.

Paul Is Arrested

ACTS 21:17–23:35

When Paul went on his third missionary journey, he travelled through Galatia and Phrygia before arriving at Ephesus, where he stayed for a while. At Ephesus, he taught and worked miracles. Seven sons of a chief priest tried to work a miracle in Jesus' name, but the demon-possessed man involved beat them up. This brought fear on the believers, and many burned their books of sorcery. Many others became believers in Ephesus, and the sales of silver Diana shrines dropped. The silversmiths got angry and started a riot against Paul, but the city clerk stopped it. Paul then left Ephesus and travelled through Macedonia and Achaia to Troas, where Eutychus died from a fall and Paul brought him back to life. From Troas, Paul stopped at several places, then returned to Jerusalem. In the temple, Paul went through certain rituals to prove he had not deserted his Jewish past, but he was falsely accused and arrested anyhow. Some men plotted to kill Paul, but his nephew learned of the plot and told the Roman commander, who then transferred Paul through Antipatris to Caesarea.

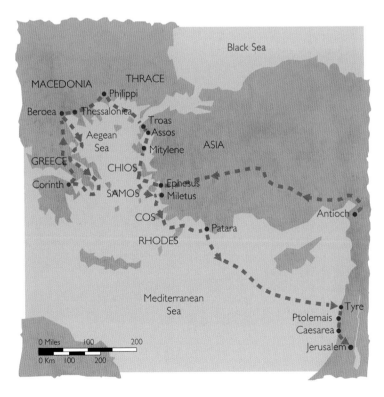

The cohort commander

The commander, Claudius Lysias, was a *chiliarch*, the leader of 1,000 men. A tribune later was the commander of a cohort, usually consisting from 360 to 600 men. Today he would be major or colonel.

The commander of the cohort stationed in the Tower of Antonia was in charge of soldiers in the nearby barracks. They were part of the Roman Tenth Legion, headquartered in Caesarea. Josephus tells us that at Herod Agrippa's death in AD 44 Rome had five cohorts stationed at Caesarea. A full legion consisted of 10 cohorts, and each cohort had 6 centurions, each in charge of 60 men.

Rome also organized an auxiliary army. The regular army was made up only of Roman citizens. But the auxiliary army, which was equal to it in size, consisted of soldiers from the provinces who were not citizens. Maybe the Antonia Fortress was staffed by auxiliaries.

The Antonia Tower where the commander or tribune was stationed was next to the temple. From the southeast, and tallest, of its four towers he could see all of the temple area. Should anything happen, the Antonia was joined to the temple by two stairways and an underground passageway. On Jewish feast

Antipatris was built by Herod the Great in honour of his father, Antipater. What remains of it today is called Tel Afek.

days Rome may have increased its military forces to 2 cohorts up to 1,200 soldiers – a small part of the total force of 400,000 believed to have been in the regular and the auxiliary armies.

Saint Paul.

The vow of Paul

It is not easy to understand the vow the Jerusalem Christians asked Paul to make. Vows were usually religious pledges made in the hope that God would do something for you. But the vow Paul and his friends made does not fit the pattern of Old Testament vows. No reference is made to eating a vowed peace offering or even to making a money offering predetermined by age, sex, and wealth – unless it is the reference in Acts 21:24 to paying expenses. Instead there are references to shaving the head and a set number of days of purification (Acts 21:24, 26). This may have been a temporary Nazirite vow, a vow for safety (see Jonah 1:16), or a rite of purification after Paul's Gentile contacts.

Antipatris

Under the safety of no less than 470 soldiers Paul was taken to Antipatris. Antipatris was a *mutatio*, or military relay station, on the border between Judea and Samaria. It was located 65 km (40 miles) from Jerusalem downhill from the mountainous Aijalon Valley into the Plain of Sharon, on the main coastal road 16 km (10 miles) north of Lydda and 40 km (25 miles) south of Caesarea, the capital of Judea at this time.

Antipatris was excavated by the Palestine Department of Antiquities in 1946. The excavations revealed that Antipatris had been built above the older Philistine town of Aphek (2000 BC).

Paul Before Felix and Festus

ACTS 24:1–25:12

A bronze prutah minted by Antonius Felix. On one side it says "Nero" and on the other side "Caesar" and a palm branch.

After returning from his third missionary journey, Paul went to the temple in Jerusalem. But he was arrested there and held prisoner. Paul's nephew learned of a plot to kill Paul and told the Roman commander, who transferred him by night to Caesarea, where Paul remained prisoner for two years. While there, Felix and Festus judged Paul.

Governor Felix

Antonius Felix, brother of Pallas, a favourite of Claudius and a freedman from the house of Antonia, Claudius' mother, got his procuratorship of Judea through his brother's influence on the emperor. His term was marked by corruption, mismanagement, and near anarchy. Tacitus, the Roman historian, not always an impartial witness, is probably correct in calling him "a master of cruelty and lust who exercised the powers of a king in the spirit of a slave". His mismanagement is revealed in the fact that it required 470 men to convey Paul safely the 65 km (40 miles) from Jerusalem to Antipatris.

Just when did Felix become governor of Judea? Tacitus and Josephus do not agree on this. Josephus says quite simply that Ventidius Cumanus became procurator in AD 48 and Antonius Felix after Cumanus' recall in AD 52. Tacitus says Cumanus was procurator of Galilee while Felix held the same office in Samaria and Judea.

Felix took Drusilla, the 15-year-old wife of Azizus, king of Emesa (a small principality northeast of Damascus), and made her his third wife. (He had also been married to the granddaughter of Mark Antony and Cleopatra.) Drusilla was also the sister of King Herod Agrippa II. She bore a son, Agrippa.

Felix's tenure was marked by many uprisings, the murder of the high priest, and the slaying of 400 of the followers of an Egyptian Jew (see Acts 21:38). When Nero recalled Felix in AD 60, a large deputation of Jews brought charges against him. His cruelties triggered a war that broke out in AD 66.

Drusilla

Drusilla, Felix's wife, was the youngest of Herod Agrippa I's three daughters. She was probably named after the sister of Herod's friend, the young emperor Caligula. Drusilla had just died at the age of 22 when Herod's daughter was born, and Herod had been in Rome at the time, AD 38. By AD 53 she broke her engagement to Epiphanes, prince of Commogene (northeast of Tarsus), because he changed his mind about converting to Judaism, and married Azizus of Emesa. In 54, however, Felix persuaded her to leave Azizus and marry him. She was 20 when Paul spoke to her and her husband. Their son Agrippa died later in the eruption of Mt Vesuvius in AD 79. Drusilla, a widow by this time, may have died with him.

Porcius Festus (AD 60–62)

We know nothing of Porcius Festus except for the brief time he was procurator of Judea. According to Josephus, he was a welcome contrast to his corrupt predecessor, Felix, and his equally corrupt successor, Albinus. Lawlessness had broken out throughout the land, foreshadowing the Jewish war that was to break out in AD 66. Festus had the difficult task of placating all groups in Judea. With near anarchy in Judea, Paul no doubt made the right decision when he rejected Festus' suggestion that he return to Jerusalem. Festus supported Herod Agrippa II in a controversy with the Jews and died before hearing from Rome on the matter.

Paul Before King Agrippa

ACTS 25:13–26:32

After Paul was arrested in the temple in Jerusalem, he was held prisoner there. But his nephew discovered a plot against Paul's life and told the Roman commander in charge. Paul was secretly transferred to Caesarea, where he was held for about two years. During this time he was judged by two procurators, Felix and Festus, and by King Herod Agrippa II.

The remains of the covered arcades in Caesarea. For about two years Paul was imprisoned in Caesarea.

King Herod Agrippa II

Born in AD 27 the oldest of the first Herod Agrippa's five children, Herod Agrippa II was the brother of Drusus, Bernice, Drusilla, and Mariamne. His mother was the daughter of Herod the Great's nephew and daughter. When his father died in AD 44, Agrippa was only 17. Emperor Claudius felt he was too young to be king of his father's territories and appointed Cuspius Fadus procurator of Palestine instead. For the next four years Agrippa used his influence to help the Jews. When he turned 21 he was appointed king of Chalcis, a region north of Caesarea Philippi and west of Damascus, which his late uncle had ruled. In AD 53, five years later, he exchanged Chalcis for his Uncle Philip's tetrarchy, including Abila. In AD 55 Nero added Tiberias and Taricheae in Galilee and Abilene in Perea with its 14 villages to Agrippa's territory. In appreciation Agrippa gave Caesarea Philippi the name Neronias. He built Jerusalem's "third wall". With his sister Bernice he tried to stop the Jewish war from starting but was unsuccessful and was wounded by a slingstone at the siege of Gamala, east of the Sea of Galilee. A friend of Vespasian's son Titus, he sided with Rome throughout the war, and when Vespasian became emperor he confirmed Agrippa in his territories and added unspecified others. Little is known of his later years except he corresponded with Josephus, who wrote *The Jewish War*. He never married. He died about AD 100.

Bernice

Bernice was the oldest of Herod Agrippa's three daughters. Born in AD 28, she was married at 13 to Marcus, the son of Tiberius Julius Alexander the alabarch. On his death she married her uncle Herod, for which her father got the little kingdom of Chalcis, west of Damascus, and to whom she bore two sons, Berniceanus and Hyrcanus. On Herod's death in AD 48, she went to live with her brother, Herod Agrippa II. She married Polemo II of Olba in Cilicia, about AD 65. Shortly thereafter she left him and returned to her brother's home, where she worked hard to prevent the outbreak of the Jewish war by confrontation with the procurator, Gessius Florus, and in other ways. Vespasian's son Titus fell in love with her during a stay in Caesarea and took her to Rome. But when Titus became emperor, AD 70, he sent her away. He died two years later. Bernice disappeared from history.

Paul's Journey Toward Rome

ACTS 27:1–8

After Paul had presented his case to King Agrippa, who was actually Herod Agrippa II, son of Herod Agrippa I, he appealed to have his case heard by Caesar. Paul had already spent two years in prison at Caesarea, and he believed he would have a fair hearing in Rome. Under Roman law, a Roman citizen who appealed to Caesar had to be sent to Caesar to be judged. Paul was placed on a ship sailing from Caesarea, then transferred to another ship at Myra, a city in Cilicia, which is in present-day Turkey. But sailing was slow because of contrary winds. By the time the ship had reached Cnidus in early October, the dangerous autumn weather had set in, and the danger of shipwreck had increased.

Ancient carved blocks from Myra.

The emperor

The Roman emperor Nero was Caesar at this time. The term Caesar was, like the term Pharaoh, a title which meant supreme ruler. Rulers over small areas, sometimes cities, were called kings, so the rulers of empires wanted a more grand term to describe their greater powers. Nero had begun to reign in AD 54, nine years before Paul arrived in Rome. His early years as Caesar were peaceful, and people were judged fairly. But in AD 64, the year after Paul was freed, Nero seemed to change. In that year much of Rome was destroyed by fire, and it was thought that Nero was responsible. Paul spent two years (AD 61–63) waiting for Nero's trial. Four years later, in AD 67, Paul was arrested again and brought before Nero for trial. This time he died as a martyr.

Sculpted head of the Emperor Nero, Caesar at the time of Paul's journey to Rome.

Ruins of Rhodes, one of the ports of call as Paul sailed to Rome.

Roman ships from Alexandria

Two ships are mentioned. The first was a ship from Adramyttium, on the coast of present-day Turkey. The second was a Roman grain freighter based in the Egyptian city of Alexandria.

At first it seems strange that Roman ships based in Alexandria, Egypt, were bringing grain to Rome. Why were Roman ships in Egypt? And why were they bringing grain to Rome? These ships transported the tribute of grain from Egypt, for Egypt was ruled by Rome at that time. There was a large fleet of these grain freighters. Alexandria was the port for Egypt. The average ship was about 350 tons but some were as large as 1,200 tons. Probably as much as 150,000 tons of grain were shipped to Rome each year from Alexandria during the first three centuries AD.

Paul's fourth and final journey – this time toward Rome.

385

Paul's Shipwreck

ACTS 27:27–28:10

When Paul was arrested in the temple in Jerusalem, some men plotted to kill him. His nephew discovered the plot and warned the Roman army commander. Paul was transferred to Caesarea, where he remained for about two years. During this time, he was judged by the two procurators, Felix and Festus, and by King Herod Agrippa II. During his trial, Paul appealed to Caesar to hear his case, and under Roman law the procurators were obligated to send him to Rome. But on the way to Rome, Paul's ship was wrecked.

Ships in Paul's day
There were two basic types of ships in the ancient world, the merchantman and the warship. The earliest Greek ship, the swift *pentekontor*, was manned by 50 oarsmen, 25 on each side, and was used for both trade and piracy. The heavy merchantman, a trading ship designed to travel day and night through stormy weather, was the type of ship on which Paul is said to have travelled on 13 occasions in Acts. There were no commercial passenger ships. Propelled by sails or long, heavy oars called sweeps, some ships were as long as 90 m (300 feet) and could carry 600 passengers.

The most common of several types of Greek warship was the *trireme*. It was a light, swift, slim ship with a distinctive high, hooked prow that ended with a bronze ram and had an eye painted on each side to ward off evil. The trireme received its name from the three rows of

BITTEN BY A SNAKE

The snake which bit Paul was probably a viper, like this Maltese example of the Mediterranean Cat Snake. Although the snake was poisonous, it could not harm the apostle, because God had promised him a safe passage (Acts 27:23–25) and nothing could stop his servant. The same Greek word for serpent is used in the Gospels, where it has a strong pictorial meaning – see for example Matt. 3:7, 12:34, 23:33 and Luke 3:7.

oarsmen, one above the other. As many as 200 men could be crammed into a tiny space. Its prows often ended in the bent neck of a goose and its stern with

Model of a Greek trireme.

the head of Minerva or some other goddess.

The design of these ancient ships was so advanced it did not change in its basic outlines over the next 18 centuries.

Malta

The island of Malta lies 95 km (60 miles) south of Sicily and 145 km (90 miles) from Sicily's capital, Syracuse. Since Syracuse was the Mediterranean's central commercial port, Malta with its good harbours could not have been more ideally located for trade. The island seems to have been settled as early as 2000 BC, but its historical beginnings date to 1000 BC, when the Phoenicians colonized the island and built the city of Malta.

After three centuries of harsh domination by Carthage, Malta became a Roman *municipium*, a privileged community. Cicero mentions its prosperous, wealthy people and the elegant houses of Malta.

Publius, Malta's "chief"

Monument inscriptions indicate that Publius was known as "chief". He may have been a Roman procurator or the leading native official.

The coastline of Malta.

Paul at Rome

ACTS 28:11–31

For about two years, Paul was imprisoned at Caesarea, and was judged by two procurators, Felix and Festus, as well as by King Herod Agrippa II. While before Festus, Paul appealed to Caesar to judge him, so he was sent to Rome. But on the way, his ship was wrecked on the island of Malta. Then he resumed his trip to Rome, where he lived in a private home while waiting for trial.

The Appian Way still exists today.

The sites of Paul's journey:

1. Syracuse
Founded by Greek colonists led by Archias in 734 BC, Syracuse, on the east coast of Sicily below the "toe" of Italy, became second only to Carthage in importance in the fifth century BC Captured by the Romans, Syracuse became a colony under Augustus. Cicero called it the loveliest city.

2. Rhegium (*today Reggio*)
On the seven-mile-wide treacherous Strait of Messina, which separates Sicily from Italy, Rhegium may have got its name from the Greek word for "tear", since it looks as if Sicily had been torn from the mainland of Italy at this point. In 280 BC, 4,000 Roman soldiers, called in to protect Rhegium, slaughtered all its citizens and settled here themselves.

3. Puteoli (*today Pozzuoli*)
A fashionable Roman resort, port, and spa on the Bay of Naples halfway between Rhegium and Rome, Puteoli was colonized from the island of Samos near Ephesus and made a Roman colony in 194 BC. In Paul's day it was the most important commercial port for the receipt of imports from the east. Seneca, the Roman author, says the residents loved to watch the arrival of Alexandrian grain ships like the one Paul travelled on. Tradition says Paul stopped off nearby to visit the Latin poet Virgil's tomb.

4. The Appian Way (*and the Forum of Appius*)
The Appian Way was the first of the famous Roman paved roads. It went from Rome south to Brundisium in the "heel" of Italy, a total of 565 km (350 miles).

The Appian Way, which is 4.5 m (15 feet) wide was started by the man after whom it was named, Appius Claudius Caecus. In 312 BC Paul went 32 km (20 miles) from Puteoli to Capua, where the road originally stopped, to reach the Appian Way, "the queen of the long roads". He then travelled 212 km (132 miles) on it to Rome. The market town, called the Forum of Appius, was on the Appian Way 70 km (43 miles) from Rome. It was a long day's journey for those Roman Christians who met Paul here.

5. Three Taverns (*or, more accurately, Three Stores*)
A stopover for travellers, 53 km (33 miles) from Rome and 16 km (10 miles) from the Forum of Appius.

Castor and Pollux
Twin sons of Zeus according to mythology, they were the children of Leda, wife of Tyndareos, king of Sparta, and the patrons of mariners. They guided sailors through their positions as the two brightest stars in Gemini. Paul's ship had their figureheads on its mast.

Ruins of the Roman Forum.

Philemon

THE BOOK OF PHILEMON

While Paul was imprisoned at Rome, he came to know a runaway slave, Onesimus, who had come to Rome after leaving his master Philemon behind at Colossae. Onesimus must have become a believer under Paul's ministry and evidently helped him there in Rome. But in time Paul sent him back to Philemon with a letter. Paul asked Philemon to forgive Onesimus and receive him as a brother in Christ.

Colossae

The Letter to Philemon is usually associated with the city of Colossae. Colossae was located in southwest Asia Minor in the valley of the Lycus River. The Lycus (now called the Çuruksuçay) flows into the Maeander River not far from Laodicea, which is located about 16 km (10 miles) west of Colossae. In its prime Colossae was a busy stopover on the main road from the east to Ephesus. The road to Sardis and Pergamum to the north also branched off at this point. Today the highway and railroad still follow the Lycus Valley trade route.

During Rome's imperial days, however, Colossae declined in importance because the branch road to the north was moved to Laodicea, and Laodicea became the more important city. Colossae, not Laodicea, appears to have been the more important centre in the days of Xerxes and Cyrus because it is mentioned as a stopover for their armies as they travelled westward.

Today Colossae is an uninhabited ruin. Motorists' guides to Turkey point out Laodicea's ruins near the modern town of Denizli but do not even mention Colossae. William J. Hamilton located the site of ancient Colossae in 1835, but the spot has never been excavated.

Ruins of Colossae.

Rembrandt's *Saint Paul in Prison*.

Several of Paul's associates seem to have come from Colossae. Epaphras came from there (Col. 1:7), and Archippus too seems to have been active in Colossae (Col. 4:17).

Onesimus

Onesimus, whose name means "useful", was one of the millions of slaves who kept the Roman Empire functioning. The brief letter that mentions him as its central subject leaves a lot of unanswered questions. Where was Paul when he met Onesimus, in Rome or in Ephesus? What did Onesimus do? What is Paul asking the recipient to do? Was the recipient Philemon or Archippus? The most common answers are that Paul was in Rome at the end of his life, that Onesimus had stolen money and run away, that Paul is asking the recipient to take Onesimus back as a Christian brother, and that Philemon is the recipient. But each question can be answered in different ways.

The Seven Churches

THE BOOK OF REVELATION

The first century was drawing to a close. The Emperor Domitian had banished the apostle John to the island of Patmos. There John wrote the last book of the New Testament, part of which is addressed to the seven churches at Ephesus, Smyrna, Pergamum, Thyatira, Sardis, Philadelphia, and Laodicea.

The location of the seven churches.

The emperor Domitian

No one expected the younger brother of Titus and younger son of Vespasian to become emperor. In fact, Titus was suspicious of him and deliberately gave him no governmental responsibilities.

Born Titus Flavius Domitianus in AD 51, Domitian was forced to flee Rome at 18 dressed in the habit of an Isis priest. When the popular Titus died at 42, Domitian was only 30, a man embittered by his father's and brother's humiliation through the years. Around AD 85 he allowed himself to be worshipped as a god. After a revolt in Germany in AD 89, Domitian became increasingly suspicious and autocratic. With spies and informers all over Rome, he even came to suspect his niece and her husband,

Flavia Domitilla and Flavius Clemens, the parents of his heir apparent. Flavius was accused of godlessness and executed; Flavia, possibly a Christian, was exiled. Domitian hated the aristocracy, and he persecuted the Christians, largely as part of his effort to enforce Nero's laws. In AD 96 his wife murdered him.

The island of Patmos

Shaped like the right half of a T, Patmos is located 60 km (37 miles) southwest of Miletus off the coast of Asia Minor in the Icarian Sea. A mountainous island covering only 39 square kilometres (15 square miles), it is 16km (10 miles) from north to south and only 10 km (6 miles) at its widest point in the north. Today it is part of "12 Islands", actually a group of 14 islands with local government and a capital in Rhodes.

During Roman times Patmos was a place of political banishment. John was banished here in AD 95 by Domitian. Per tradition he was released 18 months later under Nerva, Domitian's successor. John was head of the Ephesus church. The seven churches mentioned in Revelation 2 and 3 were all located in the area around Ephesus and may have been founded by the mother church in that city.

A bust of Domitian.

The Adoration of the Lamb by Jan van Eyck attempts to picture the vision
John received on the island of Patmos, seen in the photograph below.

Index

The format of this volume is story by story, through the Bible. Topics are indexed below in alphabetical order. With each topic are phrases which tell specifically what you will find concerning that topic on certain pages.

Aaron
priests descendants of 68
Abednego
thrown into fiery furnace 169
Abel
Cain murders him 6–7
description of 6
Abigail
brings food to David 110
Abijah
the order of 187
Abraham
moves from Ur to Canaan 12
map of his journey to Canaan
and Egypt 13
goes to Egypt with Sarah 13
family relationship to Sarah 13
parts with Lot 14
his pursuit of Lot 14
God's covenant with 15
visited by angels 16
bargains for Sodom with God 18
meaning of his name 20
unique family relationships 21
sends Hagar into wilderness 22
offers Isaac 24
Absalom
rebellion of 122
how he won people's hearts 122
Achan
his sin, Israel's defeat 78
how much he stole 79
Adam
temptation and fall 4
the family of 6
Adze
use as carpenter's tool 205
Age
old parents bear children 15
marrying at an older age 27
Agrippa (Herod)
conflict with Antipas 348
puts Peter in prison 348
rise to kingship 348
death of 348
Agrippa II (Herod)
judges Paul 383
his life and reign 383
Ahab
Elijah hides from 138
wants Naboth's vineyard 140
his wickedness 140
Ahasuerus (king of Persia)
stone relief of 173
marries queen Esther 172
palace cities of 173

Ai
Achan's sin; conquest of 78
photo of ruins today 79
location, description of 79
Aijalon, Valley of
sun, moon stand still for Joshua 80
present day photo 81
Akeldama
description, meaning 309
Alabaster
used in Egyptian furniture 45
value and uses 296
photo of alabaster jar 296
Alexandria
why Roman ships sailed from 385
Alliances
formed against Joshua 81
Aloes
use in burial 318
Altars
significance to Israel 25
materials and design 25
altar of burnt offering 127
Amenhotep II
possible Pharaoh of Exodus 56
figure of 59
Ammonites
how the nation began 19
Amon-Ra (Egyptian sun god)
God proves His power over 55
Amram
father of Moses; description 49
Ananias
and Sapphira 334
Andrew (disciple of Jesus)
leaves family business for Jesus 220
description and character of 236
Angels
compared with demons 4
visit Abraham as men 16
angels as warriors 150
Elisha's servant sees angel army 151
announce Jesus' birth 196
nature and names 203
in the life of Jesus 209
Animals
God creates 3
those used for offerings 94
Animal Skins
used in making tents 16
ancient "bottles" made from 23
use in writing 193, 223
Anna
honours Jesus in temple 198
Annas
Jesus on trial 306
powerful high priest 306

Anointing
why, how kings were anointed 100
ancient anointing horn 100
other occasions for 101
Antioch (in Pisidia)
photo of Roman aqueduct 345
Paul's first missionary journey 350
description 351
location on map 351
Antioch (of Syria)
believers first called Christians 344
description, importance 346, 347
present day photo 346
location on map 351
Antipas (Herod)
who he was; what he ruled 207, 234
beheads John the Baptist 250
his fear of killing John 250
role in New Testament events 250
chart of Herod the Great's family 251
one of Jesus' judges 307
map: where Jesus met him 311
Jesus before 311
political life 312
picture of Citadel 313
Antipatris
description 381
Antonia Fortress
description 310, 312
shown on temple diagram 311
Apis Bull
Egyptian symbol of worship 66
Apostles
taken before Council 333
Appian Way
present day photo 388
importance as Roman road 388
Aqueducts
bring water into Jerusalem 267
photos of Roman aqueducts 267, 345
Aquila
Paul works at Corinth with 372
Ararat, Mount
chart of elevations 138
Araunah's Threshing Floor
David buys 124
site of temple 124
Bible history at 124
Archelaus
his rule in Judea 204
Areopagus
what it was 368
Ark of Covenant
location, use in tabernacle 68
illustrations of 69, 74
construction, description of 74
captured by Philistines 96
Philistines return to Israel 97
David moves to Jerusalem 118

Ark (of Noah)
Noah builds 8
the people on board 8
its size, building materials, and special
features 9
purpose of 9
Armour
Israelite/Canaanite compared 80
Goliath's mighty armour 105
as defensive weapon 305
Army
description of army encampment 111
Elisha's servant sees angel army 150
drawing of Sennacherib's army 161
Rome's auxiliary army 380
Artaxerxes I (king of Persia)
helps Ezra and Nehemiah 175
palace cities of 178
description of 178
why he let Jews return 178
Ascension
Jesus ascends into heaven 328, 329
possible locations of 328
photo: Chapel of Ascension 328
why Jesus ascended 329
Asher (brother of Joseph)
short description of 45
Ashtaroth (Canaanite god)
description, worship of 87, 129
a figurine of 129, 163
on Phoenician coin 255
Asia Minor
Roman provinces of 358
Assyria, Assyrians
treatment of captives of war 113
leading captives of war 157
takes Israel into captivity 158
some kings of 159, 160
map of invasion of Israel 158
Sennacherib attacks Jerusalem 160
angel destroys army of 161
description of city siege 161
the fall of 164
great empires of the Bible 165
Astrology
ancient fortune-telling 364
Athens
description 357, 368
Paul preaches in 366
photo of Mars Hill 368
photo of Acropolis ruins 372
Atonement, Day of
significance 94
Augustus Caesar (Roman emperor)
role in Jesus' birth 194
coin of 194
description of 292
Authority
Jesus teaches with 222
Baal (Canaanite god)
description, worship of 82, 87
picture of Baal as storm god 86
description, mythology of 138
Elijah defeats prophets of 138
statuette of 142
Jehu destroys Baal worship 152

Babel, Tower of
what happened and where 10–11
reconstruction of 10–11
Babylon, Babylonians
treatment of captives of war 113
rise of empire 164
overthrows Assyria 164
great empires of the Bible 165
takes Judah into captivity 166
map of invasions 166
great empire of 166
its decline 166
Nebuchadnezzar's life and reign 168
excavations today 168
strengths of the ancient city 168
map of the empire 170
overthrown by Persians 171
Bags
the scrip 248
the money bag, or box 297
Baker, Baking
baking in ancient Egypt 41
Joseph interprets his dream 42
baking bread in oven 135
Balances
how used 171
Ballah Lake
possible Red Sea crossing 65
Banquets
see Feasts
Baptism
Jesus is baptized 208
Barabbas
who he was 311, 312
Barley
time of harvest 235
Barnabas
description and character 334
first missionary journey with Paul 350
mistaken for a god 354
Bartholomew (disciple of Jesus)
description and character of 237
Bartimaeus
Jesus heals his blindness 286
Baskets
type that hid baby Moses 48
a basket from Moses' time 48
Bathing
in David's day 120
Bathsheba
David murders for 120
another wife for David 121
Battering Ram
use in Assyrian battle 161
drawings of 161
Battle
strange battle at Jericho 76
battle spoils 78
purification rites after 78
hand-to-hand combat 80
ancient battle strategies 80
military alliances 81
Gideon and his 300 men 88
importance of army encampment 111
Saul's last battle 113
treatment of captives of war 113
how a city was captured 120

Assyrian battle tactics 167
destruction of Jerusalem in AD. 70 272
Battle Spoils
what they were 78
how divided 78
Beatitudes
what they were 239
Beatitudes, Mount of
present day photo 238
possible location of Sermon on the
Mount 238
Beautiful Gate
Peter, John heal lame man 332
description 332
photo of traditional site 332
Beds
description of 254
Bedouin
encampments of 17
photo of tents today 17
photos of Bedouin women today 22, 34
photo of Bedouin man today 183
Beersheba
photo of excavations at 20
the city in Abraham's time 20
another photo 29
photos of flocks at 31, 35
"from Dan to Beersheba" 124
Beersheba, Wilderness of
its location 23
Beggars
life as a blind person 257
why there were so many 286
Bellows
use in metalworking 67
Belshazzar (king of Babylon)
handwriting on the wall 170
his life and reign 170
Ben–ammi
ancestor of the Ammonites 19
Benefactor
meaning of the title 301
Benjamin (brother of Joseph)
description 45
Berea
description 357, 367
Bereans accept Paul 367
Bernice
chart: Herod the Great's family 251
description 383
Bethany
Jesus visits Mary and Martha 271
description of 271, 289
present day photo 271
location on map 278
Bethel
the city in the Old Testament 32
present day views 33
Bethesda, Pool of
Jesus heals man at 232
description of 232
present day photo 232
location on Jerusalem map 232
as water supply for Jerusalem 267

Bethlehem
nearby ruins 101
Jesus born in 194
Bible time citizens of 195
photo: Church of Nativity 195
Joseph afraid to settle in 204
Bethphage
description and location 289
Bethsaida
two possible locations 220, 252, 257
photos of Bethsaida Julias 257
Jesus feeds 500 at 252
Jesus heals blind man at 257
Beth Shan
events at 113
Beth Shemesh
captured ark returned to 97
present day photos 97
Betrayal
why Judas might have betrayed Jesus 298
Betrothal
description 210
Bier
use in funerals 241, 246, 279, 319
Bilhah
sons she bore for Jacob 35
Birthright
Esau sells his to Jacob 28
importance to Hebrew family 28–29
privileges and responsibilities 28–29
includes the care of widows 30
Bitter Lakes
possible Red Sea crossing 61
Black Obelisk of Shalmaneser III
photo 152
King Jehu seen on 152
description of 153
Blessing
meal for family blessing 30
passes on the family birthright 30
Blindness
gouging out a captive's eyes 88
common in Bible times 226
lives of the blind 257
causes of 257, 286
Blowpipe
use in metalworking 67
Boats
fishing boats on Sea of Galilee 243
rowing across Sea of Galilee 253
Galilean fishing boats 243, 253
see also Ships
Boaz
important descendants of 90
Bodyguard
captain of 40
Books
scrolls, materials and writing 163, 229
public reading of Bible 163
in Jesus' day 229
Book of the Law
found in Josiah's reign 162
what it was 163
where it was found 162
reading 163
Ezra reads to the people 180

Booths
why they were built 261
photo of 261
use in Feast of Tabernacles 271
Born Again
what it means 214
Bottles
made from animal skins 23, 231
ancient waterskins, wineskins 231
Bow and Arrows
examples from Bible times 108
varieties and uses 108
Bowls
who made them 205
Box
cosmetic 40
Boys
Egyptian/Hebrew contrasted 46
education of a Jewish boy 206
Bread, Breadmaking
how it was made 41, 303
unleavened bread 58
baking bread in oven 135, 303
how ancient bread looked 257, 303
Breastpiece
of high priest 68
drawing 93
description of 112
Bricks, Brickmaking
those used in ziggurats 11
how bricks were made 47
description, size of Egyptian 54
Nebuchadnezzar's inscription 169
baked in furnace 169
Brides
in weddings of Jesus' day 210
parable of, and meaning 231
Bronze Serpent
plague of serpents 72
Brothers
Joseph's 11 brothers 45
Bulls
the Golden Calf 66
as a symbol of worship 66
how golden calf was made 67
Jeroboam makes golden calves 130
the fattened calf 276
Bulrushes
description of 48
Burial
funerals in Jesus' day 241, 246
preparing body for 246, 278
caves used as tombs 278, 318
ancient customs of 318
Burning Bush
Moses talks with God at 52
Burnt Offerings
explanation and uses 25
various types of 94
often given before battle 99
Burnt Offering, Altar of
description of 127
Bushes
Moses sees burning bush 52
Butler
see Cupbearer
Caesar
description of the title 292

Caesarea
city rises to importance 342
Hecrod's building project 342
location on map 344
Paul taken to as prisoner 380
map of Paul's trip to 380
photos of ruins at 383
Caesarea Philippi
Jesus visits 258
description 258
present day photos 258–259
location on map 259
Caiaphas
location of house on map 297, 333
Jesus on trial before 297
description and character 306
photo of his neighbourhood 307
Cain
murders his brother Abel 6–7
the life of 6
living in the land of Nod 6
Calendar
the Jewish calendar 58
Calf
see Bulls
Camels
photos today 22, 27, 39, 199
suitable for desert travel 200
clothing of camel's hair 207
Camps
see Encampments
Cana
Jesus changes water to wine at 210
photo of traditional site 210, 211
map of traditional site 210
possible locations of 211
nobleman's son healed by Jesus 216
Canaan, Canaanites
Abraham migrates to 12
map of Abraham's journey to 13
the land before it became Israel 14
compared to Egyptian lifestyles 46
a fertile land of plenty 71
battle strategies 80
when Joshua invaded 81
idol worship in 86
Capernaum
present day photo 216
location on map 217
Jesus moves to 219
description and importance 219
Jesus' healing at synagogue 222
Jesus' miracles there 222
Jesus' curse on 222
photo of synagogue ruins 222
description of synagogue at 222
houses in 224
Peter's house at 224
Jesus heals man with demons 244
woman healed by touching hem of Jesus' cloak 245
Jesus raises Jairus' daughter 246
Captain of Bodyguard
duties of 40
Captives, Captivity
striking prisoners of war 47
humiliation of captured kings 113
torture of captured kings 113, 166
treatment of captives of war 113, 166

Israel taken into captivity 158
Judah's later captivity pays off 158
period between the captivities 159
captives of war before Sennacherib 160
exiles return to Jerusalem 174

Caravans
characteristics of 39
travel by 39, 202–203
photo of caravan today 39
at ancient inns 195
caravan routes to Egypt 202–203

Carmel
location and description 110

Carmel, Mount
Elijah defeats prophets of Baal 136
location on map 137
photo of Carmel range 137
chart of elevations 138

Carob Pods
connection with prodigal son 276
use and description 276
picture of 276

Carpenters
work and tools 117, 205
things a carpenter made 205

Carts, Wagons
use of oxcarts 97
illustrations of oxcarts 97

Cast Nets (fishing net)
fishing net, use of 220, 262, 327

Catacombs
development, use in burial 279

Caves
photo of cave near Adullam 109
used as tombs 278, 318

Cedars of Lebanon
use in temple construction 127

Celebrations
victory celebrations 107
in song and dance 118

Cenchraea
Paul's second missionary tour 357
location 357

Census
for tax rolls 229

Centurions
Jesus heals servant of 240
of the New Testament 240
position in Roman army 240, 380
as backbone of Rome's army 345

Chariots
Egyptian 60
in Elijah's time 143
Assyrian 159
Persian 172
uses of 339

Chemosh
description, worship of 129

Cherubim
what they were 4, 203

Chief Priests
description 298

Children
born to very old parents 15
stigma of bearing no children 22, 144, 187
importance to family 22
purification from childbirth 198
sold into slavery to pay parents' debts 265, 277

Jesus with 282
why Jesus noticed them 282
and God's kingdom 282

Christians
see Church

Chronology
time frames of Old and New Testament 334

Church
believers multiply 335
when the Gospel began to spread 335
at Antioch 346
John writes to seven churches 392

Circumcision
ceremony, symbolism of 192, 198

Cisterns
description and uses 38

Citadel
description 312
photo of ruins 313

City
ancient Sumerian city 12
storage cities of Egypt 50
fortified cities 76
the city elders 101
victory celebrations 107
how a city was captured 120
drawings of city siege 120
activities at the city gate 122
Assyrian siege 161
besieging Jerusalem in AD 70 272
duties of city clerk 377

City Gate
activities at 122
photo 122
entering Eye of the Needle 283

City-States
what they were 81

Claudius (Roman emperor)
description of 347

Clay
use in pottery making 84
use in letter writing 147

Cleopas
who he was 322

Clerk
duties of city clerk 377

Cloak
Joseph's colourful cloak 36
varieties, symbolism of 36
its many uses 36, 139
drawn from ancient monuments 37
valuable gift for a friend 106
making of 139
woman healed by touching hem of Jesus' cloak 245
appearance in Jesus' day 245, 286
of a beggar 286

Cloth
photo of Bedouin's cloth 36
weaving 88
value of purple cloth 363

Clothing
varieties and uses of cloak 37, 139
of high priest 68, 93
sheep and wool 110
making a cloak 139
value, status of purple clothing 171

Cloud
God sends pillar of cloud 60

Coffins
use in burial 278

Cohort
division of Roman army 380
description of its commander 380

Coins
drachma (half-shekel) 79, 212, 262, 293, 298
half-shekel (drachma) 79, 212, 262, 289, 293, 298
of Augustus Caesar 194
denarius 194, 212, 289, 292
tetradrachm (shekel) 198, 212, 213, 262, 265, 275, 291
shekel (tetradrachm) 198, 212, 213, 262, 265, 275, 291
acceptable in temple 212, 213, 262
assarion 212
didrachma 212, 262
of Herod the Great 212
quinarius 212
sesterce 212
of Herod Antipas 229, 312
of Pontius Pilate 229
of Herod Philip II 250
ancient Phoenician 255
half-shekel of Jewish revolt 262
coins of Jesus' time 265, 275
lepton (widow's mite) 265, 293
quadrans 265, 293
widow's mite (lepton) 265, 293
invention of 275
mina 288
thirty pieces of silver 298
of Herod Agrippa I 348
lictors 373

Collosae
Paul writes to Philemon 390
description of city 390
present day photo 390

Columns
see Pillars, Columns

Contract
ancient Assyrian contract 15
custom of giving a sandal away 91
use in betrothal 189

Cooking
methods of cooking meat 30

Corinth
description 357, 370
Paul works with Priscilla and Aquila 370
its reputation in Paul's day 370
photos of 370–372
Gallio judges Paul at 372

Cornelius
centurion baptized by Peter 344
description 345

Cornerstone
Book of the Law possibly found in 162

Cosmetics
ancient makeup, ingredients 153
kohl jars, cosmetic bowl 153

Couches
Romans recline on to eat 301
drawing of 301

Council
see Sanhedrin

Courtyards
of Bible-time house; drawing 145
of Bible-time inn 270
diagram of temple courtyards 290
Covenant
God's covenant with Abraham 15
types of covenants 15
between David and Jonathan 106
Creation
God makes the world 2–3
Crooks
picture of shepherd's rod 196
Cross
Jesus on His way to 314
Jesus crucified on 315
Crown
Jesus' crown of thorns 313
Cups
divination cup 45
photo of ancient drinking cup 45
varieties and materials 302
ceremonies and symbolism 302
Cupbearer
the duties of 41
picture of 177
Cyprus, island of
description 335
Cyrus (king of Persia)
a competent ruler 171
appointment of Darius the Mede 171
lets exiles return to Jerusalem 174
description of 174
Dagon (Philistine god)
description, priests of 89, 96
drawing from ancient relief 96
Dagon, Temple of
construction, design of 89
many built in Philistia 89
Damascus
conflicts with Samaria 149
Paul meets Jesus on road to 340
the city in Paul's day 340
Paul escapes from 342
Dan (brother of Joseph)
short description of 45
Dan (city)
"from Dan to Beersheba" 123
Dance
as expression of worship 119
Salome's evil dance 251
Daniel
refuses king's food 168
handwriting on the wall 170
his rank as Babylonian ruler 170
thrown into lions' den 170
Darius the Great
the homes, or palaces, of 176, 177
stone relief of 177
searches for Cyrus' decree 180
Darius the Mede
tricked into sentencing Daniel 170
who he was 171
David
Samuel anoints him 100
why, how he was anointed 100
plays music for Saul 102
kills Goliath 102
friendship with Jonathan 106

Jonathan's gifts for 106
Saul tries to kill him 107
Jonathan warns him of Saul 108
summary of flight from Saul 109
Abigail shares food with 110
spares Saul's life 111
map of flight from Saul 111
made king of Judah 114
why Hebron chosen as capital 115
becomes king of all Israel 116
why Jerusalem chosen as capital 116
captures Jerusalem 117
moves ark to Jerusalem 118
music experience and programmes 119
and Bathsheba 120
other wives of 121
chart of his family 121
Absalom rebels against 122
buys Araunah's threshing floor 124
traditional tomb of 331
Deacons
the appointment of 336
Dead Sea
the sea and surrounding area 18–19
photo of, coated with minerals 18
present day photos 18, 19, 271, 273
chart of elevations 138
Deafness
Jesus heals deaf and dumb man 256
Death
wealth buried with Pharaoh 60
funerals in Jesus' day 241
hired mourners 246
caves used as tombs 278, 319
preparing body for burial 279
ancient burial practices 318
Debts, Debtors
cloak a security for debt 37
wife, children sold as slaves 265, 277
Jesus' parable of two debtors 265
consequences for debtors 265
Decapolis
what and where it was 259
Delilah
deceives Samson 88
Delphi
centre of worship 364
photo of 365
Demons
as compared to angels 4
communicating with 112
Jesus heals man with 244
explanation of 244
meaning of "legion" 244
Jesus' power over 244
Denarius
a day's wage 284
Derbe
Paul's first missionary journey 351
location on map 354
Desert
see Wilderness
Diana (Ephesian goddess)
description, worship of 376
statue of 376
Diana, Temple of
column from the temple 377
Diaspora
the Jewish Diaspora 367

Disciples of Jesus
Jesus calls four of them 220
accused of working on the Sabbath 233
Jesus chooses the Twelve 236
list, description of 236–237
sent by Jesus two by two 248
ask Jesus who is the greatest 264
at the Last Supper 300
at Pentecost 330
Disease
see Sickness
Divination
divination cups 45
description, practices of 112
Doctors
helpless against disease 226
Dogs
description of 277
Dome of the Rock
present day photo 25
background of temple site 124, 127
Domitian (Roman emperor)
description 392
Donkeys
importance of 289
Jesus enters Jerusalem on 289
Doors
entering Eye of the Needle 283
Dorcas
Peter raises at Joppa 343
traditional tomb of 343
Dothan
Joseph sold as a slave at 38
description of the city 38–39
location on map 38, 46, 151
present day photo 150
Elisha's servant sees angel army 150
Dowry
customs of marriage dowry 35
Drag Nets
fishing net, use of 220, 262, 327
Dreams
importance placed on 37
dream interpreters 37
throughout the Bible 42
Drinks
duties of a cupbearer 41
drinking and divination cups 45
Drusilla
chart: Herod the Great's family 251
description 382
Dumbness
Jesus heals dead and dumb man 256
Dungeons
cisterns used as 38
life in 40–41
Dura, Plain of
description 169
Dust
shaking dust from feet 248
Dyes
source of 134
value of purple clothing 171
Ebal, Mount
description 215
Ebony
used in Egyptian furniture 45

Eden, Garden of
Adam and Eve tempted by Satan 4
description of 4
Edom, Edomites
Esau the ancestor of 29
Education
of Jewish boys 206
at Jewish synagogue 218
Egypt, Egyptians
Abraham and Sarah travel to 12–13
picture of sphinx 13
a slave's life in 39
travelling from Canaan to 45
silver cup from 45
Jacob and family move to 46
compared to Canaanite lifestyles 46
negative view of Hebrews 46
why Hebrews were made slaves 50
distaste for shepherds 51
the plagues of Egypt 54–55
dependence upon Nile River 54–55
some gods of 55
when Joseph ruled in 56
Hyksos invaders in 56
which Pharaoh oppressed Hebrews 56
loss of Hebrew slaves a blow 59
jewellery 59
painting of chariot 60
what the Hebrews left behind 60
law codes of 64
great empires of the Bible 165
Jesus and family flee to 202
Jesus' home in 202
distance from Palestine 203
Ein Gev
area where Jesus healed man with
demons 242
photo of area 242
Ein Karem
traditional home of Elizabeth 191
location on map 191
description of 191
Elah, Valley of
present day photo 101
Elders
position of a city elder 101
as a synagogue ruler 246
Eli
duties as high priest 94
Eliezer (Abraham's servant)
finds Isaac a wife 30
map of his route to Haran 30
Elijah
hides from Ahab; ravens feed 130
and widow of Zarephath 134
and prophets of Baal 136
God speaks at Mount Sinai 138
his journey to Mount Sinai 138
gives cloak to Elisha 139
map of his travels 139
differences from Elisha 139
taken to heaven in whirlwind 142
kings of his day 142
Elisha
Elijah gives cloak to 139
differences from Elijah 139
kings of his day 143
meets Shunammite couple 144
his gift to Shunammite 144

raises Shunammite boy 144
Naaman healed of leprosy 146
his greedy servant 148
shows servant angel army 150
Syrians struck blind 151
a diplomat of peace 151
Elizabeth
her miracle baby 189
Mary visits 190
relation to Mary 190
Embrace
common custom among men 35
Emmaus
Jesus on the road to 322
photos 322, 323
possible locations 323
Emperors
Roman emperors of New Testament 292
Empires
great empires of the Bible 165
empires of the ancient world 170
Encampments
of ancient Bedouin 17
description of army encampment 111
Endor
Saul visits witch of 112
En Gedi
present day photos 111
En Rogel
description, events at 122
present day photo 123
Ephah
measurement in Israel 62
Ephesus
description 357, 374
books of evil burned at 374
photo of ruins at 375
the silversmith riot 376
location on map 392
John writes to church at 392
Ephod
used to consult God's will 112
Ephraim, Forest of
Absalom defeated at 123
Epicureans
who they were 369
Esarhaddon (king of Assyria)
mistakenly rebuilds Babylon 164
Esau
causes of strife with Jacob 21
birth of 26
sells birthright to Jacob 28
preferred by Isaac 28
the man and his character 29
Jacob steals family blessing from 30
Eshcol, Valley of
photo of 71
Esther
the story of 172
times that led to her story 172
meaning of her name 172
when she lived 173
Ethiopian
meets Philip on Gaza Road 339
who he was 339
map: location of his country 339
Eutychus
Paul raises him from death 378
description 378

Eve
temptation and fall 4
the family of 6
Exodus
possible pharaohs of 49, 60
the Hebrews leave Egypt 58
map of the route of 61
map from Sinai to Jordan River 75
Eyes
gouging out a captive's eyes 88
Eye of the Needle
explanation of 283
Ezra
exiles return to Jerusalem 174
map of route to Jerusalem 175
reads Book of the Law 180
his leadership and reforms 180
Family
how families grew into nations 11
stigma of having no children 23, 187
children's importance to 23
importance of family birthright 28–29
strife in Jacob's family 38
Egyptian/Canaanite lifestyles 46
redemption of the firstborn 198
family chart of Herodias 251
chart of Timothy's family 361
Famine
its causes and impact 13, 132
widows first to suffer 134
Farmer, Farming
his work in ancient Egypt 43
planting near the Nile River 55
importance of rain to 137
ploughing and planting 139, 242
Farthing
coin of Jesus' time 293
Fasting
Jewish custom of 281
Fattened Calf
sign of hospitality 276
Feasts, Festivals
the marriage feast 35, 210
Feast of Unleavened Bread 59, 92
Feast of the New Moon 108
why feasts were given 151
the Babylonian feast 170
Feet
shaking dust from feet 248
symbolism of washing feet 302
Felix (governor of Judea)
Paul on trial before 382
his term as governor 382
Fertile Crescent
important role in Bible times 12
Festus (governor of Judea)
Paul on trial before 382
his term as governor 382
Fields
the Potter's Field 309
Akeldama, field of blood 309
Figs, Fig Tree
importance of figs in Bible lands 294
photo of fig tree 294
Fish, Fishing
God creates 2
in Egyptian diet 62
Jesus' miracle of 219
disciples' fishing business 219

fishing nets 220, 262, 327
fishing boats on Galilee 243
Peter finds tax money in 262
fishing in Jesus' day 262
Jesus' miracle after Resurrection 326
fishing on Sea of Galilee 326
importance as food 327
Flocks
watering at a well 34
photos of 183
often tended far from home 56
a measure of wealth 183
Flood
events that led to the Flood 8
Noah and his family saved from 8–9
when it happened 8
sources of water for 9
Food
impact of famine on food supply 13
description of manna 62
of Egypt, desired by Israelites 62
provided by sheep 110
carob pods eaten by poor 276
of Passover meal 300
Forgiveness
Jesus' forgiveness of sins angers religious
leaders 227
Fortifications
see Walls, Fortifications
Fortune-telling
description 364
Frankincense
use with shewbread 109
how it was extracted 201
a gift to Jesus; significance 201
Friendship
between David and Jonathan 106
Fringes
on Jewish clothing 245
Funerals
in Jesus' day 241, 246
hired mourners at 246
Furnace
Daniel's friends thrown into 169
use of ancient furnaces 169
Furniture
tabernacle furniture 68
of average house 145
Gabriel
announces John's birth to Zacharias 186
announces Jesus' birth to Mary 188
description 188
photo of Gabriel's Church 189
Gad (brother of Joseph)
short description of 45
Galilee
map of two routes to Jerusalem 214
Jesus' healing tour of 226
map of the region 226
why Jesus left 255
description of 256
its border with Samaria 280
Galilee, Sea of
chart of elevations 138
fishing business on 219, 325
the fish of 219
description of 219, 235, 326
map of 220
Jesus teaches by 235

Jesus' ministry around 235
other names for 235
photos of 235, 238, 243, 253, 256
Jesus calms a storm on 243
storms on the sea 243
fishing boats on the sea 243
Jesus walks on 253
rowing across 253
Gallio
judges Paul at Corinth 372
who he was 372
Garden of Eden
and the Fall 4
Garden Tomb
traditional tomb of Jesus 318
photo 319
possible locations 320
history of 320
Garrisons
Philistine garrisons (outposts) 99
Gates
activities at the city gate 122
photo of city gate 122
the gates of Jerusalem 178
Gaza
Samson a prisoner at 89
description and location 89
Gennesaret, Plain of
Jesus heals people there 254
description 254
present day photos 254
location on map 255
Gentiles
in the region of Decapolis 259
how Paul preached to 353
why many attracted to Judaism 367
Gentiles, Court of (temple)
diagram of 186, 291
Jesus cleanses temple there 212
model of 291
Gerizim, Mount
Samaritans worship on 215
Geshem
who he was 179
Gethsemane, Garden of
Jesus prays there 304
possible locations of 304
Judas betrays Jesus at 304
photo 304
Gibeah
location on map 98
Saul's capital city 99
present day photo 103
Gibeon
Gibeonites trick Joshua 80
Joshua fights for 80
location on map 81
Gideon
his call and tests 82
his 300 men in battle 84
Gifts
Jonathan's gifts for David 106
Elisha's gift to Shunammite 144
Gihon Spring
picture of water supply tunnel 116
a source of Jerusalem's water 266
Gilboa
Saul's last battle at 113
present day photo 113

Gilgal
location and meaning 75
photo of area today 99
Saul wrongly sacrifices at 99
location of map 115
Gill Net (fishing net)
use of 327
Girdle
clothing worn by John the Baptist 207
as part of men's clothing 245
Glassmaking
industry of 134
Gleaning
explanation of 91
Goats
goats' hair used in tentmaking 16
photos of 31, 295
Gods, Goddesses
God proves His power over Egyptian
gods 59
some Egyptian gods 55
bull worship 66
Baal as storm god 86
those worshipped by Solomon 129
yearly festival for Marduk 169
sculpture of Zeus 355
Gold
Nebuchadnezzar's image of 169
wise men's gift to Jesus 201
Golden Calf
Israelites worship 66
how it was made 66
Apis bull 66
Jeroboam makes 130
Golden Candlestick
see Lampstand (of tabernacle)
Golden Gate
Jesus enters triumphantly 289
Golgotha
traditional locations 316
photos 316
Goliath
David kills 104
his armour and fighting skill 105
Good Samaritan
parable of 270
location of the inn of 270
present day photo of the inn of 270
Gordon's Calvary
traditional site of crucifixion 316
photo of 316
Goshen
the land of 46
location on map 46
Gospel
when it began to spread 334
Government
Philistine/Israelite compared 88
Governor
Joseph becomes 42
Joseph rules Egypt as 44
Joseph's life as 44–45
Grain
use in breadmaking 41
Egyptian storehouses 43
planting and harvesting 43
where it went after harvest 43
separating grain from stalks 43, 83
prisoners grind grain 89

illustrations of 90
grinding it in millstones 124

Granaries
see Storehouses

Grapes
growing and eating of 71, 140
trampled in winepress 83

Greece, Greeks
great empires of the Bible 165
map of the empire 171

Greetings
customs of Jesus' day 325

Grinding
punishment for prisoners 89
illustrations of 264
millstones and hand mills 264

Guards
the temple guards 333

Guests
at the king's table 108
hospitality toward 271
killing the fattened calf for 276

Hagar
sent into wilderness 22

Hair
Egyptian hairstyles 46
women and long hair 145

Hakilah, Hill of
location, events at 111

Ham
nations that descended from 9

Hannah
her bargain (vow) with God 93

Haran
Abraham moves to 12
map of Eliezer's route to 27
Jacob travels to 32
importance to Israel's history 33
map of Jacob's route to 33

Harems
common in ancient times 13
photo of ruins at Persepolis 173

Harod, Spring of
present day photo 85

Harps
explanation and uses 102
carving with 103

Harvest
dependence upon rain 138
wheat and barley harvest 233

Hatshepsut
possible princess who found baby Moses 48–49
why she would have accepted Moses 49

Hebrews
as viewed by Egyptians 46
become slaves in Egypt 47
possible Pharaohs of the oppression 49, 56
why they were wanted as slaves 50
Passover celebration 56
the Jewish calendar 58
exiles return to Jerusalem 174
see also Israel, Israelites; Jews

Hebron
photo 115
why chosen as capital of Judah 115
location on map 115

Hermon, Mount
chart of elevations 138
present day photo 261
possible site of Transfiguration 261

Herods
the rule of 234
intermarriage of 250
family chart 251

Herod the Great
rises to power 190
wise men visit 199
feared Jesus' birth 200
kills baby boys in Bethlehem 202
death of 204
kingdom divided among sons 207
builder of the temple 213
reign and successors 234
family chart 251
extent of his kingdom 256
his palace 310, 312
building projects in Caesarea 342

Herodians
description 234, 292

Herodias
who she was 251
family chart of 251

Hezekiah (king of Judah)
Sennacherib goes against 160
the godly reign of 160
preparations for Assyrian attack 160
his prayer; Assyrians destroyed 161

Hezekiah's Tunnel
picture 267

High Priest
clothing of 68, 98
duties of 98
political office in Jesus' day 306
inside the palace of 308

Hinnom Valley
location on map 179
near Kidron 309

Hobah
Abraham rescues Lot at 14

Hoes
ancient farmers using 242

Holy of Holies (temple)
only high priest can enter 94

Holy Place (temple)
angel visits Zacharias 186
diagram of 186
description, furniture in 187

Holy Sepulchre, Church of
traditional site of crucifixion 316

Holy Spirit
disciples receive at Pentecost 330

Honey
food for John the Baptist 207

Hooks
fishing with 262

Horeb, Mount
see Mount Sinai

Horns
animal horns used as trumpets 77, 84

Horns of Hattin
possible location of Sermon on the Mount 238
present day photos 239

Horse
painting of a chariot horse 60

Hospitality
towards guests, strangers 271
killing the fattened calf 276
customs of greeting 325

Houses
of ancient Ur 12
of wealthy Egyptians 44–45
room built on roof of 144
layout of average house 144
courtyard of ancient house 145
a Palestinian house 191
drawing of 191
Peter's house at Capernaum 224
materials, construction in New Testament times 224
roofs of 227
sizes of 227
hospitality towards strangers 271
of the wealthy 277

Hyksos
relationship to Joseph's rule 56

Hyssop
its role in Passover ceremony 56

Iconium
description 351, 354
location on map 354
present day photo 361

Idols, Idolatry
Egyptian idol 65
how golden calf was made 70
bull worship 70
idol worship in Canaan 86
how Solomon turned to idolatry 129
idols worshipped by Solomon 129
picture of 129
reforms of Hezekiah 160
reforms of Josiah 162

Incense
heathen incense altars 86

Incense, Altar of
location, use in tabernacle 68

Inheritance
importance of family birthright 28

Ink
use in ancient writing 147
ancient ink 193

Inns
of Bible times 195, 270
offer safety to travellers 203
picture 270
Inn of Good Samaritan 270

Innkeepers
description of 270

Isaac
the birth of 20
unique family relationships 20
meaning of his name 20
his life and character 20–21
Abraham offers 24
marries Rebekah 26
Jacob and Esau are born 27
prefers Esau over Jacob 28
Jacob deceives him 30
sends Jacob to Haran 32

Isaiah
the story of 156
when he was a prophet 156
map of Bible world in his day 156
his influence on Judah 157

Ishmael
sent into wilderness with Hagar 22
who he grew up to be 22
Ishtar Gate
reconstruction of 168
Ishtar, Temple of
thought to be Tower of Babel 11
Israel, Israelites
Joseph's brothers its ancestors 45
Passover celebration 56
the Exodus from Egypt 58
led by pillar of cloud, fire 60
problems of crossing wilderness 60
map of route from Egypt 61
what they left in Egypt 61
where they crossed the Red Sea 61
God sends manna in wilderness 62
foods they desired from Egypt 62
grumbling and complaining of 62
laws compared with other lands 64
worship golden calf 66
living amidst calf worship 66
chart of tribes' arrangement around
    tabernacle 69
as the Promised Land 70
dimensions and boundaries of 71
map of Exodus to Kadesh Barnea 73
finally enter Promised Land 74
route from Sinai to Jordan River 75
inferior battle strategies 80
God the key to victory 80
travelling to yearly sacrifice 92
why they wanted a king 98
map of Saul's kingdom 98
Philistine oppression of 99
a festive people 108
why David chose Jerusalem as capital 116
wealth in Solomon's day 128
the kingdom divides 130
see also Israel, Kingdom of, for remaining
    Old Testament events
weather cycles of 132, 194
historical setting of Jesus' day 190
territories in Jesus' day 207
Roman control over 264
Israel, Kingdom of
chart of kings 101
Ish-Bosheth made king of 114
division of kingdom 130
Shishak invades 130
map of divided kingdom 131
background to division of 132
constant conflict with Syrians 147, 151
chart of kings: Joash to Hoshea 157
taken into captivity 158
why it fell before Judah 158
map of Assyrian invasion 158
period between the captivities 160
Israel, Pool of
supplies water for Jerusalem 266
Issachar (brother of Joseph)
short description of 45
Jacob
unique family relationships of 20–21
meaning of his name 20
causes of strife with Esau 21
birth of 26
buys Esau's birthright 28
preferred by Rebekah 28

deceives Isaac 30
dreams of ladder to heaven 32
map of his journey to Haran 33
meets Rachel at well 34
marries Leah and Rachel 35
gives Joseph colourful cloak 36
family moves to Egypt 46
Jacob's Well
description of 215
photo of today 215
Jairus
Jesus raises his daughter 246
as a synagogue ruler 246
James (son of Alphaeus)
short description of 237
James (son of Zebedee)
leaves family business for Jesus 220
possible relation to Jesus 221
description and character 236
Japheth
the nations that descended from 9
Jars
ancient cosmetic jars 153
photo of alabaster jar 296
Jason
who he was 366
Javelins
of Goliath 105
what they looked like 107
as offensive weapon 305
Jehu (king of Israel)
becomes king, kills Jezebel 152
his zealous reign 152
his "picture" on black obelisk of
    Shalmaneser III 152
Jeremiah
the story of 164
map of his world 164
his efforts in Judah 165
Jericho
Joshua captures 76
walls excavated 76
climate, strategic location 76–77
example of fortified city 77
location on map 77
the Jericho Road 270
a city of many priests 270
the city in Jesus' day 286
photo of 286
palm trees 288
Jericho Road
description of 270
Jeroboam (king of Israel)
makes golden calves 130
Jerusalem
Dome of the Rock 25, 124, 127
David captures 116
the city in David's day 116
why David chose as Israel's capital 116
picture of water supply tunnel 116
diagram of water supply tunnel 117
David moves ark to 118
photo of city walls 125, 178
chart of elevations 138
destroyed by Nebuchadnezzar 166
summary of history 167
exiles return to 174
map of Ezra's journey to 175
Nehemiah rebuilds the walls of 178

map at time of Nehemiah 179
water systems for 232
Pool of Bethesda 232
the Pool of Siloam 232, 266
pools, water systems of 266
Jesus weeps for 272
destruction in AD 70 272
Jesus enters triumphantly 289
photo of Kidron Valley 289
map of Jesus' last week in 297
photo of Mount of Olives 299
traditional site of Upper Room 301
location of Akeldama 309
photo of Via Dolorosa 314
photo of Gordon's Calvary 316
photo of Church of Holy Sepulchre 317
Jesus
birth announced 188
when birth announced 188
miracle of His birth 189
meaning of name 189
names of 189
historical setting of 190
relation to John the Baptist 193
birth, date of birth 194
birth announced to shepherds 196
prophecies of His birth 197
honoured by Simeon, Anna 198
political background to birth 199
wise men's gifts to 201
parents take Him to Egypt 202
His home in Egypt 204
return from Egypt 204
works as a carpenter 205
childhood timetable 205
talks with teachers as a boy 206
baptized by John 208
revealed as God's Son 208
Satan tempts Him 209
changes water to wine 210
cleanses temple 212
why He disliked money-changers 212
Nicodemus visits Him 214
talks with woman at well 215
heals nobleman's son 216
visits Nazareth synagogue 218
moves to Capernaum 219
miracle of fish 219
calls four disciples 220
disciples leave businesses for 220
healing at Capernaum synagogue 222
miracles at Capernaum 222
teaching with authority 222
and evil spirits 223
heals Peter's mother-in-law 224
contrasted with Peter 224
diseases He healed 225
healing tour of Galilee 226
paralytic through roof 227
calls Matthew 228
eats with tax collectors 228, 230
His view of sinners 230
criticized by John's disciples 231
heals at Pool of Bethesda 232
disciples eat grain on Sabbath 233
heals a withered hand 234
teaches by Sea of Galilee 235
chooses 12 disciples 236
Sermon on the Mount 238

heals centurion's servant 240
raises widow's son at Nain 241
parable of the sower 242
calms a storm at sea 243
heals man with demons 244
His power over demons 244
woman healed by touching hem of His cloak 245
clothing He would have worn 245
raises Jairus' daughter 246
recognizing His miracles 247
sends disciples two by two 248
feeds 5000 252
walks on the water 253
healing at Gennesaret 254
reputation as miracle worker 254
heals Syrophoenician woman 255
why He left Galilee 255
map of travels in Tyre, Sidon 255
heals deaf and dumb man 256
lands where He walked 256
heals blind man at Bethsaida 257
at Caesarea Philippi 258
as the Son of man 258
transfiguration of 260
fish supplies tax money 262
disciples ask who is greatest 264
heals man at Pool of Siloam 266
as the Good Shepherd 268
table of parables 269
parable of the Good Samaritan 270
visits Mary and Martha 271
Mary, Martha show their love for 271
weeps for Jerusalem 272
parable of lost sheep 274
why He taught in parables 274
parable of lost coin 275
parable of Prodigal Son 276
parable of rich man and Lazarus 277
raises Lazarus 278
heals 10 lepers 280
parable of Pharisee and publican 281
with children 282
and the rich young ruler 283
parable of labourers in vineyard 284
heals blind Bartimaeus 286
last journey to Jerusalem 287
and Zaccheus 288
Triumphal Entry into Jerusalem 289
teaches in the temple 290
widow's mite 293
Mary anoints feet of 296
map of Jesus' last week 297
at the Last Supper 300
prays in Gethsemane 304
Judas betrays Him 305
on trial before Council 306
Peter denies Him 308
before Pilate 310, 311
map of His movements under arrest 311
before Herod Antipas 312
scourged, mocked by soldiers 313
on way to cross 314
crucifixion of 316
why Pilate condemned Him 316
events the day He died 317
His body is buried 318
rises from the dead 320, 321
sees Mary Magdalene at tomb 321

on the Road to Emmaus 322
Thomas doubts His resurrection 324
fact of His resurrection 324
events of His 40 days after Resurrection 325
miracle of fish after Resurrection 326
ascends into heaven 328
when He ascended 329

Jethro
Moses' father-in-law 50
description of 50

Jews
the Jewish calendar 58
carving of captive Jew 130
exiles return to Jerusalem 174
historical setting of Jesus' day 190
ceremony of circumcision 198
education of a Jewish boy 206
hatred for Samaritans 215
revolt against Romans 272
pigs an "unclean" food 276
why they hated tax collectors 288
daily prayer times 332
why many disliked Paul 353
how Paul preached to 353
Jewish Diaspora 367

Jewellery
nose rings and bracelets 26
from ancient Egypt 59
where Hebrews' jewellery came from 67

Jezebel
kills Naboth for vineyard 140
Jehu kills her 152

Jezreel
Naboth's vineyard at 140
present day photo 140
Jehu kills kings of Israel and Judah 152

Jezreel Valley
fertile region of 144

Joab
leads raiding party into Jerusalem 117

Job
the story of 182
plot of the Book of Job 182

Jochebed (mother of Moses)
description 49

John (disciple of Jesus)
leaves family business for Jesus 220
possible relation to Jesus 221
description and character 236
visits Jesus' tomb 320
heals lame man at Beautiful Gate 332
before Jewish Council 333
writes to seven churches 392

John the Baptist
birth announced by angel 186
when birth announced 186
historical setting of 190
traditional birthplace 191
birth of 192
a Nazirite 192
a forerunner to Messiah 193
relation to Jesus 193
preaches in the wilderness 207
clothing and food of 207
baptizes Jesus 208
meaning of his name 208
disciples criticize Jesus 231
his disciples 231

beheaded by Herod Antipas 250
why John was beheaded 250

John Mark
Paul, Barnabas argue about 356

Jonah
the story of 154
when his story took place 154

Jonathan
friendship with David 106
his gifts for David 106
warns David of Saul 108

Joppa
Peter raises Dorcas at 343
description, history of 343
present day photo 343
location on map 344
site of Simon the Tanner's house 344

Jordan River
the Israelites cross 74
location, history of 74, 208
photos near Sea of Galilee 208, 257

Jordan Valley
the land chosen by Lot 14

Joseph of Arimathea
buries Jesus' body 318
who he was 318
traditional site of Arimathea 318

Joseph (son of Jacob)
his colourful cloak 36
sold as a slave 38
in Potiphar's house 40
thrown into prison 40
his work as a steward 40
the baker 41
the cupbearer 41
Pharaoh makes him governor 42
manages Egypt's grain 43
brothers come to buy grain 44
his life as governor 44–45
his silver drinking cup 45
his 11 brothers 45
map of journey from Canaan 46
family moves to Egypt 46
why he rose to power in Egypt 56

Joseph (Mary's husband)
flight to Egypt 202
return from Egypt 204
fear of Archelaus 204
sets up carpenter's shop 205
picture of Church of Joseph 205

Joshua
crossing the Jordan River 74
Achan's sin; Ai conquest 78
sun and moon stand still 80
map of victory over five kings 81

Josiah (king of Judah)
Book of the Law found 162
godly reign and reforms 162

Judah (brother of Joseph)
short description of 45

Judah, Kingdom of
chart of kings 101
David becomes king of 114
map of, in David's time 115
why Hebron the capital of 115
division of kingdom 130
Shishak invades 130
map of divided kingdom 131
background to division 132

decline in Isaiah's day 156
chart of kings: Amaziah to Zedekiah 157
why Israel captured first 158
later captivity pays off 158
period between the captivities 160
Jeremiah's ministry in 164
Babylon takes into captivity 166

Judas (disciple of Jesus)
see Thaddaeus

Judas Iscariot
short description of 237
plans to betray Jesus 298
why he might have betrayed Jesus 298
betrays Jesus 305
hangs himself 309

Judea
present day photos 175, 207
description of the region 256
location on map 256

Judea, Wilderness of
present day photos 207

Judgement Seat
Roman 311

Judges of Israel
chart of 87

Jugs
from Bible times; photo 85, 135, 145, 148
from Elijah's time 135

Kadesh Barnea
description, location 70
photo today 70
location on map 73

Kerith Brook
Elijah hides by 133
photo of traditional site 133

Kidron Valley
present day photo 289

Kings
ancient harems 13
map of Joshua's victory over 81
life of a captured king 88
Saul is anointed as 98
why Israelites wanted one 98
advantages, disadvantages of 98
why, how they were anointed 100
chart of kings 101
sitting at the king's table 108
torture of 113, 166
example of a wicked king 140
the king's seal 141
God's prophets and 142
of Elijah's, Elisha's day 142, 143
chart of Israel's, Judah's prophets and
  kings 157
some kings of Assyria 159, 160
placing foot on neck of 166
obeying king's command 169
palaces of Persian kings 176

Kingdom of God
explanation 207
people's ideas about 264
children's importance in 282

Kiriath Jearim
people receive the ark 96, 97
ark of covenant at 118
present day photo 118

Kissing
common custom among men 35, 305

Labourers
see Workers

Ladder
Jacob's ladder 32

Lamps
photos of 95, 294
use of olive oil in 95, 294
description and varieties 294

Lampstand (of tabernacle)
location, use in tabernacle 68
importance to Israelites 95
how it was made 95
photos of 95, 129

Lanterns
uses in New Testament times 305

Laodicea
John writes to church at 392

Last Supper
preparations for 300
Jesus and disciples at 300–303

Law, Law Codes
the Ten Commandments 64
law codes of other lands 64
Book of the Law 162
oral law of Pharisees 230
the Areopagus 368

Laying on of Hands
significance in Jesus' day 282

Lazarus
parable of rich man and 277

Lazarus (brother of Mary, Martha)
his family 271
Jesus raises from the dead 278
description and character 278

Leaders
religious, civil, military 216

Leah
marries Jacob 35

Leather
used in shields and armour 305

Leaven
use forbidden at Passover 58
explanation 257

Legion
division of Roman army 240, 380

Legion (demons)
meaning of the name 244

Lentils
photo of 28
common use as a vegetable 29

Lepers, Leprosy
the life of a leper 146–147, 280
types of leprosy 146, 280
purification of healed sufferers 146
photos of sufferers 146, 280
Jesus heals 10 lepers 280
ceremony of cleansing 280

Letters
writing materials for 147

Levi (brother of Joseph)
short description of 45

Levites
collecting the tithe 181

Lions
Daniel thrown into lions' den 171
description of lions' den 171

Liquid Measures
diagram 211

Locusts
ancient food 207
photo of 207

Looms
weaving on 89

Lot
parts with Abraham 14
the land he chose 14
deceived by his daughters 19

Lots
use in magic, occult 112
casting lots to determine priest to enter
  holy place 187

Lydians
invention of the coin 275

Lyres
explanation and uses 102

Lystra
Paul's first missionary journey 351
description 351, 354
Paul and Barnabas mistaken for gods 354,
  355
location on map 354, 357
Paul meets Timothy at 360

Macedonia
Paul's call to 358
description of the region 358
photo of the area 358

Machaerus
connection with John the Baptist 250
description of 250
location on map 250

Magdala
description 321
present day photo 321

Magi
see Wise Men

Magic, Magicians
magic, occult in Israel 112
what they did 364

Mahanaim
David flees from Absalom to 123

Mail
Goliath's coat of mail 105

Mallets
photo of ancient mallets 205

Malta
Paul shipwrecked on 386
description 386
picture of coast 387

Mamre
Abraham's activities at 16

Manger
description 194
photo of ancient manger 194

Manna
God sends to Israelites 62
what it was 62

Maon
location and description 110

Maon, Wilderness of
a hideout for David 110

Marduk (Babylonian god)
yearly festival for 169
drawing of 169

Marketplace
activities at 254
Greek and Jewish compared 284
activities at Greek marketplace 366

Marriage, Weddings
mates chosen by parents 26
marrying at an older age 27
the marriage feast 35, 217
the dowry 35
the wedding veil 35
betrothal 195
weddings in Jesus' day 210
customs for widows 293

Mars Hill
Paul preaches at 368
present day photo 368
and the Areopagus 368

Martha
Jesus visits Mary and Martha 271
her family 271

Mary (Jesus' mother)
Jesus' birth announced 188
a miracle birth 189
visits Elizabeth 190
relation to Elizabeth 190
flight to Egypt 202
return from Egypt 204

Mary (mother of John Mark)
description of her house 348

Mary (Lazarus' sister)
Jesus visits Mary and Martha 271
her family 271
anoints feet of Jesus 296

Mary Magdalene
sees Jesus at tomb 321
description and character of 321

Masons
stonemasons 127

Mats
used as ancient beds 254

Matthew (disciple of Jesus)
Jesus calls him 228
his job and personality 228, 237
Jesus eats at his house 230

Matthias
disciple who replaced Judas 330

Meals
preparing meal for family blessing 30
the Passover meal 300

Measures
see Weights, Measures

Meat
cooking it in a pot 31

Media, Medes
justice system 64
who they were 170

Mediums
magic, occult in Israel 112
what they did 364

Melchizedek
who he was 14

Men
God creates 3
custom of kissing 35
the good and evil man 182
clothing in Jesus' day 245

Menorah
see Lampstand (of tabernacle)

Merchants
travel by caravan 202

Merneptah
possible Pharaoh of Exodus 49, 56

Merti
Egyptian governor 43

Meshach
thrown into fiery furnace 169

Mesopotamia
dominant nations in Bible times 12

Messengers
what they did 103

Messiah
birth announced 188
John a forerunner to 192
first public announcement of birth 196
meaning of the word 307

Metalworking
the art of 66
photo of 67

Midian
Moses flees to 50
description of the region 50
map of Moses' journey to 51

Mills
illustrations of large mill 88, 264

Millstones
illustration of 134, 264
types and uses 264

Mina
money of Jesus' day 288
value of 288

Minerals
taken from Dead Sea 19

Miracles
Israelites didn't learn from 63
Jesus' miracles of healing 217
Jesus' miracles at Capernaum 222
recognizing Jesus' miracles 247
Jesus' reputation as miracle healer 254

Mite
a coin of Jesus' day 293
photo of 293
story of widow's mite 293

Mizpah
Saul made king at 98
location on map 98, 115, 131

Moab (son of Lot)
ancestor of the Moabites 19

Moabites
how the nation began 19

Moulds
use in brickmaking 47
photo of 47
use in metalworking 67

Molech
description, worship of 129

Money
the shekel 79, 148
a talent of silver 148
use in betrothal 189
debts and debtors 265
of Jesus' time 265, 275
a day's wage in Jesus' time 284
difficult to place value on 288
the money bag, or box 297
thirty pieces of silver 298
see also Coins

Money-changers
their work and duties 212, 291

Moon
God creates 3
stands still for Joshua 80

Mordecai
cares for Esther 172
his work 172

Moriah, Mount
Abraham offers Isaac on 24
Bible events that happened there 24
map of Abraham's journey to 25

Mortar
from Elijah's time 134

Moses
birth of 48
who rescued him from Nile 48–49
possible Pharaohs of his time 49
when he was born 49
his parents 49
flees to Midian 50
settles with people he was taught to hate 51
map of journey to Midian 51
marries Zipporah 51
40-year divisions of his life 51
and the burning bush 52
as shepherd at Mount Sinai 52
the plagues in Egypt 54
God's power greater than Egyptian gods 55
the first Passover 56
the Exodus from Egypt 58
the Red Sea parts 60
events at Rephidim 63
receives Ten Commandments 64
the golden calf 66
instructions for tabernacle 68
instructions for priests, offerings 68
sends spies into Promised Land 70
the bronze serpent 72

Mountains
important mountains in the Bible 24–25
chart of important elevations 138

Mourners, Mourning
during funeral procession 241
hired mourners 246

Murex (shellfish)
example of 363
a source of purple dyes 375

Music, Musicians
plays important role in Israel 77
David plays music for Saul 102
common language of Bible times 103
importance of musicians 103
performing in streets 103
at victory celebrations 107
song, dance in Israel 118
David's experience with 119

Musical instruments
trumpet and its uses 77
explanation of harp, lyre 102
music and musicians 103

Myrrh
wise men's gift to Jesus 201
significance of 201
photo of 201
use in burial 319

Naaman
healed of leprosy 146
map of journey to Elisha 147

Nabonidus (king of Babylon)
attitudes as king 170

Naboth
Jezebel kills him for vineyard 140
Nain
Jesus raises widow's son at 241
present day photo 241
description of the town 241
location on map 241
Names
changing names in Bible times 15
of Jesus 189
of Jesus' followers 347
Naphtali (brother of Joseph)
short description of 45
Nard
see Spikenard
Nathanael
see Bartholomew
Nations
that descended from Ham, Shem, and
Japheth 9
how nations began 11
importance of Fertile Crescent to 12
Nativity, Church of the
present day photo 195
Nazareth
Jesus' birth announced at 188
description 188
photos 189
Jesus' family moves to 204
Jesus' trip from Egypt to 204
Jesus visits synagogue at 218
as Jesus' hometown 218
traditional site of synagogue 218
Nazirite
conditions of Nazirite vow 87
breaking Nazirite vow 87
lifestyle of 192
Neapolis
Paul's second missionary tour 356
description 356
location on map 357
Near East
home of earliest civilizations 2
Nebi Samwil
traditional site of Samuel's tomb 112
description of 112
Nebo, Mount
location on map 77
Nebuchadnezzar II
Babylon flourishes under 164
carries Judah into captivity 166
map of invasions 166
life and reign of 168
Neck
custom of placing foot on 166
Needle's Eye
what it was 283
Negev
wilderness south of Canaan 73
present day photo 73
Nehemiah
prays for homeland 176
rebuilds Jerusalem walls 178
wise character of 179
Nero (Roman emperor)
his reign as Caesar 384
Paul's connection with 384
Nets
fishing nets 219–221, 262–263, 327

New Moon, Festival of
explanation 108
Nicanor Gate
possibly the Beautiful Gate 332
Nicodemus
visits Jesus 214
description and character 214
where he met Jesus 214
helps to bury Jesus' body 318
Night
caravans offer protection from 39
watches of 217
the fourth watch 253
Nile River
crucial to Egyptian farming 43, 54
Egypt depends upon 54
Nimrud
ruined temple thought to be Tower
of Babel 11
Nineveh
Jonah at 154
great Assyrian city 154
why Jonah afraid to go to 154
Noah
builds the ark 8
the Great Flood 8
the life of 8
Nob
David flees from Saul to 109
location, events at 109
present day photo 109
Nobleman
Jesus heals his son 216
job and duties of 216
Nod
land where Cain lived 7
Nomads
life in the wilderness 60
Nose Rings
worn by ancient Bedouin women 26
Nurse
a daughter's personal servant 35
Oasis
welcome sight in the wilderness 60
description of 63
Obedience
Noah's great test of 8
Obelisk
black obelisk of Shalmaneser III 152
Offerings, Sacrifices
Abraham offers Isaac 24
altars for 25
burnt offerings 25
God's instructions about 68
purpose of 92
the yearly sacrifice 92
those given at tabernacle 94
Saul sacrifices wrongly 99
offered by Saul wrongly 99
the temple sheep 196
three o'clock sacrifice 196
animals used for 213
related to man's wealth 213
to declare lepers clean again 280
temple collection vessels 293
Oil
holy anointing oil 100
variety of uses 101

Ointment
Mary anoints Jesus with 296
alabaster ointment jar 296
nard and spikenard 296
Olives, Mount of
a mountain of tears 122
photos of 299, 329
possible locations of Gethsemane 304
Jesus ascends to heaven 328
Olive Trees
photo of 304
importance to Israel 305
Omer
measurement in Israel 62
Onesimus
runs away from Philemon 390
who he was 390
Ossuary
use in burial 278
Ovens
use in breadmaking 41, 135
Oxcarts
travel by, description of 97
photo of 97
Palace
how David saw Bathsheba from 121
Solomon's palace 126
of different Persian kings 176
inside the high priest's palace 308
Herod the Great's palace 310, 312
Palestine
see Israel, Israelites
Palm Trees
at Jericho 288
Paphos
Paul's first missionary journey 350
description 350
Papyrus
also known as bulrushes 48
uses of 48
ancient basket made from 48
use in ancient writing 147
Parables
teaching in 242
table of 269
Parents
choosing a wife for their son 26
Parthians
rivalry with Rome 199
Passover
Hebrews celebrate first Passover 56
when it began 56
what it is 56
the ceremony (ritual) of 56
as the yearly sacrifice 92
Israelites travel to Shiloh for 92
New Testament celebration 206
the meal of 300
photo of Passover bread 300
Patmos (island of)
John writes to seven churches 392
description 392
Patriarchs
their ages, from Noah to Abraham 8–9
families of Abraham, Isaac, Jacob 21
Paul
centurions he met 240
blinded on Damascus Road 340
escapes from Damascus 341

map of his early events 347
first missionary journey 350
cities he visited on first missionary
  journey 350–351
map: first missionary journey 351
at Antioch in Pisidia 352
why Jews disliked him 353
how he preached to Jews and Gentiles
  353
mistaken for a god 354–355
cities he visited on second missionary
  journey 356–357
map: second missionary journey 357
call to Macedonia 358
meets Timothy 360
Lydia becomes a believer 362
helps Philippian jailer 364
preaches at Thessalonica 366
Bereans accept him 367
at Mars Hill in Athens 368
with Priscilla and Aquila 370
Gallio judges him at Corinth 372
books of evil burned at Ephesus 374
silversmith riot in Ephesus 376
raises Eutychus at Troas 378
arrested in Jerusalem 380
before Felix and Festus 382
before Herod Agrippa II 383
journey toward Rome 384
his life in Rome 384
shipwreck 386
arrives in Rome 388
stops on journey to Rome 388–389
writes to Philemon 390

Peace
how Elisha achieved it 150
Peace Offerings
what they were 99
Pens
made from reeds 147, 193
use in writing 193
Pentecost
disciples receive Holy Spirit 330
meaning 330
the nations of 331
Perea
description of the region 256, 282
Perfection
Jesus' meaning of 283
Perga
Paul's first missionary journey 351
description 351
location on map 351
Pergamum
John writes to church at 392
location on map 392
Persepolis
photo of 173
Persia, Persians
justice system 64
great empires of the Bible 165
overthrow of Babylon 167
map of the empire 170
who they were 171
background of the empire 172
drawings of Persian methods of travel
  172
places of Persian kings 173

Pestle
use in breadmaking 41
from Elijah's time 134
Peter (disciple of Jesus)
miracle of fish 219
leaves family business for Jesus 220
Jesus heals his mother-in-law 224
contrasted Jesus 224
his house at Capernaum 224
church ruins over home of 225
description and character of 236
finds tax money in fish 262
denies Jesus 308
visits Jesus' tomb 320
heals lame man at Beautiful Gate 332
before Jewish Council 333
raises Dorcas at Joppa 343
baptizes Cornelius 344
thrown into prison 348
angel releases from prison 348–349
Pharaoh
his orders to taskmasters 47
possible Pharaohs of Hebrew oppression
  and Exodus 47, 56
statue of 54
hopeless trust in his gods 55
the great wealth of 60
Pharisees
their view of sinners 230
description and beliefs of 230, 281, 292
accuse Jesus' disciples of working on
  Sabbath 233
their Sabbath rules 233
connection with Herodians 234
the Pharisee and publican 281
strictly followed the Law 281
Philadelphia
John writes to church at 392
location on map 392
Philemon
Paul writes to 390
Philip (disciple of Jesus)
description and character 236
Philip (the Evangelist)
preaches in Samaria 339
meets Ethiopian 339
description of 339
Philip I (Herod)
chart: Herod the Great's family 251
Philip II (Herod)
coin of 250
chart: Herod the Great's family 251
Philip's Springs
significance of 339
map location 339
Philippi
Paul's second missionary tour 356
description 356, 362
Lydia becomes a believer 362
photo of ruins at 363
jailer becomes a believer 364
location on map 365
Philistia
location on map 104
Philistines
advanced battle strategies 80
system of government 88
five Philistine rulers 88

capture the ark of the covenant 96
ark brings plagues to 96
oppression of Israel 99
Phoenicians
picture of Phoenician merchant ship 154
Phylacteries
examples of 57
Pigs
Jews consider "unclean" food 276
Pigeons
offering for the poor 198
Pilate, Pontius
one of Jesus' judges 307
Jesus before 310
description, political life 311
sentences Jesus 312
why he condemned Jesus 316
Pillars, Columns
main support of Philistine temple 89
ruins in Ephesus 356
from temple of Diana 377
Pillows
ancient Egyptian headrests 42
photo of 42
Pinnacle of Temple
photo 209
Pit
cisterns 38
Pitchers
used to draw water from well 27
Plagues
the plagues in Egypt 54–55
the plague of serpents 72
fear and disaster 96
Plants
God creates 3
Planting
near the Nile River 54–55
in Bible times 242
Ploughs
construction and uses 139
Ploughing
description 139
Ploughshares
what they were 139
Polygamy
in the Bible 129
Pomegranates
popular fruit in Bible lands 4
photo of 4
Pompey (Roman general)
his siege of Jerusalem 190
Pontius Pilate
see Pilate, Pontius
Pools
Pool of Siloam 266
other pools of Jerusalem 266
Poor
life of poor people 277
exploited by the rich 277
New Testament beliefs about 283
Porticoes
the Royal Portico at temple 290
Possessions
should we sell ours 283
Potiphar
Joseph a slave 40
a description of 40

Pots
ancient cooking pot 31
woman carrying water pot 215
Potter's Field
what it was 309
Pottery
cooking pot 31
jugs from Elijah's day 135
used as writing material 147, 193
pottery styles aid in dating 148
pottery-making techniques 148
Praetorium
what it was 311
Prayer
photo of man at prayer 245
daily prayer times 332
Precipitation, Mount of
present day photo 218
Priests
God's instructions about 68
duties, eligibility 68
clothing of high priest 68
duties with offerings 94
anointing a king of Israel 100
Elijah and priests of Baal 136
lifestyles of heathen priests 136
order of Abijah 187
ceremony of cleansing lepers 280
who chief priests were 298
Priscilla
Paul works at Corinth with 370
Prisms
of Sargon II 159
of Sennacherib 160
Prisons
cisterns used as 38
life in 40
debtors thrown into 265
Prisoners
life in prison 44
ancient drawing of possible prisoners of
war 83
grinding grain in prison 88
treatment of prisoners of war 113
debtors as 265
Procurators
Roman rulers in Jesus' day 207
Promised Land
Moses sends spies into 70
description 70
Israelites finally enter 74
Israelites never fully conquer 82
Prophecies
about Jesus 184
about Jesus' birth 197
Prophets
anointing a king of Israel 100
Elijah and prophets of Baal 136
work of God's prophets 142
chart of Israel's, Judah's prophets and
kings 157
Proselytes
who they were 290
Ptolemies
when they controlled Israel 264
Publius
who he was 387

Purification Rites
after a battle 78
from childbirth 198
Purple
value of purple clothing 171, 363
a source of purple dyes 363
Puteoli
an ancient Roman resort 388
Pyramids
photo of 46
Quarry
quarrying stones for temple 127
Rachel
meets Jacob at well in Haran 34
marries Jacob 35
Rain
importance to Israel 132–133, 137
in winter 194
Ram
photo of 24
Ramah
Samuel's hometown 92
Ramses II
possible Pharaoh of Hebrew oppression
49, 56
statue of 54
mummy of 55
Ravens
feed Elijah 132
picture 133
Reading
public reading of Book of Law 163
Rebekah
marries Isaac 26
gives birth to Jacob and Esau 27
prefers Jacob over Esau 28
description of 31
Red Sea
the parting of 61
where the Israelites crossed 61
Reeds
used by ancient carpenters 117
use in writing 193
Religious Leaders
angered when Jesus forgives sins 227
failure to recognize Jesus' miracles 247
who they were 292
why they wanted Jesus killed 316
conspire against Resurrection 324
see also Pharisees, Sadducees, Chief
Priests, Sanhedrin
Rephidim
location on map 61
Moses gets water from a rock 63
description of 63
Resurrection
Jesus rises from the dead 320, 321
fact of Jesus' resurrection 324
events of Jesus' 40 days after 325
Reuben (brother of Joseph)
short description of 45
Riches
see Wealth
Rimmon
a god of Syria 148
sculpture of 149
Rings
ancient nose rings 26

signet rings 43
photo of earrings 59
Rivers
Egypt's dependence upon Nile 54
see also Jordan River
Roads
travel on ancient roads 33
caravan travel 39, 202
Bible-time inns 195
travel conditions in Jesus' day 202
the Jericho Road 270
the Via Egnatia 358
the Appian Way 388
Robe
see Cloak
Rod
fishing with a rod 263
see also Staff
Rome, Romans
great empires of the Bible 165
maps of the empire 171–172, 240
rivalry with Parthians 199
their control over Israel 207, 264
Roman taxes 228
organization of government 229
organization of the army 240
destruction of Jerusalem in AD 70 272
the Arch of Titus in Rome 272
emperors of New Testament times 292
civilization 345
types of provinces 358
Roman citizenship 364
the auxiliary army 380
Paul's journey toward Rome 384
Paul's life in Rome 384
Paul arrives in Rome 388
Roof
how David saw Bathsheba from 121
room built on roof of house 144
of Bible-time houses 227
Rooms
room on roof a sign of prosperity 144
the Upper Room 300, 325, 330
Royal Portico
description 291
model of 291
Ruth
the story of 90
important descendants of 90
as a widow 90
map of her journey from Moab 91
Sabbath
Sabbath call to worship 218
Pharisees' rules about 233
Sabbath day's journey 233
Sackcloth
symbol of mourning 180
Sacrifice
see Offerings
Sadducees
description, beliefs of 281, 333
Sailing
fair weather months of 155
on Mediterranean Sea 352
Salamis
Paul's first missionary journey 350
description 350
Salome (daughter of Herodias)
her dance 251

chart: Herod the Great's family 251

Salome (wife of Zebedee)
her work 220

Samaria (city)
location on map 147
conflicts with Damascus 149
photo of 150
city and region distinguished 151

Samaria (region)
background and history 215, 270
description of the region 256
location on map 256
its border with Galilee 280

Samaritans
origin 215, 270
hated by Jews 215, 270
parable of Good Samaritan 270
description 270

Samson
birth of 86
breaking the Nazirite vow 87
Delilah deceives him 87
a prisoner of the Philistines 88
grinding grain in prison 88

Samuel
birth of 92
traditional site of tomb 93, 112
serves at the tabernacle 94
God speaks to in tabernacle 94
anoints Saul king 98
anoints David king 100

Sanballat
description of 179

Sandals
photo of 52
example of ancient sandals 53
uses and customs for 53
used in business contracts 95

Sand Viper
common poisonous snake 72

Sanhedrin
explanation 214, 333
getting membership in 283, 333
Jesus on trial before 306
Peter and John before 333

Sanitation
poor in New Testament times 226

Sapphira
description 334

Sarah
Abraham and Sarah go to Egypt 13
relation to Abraham 13
birth of Isaac 20
meaning of her name 20

Sarcophagus
use in burial 278

Sardis
John writes to church at 392
location on map 392

Sargon II (Assyrian king)
carries Israel into captivity 159

Satan
tempts Adam and Eve 4
tempts Jesus 209
methods of temptation 209

Saul
anointed king by Samuel 98

map of his kingdom 98
the sacrifices he gave 99
David plays music for 102
tries to kill David 107
David spares his life 111
visits witch of Endor 112
dies in battle 113

Saul (the apostle)
see Paul

Scourges
types and uses 213
illustration of 213
as punishment 312

Scribes
their work and training 163
public reading of Bible 163

Scrip
what it was 248

Scrolls
how they were made 163, 223
materials for 163, 223, 375
illustrations 163, 181, 223
writing practices on 375

Seas
chart of important elevations 138

Seals
the king's seal 141
description and use 141
an imprint of ancient seal 141

Seine net
fishing with 263

Seleucia
Paul's first missionary journey 350
description of city 350

Seleucids
when they controlled Israel 264

Sennacherib (king of Assyria)
goes against Hezekiah 160
helpless against God's power 161
prism 160
his cavalry 161

Seraphim
and angels 203

Septuagint
helped Gentiles become believers 367

Sergius Paulus
becomes a believer 353

Sermon on the Mount
Jesus teaches 238
possible locations of 238

Serpents
the bronze serpent 72
types in Bible lands 72
worshipped in Egypt 72

Servants
servant girls as substitute wives 23
value of a trusted servant 26
duties of a slave girl 147
Elisha's greedy servant 148
hired servants sign of wealth 220

Seth
his family descendants 7

Seven
significance of the number 337

Shadrach
thrown into fiery furnace 169

Shalmaneser III (king of Assyria)
black obelisk of 152

Sharon, Plains of
description of 343

Shearing
shearing sheep 110
photo of 110

Sheba, Queen of
her visit to Solomon 128

Sheep
photos 7, 24, 35, 110, 196, 268, 295
variety of products from 110, 295
importance and characteristics 110, 274, 295
shearing sheep 110
temple sheep 196
how a good shepherd cares for 268
the sheepfold 268
parable of the lost sheep 274
protection of 274

Sheepfold
shelter for sheep 268

Shekel
standard weight for money 79
half-shekel of Jewish revolt 79
photo of half-shekel 79, 298

Shem
nations that descended from 9

Shepherds
present day photo 7
job despised by Egyptians 51
tending flocks far from home 52
pictures of shepherd tending sheep 114, 268
description of shepherds who visited Jesus 196
angels announce Jesus' birth 196
Jesus, the Good Shepherd 268
qualities of a good shepherd 268
guarding the sheepfold 268
work of 274

Shepherdess
Rachel 34
Zipporah 51–52

Shewbread
explanation and priests' ritual 109
ingredients kept a secret 109

Shewbread, Table of
location, use in tabernacle 68

Shields
as defensive weapon 305

Shiloh
journey for yearly sacrifice 92

Shinar, Land of
Tower of Babel built there 10

Ships, Shipping
bireme sculpture 154
Phoenician ships 154, 155
description of ships and sailing 155
fishing boats on Sea of Galilee 243, 253
shipping in Paul's day 353, 385
shipping season 353
kind Paul travelled on 384
work of Roman merchant ships 385
capacity and cargo of Roman ships 385
trireme 386
model of trireme 386
stars used in navigation 389

Shishak
invades Israel and Judah 130

Shofar
  picture of 77
Shoes
  see Sandals
Shunem
  couple make room for Elisha 144
  Elisha raises Shunammite boy 144
  description and events at 144
  painting of 144
Sickness
  plagues in Bible times 96
  leprosy 146, 280
  Jesus' miracles of healing 217
  diseases of Jesus' day 226
  why disease so common 226
  diseases Jesus healed 226
  woman with issue of blood 245
Sidon
  the region of 255
  map of Jesus' travels in 255
  description of city 349
Signet Rings
  uses, symbolism of 43
  photo of 43
Silas
  on Paul's second missionary tour 356
  meaning of his name 359
Siloam, Pool of
  Jesus heals blind man at 266
  description and location 266
  location on map 266
  present day photo 267
Silver
  a talent of silver 148
  30 pieces of 298
Simeon
  praises God for seeing Jesus 198
Simeon (brother of Joseph)
  short description of 45
Simon the Tanner
  traditional site of his house 344
  his work 344
Simon the Zealot (disciple of Jesus)
  short description of 237
Sinai, Mount
  Moses talks with God at 52
  location on maps 52, 73
  present day photos 52, 53, 65
  photo, St Catherine's Monastery 53
  God gives Moses Ten Commandments 64
  Elijah's journey to 138
  chart of elevations 138
Sinai Peninsula
  location on map 77
Singers
  at victory celebrations 107
Singing, Songs
  at victory celebrations 107
  as expression of worship 118
  songs found in Bible 119
Sinners
  Jesus eats with 228–230
  two views of 230
Slaves, Slavery
  Joseph sold into 38
  slave's life in Egypt 39
  slaves of wealthy household 40
  Hebrews become slaves in Egypt 47

  oppression by taskmasters 47
  why Hebrews were wanted as slaves 50
  Egypt's great loss of 59
  children sold into slavery to pay parents'
    debts 265, 277
Slings, Slingers
  a deadly weapon 105
  slinger's skill in David's day 105
Smyrna
  John writes to church at 392
  location on map 392
Snake
  picture of viper 72, 387
  see also Serpents
Sodom
  the destruction of 18
  possible location of 18
Soldiers
  purification rites for 78
  Israelite vs. Canaanite 80
  life of a captured warrior 88
  Goliath a champion fighter 105
  angels as warriors 150
  Assyrian soldiers, weapons 161
  obeying king's command 169
  weapons and armour in New Testament
    times 305
  Romans who crucified Jesus 317
Solomon
  wisdom of 126
  his palace 126
  builds the temple 126–127
  his wealth; Queen of Sheba 128
  how he got his wealth 128
  map showing trading links 128
  turns from God 129
  his many wives bring trouble 129
  gods that he worshipped 129
Solomon's Pools
  a source for Jerusalem's water 232
Solomon's Porch
  description 290, 332
Son
  parents choose a wife for 26
  privilege of family birthright 28
  ceremony of circumcision 192
  parable of prodigal son 276
Son of Man
  Jesus as 258
Sorcery, Sorcerers
  magic, occult in Israel 112
  ancient fortune-telling 364
Soup
  making lentil soup 29
Sower, Sowing
  in ancient harvest scenes 242
  Jesus' parable of the sower 242
  how it was done 242
  see Planting
Spears
  of Goliath 105
  what they looked like 107
  as offensive weapons 305
Sphinx
  photo 13
Spices
  use in burial 279
Spies
  Moses sends into Promised Land 70

Spikenard
  as a fragrant ointment 296
Springs of Water
  the spring at En Rogel 122
  present day photo of En Rogel 123
Staff
  picture of shepherd's rod 196
  description and uses of 249
  photo of 249
Star of Bethlehem
  wise men follow 199
  description 200
Stars
  God creates 3
  used in ship navigation 389
Stephen
  stoned to death 338
Steward
  the job and its duties 40
Stoics
  who they were 369
Stones
  used as well coverings 34
  quarrying, stonecutting 127
Stonecutting
  description, drawings of 127
Storage Cities
  of ancient Egypt 50
Storehouses
  function of in ancient Egypt 43
  model of granary 44
  storage cities of ancient Egypt 50
Storms
  Jesus calms storm on sea 243
  on the Sea of Galilee 243
Straight Street
  description, importance 340–341
Strainer
  ancient example 145
Strangers
  hospitality toward 271
Stylus
  an ancient "pen" 147, 193
Suez, Gulf of
  possible Red Sea crossing 61
Sumerians
  young Abraham lives among 12
Sun
  God creates 3
  stands still for Joshua 80
  the ancient time clock 217
Sundials
  an ancient timepiece 217
Supernatural
  unseen world around us 150
Susa
  Shushan palace at 173, 176, 177
Swaddling Clothes
  of the baby Jesus 196
Swords
  as an offensive weapon 305
Sycamore Tree
  explanation 288
  photo 288
Sychar
  village of woman at the well 215
Synagogue
  Jesus visits at Nazareth 218

description and uses of 218
at Capernaum 222
photo: ruins at Capernaum 222
construction and arrangement 223
activities at 223, 373
description of the inside 223
drawing of the interior 223
the synagogue ruler 246
why they began 373

Syria, Syrians
constant conflicts with Israel 147, 151
who they were 150
Elisha strikes them blind 151
why they always fought with 151

Syrophoenician Woman
Jesus heals 255
who she was 255

Tabernacle
where precious metals came from 67
God instructs Moses about 68
arrangement and construction 68
the furniture of 68
model of 68, 92
arrangement of tribes around 69
differences between Moses; and Samuel's
   day 92
Samuel serves at 94
the offerings at 94

Tabgha
possible site of feeding of 5000 252

Table
sitting at the king's table 108

Tablets
ancient contract on clay tablet 15
Code of Hammurabi 64
writing tablets 193

Tabor, Mount
possible site of Transfiguration 25, 261
location on map 98
chart of elevations 138
present day photos 260

Talent (money)
worth of a talent 148

Tallith
photo of 245
a part of men's clothing 245, 286

Tambourines
description of 119

Tanner, Tanning
the work and attitudes toward 344–345

Tannur
ancient type of oven 41, 125

Tarsus
description of Paul's hometown 341–342
present day photo 342
location on map 347

Taskmasters
oppression of Hebrew slaves 47

Tax Collectors
their work in Jesus' time 228
abuses of 228
two types of 281
parable of Pharisee and 281
the chief tax collector 288

Taxes
collected by Pharaoh 50
work of tax collector 228
Roman taxes in Jesus' day 228
of religious leaders 228

in Bible times 262
temple tax 262
Roman tribute tax 292

Teachers, Teaching
Jesus visits as a boy 206
who they were 206
teaching in parables 242

Temples
construction, design of Philistine temples
   89

Temple in Jerusalem
photos of site today 29, 124, 125
where it was built 124
David's, Solomon's part in 126
Solomon builds 126–127
history after Jesus' day 127
materials, construction 127
where Book of Law was found 162
Zerubbabel begins work on 174
floor plan 186
history of 186
division of priests at 187
the temple sheep 196
Jesus cleanses 212
Court of Gentiles 212–213
money-changers in 212, 291
built by Herod the Great 213, 290
Jewish coins acceptable in 213
the temple tax 228, 262
Jesus' view from Mount of Olives 289
model of Royal Portico 291
description of temple treasury 293
description of Solomon's Porch 332
the temple guard 333

Temptation
Adam's and Jesus' compared 209
Satan's methods of 209

Temptation, Mount of
present day photo 209

Ten Commandments
God gives to Moses 64
summary of 64

Tents
how they were made 16
materials used in making 16
how people lived in them 17
picture of Bedouin tent today 17
description of tentmaking 371

Tetradrachms
of the sanctuary 198
picture 212, 265
coins for temple tax 213, 262, 291
of Tyre 275

Thaddaeus (disciple of Jesus)
short description of 237

Thessalonica
Paul's second missionary tour 356
description 356–357, 366
location on map 357
Paul preaches at 366
present day photo 366

Thieves
a danger to travellers 203, 270

Thomas (disciple of Jesus)
short description of 236
doubts Jesus' resurrection 324
description and character of 324

Thorns
Jesus' crown of 313

Threshing
in ancient Egypt 43

Threshing Floor
Araunah's threshing floor 124
daily activities at 125

Threshing Sledge
drawing of 125
description of 125

Thummim
used to seek God's will 112

Thutmose I
possible connection with Moses 49

Thutmose II
possible connection with Moses 49

Thutmose III
possible Pharaoh at Moses' birth 56

Thyatira
important commercial centre 363
location on map 392
John writes to church at 392

Tiberius Caesar (Roman emperor)
ruler over John and Jesus 207
bust of 273, 292
coins of 292, 293
description 292

Time
telling time in Jesus' day 217
periods of the day 284

Timothy
Paul meets Timothy 360
description and character 360–361
chart of his family 361

Tithe
in days of Ezra 181
explanation 281

Titus (Roman emperor)
destroys Jerusalem in AD 70 272

Tobiah
description of 179

Tombs
caves used as 278
women visit Jesus' tomb 318
varieties of 318
the Garden Tomb 320–321
Peter, John visit Jesus' tomb 320

Tools
for a carpenter 205

Torches
uses of 85, 305

Torture
of prisoners of war 113

Towers
the Tower of Babel 10
ancient ziggurats 10

Towers' Pool
supplies water for Jerusalem 267

Trade
flourished in Solomon's day 128
map of trading links 128

Transfiguration
of Jesus 260
its meaning 260
possible locations of 261

Travel
roads in Jacob's day 32
by caravan 39, 202
Israelites cross the wilderness 60
to Shiloh, for yearly sacrifice 92
with wagons and oxcarts 97

Bible-time inns 195
wise men on camels 199, 200
travel conditions in Jesus' day 203
dangers of 203
on the Jericho Road 270
by donkey 289

Treasury
shown in temple diagram 186, 290
description of temple treasury 293

Tribune
Roman army commander 380

Tribute
Roman tribute tax 292

Triumphal Entry
Jesus enters Jerusalem 289

Troas
description 356, 378
Paul raises Eutychus 378
present day photo 379

Trumpets
description and varieties 77
picture of shofar 77
the trumpet of Gideon 84
from Bible times; photo 84
signals start of Sabbath 218
as temple collection vessels 293

Tunic
a part of men's clothing 245

Turan
disciples pick grain on Sabbath 233
possible location of 233

Turtledoves
offering for the poor 198

Tyre
the region of 255
map of Jesus' travels in 255
description of the city 349

Unleavened Bread
description, varieties 58
photo of 58
symbolism at Passover 59

Unleavened Bread, Feast of
description 59, 92, 348

Upper Room
traditional site of 300, 325, 330
Last Supper in 300
Pentecost at 330

Ur
Abraham journeys from 12
description of the ancient city 12
map showing location of 13
present day photo near 180

Urim
used to seek God's will 112

Uz, Land of
Job's homeland 183
possible location 183

Veil
the wedding veil 35

Veil (of tabernacle, temple)
location, use in tabernacle 68

Ventriloquism
use in magic, occult 112

Via Dolorosa
traditional route of Jesus to cross 314

the 14 stations of 314–315
photo 314

Vineyards
story of Naboth's vineyard 140
activities at 140, 284
photos today 284, 285
parable of workers in vineyard 284

Viper
carpet 72
sand 72
Paul bitten by 387

Vows
the Nazirite vow 87
Hannah's bargain with God 93
Herod Antipas' foolish vow 250
of Paul and friends 381

Wagons
see Carts, Wagons

Walls, Fortifications
a fortified city 76
Philistine garrisons 99
photo of Jerusalem walls 125, 178
varieties of workers on Jerusalem walls
178
Nehemiah and Jerusalem walls 178

War
see Battle

Warriors
angels as warriors 150
see also Soldiers

Washing Feet
of guests 271, 302

Watches
night watches 84, 217, 348
the middle watch 84
the fourth watch 253

Watchman
duties of 123

Water, Water Systems
importance of wells to a city 27
drawing water from well 27, 215
watering flocks at well 34
God gives water from a rock 63
bathing in David's day 120
Jerusalem's water systems 232, 266–267
Jerusalem's water problems 266

Waterskins
photo of 23
description of 231

Wax
used on writing tablets 193

Wealth
of an ancient Pharaoh 60
Solomon's wealth 128
flocks an ancient measure of 183
parable of rich man and Lazarus 277
life of wealthy people 277
Jesus and rich young ruler 283
description of rich young ruler 283
using it for Jesus 283
New Testament beliefs about 283

Weapons
sling, slingers in David's day 104
of Goliath 105
photo of ancient sword 106
what a spear looked like 107
Assyrian weapons, soldiers 161
used in New Testament times 305

Weather
weather cycles in Israel 132–133

Weaving
how it was done 88–89

Weights (fishing)
attached to fishing nets 262

Weights, Measures
omer and ephah 62
use of the shekel 79
how used on balances 171
photo of 171
liquid measures 211

Wells
importance to a city 27
activities at 27
drawing water from 27, 215
well coverings 34
watering flocks at 34
women at 34
Jesus meets woman at well 215
description of Jacob's well 215

Western Wall
photo of 125

Wheat
beating out wheat for bread 83
pictured in Bible lands today 90, 233
time of harvest 233

Whips
types and uses of scourges 213
photo of Roman scourge 213

Wicks
trimming lamp wicks 295

Widows
protected by birthright 30
difficult life of 90, 293
gleaning the fields 91
the first to suffer 134
customs of remarriage 293

Wife
see Wives

Wilderness
between Egypt and Canaan 60
Israel's problems crossing 60
map of Israel's route through 75
camels travel in 200
photo of Judean wilderness 207

Wine
symbolism at Passover meal 300

Winepress
drawings of its operation 83, 285
how it was used 83

Wineskins
example of 231
parable of, and meaning 231
description of 231

Winnowing
what it was 43

Winter
in Israel 194

Wise Men
follow star 200
who they were 200
how many 200
visit Jesus 201
their gifts to Jesus 201

Witches
Saul visits witch of Endor 112

magic, occult in Israel 112
Wives
   servant girls as substitute wives 23
   stigma of having no children 23, 187
   parents choose wife for son 26
   David's wives 121
   Solomon's many wives 129
   polygamy in the Bible 129
Wizards
   magic, occult in Israel 112
Women
   ancient harems 13
   photos of Bedouin women today 22, 34
   stigma of bearing no children 23, 187
   daily visits to the well 34
   lifestyles in Egypt 46
   finery of Egyptian women 59
   using cosmetics 153
   purification from childbirth 198
   Jesus talks with woman at well 215
   as hired mourners 246
   visit Jesus' tomb 318
Women's Court   (temple)
   shown in temple diagram 186
Workers
   parable of workers in vineyard 284
   a day's wage 284
World
   the Bible world 2
Worship
   ziggurats ancient centre of 10
   bull worship affects Israel 66
   Baal worship 82
   idol worship in Canaan 86
   strange worship of Dagon 96
   worship at synagogue 218
Writing
   signet rings as signatures 43
   the king's seal 141
   imprint of ancient seal 141
   ancient letters, pens 147
   scrolls; materials and writing 163, 375
   work of scribes 163
   handwriting on the wall 170
   writing tablets; use, materials 193
   ancient materials for 193
   ancient writing practices 375
Xerxes
   see Ahasuerus

Yarn
   how it was made 89
Yeast
   use forbidden at Passover 58
Yoke
   drawing, photo of 139
Zaccheus
   meets Jesus 288
Zacharias
   John's birth announced to 186
   loss of speech 192
Zarephath
   Elijah and widow of 134
   the town in Elijah's day 134
Zealots
   political beliefs 237
Zebedee (father of James and John)
   his family fishing business 220
Zebulun (brother of Joseph)
   short description of 45
Zerubbabel
   who he was 174
   begins work on temple 174
   his enemies 174
Zeus
   picture of 355
Ziggurats
   what they were and represented 10–11
   Tower of Babel an example 11
   building materials for 11
Zilpah
   sons she bore for Jacob 35
Zipporah
   Moses marries 51
   description of 51
Zoar
   Lot flees from Sodom 19

ACKNOWLEDGEMENTS

The artwork for this book came from a variety of sources including the The Walters Art Museum, The Metropolitan Museum of Art, The Smithsonian American Art Museum, the Louvre, the Cleveland Museum of Art, the Brooklyn Museum, iStockphoto, Pixaby, 123rf, Shutterstock, Alamy, and more. Specific photo and illustration credits are as follows: Abigail Clark (23, 40, 151, 285, 290–291), Deror Avi (32, 33), Tony Dover (41, 96, 109), Dennis Jarvis (54), Vladimir Mazuranic (67), Alex Ostrovski (79), MKcray (80), Yair Aronshtam (85), Avraham Gracier (93), Adam Zartal (99), Margaret Bustard (105, 317, 327, 343), Cantonal Museum of Archaeology (106), Bahnfrend (118), Netanel H (150), O.S.M Amin (159), Shai Halevi/Israel Antiquities Authority (162), Tony Cantale: (175), Chris Lloyd and Abigail Clark (197, 231), Peter van der Sluijs (193), Tamar Hayardeni (209), Ned Bustard (212), Jeremiah K Garrett (215), Avishai Teicher (218), Classical Numismatic Group (229, 312, 348, 376), Chris Lloyd (233), Olevy(238), Bukvoed (239), Sandy Connor (261), Marion Doss (279), F. Nigel Hepper and Abigail Clark (288), Konrad Summers (303), Joseolgon (306), Alzbeta (309), Юкатан (316), Berthold Werner (320), Hanay (321), Neu Aloyse (322), Heritage Conservation Outside The City (323), Bernard Gagnon (346), Christophe Jacquand (347), Dosseman (354), DocWoKav (363), Nicholas Hartmann (371), Yevlem (382), Nachtbold (387), Jeffrey Sciberras (387), Alexander Savin (390).

The maps were created by Tony Cantale, Keith Jackson, and Amy Clark.

The diagrams were made by Tony Cantale, Ned Bustard, and Abigail Clark.